Tomáš Janík, Petr Knecht (Hg./Eds.)

New Pathways in the Professional Development of Teachers

Neue Wege in der Professionalisierung von Lehrer/-inne/-n

Austria: Forschung und Wissenschaft

ERZIEHUNGSWISSENSCHAFT

Band 7

LIT

New Pathways in the Professional Development of Teachers

Neue Wege in der Professionalisierung von Lehrer/-inne/-n

edited by/herausgegeben von

Tomáš Janík and Petr Knecht

LIT

Lektorierung der Texte in deutscher Sprache und Gesamtlayoutierung: Renate Seebauer, Wien
Redaktionsschluss: 26. März 2010; 12:00
Die Autorinnen und Autoren sind allein für den Inhalt ihrer Beiträge verantwortlich.

Bibliographic information published by the Deutsche Nationalbibliothek
The Deutsche Nationalbibliothek lists this publication in the Deutsche Nationalbibliografie; detailed bibliographic data are available in the Internet at http://dnb.d-nb.de.

ISBN 978-3-643-50153-0

A catalogue record for this book is available from the British Library

Krotenthallergasse 10/8
A-1080 Wien
Tel. +43 (0) 1-409 56 61
Fax +43 (0) 1-409 56 97
e-Mail: wien@lit-verlag.at
http://www.lit-verlag.at

LIT VERLAG Dr. W. Hopf
Berlin 2010
Fresnostr. 2
D-48159 Münster
Tel. +49 (0) 2 51-620 320
Fax +49 (0) 2 51-922 60 99
e-Mail: lit@lit-verlag.de
http://www.lit-verlag.de

Distribution:
In Germany: LIT Verlag Fresnostr. 2, D-48159 Münster
Tel. +49 (0) 2 51-620 32 22, Fax +49 (0) 2 51-922 60 99, e-Mail: vertrieb@lit-verlag.de

In Austria: Medienlogistik Pichler-ÖBZ, e-mail: mlo@medien-logistik.at

In Switzerland: B + M Buch- und Medienvertrieb, e-mail: order@buch-medien.ch

In the UK: Global Book Marketing, e-mail: mo@centralbooks.com

In North America by:

Transaction Publishers
New Brunswick (U.S.A.) and London (U.K.)

Transaction Publishers
Rutgers University
35 Berrue Circle
Piscataway, NJ 08854

Phone: +1 (732) 445 - 2280
Fax: + 1 (732) 445 - 3138
for orders (U. S. only):
toll free (888) 999 - 6778
e-mail: orders@transactionpub.com

Inhaltsverzeichnis

Introduction: New Pathways in Professional Development of Teachers

Referate im Plenum

Beiträge in deutscher Sprache

Papers Submitted in English

INTRODUCTION: NEW PATHWAYS IN PROFESSIONAL DEVELOPMENT OF TEACHERS

Professional development of teachers is a theme which is discussed intensively in the context of the ongoing school reforms in Europe. This provides many impulses for educational theory as well as educational research and educational practice. Many questions concerning professional development of teachers need to be answered or clarified.

The conference volume *New Pathways in the Professional Development of Teachers* provides an opportunity to present innovative concepts, models and instruments in the pre-service as well as in-service teacher education in the context of trends in educational policy. Theoretical and research papers are presented as well as descriptions of practical activities in teachers' professional development courses.

The questions focusing on professional development of teachers are accompanied by increasing interest, especially within the educational sciences as well as within other disciplines. How do we explore, develop or even approach teachers' expertise? This is an everlasting question, and the answer was one of burning issues during the conference.

This volume gathers the majority of the contributions which were presented during the conference *New Pathways in the Professional Development of Teachers,* which was held at Faculty of Education, Masaryk University in Brno, Czech Republic in June 2010. More than sixty participants attended the conference, coming from thirteen different countries. In this introduction we would like to give an overview of the conference and the contents of this volume. The following collection is composed of 48 papers, all of which were pre-reviewed and revised if needed.

Invited papers

Four invited papers provided in this conference volume an introduction to the main theoretical and empirical aspects of the professional development of teachers. J. Mayr and M. Píšová presented interdisciplinary conceptual frameworks and methodologies connected to teachers education and teachers' expertise. J. Kühnis and P. Jelemenská reflected on key issues in physical education and biology teacher training.

Working Session 1: Interdisciplinary theoretical and empirical pathways to the professional development of teachers

This working session invited interdisciplinary theoretical and empirical papers which focused on the following themes: Theory of teaching as a profession; historical as well as current trends in the professional development of teachers;

theoretical approaches supporting pre-service as well as in-job teachers' professional development (e.g. Inquiry-Based Learning, Teachers self-reflection and self-regulation, teachers' competencies etc.).

Working Session 2: Subject-specific theoretical and empirical pathways to the professional development of teachers

This workshop included papers that focused on subject-specific theoretical and empirical ways to the professional development of teachers. The papers reflected aspects such as developing Pedagogical Content Knowledge, teaching practice during the pre-service teachers training, In-Service Teacher Training and the quality of instruction in different school subjects. The papers addressed biology and foreign language teachers predominantly; several papers reflected on arts, physical education and ballet teachers.

Working Session 3: Practical pathways in the professional development of teachers

In this workshop, practical approaches to fostering the professional development of teachers were presented. The papers covered a range variety of themes: Teacher training curricula in different countries, traditional or innovative teacher training courses and practical teacher training activities, e.g. using video recordings of lessons in teachers training.

Some concluding remarks

This conference volume provides a wide overview of current theoretical, empirical as well as practical questions, methodologies and results. The papers utilised a range of different research methodologies, examined a variety of learning environments and discussed many practical approaches to support professional development of teachers. The conference presented an opportunity to exchange points of view from different perspectives and cultural backgrounds.

We hope that this volume – taking into account the diversity and the quality of the papers – constitutes a valuable source book for educational theorists, educational researchers, teacher trainers as well as teachers. Often, the most useful and challenging information can be found in the papers far from our own traditions of educational theory or practice. Therefore we are hopeful that this volume provides many valuable pathways to the professional development of teachers.

Tomáš Janík & Petr Knecht
Brno, Czech Republic
June 2010

EIN LEHRERSTUDIUM BEGINNEN - KONZEPTE UND BEFUNDE ZUR GESTALTUNG VON BERUFSINFORMATION, LAUFBAHNBERATUNG UND BEWERBERAUSWAHL

Johannes Mayr, Alpen-Adria-Universität Klagenfurt, Österreich

In vielen europäischen Ländern droht ein gravierender Lehrermangel. Dieser Mangel betrifft vor allem bestimmte Schularten – insbesondere solche mit geringerem Prestige bzw. schwierigen Schüler/-inne/-n – und er betrifft vor allem bestimmte Fächer – wie etwa Mathematik und die Naturwissenschaften. Die Schulbehörden der betroffenen Länder starten deshalb verschiedene Aktivitäten, um die benötigte Anzahl von Lehrkräften zu rekrutieren. Dabei sehen sie sich gezwungen, auch auf Personen zurückzugreifen, die kein Lehramtsstudium absolviert haben bzw. Lehrkräfte auch in Fächern einzusetzen, für die sie nicht ausgebildet sind.
Diesem Bemühen der Schulbehörden steht ein anderes Ziel gegenüber: Man möchte nicht nur ausreichend viele Lehrkräfte zur Verfügung haben, sondern möglichst gute. Das ist verständlich, ist doch die Qualität der Lehrkräfte – neben den Merkmalen der Schüler/-innen – der wesentlichste Einflussfaktor auf die Schülerleistungen (McKinsey, 2007).

Schlüsselbegriffe: Lehrermangel, Empfehlungen zur Lehrerlaufbahn, Selbsterkundung

Bereits 2005 wurden in der OECD-Studie *Teachers matter* Maßnahmen vorgeschlagen, wie man gute Lehrkräfte gewinnen, ausbilden und im Beruf halten kann. In ähnlicher Weise werden im österreichischen Nationalen Bildungsbericht (Mayr & Neuweg 2009) Empfehlungen gegeben, die sich ebenfalls auf die gesamte Lehrerlaufbahn beziehen. Im Folgenden erfolgt dem gegenüber eine Fokussierung auf die Phase der Laufbahnwahl und den Einstieg ins Lehrerstudium. Die Darstellung folgt dabei teilweise einem Positionspapier, das von der Arbeitsgruppe Eignungsabklärung (2009) im Auftrag des österreichischen Ministeriums für Unterricht, Kunst und Kultur erstellt wurde.

1 Information und Selbsterkundung

Um ausreichend viele potenziell geeignete Personen für ein Lehrerstudium bzw. den Lehrerberuf zu interessieren, muss dieser Beruf zunächst so weiterentwickelt werden, dass er für ambitionierte junge Menschen anziehend ist – zumindest sind glaubwürdige Schritte in diese Richtung zu setzen. Das hieße z. B. höhere Anfangsgehälter zu bezahlen, mehr Gestaltungsspielraum an den Schulen zu ermöglichen und differenziertere Karrieremöglichkeiten vorzusehen (Strittmatter, 2007; Nieskens, 2009). Dieses dann geschärfte, attraktiver gewordene Bild von Lehrerberuf wäre in der öffentlichen Wahrnehmung zu positionieren und gezielt an Studieninteressierte heranzutragen – ohne die weiter bestehenden Probleme des Berufs und seines Umfeldes auszuklammern. Es geht also darum, *realitätsbezogen* und zugleich *zukunftsorientiert* über den Lehrerberuf zu *informieren.*

An einer Lehrerlaufbahn interessierte Personen sollten darüber hinaus veranlasst werden, ihre persönliche Neigung und Eignung zum Lehrerberuf zu klären, also die Passung zwischen den eigenen Voraussetzungen und dem beruflichen Anforderungsprofil zu überprüfen. Dabei können wissenschaftlich fundierte Test- und Selbsterkundungs-Verfahren einen wichtigen Beitrag leisten und zu einer wünschenswerten Selbst-Selektion beitragen. Diese Wirkung können sie allerdings nur entfalten, wenn sie nicht erst zu Studienbeginn, sondern bereits in der Phase der Studienwahlentscheidung eingesetzt werden (Mayr 2002). Aus diesem Grund ist der österreichische Pilotversuch „Studienchecker" zu würdigen, bei dem bereits Schüler/-inne/-n der vorletzten Klasse der höheren Schule Verfahren zur Selbsterkundung und gezielte, auch individuelle Beratung angeboten wird. Manche dieser Verfahren lassen sich kostengünstig auch über das Internet bereitstellen (Hell, in Druck), was erhebliche Kostenvorteile mit sich bringt und kein Nachteil zu sein braucht, wenn zusätzlich eine persönliche Laufbahnberatung bereit steht.

2 CCT - Career Counselling for Teachers

Ein solches webbasiertes, speziell für den Lehrerberuf gedachtes Beratungsangebot entstand unter dem Titel *CCT – Career Counselling for Teachers* im Zuge einer Zusammenarbeit von Lehrerbildungseinrichtungen aus sechs europäischen Staaten. Die CCT-Website vereint die oben angesprochenen Funktionen der Information über den Lehrerberuf und der Selbsterkundung und rückt bereits in der Phase der Studien- und Berufswahl die gesamte Lehrerlaufbahn in den Blick – einschließlich der späteren Um- und Aufstiegsoptionen. CCT bietet u.a. folgende Inhalte:

Informationen über das Bildungswesen, den Lehrerberuf, die Arbeitsmarktsituation, die Ausbildungsangebote, Karrieremöglichkeiten im Bildungswesen und Beratungseinrichtungen sowie *Links* zu weiterführenden Informationen.

Selbsterkundungs-Verfahren: Fragebögen, Checklisten und Tests, mit denen die persönlichen Voraussetzungen für eine erfolgreiche und befriedigende Berufstätigkeit als Lehrer/-in bzw. für spezielle Karrieren im Bildungswesen (zum Beispiel als Schulleiter/-in) geklärt werden können. Die Verfahren sind *online* bearbeitbar und liefern individualisierte Ergebnisrückmeldungen.

Geführte Touren: Für wichtige Entscheidungssituationen – etwa die Entscheidung für oder gegen ein Lehrerstudium – wird eine Abfolge ausgewählter Informationstexte und Selbsterkundungs-Verfahren angeboten, die mit einer zusammenfassenden Interpretation und Empfehlungen für weitere Abklärungen endet. Dieses Resümee sowie alle Detailergebnisse können von den Benützer/-innе/-n später jederzeit wieder abgerufen werden.

Reportagen: Berichte von Schüler/-inne/-n, Lehrerstudent/-inn/-en und Lehrer/-inne/-n aus ihrem Leben – als Reflexionsanstoß für alle, die sich in einer ähnlichen Laufbahnsituation befinden.

CCT ist derzeit das am weitesten verbreitete Online-Beratungsprogramm für den Lehrerberuf. In *Österreich* wird es vom Ministerium für Unterricht, Kunst und Kultur unterstützt und an allen Pädagogischen Hochschulen sowie den meisten Universitäten verwendet. In *Deutschland* ist es in mehreren Bundesländern sogar ein verpflichtender Teil des Zulassungsverfahrens zum Lehrerstudium, so dass es jährlich von vielen Tausenden Studienanfänger/-inne/-n durchlaufen wird.

Die *Evaluierungsergebnisse* belegen, dass die Auseinandersetzung mit CCT von den Benützer/-inne/-n als informativ empfunden wird, dass sie dadurch auf Tätigkeitsfelder von Lehrer/-inne/-n und berufliche Belastungen aufmerksam werden, die ihnen zuvor noch nicht bewusst gewesen waren. Die Benützer/-innen gewinnen also ein realistischeres Bild der Schulwirklichkeit.

Zugleich wird ein positives Bild vom Lehrerberuf vermittelt, das ihn als vielfältigen und zugleich herausfordernden Beruf zeigt und Personen mit guter Passung eine attraktive Berufslaufbahn verspricht. Solche Studieninteressierten erleben die Rückmeldungen als Ermutigung, tatsächlich ein Lehrerstudium zu beginnen. Personen mit ungünstigen Voraussetzungen berichten gegenteilige Impulse. Damit übt CCT eine wünschenswerte Steuerungsfunktion aus (Nieskens & Müller, 2009).

3 Zulassungsverfahren zum Lehrerstudium

Durch die skizzierten Maßnahmen der Information und Selbsterkundung lassen sich zwar gut geeignete Personen auf den Lehrerberuf aufmerksam machen und für diesen gewinnen, problematische Personen jedoch nur bedingt vom Lehrerberuf fernhalten (Mayr, Gutzwiller-Helfenfinger & Nieskens, 2009). Es sind deshalb zusätzlich Maßnahmen der *Fremd-Selektion* vor Aufnahme ins Lehramtsstudium zu überlegen. Da dieses Studium – im Gegensatz zu den meisten anderen Studienrichtungen – auf einen bestimmten Beruf vorbereitet, sollten sich die Auswahlkriterien nicht nur auf den Studienerfolg beziehen, sondern auch aussagekräftig im Hinblick auf die spätere Berufsbewährung sein. Dazu gehören berufsrelevante Dispositionen, die nur beschränkt im Studium verändert werden können, etwa Berufsmotivation, Kontaktbereitschaft und psychische Stabilität (Hanfstingl & Mayr, 2007).

Um das Vorliegen solcher Merkmale mit vertretbarer Zuverlässigkeit feststellen zu können, sind wissenschaftlich abgesicherte Assessments erforderlich. Solche werden in manchen Ländern seit Jahren angewandt, darunter auch im „PISA-Musterland" Finnland (Kohonen, 2007). Im deutschen Sprachraum gibt es dagegen erst wenige diesbezügliche Erfahrungen und noch weniger Evaluierungsstudien (Mayr, Eder & Fartacek, 1985; Trapmann, Hell & Schuler 2008). Eindeutig lässt sich jedoch sagen, dass diese Prozeduren überaus personalintensiv sind und deshalb eine *Kosten-Nutzen-Abwägung* erforderlich ist. Diese fällt vor allem dann ungünstig aus, wenn – anders als in Finnland – letztlich ein Großteil der Bewerber/-innen aufgenommen wird bzw. wegen des Lehrermangels aufgenommen werden muss. Die Entscheidung über den Einsatz solcher Verfahren sollte allerdings nicht ausschließlich an den dadurch erzielten Verbesserungen in der „Trefferquote", also dem Rekrutieren gut geeigneter bzw. dem Abhalten problematischer Lehramtsaspirant/-inn/-en gemessen werden: Das Durchlaufen eines anspruchsvollen Bewerbungsverfahrens verbessert nämlich die Bindung an die Ausbildungsinstitution und die Studienmotivation (Spiel, Litzenberger & Haiden, 2007).

4 Reflexions-, Qualifizierungs- und Selektionsprozesse in der ersten Phase des Lehrerstudiums

Die Aussicht, bereits in frühen Abschnitten des Studiums mit Kindern und Jugendlichen arbeiten zu können, scheint sich günstig auf die Rekrutierung intrinsisch für den Lehrerberuf motivierter Personen auszuwirken (Mayr, 2009). Das Ziel solcher Praktika sollte jedoch nicht sein, rasch berufspraktische Kompetenz zu erwerben, sondern zunächst einen distanzierten Blick auf die Schule werfen zu können, die bisher nur aus der Schülerperspektive vertraut war. Erste Handlungserfahrungen in der Rolle als Lehrende/-r sollten jedoch ermöglicht werden, da sie zur weiteren *Selbst-Überprüfung* der Berufswahl anregen, individuellen *Entwicklungsbedarf* aufzeigen und Ansatzpunkte für *Beratung* bieten (Mayr & Neuweg, 2009).

Das deutsche Bundesland Nordrhein-Westfalen setzt diesen Schritt der Praxiskonfrontation bereits *vor dem Studium*: Am Lehrerberuf interessierte Personen werden für die Dauer von 20 Tagen als Praktikant/-inn/-en an einer Schule aufgenommen und von Mentor/-inn/-en begleitet. Diese führen mit ihnen Beratungsgespräche, in die auch Erkenntnisse aus dem Online-Programm CCT einfließen. Bereits im Zuge dieses Praktikums wird mit dem Führen eines Portfolios begonnen, das auch schon Entwicklungsschritte für das spätere Studium vorbereitet und damit die Brücke von der Berufsklärungsphase hinein ins Studium schlägt (MSW, o.J.; Oelkers, 2009).

Solche Formen der Praxisbegegnung dienen der Selbstklärung der Laufbahnwahl und intendieren im Allgemeinen keine Fremd-Selektion. In späteren Praktika kann die Beobachtung des Handelns der Studierenden im Praxisfeld und ihres Kompetenzzuwachses jedoch eine taugliche Grundlage auch für institutionelle Entscheidungen sein, ob das Lehrerstudium fortgesetzt werden darf. An den Schweizer Pädagogischen Hochschulen wird eine solche Entscheidung meist bereits Ende des ersten Studienjahres explizit angestrebt (Criblez & Lehmann, 2007). Dafür wurden elaborierte Beobachtungsschemata und Vorgangsweisen entwickelt, die eine möglichst zuverlässige Entscheidungsfindung ermöglichen sollen. Hinsichtlich ihrer Aufwändigkeit ähneln diese Prozeduren den Assessments vor Studienbeginn, sie versprechen jedoch eine weitaus höhere – allerdings erst empirisch nachzuweisende – Validität. Zweifellos haben sie aber den Vorzug, dass in den meisten Fällen die Qualifizierungsabsicht und die Entwicklungsberatung im Vordergrund stehen, nicht die Selektion (Fuchs, Lauener & Luthiger, 2008).

5 Eignungsabklärung und Qualifizierung als Kontinuum

Die skizzierten Informations- und Reflexionsangebote sowie die Maßnahmen zur Eignungsüberprüfung sollten günstigerweise aufeinander bezogen konzipiert und so gestaltet sein, dass sie von den angehenden Lehrpersonen als hilfreiche Anstöße zu ihrer Professionalitätsentwicklung erlebt werden. Die Arbeit mit Portfolios (Schratz & Tschegg 2001) kann eine solche Perspektive fördern, speziell wenn sie von Beginn an phasenübergreifend konzipiert ist oder sogar die Zeit vor dem Studium mit einbezieht.

Literaturangaben

ARBEITSGRUPPE EIGNUNGSABKLÄRUNG (2009): Ein Lehrerstudium beginnen. Positionspapier zu Berufsinformation, Selbsterkundung und Studierendenauswahl. Stand: 29. März 2009.

CCT – CAREER COUNSELLING FOR TEACHERS: www.cct-austria.at; www.cct-germany.de; www.cct-switzerland.ch

CRIBLEZ, L. & LEHMANN, L. (2007): Verfahren zur Auswahl von Lehrerinnen und Lehrern in der Schweiz. Journal für Lehrerinnen- und Lehrerbildung, 7 (2), 33-40.

FUCHS, M., LAUENER, H. & LUTHIGER, H. (2008): Potenziale entdecken – Grenzen wahrnehmen. Seminar, 14 (2), 23-40.

Hanfstingl, B. & Mayr, J. (2007): Prognose der Bewährung im Lehrerstudium und im Lehrerberuf. Journal für Lehrerinnen- und Lehrerbildung, 7 (2), 48–56.

HELL, B. (in Druck): Selbsttests zur Studienorientierung: nützliche Vielfalt oder un-nützer Wildwuchs? In G. Rudinger (Hg.), Self-Assessment an Hochschulen: Von der Studienfachwahl zur Profilbildung. Bonn: Vandenhoeck & Ruprecht.

KOHONEN, V. (2007): Auswahlverfahren für Lehramtsstudierende in Finnland. Journal für Lehrerinnen- und Lehrerbildung, 7 (2), 26-32.

MAYR, J. (2002): Qualitätssicherung durch Laufbahnberatung: Zur Rolle von Selbsterkundungs-Verfahren. In H. Brunner, E. Mayr, M. Schratz & I. Wieser (Hg.), Lehrerinnen- und Lehrerbildung braucht Qualität. Und wie!? (S. 413-434). Innsbruck: Studienverlag.

MAYR, J. (2009): LehrerIn werden in Österreich: empirische Befunde zum Lehramtsstudium. Erziehung und Unterricht, 159 (1-2), 14-33.

MAYR, J., EDER, F. & RIEDL, J. (1985): Evaluierung eines Verfahrens zur Auswahl von Lehramtsstudenten. In F. Buchberger & H. Seel (Hg.), Materialien zur Lehrerbildung für die Schulreform (S. 136-144). Linz/Brüssel: Association for Teacher Education in Europe.

MAYR, J., GUTZWILLER-HELFENFINGER, E. & NIESKENS, B. (2009): Online counselling for teacher training applicants: Voluntary versus bound. Poster presented at the European Conference on Educational Research (ECER), Vienna, 29 September 2009.

MAYR, J. & NEUWEG, G. H. (2009): Lehrer/innen als zentrale Ressource im Bildungssystem: Rekrutierung und Qualifizierung. In W. Specht (Hg.), Nationaler Bildungsbericht Österreich 2009. Band 2: Fokussierte Analysen bildungspolitischer Schwerpunktthemen (S. 99-119). Graz: Leykam.

MCKINSEY (2007): How the world's best-performing school systems come out on top.
www.mckinsey.com/clientservice/socialsector/resources/pdf/Worlds_School_Systems_Final.pdf

MSW (2010): Das Eignungspraktikum. Ein neues Praxiselement in der Ausbildung zukünftiger Lehrerinnen und Lehrer in Nordrhein-Westfalen. Standardvortrag des Ministeriums für Schule und Weiterbildung (MSW) des Landes Nordrhein-Westfalen (Power Point Präsentation).

NIESKENS, B. (2009): Wer interessiert sich für den Lehrerberuf – und wer nicht? Berufswahl im Spannungsfeld von subjektiver und objektiver Passung. Göttingen: Cuvillier.

NIESKENS, B. & MÜLLER, F. (2009): Web-basierte Selbsterkundung persönlicher Voraussetzungen und Interessen. Erziehung und Unterricht, 159, 41-49.

OECD (2005): Teachers matter: Attracting, developing and retaining effective teachers. Paris: OECD.

OELKERS, J. (2009): "I wanted to be a good teacher...". Zur Ausbildung von Lehrkräften in Deutschland. Studie. Berlin: Friedrich Ebert Stiftung.

SCHRATZ, M. & TSCHEGG, K. (2001): Das Portfolio im Kontinuum unterschiedlicher Phasen der Lehrerbildung. Journal für Lehrerinnen- und Lehrerbildung, 1 (4), 17-25.

SPIEL, C., LITZENBERGER, M. & HAIDEN, D. (2007): Bildungswissenschaftliche und psychologische Aspekte von Auswahlverfahren. In C. BADELT, W. WEGSCHEIDER & H. WULZ (Hg.): Hochschulzugang in Österreich (S. 479-552). Graz: Leykam.

STRITTMATTER, A. (2007): Gute Lehrkräfte gewinnen ist mehr als eine Selektionsaufgabe. Journal für Lehrerinnen- und Lehrerbildung 7 (2), 9-19.

STUDIENCHECKER. Pilotprojekt des BMUKK und des BMWF. www.studienchecker.at

TRAPMANN, S., HELL, B. & SCHULER, H. (2008): Konstruktion und Evaluation eines mehrstufigen Auswahlverfahrens für Lehramtsstudierende im Fach Biologie an der Universität Hohenheim. In H. Schuler & B. Hell (Hg.), Studierendenauswahl und Studienentscheidung (S. 168-177). Göttingen: Hogrefe.

Kontakt:
Johannes MAYR: Johannes.Mayr@uni-klu.ac.at

TEACHER EXPERTISE: KEY CONCEPTS AND RESEARCH METHODOLOGIES

Michaela Píšová, Masaryk University Brno, Czech Republic

The ongoing discussion concerning quality in education concurrently addresses one of its central challenges – the professionalization of a teacher. It is within this context that our paper aims to shed some light on the concept of expertise in the teaching profession. A brief survey of current research on teacher expertise is provided, focusing mainly on approaches to the study of expertise and main trends in research of the phenomenon, at the same time discussing the underlying and crucial question – how to define and identify an expert teacher.

Keywords: Teacher professionalization, teacher expertise, teaching profession, expert teacher

1 Introduction

In any discussion of expertise it is important to be aware of the fact that even though the field of scientific research of this phenomenon has "matured up to the point warranting the publication of its first handbook" (Ericsson et al., 2006, p. 3), the discourse is still hampered by a lack of terminological or even conceptual clarity. Therefore it should be clearly stated at the very beginning that this paper deals with expertise *in* the teaching profession rather than expertise *of* the teaching profession. The latter might bring in a slightly different discourse perspective with a sociological 'flavour' (cf. e.g. Welker, 1991 and others). Furthermore, the terms 'expertise' or 'expert teacher' have been neither used universally nor defined in a consensual way; various authors adopt different terms for the same notion (e.g. excellence, effectiveness, superiority; experienced teacher, quality teacher, effective teacher, competent teacher, exceptional teacher, etc.). For the purpose of further discussion we will build on one of the most authoritative definitions, namely that by ERICSSON (2006, p. 3) who perceives *expertise* as "the characteristics, skills and knowledge that distinguish experts from novices and less experienced people". These characteristics, skills and knowledge underpin "superior reproducible performances of representative tasks" in the profession, i.e. *expert performances.* An *expert*, then, is "someone widely recognized *(sic!)* as a reliable source of knowledge, technique, or skill whose judgement is accorded authority and status by the public or his or her peers. Experts have prolonged or intense experience through practice and education in a particular field" (Wikipedia, 2005, cited in Ericsson, 2006, p. 3). Though interest in superior performances in various areas of human activity can be traced to the very beginnings of Western civilisation, serious scientific attempts to capture the essence of these performances date back to the 19th century when two of the main theories were formulated and investigated: the theoretical concept of innate general mental capacities as a source of exceptional achievements, and the second widely accepted theoretical framework of expertise as extended experience. It is not the aspiration of this paper to provide an exhaustive diachronic survey of the study of expertise; suffice to say that the research reflected the dominant paradigms of its time, be it the process-product (essentially behaviourist) or cognitive one (for more detailed information see Johnson, 2005, pp. 11-33, or Feltovich et al., 2006, pp. 41-68). But it should be noted that the last decades witnessed a shift of research priorities from other domains towards *expertise in professions* in accord with the function of professional experts as key agents in social and economic life (Tynjälä et al., 1997, pp. 475-6). It is also obvious that rapid social and cultural changes, as well as changes in knowledge production, influence the nature and content of professional expertise and bring in a need to add a future perspective or dimension to its perception. This in particular applies to the teaching profession: expert teachers must continually invest in reconstruction of their expertise in response to the ongoing contextual development, but at the same time it is the teachers and "educational systems that are expected to produce (future) experts for working life" (ibid.).

2 Research on expertise in the teaching profession

2.1 Approaches to the study of expertise

Research of expertise in the teaching profession has been inspired by studies on expertise in other domains. According to CHI (2006, pp. 21-23), two main approaches to the study of expertise in general can be identified in psychological research; she chose to label them the *absolute approach* and the *relative approach*. The former way is to study exceptional individuals in order to understand how they perform in their domain of expertise. Here "the tacit assumption is that greatness ... arises from chance and unique innate talent" (Simonton, 1977, cited in Chi, 2006, p. 22) The latter approach is based on comparative studies of experts and novices, therefore it allows for a slightly less precise definition of expertise as experts are assessed on a comparative (relative) continuum. On the other hand, in addition to description and understanding of expertise, its goal is to find out how experts became experts so that others may shape their professional trajectories that way.

The study of expertise in the teaching profession has deployed similar approaches since the 1980s. A slightly different organisational principle for their categorisation was provided by TSUI (2005, pp. 167-189, see also Tsui, 2003): she made a distinction between studies of *expertise as a state* and those with a *developmental perspective*. Within research of expertise as a state which is – or rather may be – reached after years of experience most of the studies took the form of novice-expert comparisons. A number of them (e.g. Berliner et al., 1988; Peterson and Comeaux, 1987, etc.) were carried out in laboratory settings, other studies (e.g. Leinhardt, 1989; Turner-Bisset, 2001, etc.) adopted a naturalistic approach where the investigations were conducted in a classroom setting. Later on, the limitations of the novice-expert comparisons were recognised and the studies were criticised by BEREITER and SCARDAMALIA (1993) and others for overestimation of the role of practice as the main source of expertise and for provision of a static and uniform view of the nature of teacher expertise. One of the proposed solutions rested in broadening the definition of expertise. TYNJÄLÄ et al. (1997, p. 478) summarised recent arguments for considering the concept of *wisdom* as an alternative perspective for defining and conceptualising expertise

and claimed that "expertise as comprehensive wisdom includes, in addition to a cognitive dimension, the affective and volitive aspects of human action."
Other studies, however, in reaction to the identified limitations, set upon a different route to the research of teacher expertise: they adopted a developmental perspective. In other words, they examined the acquisition and maintenance of expertise (Bereiter, Scardamalia, 1993; Tsui, 2003, etc.). Thus, expertise has been understood as a process rather than state.

2.2 Main trends in research on expertise in the teaching profession

Research within the above approaches was rooted in various paradigms over time. With reference to SHULMAN'S emphasis on the need of *disciplined eclecticism* in educational research (1986, p. 33), we will attempt to present the three currently dominant paradigms in the study of teacher expertise as this paradigmatic plurality yields fairly different characteristics of the phenomenon, with each of them capturing its specific aspects.
The first influential theoretical position developed as a reaction to the rationalist information processing approach in cognitive psychology linked to the work in the field of artificial intelligence. Building on the work by FULLER and BOWN (1975, in Zeichner, 1981/2) and by DREYFUS and DREYFUS (1986) and their general stage model of professional development, as well as on further research findings concerning novice and expert teachers, BERLINER (e.g. 1995 and elsewhere) developed a five-stage model of teacher professional development. The top stage – an expert teacher – is characterised as intuitive or even arational (Berliner, 2004, p. 22). Expert knowledge is seen as embedded in the expert's action, tacit, non-reflective and automatic. The core of human expertise is 'knowing how' rather than 'knowing that' (cf. also Eraut, 1994, p. 15, who distinguished propositional knowledge that underpins or enables professional action, and practical know-how, which is inherent in the action and cannot be separated). The label attached to this theoretical position usually reads *expertise as intuition and tacit knowledge*.
Research in cognitive psychology in the late 80s and 90s, however, led to a considerably different view of *expertise as conscious deliberation and an organised knowledge base*. Fundamental differences from the previous position may be formulated in the following way:

- expertise is based on a highly organised and elaborate knowledge base, which enables a deeper and more precise perception of issues and provides immediate access to optimal solutions of pedagogical situations;
- experts do not rely solely on intuition, they constantly monitor their professional behaviour and actions;
- self-reflection is a necessary prerequisite for achieving and maintaining expertise.

GLASER and CHI (1988) provided an overview of the field and formulated seven characteristics of experts which they considered generalisable:
- experts excel mainly in their own domains and well-known contexts. In other domains or contexts they are likely to behave more like novices;
- experts perceive large meaningful patterns in their domains. This perceptual ability reflects an organisation of the knowledge base;
- experts are fast; they are able to solve pedagogical situations very quickly and in a flexible way as some aspects of their actions are automated which frees their mental capacity for 'processing' other aspects;
- experts see and represent a problem at a deeper and more principled level than novices; novices tend to represent a problem at a superficial level;
- experts spend a great deal of time analysing a problem qualitatively, whereas novices plunge immediately into attempting to solve the problem. This is particularly true with the so-called ill-defined situations;
- experts have strong self-monitoring skills and self-knowledge, they are more aware than novices of when they make errors (see also Eraut, 1994; Tsui, 2003; Berliner, 1995; Chi, 2006, etc.).

It should be noted that the first characteristic feature, namely domain- and context-dependence of experts, was questioned by HATANO and INAGAKI (1986; see also Berliner, 2001), who claimed that exceptional – as opposed to *routine* – experts are *adaptive* (see also Bereiter and Scardamalia, 1993, who talked about crystallised vs. fluid expertise). However, CHI (2006, pp. 23-27) in her summary of ways in which experts fall short, provides further evidence concerning domain-limitedness, context-dependence and inflexibility of experts (in addition to other issues).
The third theoretical position is based on criticism of expert–novice comparisons. BEREITER and SCARDAMALIA (1993) in their research of novice and

expert writers found out that the latter actually worked much longer and harder and consequently produced work of a much higher quality (see also Wineburg, 1991, 1994). Rather than comparing experts with novices, they proposed to look for differences amongst experts and experienced non-experts. In this way, they believed, the critical developmental aspects of expertise may be discovered. This dynamic view, the perspective of *expertise as a process,* opened up a new horizon in the study of the phenomenon. The authors suggested that fundamental differences between experts and experienced non-experts include the ability and willingness of the former to 'work consistently on the edge of their competence' (ibid., p. 34), i.e. to *reinvest their mental resources* freed up by the use of routines to tackle more challenging problems or problematise seemingly routine operations. Further on, they refer to another characteristic of experts, the so-called *progressive problem solving* (experts, according to the authors, consistently extend their competence by choosing to solve problems that are progressively more difficult). So far, however, there have, to the best of my knowledge, been only a few studies conducted from the perspective of expertise as a process (e.g. Bullough and Baughman, 1997; Tsui, 2003).

2.3 Identification of an expert teacher

We presented a brief survey of the three main trends in research on expertise in the teaching profession which, all in their specific way, attempt to contribute to our understanding of the nature of expertise. The underlying and crucial question in any of the trends, is, of course, how we can *define and identify an expert teacher*. In the above studies, little attention was given to the consistency of the selection of criteria used to identify expert teachers which may raise doubts about the validity of the studies. It is obviously much easier to identify an expert in some other domains such as sports, computer science etc. However, identification of experts in professions in general and in teaching specifically poses a true challenge. As a set of objective criteria has not yet been established (and may never be), it may be useful to refer to a study conducted by PALMER et. al. (2005). The authors examined 27 studies from the perspective of the marker variables used to identify expert teachers and found out that these included:

- *Years of experience in the profession*: the most frequent requirement was between 5 and 10 years of practice (further in the discussion the authors strongly recommend to take into consideration also the context and require at least 3 years in the same instructional context);

- *Professional or social group membership* (e.g. status as cooperating or mentor teacher etc.). Some other sources (e. g. Tsui 2005, p. 169) talk in this sense rather about nominations or recommendations from the school administrators, about social recognition, etc.;
- *Performance criterion:* either normative (5 studies), criterion-based (9 studies) or mixture of both (2 studies);
- *General criteria*, such as 'based on Berliner criteria'.

In the discussion about common criteria for identifying expert teachers, Tsui (2005, pp. 170-171) reminds us of "cultural differences in perceptions about what constitutes expertise in teaching" and expresses doubts "whether it is at all possible or even meaningful to establish criteria which could be applied across cultures".

A promising attempt to solve the problem was provided by STERNBERG and HORVATH (1995) who sketched out a prototype view of teacher expertise: "a featural model of similarity based categorisation" (p. 9). Drawing on work of other researchers, they proposed three critical prototypical features which distinguish expert teachers from novices and represent a core of clusters of similar features: *knowledge, efficiency* and *insight.* This prototype model was considered particularly useful as it allows for variations and diversity among expert teachers. It was adopted by BOND ET AL. (2000) in their sophisticated study aimed at establishing and validating professional standards for the National Board of Professional Teaching Standards. They worked with thirteen prototypical features of expertise and created measures for each of them. These features or characteristics to be held by expert teachers were: *better use of knowledge; extensive pedagogical content knowledge, including deep representations of subject matter knowledge; better problem solving strategies; better adaptation and modification of goals for diverse learners including better skills of improvisation; better decision making; more challenging objectives; better classroom climate; better perception of classroom events including a better ability to read the cues from learners; greater sensitivity to context; better monitoring of learning and providing feedback to students; more frequent testing of hypotheses; greater respect for learners; and a greater display of passion for teaching.* These prototypical features were deployed in a comparative study of a group of Board certified teachers (experts) and a comparison group of experienced and well-prepared teachers. The outcomes, no matter how remarkable they are considered e.g. by BERLINER (2004, p. 24), in our opinion provide validation of the assessment procedure used by the Board rather than a generalisable and objective tool for identification of expertise (cf. also Tsui, 2005, p. 170).

2.4 Research methodologies

Most research on expertise has been conducted in the field of cognitive psychology; expertise in the teaching profession, as mentioned above, has had a much shorter history and consequently has harvested fewer studies so far. This, in a way, influences the following survey of research methodologies applied in the study of expertise. Building on ERICSSON ET.AL. (2006, sections 2 and 3), we may divide the studies and the core methods they deployed into two main groups:

- *Methods for studying the structure of expertise:* ethnographic observation of work practices in natural settings, psychometric methods, laboratory studies, simulations, concept maps, verbal methods (think-aloud protocols), etc.
- *Methods for studying the acquisition and maintenance of expertise: l*aboratory studies, retrospective interview/life stories, clinical writing, analyses of documents, etc.

Research on expertise as a developmental process typically includes longitudinal studies. TYNJÄLÄ ET AL. (1997, p. 490) also strongly recommend theoretically grounded intervention studies, action research, etc.

3 Conclusion

This paper presented a brief survey of research on expertise in the teaching profession. The last approximately three decades witnessed a worldwide growing interest in this area, which stemmed from the recognition of the great social and economic importance of increasing the quality in education at schools or other educational institutions in accordance with the imperative of life-long learning. Furthermore, as TSUI (2005, pp. 184-185) noted, "much of the work on expertise in teaching ….has been motivated by the need to raise the status of the teaching profession by demonstrating to the public that like experts in other professions, experts in teaching possess knowledge and skills which are no less sophisticated." Research on expertise, its identification, development and assessment is also a vital prerequisite for setting the standards that would stand as goals towards which the members of the profession may aspire. Last but not least, learning about expertise and its acquisition may be critical for reshaping and transforming pregraduate teacher education – the idea of learning from experts in this particular area has been advocated by BERLINER (2001 and elsewhere).

Bibliography

ANDERSON, L.W. (Ed.): International Encyclopedia of Teaching and Teacher Education. Oxford : Elsevier Science Ltd, 2nd edition, 1995.

BEREITER, C.; SCARDAMALIA, M.: Surpassing ourselves: An inquiry into the nature and implications of expertise. Chicago : Open Court Publishing, 1993.

BERLINER, D.C.; STEIN, P. SABERS, D.; CLARRIDGE, P.B.; CUSHING, K.; AND PINNEGAR, S.: Implications of Research on Pedagogical Expertise and Experience for Mathematics teaching. In: Grouws, D.A.; Cooney, T.J. (Eds.): Perspectives on Research on Effective Mathematics Teaching. Reston : National Council of Teachers of Mathematics, 1988.

BERLINER, D.: Teacher Expertise. In: Anderson, L.W. (Ed.): International Encyclopedia of Teaching and Teacher Education. Oxford : Elsevier Science Ltd, 2nd edition, 1995, p. 46-52.

BERLINER, D. C.: Learning About and Learning From Expert Teachers. In: International Journal of Educational Research, 35, pp. 463-482, 2001.

BERLINER, D.: Expert teachers: Their characteristics, development and accomplishments. De la teoria?.a l'aula: Formacio del professorat ensenyament de las ciències socials. Departament de Didàctica de la Llengua de la Literatura I de les Ciències Socials. Universitat Autònoma de Barcelona, 2004.

BOND, L.; SMITH, T.; BAKER, W.K.; HATTIE, J.A.: The certification system of the National Board for Professional Teaching Standards: A construct and consequential validity study. Greensboro : University of North Carolina, 2000.

BULLOUGH, R. BAUGHMAN, K.: First year teacher eight years later: An inquiry into teacher development. New York : teachers College Press, 1997.

CHI, M.T.; GLASER, R.; FARR, M.J. (Eds.): The Nature of Expertise. Hillsdale : Erlbaum, 1988.

CHI, M. T.H.: Two Approaches to the Study of Experts´ Characteristics. In: Ericsson, K.A.; Charness, N.; Feltovich, P.J.; Hoffman, R.R. (Eds.) The Cambridge Handbook of Expertise and Expert Performance. Cambridge : Cambridge University Press, 2006, pp. 21-31.

DREYFUS, H. L., & DREYFUS, S. E.: Mind over machine. New York: Free Press, 1986.

ERAUT, M.: Developing Professional Knowledge and Competence. London : The Falmer Press, 1994.

ERICSSON, K.A.; CHARNESS, N.; FELTOVICH, P.J.; HOFFMAN, R.R. (Eds.): The Cambridge Handbook of Expertise and Expert Performance. Cambridge : Cambridge University Press, 2006.

FELTOVICH, P.J.; PRIETULA, M.J.; ERICSSON, K.A.: Studies of Expertise from Psychological Perspective. In: Ericsson, K.A.; Charness, N.; Feltovich, P.J.; Hoffman, R. R. (Eds.): The Cambridge Handbook of Expertise and Expert Performance. Cambridge : Cambridge University Press, 2006, pp. 41-68.

GLASER, R.; CHI, M.T.: Overview. In: Chi, M.T.; Glaser, R.; Farr, M.J. (Eds.): The Nature of Expertise. Hillsdale : Erlbaum, 1988.

HATANO, G.; INAGAKI, K.: Two Courses of Expertise. In: Stevenson, H.; Azuma, H.; Hakuta, K. (Eds.) Child Development in Japan. New York : W.H.Freeman, 1986.

JOHNSON, K. (Ed.): Expertise in Second Language Learning and Teaching. Basingstoke/New York : Palgrave MACMILLAN, 2005.

JOHNSON, K.: The 'General' Study of Expertise. In: Johnson, K. (Ed.) Expertise in Second Language Learning and Teaching. Basingstoke/New York : Palgrave Macmillan, 2005.

LEINHARDT, G. A.: Contrast of Novice and Expert Competence in Mathematics Lesson. In: Lowyck, J.; Clark, C.M (Eds.) Teacher Thinking and Professional Action. Leuven : Leuven University Press, pp. 75-98, 1989.

LEINHARDT, G.; BECK, I.L.; STAINTON, C. (Eds.): Teaching and Learning in History. Hillsdale : Lawrence Erlbaum Associates, 1994.

LOWYCK, J.; CLARK, C.M (Eds.): *Teacher Thinking and Professional Action.* Leuven : Leuven University Press, 1989.

PALMER, D.J.; STOUGH, L.M. BURDENSKI, T.K.; GONZALES, M.: Identifying Teacher Expertise: An Examination of Researchers´ Decision Making. In: Educational Psychologist, Vol. 40, No 1, pp. 13-25,

PETERSON, P. L., & COMEAUX, M. A.: Teachers' schemata for classroom events: The mental scaffolding of teachers' thinking during classroom instruction. In: Teaching and Teacher Education, 3, 319-331, 1987.

SHULMAN, L.B.: Paradigms and Research Programs in the Study of Teaching:

A Contemporary Perspective. In: Wittrock, M.C. (Ed.): Handbook of Research on Teaching. New York : MacMillan, 3rd Edition, pp. 3-36, 1986.

STERNBERG, R.J.; HORVATH, J.A.: A Prototype View of Expert Teaching. In: Educational Researcher, August-September, pp. 9-17, 1995.

STEVENSON, H.; AZUMA, H.; HAKUTA, K. (Eds.): Child Development in Japan. New York : W.H.Freeman, 1986.

TURNER-BISSET, R.: Expert Teaching: Knowledge and Pedagogy to Lead the Profession. London : David Fulton Publishers, 2001.

TSUI, A. B.M.: Understanding Expertise in Teaching. Cambridge : Cambridge University Press. 2003.

TSUI, A. B.M.: Expertise in Teaching: Perspectives and Issues. In: Johnson, K. (Ed.): Expertise in Second Language Learning and Teaching. Basingstoke/New York : Palgrave Macmillan, pp. 167-189, 2005.

TYNJÄLÄ, P.; NUUTINEN, A.; ETELÄPELTO, A.; KIRJONEN, J.; REMES, P.: The Acquisition of Professional Expertise – a challenge for educational research. In: Scandinavien Journal of Educational Research, Vol. 41, Nos 3-4, pp. 475-493, 1997.

WINEBURG, S.S.: Historical Problem Solving: A Study of the Cognitive Processes Used in Evaluation of Documentary and Pictorial Evidence. In: Journal of Educational Psychology, No. 83, pp. 73-78, 1991.

WINEBURG, S.S.: The Cognitive Representation of Historical Texts. In: Leinhardt, G.; Beck, I.L.; Stainton, C. (Eds.): Teaching and Learning in History. Hillsdale : Lawrence Erlbaum Associates, 1994.

WITTROCK, M.C. (Ed.): Handbook of Research on Teaching. New York : MacMillan, 3rd Edition, 1986.

WOLKER, R.: Expertise and the Teacher as Expert: Rethinking a Questionable Metaphor. In: American Educational Research Journal, Vol. 28, No.1, pp. 19-35, 1991.

ZEICHNER, K.M. Reflective Teaching and Field-Based Experience in Teacher Education. In: Interchange, 1981/1982, Vol. 12, No. 4.

Contact:
Doc. PhDr. Michaela PÍŠOVÁ, M.A., Ph.D.: pisova@ped.muni.cz

Fachdidaktisch-pädagogisches Coaching aus der Sicht der Didaktischen Rekonstruktion – Ein Beitrag zur theoretischen Differenzierung für den Biologieunterricht

Patrícia Jelemenská
Austrian Educational Competence Centre Biology (AECC-Bio),
Universität Wien, Österreich

Fachdidaktisch-pädagogisches Coaching (FPC) ist ein Ansatz, um die Kluft zwischen Ergebnissen der erziehungswissenschaftlichen Forschung und deren Nutzung in Praxisfeldern zu überwinden (Staub 2004). In der vorliegenden Studie wird der lerntheoretische Rahmen des FPC anhand der Didaktischen Rekonstruktion (DR) (Kattmann et al. 1997) differenziert, indem der Schwerpunkt auf die Auswahl und Strukturierung von Inhalten für das Lernen gelegt wird, um die Schüler/-innen zu reflektiertem Wissen zu führen (Jelemenská 2006).

Schlüsselbegriffe: Coaching, didaktische Rekonstruktion, Biologieunterricht, reflektiertes Wissen, *„conceptual reconstruction"*

1 Einleitung

Die Bildungsdiskussion über die Verbesserung des Unterrichts wurde in den letzten Jahren vor allem durch internationale Vergleichsstudien wie PISA (OECD) und TIMSS (IEA) ins Rollen gebracht. Die normative Wirkung verstärkte in der Bildungsdiskussion durch Kompetenzmodelle u.a. ebenso eine differenzierte Betrachtung der Schülerleistungen. Die veränderten Anforderungen an die Unterrichtskultur spiegeln sich in unterschiedlichen Ansätzen der Lehrer/-innenfortbildung wider. Bei der Initiative IMST (Österreich) werden innovative Ideen der Lehrer/-innen unterstützt, bei SINUS (Deutschland) werden die Lehrkräfte durch fachdidaktische Ansätze gefördert (s. n. Krainer 2007). Im angloamerikanischen Sprachraum wurde, um die Einführung der Standards und damit die Lehrer/-innen bei der Veränderung der Unterrichtskultur zu unterstützen, der Ansatz des Fachdidaktisch-pädagogischen Coaching (FPC) (West & Staub 2004) entwickelt. Orientiert an *„knowledge based constructivism"* (KBC) (Resnick & Hall 1998) wird die Praxis theoriegeleitet unterstützt. In der vorliegenden Studie wird der lerntheoretische Rahmen FPC anhand der Grundannahmen der DR (Kattmann et al. 1997) differenziert, wobei die innovativen Ideen der Lehrer/-innen gezielt aus einer fachdidaktischen Perspektive gefördert und gegebenenfalls entwickelt werden.

2 Hauptziele der Studie

- Die Unterrichtsgestaltung und Strukturierung des Biologieunterrichts werden ausgehend von den Überzeugungen der Lehrer/-innen im Rahmen des FPC unter Grundannahmen der fachdidaktischen Grundlagenforschung (DR) reflektiert und weiterentwickelt.
- Mit Hilfe des FPC sind Lernumgebungen für Lehrer/-innen zu entwickeln, in denen über die Gestaltung und Strukturierung des Biologieunterrichts reflektiert werden kann.
- Das Lernen der Lehrer/-innen soll anhand fachdidaktischer Kriterien analysiert werden. Mit praxisnah angelegten Fallstudien sollen die Überzeugungen und Vorstellungen zur wirksamen Unterrichtsgestaltung und zu deren Veränderung erfasst werden.

3 Fachdidaktisch-pädagogisches Coaching

Die persönliche Bereitschaft der Lehrer/-innen, über ihren eigenen Unterricht kontinuierlich zu reflektieren, ist ein Merkmal von Professionalität (Resnick & Hall 1998). Die Interaktion zwischen Wissenschaft und Praxis als Kokonstruktion von theoriebasierten Settings und Tools zur Entwicklung innovativer Praxis (Staub 2004) veranschaulicht die Abbildung 1. Die Modifizierung der Abbildung unter den Annahmen der DR ist Schwarz hervorgehoben.

Wesentlich bei FPC ist es, zu einer Abkehr von „mechanisch implementierten curricula“ (US-Curriculum als Handbuch) bereits bei der Unterrichtsplanung anzuleiten (West & Staub 2003, Staub 2004). Da die Rolle des Coachs von einer Lehrerperson übernommen wird, sind für die Vor- und Nachbesprechungen die Lehr-Lernprinzipien sowie ein Leitfaden zur Gestaltung des Unterrichts vorgegeben (Abb. 1 „Theorie“: KBC). Mit dem Leitfaden wird auf die Klärung der sachlichen Lernziele, Durchdenken der Unterrichtsinhalte in Bezug auf Vorwissen der Schüler etc. hingewiesen. Aus der veränderten Praxis sollen die exemplarischen Beispiele zu Tools, Settings und die theoretische Erklärung als Prototypen dienen und zum Gegenstand von weiteren empirischen Forschungsarbeiten werden (Abb. 1 „Relevanzgewinn“).

Da bei der DR für das Lernen das Verständnis der zentralen biologischen Begriffe (z.B. Selektion) zentral ist, wird nicht nur das Vorwissen, sondern vor allem das Schülerverständnis beachtet. Der Ausgangspunkt der DR im Sinne von Grundlageforschung (Kattmann et al. 1997) setzt bei der Reflexion der lernhinderlichen und lernförderlichen Inhalte und der entsprechenden Struktur des Biologieunterrichts an. Bei der Unterrichtsgestaltung sollen die lernförderlichen Ansätze in den Schülervorstellungen zu fachlich geklärten Sichtweisen differenziert und modifiziert werden (*„conceptual reconstruction"* s. z.B. Kattmann 2007). Da die Lehrer/-innen aus persönlichen Überzeugungen, subjektiven Theorien (z.B. Groeben et al. 1998) handeln, deren Wirksamkeit durch die Erfahrungen aus der Praxis unterstützt wird, ist beim FPC zwischen den fachdidaktischen und praxisbasierten Zugängen zu unterscheiden. Die dahinter stehenden Prozesse sind in Abb. 1 durch die Prozesspfeile verdeutlicht. Für die Reflexion der Unterrichtsplanung sind jedoch die Grundannahmen der DR bei dem FPC zentral. Durch „Abfolge der Interaktion" werden deren Phasen im FPC angegeben. Bei den Überlegungen zur DR werden z.B. die pädagogischen Komponenten nicht automatisch eingeschlossen (Kattmann 2007). Die Strategien für *„conceptual reconstruction/change"* sind jedoch nur dann effizient, wenn sie in entsprechende Lernumgebungen mit zusätzlichen Merkmalen eingebettet sind (Treagust & Duit 2008). Aus der Verbindung von Theorie und Praxis beim FPC können Hinweise zu solchen zusätzlichen Aspekten für wirksame Lernumgebungen gewonnen werden.

Abb. 1: Interaktion bei FPC (modifiziert nach Staub 2004)

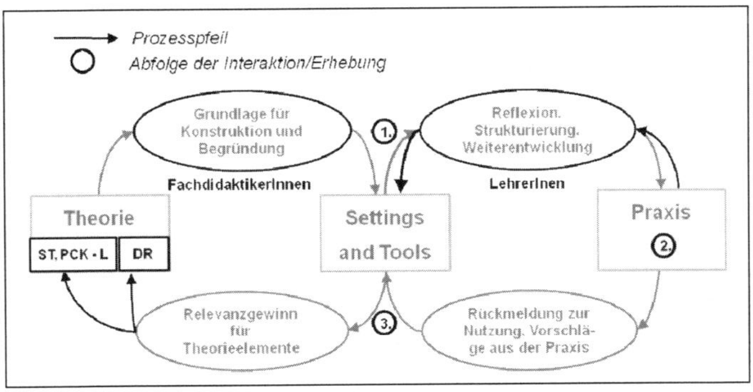

4 Methoden

FPC findet in Blöcken statt, wobei ein Block aus vier bis fünf Unterrichtstunden besteht. Die Blöcke können über mehrere Schuljahre verteilt sein. Dokumentiert werden Vorstellungen von zwei Lehrer/-inne/-n im Sinne von Fallstudien. Die Daten werden mit Hilfe der Unterrichtsmaterialien, des problem-

zentrierten Interviews und anschließender Validierung der Aussagen erhoben, wobei die Veränderungen der Lehrervorstellungen mittels retrospektiver Befragung zum Lernprozess erfasst werden (Abb. 1). Die Lehrervorstellungen werden im Sinne der subjektiven Theorien rekonstruiert (Groben et al. 1998) und auch unten dem Aspekt des P*edagogical Content Knowledge* (PCK) betrachtet (z.B. Kind 2009). Mit der DR ergibt sich eine besondere Verschränkung von bestimmten Wissensbereichen von PCK.
Das Verständnisniveau der Schüler/-innen wird per Video und durch die von den Schüler/-innen ausgefüllten Materialien erhoben. Die Auswertung der Interviews- und Videotransskripte findet mit Hilfe der qualitativen Inhaltsanalyse (Gropengießer 2005) computergestützt statt.

5 Ausgewählte bisherige Ergebnisse

Hier wird auf Ergebnisse der Fallstudie von Frau SCHWARZ eingegangen. Für Frau Schwarz ist es von zentraler Bedeutung, dass sich Evolution als roter Faden durch alle Schulstufen des Biologieunterrichts zieht. Sie steht der Anforderung, Schülervorstellungen bei der Planung des Unterrichts einzubeziehen, zunächst kritisch gegenüber: „*Ich habe eigentlich schon ziemlich viel über Schülervorstellungen gehört und auch über die Bedeutung von Schülervorstellungen für einen erfolgreichen Unterricht. Ich persönlich habe stark angezweifelt, ob das wirklich so eine große Rolle spielt. Ich habe mir gedacht, wenn der Unterricht einfach gut strukturiert abläuft und wenn ich versuche diese Dinge einfach zu erklären, dann müssten die Schülerinnen und Schüler das auch begreifen. Ich war der Meinung das geht so.*“ Anhand ihrer Erfahrungen mit Schwierigkeiten der Schüler/-innen mit dem Verständnis biologischer Begriffe und aus der zusätzlichen kritischen Überprüfung des Schülerverständnisses am Anfang des 1. FPC Blocks ändert Frau SCHWARZ ihre Einstellung: „*Aufgrund des bislang stattgefundenen Unterrichts und der näheren Betrachtung der Schülerantworten nach meinem Unterricht, habe ich aber deutlich gesehen, dass das nicht stimmt.*“
Am Anfang des 2. Blocks von FPC wurde der Zusammenhang zwischen eigenen Schwierigkeiten beim Verständnis des Themas (und damit der Unterrichtsgestaltung des 1. Blocks) und möglichen Schwierigkeiten bei den Schüler/-inne/-n vertieft reflektiert: „*Als ich mich mit den Darwinfinken auseinander gesetzt habe, hat es einige Fragen gegeben [...]. Beispielsweise wird die Ausgangspopulation der Darwinfinken in einem Artikel als insektenfressender Mittlerer Baumfink beschrieben. Etwas, was ich nicht beantworten konnte, aber die Frage kommt auch bei Schülern, ist das, dass*

man sagen kann, wie wird aus einem Insektenfresser ein Körnerfresser? [...] Diese Frage ist aufgrund des Unterrichts aufgetreten, aber wenn man sich nur an das Schulbuch hält, tritt sie nicht auf, weil es da gar nicht drin steht. Da steht sehr einfach drin, es gibt eben eine Finkenart, die vom Festland auf die Insel geflogen ist und die hat sich dort niedergelassen, und entsprechend den Lebensbedingungen auf dieser Insel konnte sie sich anpassen.“
Frau SCHWARZ spricht in diesem Zusammenhang zwei wichtige lernhinderliche Inhalte für das Verständnis der Selektion an (die später im FPC ausgeführt worden sind): Typisierung und Vernachlässigung der Variation der Merkmale in der Population (vgl. dazu z.B. Kattmann 2009). Diese Ergebnisse aus dem Interview zu dem ersten Block deuten bereits darauf hin, dass von Frau SCHWARZ nicht nur aufgrund der fachlichen Auseinandersetzung, sondern durch die Reflexion des eigenen Verständnisses und der Schwierigkeiten der Schüler/-innen wesentliche Konsequenzen für das eigene Lehren gezogen werden. Die lebensnahen Kontexte der Schüler/-innen werden herangezogen, um die Bedeutung der Variation in einer Population (bzw. Art) in Betracht ziehen zu können.

Danksagung: Den Kolleg/-inn/-en aus der Unterrichtspraxis danke ich für die Zusammenarbeit und dem IMST-Fond für die finanzielle Unterstützung.

Literaturangaben

GROEBEN, N. ET AL. (Hg.): Das Forschungsprogramm Subjektive Theorien. Eine Einführung in die Psychologie des reflexiven Subjekts. – Tübingen: Francke, 1988.

GROPENGIEßER, H.: Qualitative Inhaltsanalyse in der fachdidaktischen Lehr-Lern-Forschung. In: Mayring, P. & Gläser-Zikuda M. (Hg.). Die Praxis der Qualitativen Inhaltsanalyse. – Weinheim und Basel: Beltz, 2005.

JELEMENSKÁ, P.: Biologie verstehen: ökologische Einheiten. Beiträge zur Didaktischen Rekonstruktion 12. – Oldenburg: Didaktisches Zentrum, 2006.

KATTMANN, U. ET AL.: Das Modell der Didaktischen Rekonstruktion. Ein Rahmen für naturwissenschaftliche Forschung und Entwicklung. In: ZfDN 3/1997, 3-18.

KATTMANN, U.: Didaktische Rekonstruktion. Eine praktische Theorie. In: Krüger, D. & Vogt, H. (Hg.). Theorien in der biologiedidaktischen Forschung. – Berlin: Springer, 2007.

KATTMANN, U.: Vielfalt der Menschen. In: UB 33/2009, 2-10.

KIND, V.: Pedagogical content knowledge in science education: perspectives and potential for progress. In: Stud Sci Educ 2/2009, 169-204.

KRAINER, K.: Die Programme IMST und SINUS: Reflexionen über Ansatz, Wirkungen und Weiterentwicklungen. In: Höttecke, D. (Hg.). Naturwissenschaftlicher Unterricht im internationalen Vergleich. – Münster: LIT-Verlag, 2007.

RESNICK, L. B. & HALL, M. W.: Learning organizations for sustainable educational reform. In: Daedalus 4/1998, 89-118.

STAUB, F.C.: Fachspezifisch-Pädagogisches Coaching: Ein Beispiel zur Entwicklung von Lehrerfortbildung und Unterrichtskompetenz als Kooperation. ZfE 3/2004, 113-141.

TREAGUST, D.F. & DUIT, R.: Conceptual change: A discussion of theoretical, methodological and practical challenges for science education. CSSE 3/2008, 297-328.

WEST, L. & STAUB, F.C.: Content-Focused Coaching SM. Transforming Mathematics Lessons. - Institute of Education: University of Zürich, 2003.

Kontakt:
Patricia JELEMENSKÁ: patricia.jelemenska@univie.ac.at

SPORTLEHRERAUSBILDUNG IN DER SCHWEIZ – ZWISCHEN QUALITÄTSSICHERUNG, STANDARDISIERUNG UND PROFESSIONALISIERUNG

Jürgen Kühnis, Pädagogische Hochschule Zentralschweiz, Schweiz

Im Zuge der europäischen und nationalen Bildungsreformen sowie veränderter gesellschaftlichen Rahmenbedingungen wurden die Ansprüche an das Schulsystem und die Lehrerbildung stetig erweitert. In diesem Kontext haben sich auch das Anforderungsprofil und Berufsfeld von Sportlehrpersonen gewandelt sowie die Bestrebungen zur Qualitätssicherung verstärkt. Im vorliegenden Beitrag wird die gegenwärtige Bildungsdebatte innerhalb der Sportlehrer/-innenausbildung in der Schweiz skizziert und eine Übersicht zu aktuellen Herausforderungen und Problemfeldern eröffnet.

Schlüsselbegriffe: Sportlehrer/-ausbildung, Qualität in der Sportlehrerausbildung, Bewegungskultur; Gesundheit

1 Erweitere Bildungsansprüche und pluralisierte Bewegungskultur

Das einzig Konstante ist der Wandel. Die heutige gesellschaftliche und bildungspolitische Konstellation stellt das Bildungssystem und die Lehrerbildung vor immer größere Herausforderungen. Die veränderten soziodemographischen Rahmenbedingungen[1], die konsumorientierte Alltagsgestaltung vieler Heranwachsender, die Forderung nach Bildungsstandards, die Umsetzung der Bologna-Reform oder die Auswirkungen der PISA-Studie haben zu einem erweiterten Anforderungskatalog geführt und auch die Diskussion um die Bildungsinhalte und Qualitätssicherung verstärkt.

Im Zuge der gesellschaftlichen Modernisierungsprozesse hat sich auch die Sportwelt gewandelt – sie ist vielfältiger und unübersichtlicher geworden. Die Diversifikation und wachsende Popularität neuer Sportformen haben zu einer enormen Optionsvielfalt und zugleich einem neu akzentuierten Sportverständnis geführt. Abgrenzend zum traditionellen Sport hat sich eine Bewegungskultur mit neuen Sinnmustern und Organisationsformen entwickelt. „Indem der Sport Fernsehprogramme füllt, Unterhaltung bietet, Modetrends beeinflusst und Vorstellungen davon liefert, was z.B. sportlich oder fair ist, bestimmen seine Sinn- und Handlungsmuster das übrige kulturelle Leben mit. (…) Wie nie zuvor besitzt der Sport eine alltags- und lebensorganisierende Wirkung und ist Kristallisationspunkt sich wandelnder sozialer und psychosozialer Bedürfnisse“ (Weiss 2007, S. 9). Parallel zu dieser „Versportlichung“ lässt sich bereits im Kindes- und Jugendalter eine divergierende Tendenz in Richtung inaktiver Lebensführung, Verschlechterung der motorischen Fitness und Zunahme von Gesundheitsgefährdungen (z.B. Übergewicht) feststellen (Brettschneider et al. 2006, Bös 2003, Kühnis 2009). Entsprechend brisant verläuft die gegenwärtige Diskussion über den Gesundheits- und Bewegungsstatus der nachwachsenden Generation. In diesem ambivalenten Bedingungsgefüge situiert sich auch die heutige Sportlehrerausbildung und der Schulsport.

2 Das Sportstudium in der Schweiz ist in Bewegung – aber wohin?

Seit der Bologna-Reform, welche von der Schweiz im Jahre 1999 ratifiziert wurde, hat sich die Ausbildungslandschaft im Bereich Sport grundlegend verän-

---

[1] Z.B. die Zunahme von Scheidungsraten und der Erwerbstätigkeit von Müttern, die Integration von ausländischen Kindern und der wachsende Anteil verhaltensauffälliger Kinder.

dert. Sportunterricht erteilende Lehrpersonen werden heute an universitären, eidgenössischen und pädagogischen Hochschulen ausgebildet. Für die eidgenössischen Hochschulen in Zürich (ETH) und Magglingen (EHSM) ist der Bund; für die anderen Institutionen sind die jeweiligen Kantone zuständig. Durch die Netzwerkkonferenz Sportstudien Schweiz (www.sportstudien.ch) übt der Bund die Oberaufsicht aus. In diesem Organ sind alle Hochschulen vertreten, die Sportstudiengänge anbieten. Lehrpersonen für die Kindergarten-, Primar- (1.-6. Kl.) und Sekundarstufe I (7.-9. Kl.) werden in der Regel an Pädagogischen Hochschulen ausgebildet und erwerben eine Mehrfächerqualifikation (inkl. Sport). Studierende mit Berufsziel „Sekundarstufe II" müssen zusätzlich zum sportwissenschaftlichen Masterabschluss an einer universitären Hochschule eine fachdidaktische Ausbildung (höheres Lehramt) absolvieren. Im Gegensatz zum System vieler Universitäten in Deutschland oder Österreich besteht an schweizerischen Hochschulen keine Wahloption zwischen Lehramtsstudium oder Sportwissenschaft.

2.1 Vom Sportlehrer zum Sportwissenschaftler?

Die langjährige Tradition der eidgenössischen Sportlehrerdiplome ist 2005 nach 81 Jahren Laufzeit durch zweistufige Bachelor-/Masterstudiengänge abgelöst worden. Im Zuge dieser Umstrukturierung und universitären Integration sind neue Studienprofile mit unterschiedlichen Lehr- und Forschungsschwerpunkten entstanden. Während beispielsweise an der Universität Bern sozial- und verhaltenswissenschaftliche Fragen im Vordergrund stehen, fokusiert die ETH Zürich eine naturwissenschaftliche Ausrichtung und die Universität Basel den Gesundheitsbereich. Derzeit existieren 12 Masterausbildungen u.a. mit der Vertiefung in Sozialwissenschaften, *Excercise & Health Sciences* oder Sportmanagement. Wenngleich diese Neuausrichtung eine Mehrfachqualifikation und neue Berufsfelder (z.B. im Bereich Gesundheit, Tourismus) sowie eine breite nationale Sportforschung und Nachwuchsförderung eröffnet hat, sind im Gegenzug die fachdidaktischen und sportpraktischen Ausbildungsinhalte gekürzt worden. Diese Tendenz zur Verwissenschaftlichung bzw. Entpädagogisierung des Studiums wird kontrovers diskutiert und der Verzicht auf eine einphasige, berufsnahe Lehrerausbildung bedauert. Aufgrund der Dysbalance zwischen Fachwissenschaft, Sportdidaktik und Berufspraxis sowie der grossen Variabilität der Inhalte, Fächerkombinationen und ECTS-Dotierung wird die Unterrichtsbefähigung der Hochschulabgänger/-innen und die Gewährleistung eines qualitativ guten Sportunterrichts zunehmend in Frage gestellt. Zudem sind die Zugangsvoraussetzungen unterschiedlich geregelt; nicht alle Sportinstitute und Pädagogischen Hochschulen führen eine sportpraktische Eignungsprüfung durch.

3 Sonderfall Sportunterricht: Rahmenbedingungen und Statusprobleme

Der Sportunterricht besitzt im Schweizer Schulsystem eine Sonderstellung. Im Gegensatz zu anderen Fächern ist der Schulsport schweizweit durch Vorgaben geregelt und verfügt über ein eidgenössisches Lehrmittel. Bereits 1874 wurde der Sportunterricht als obligatorisch erklärt und 1987 via Verordnung zum Bundesgesetz über die Förderung von Turnen und Sport aus dem Jahre 1972 das Drei-Stunden-Obligatorium eingeführt. Trotz dieser gesetzlichen Verankerung wird dieses Obligatorium bis heute nicht in allen 26 Kantonen (v.a. der Westschweiz) gesetzeskonform umgesetzt (Pühse et al. 2005). Dieser Sachverhalt ist u.a. auf die Schnittstellenproblematik zwischen Bund und Kantonen zurückzuführen, d.h. der Bund erlässt Gesetze; die Kantone sind in Bildungsentscheidungen jedoch autonom und tragen die Kosten. Das Tauziehen um die dritte Sportlektion ist deshalb ein politischer Dauerbrenner, der durch die medienwirksame PISA-Studie eine neue Kürzungsdebatte zugunsten der Kernfächer entfacht hat. Auch der freiwillige Schulsport sowie ergänzende Sportangebote (z.B. Sportlager) wurden im Zuge von kantonalen Sparmaßnahmen in den letzten Jahren drastisch reduziert. Als musisches Fach kämpft der Sportunterricht seit jeher um seine schulische Gleichstellung und Legitimation. Sport ist selten promotionsrelevant und der Berufsstatus entspricht meist folgendem Bild: „Häufig erlebt man eine randständige Beachtung der ‚Sportler': bei Kollegen, Eltern, Ärzten, Politikern. Die Sitzordnung im Lehrerzimmer (eine kleine Ecke ganz hinten für die Kolleginnen und Kollegen in Sportbekleidung, da sie die Pausen meist ohnehin in der Umkleide verbringen), die Beschränkung des Sportthemas auf Wettkampferfolge in den Elternbriefen und Jahresberichten, die Seltenheit von Elternbesuchen in der Sprechstunde, die Nonchalance, mit der Sportbefreiungen ausgesprochen werden und Sportstunden gekürzt werden: das alles spricht eine deutliche Sprache der Missachtung des Faches und seiner Repräsentanten" (Kugelmann & Klupsch-Sahlmann 2000, S. 6). „Sportlehrer sind im Vergleich zu ihren Kollegen in vielen Kantonen schlechter bezahlt und müssen zudem noch mehr Pflichtstunden unterrichten" (Pühse et al. 2005, S. 21).

3.1 Anspruch und Anforderungsprofil

Unterscheidungsmerkmale zu anderen Fächern finden sich auch in der pädagogischen Orientierung des Schulsports. Seit den 1876 erschienenen schweizerischen Turnschulen bis zum aktuellen Sportlehrmittel von 1997 wurden Bewegung, Spiel und Sport stets als Anliegen einer umfassenden Persönlichkeitsbildung verstanden. D.h. der Körper ist nicht nur ein „Stativ" für den Kopf, sondern Bewegung gilt als Motor der kindlichen Entwicklung und stellt ein Medium der Körper- und Umwelterschliessung dar (Zimmer 2009). Im Sportunterricht werden vielfältige physische, kognitive und soziale Lernfelder eröffnet und alle Kinder zugleich zu einem Mindestmass an wöchentlicher Sportaktivität verpflichet (Kühnis 2009). Die Förderung von vielseitigen und erlebnisbetonten Erfahrungen, die Vermittlung eines breiten Bewegungsrepertoires sowie die sinnhafte Erschliessung der körperlichen Betätigung gelten heute als zentrale Grundanliegen des Sportunterrichts. Das Ausleben des Bewegungsdranges, der Ausgleich zum sitzlastigen Alltag, das Entdecken des Körpers und seiner Leistungsgrenzen, der soziale Austausch und Vergleich mit Gleichaltrigen sind beispielhafte Sinnrichtungen eines mehrperspektivischen Bewegungs- und Sportverständnisses, wie es im aktuellen Schweizer Lehrmittel (ESK 1997) vertreten wird.

Das Tätigkeitsfeld und Anforderungsprofil von Sportlehrpersonen gestaltet sich heute sehr facettenreich. Die steigende Prävalenz von Übergewicht und Inaktivität, die Heterogenität motorischer Voraussetzungen, die Integration von Migrantenkindern, die Sensibilisierung von Heranwachsenden für einen aktiven Lebensstil sowie die Qualitätssicherung des Unterrichts erfordern eine hohe Flexibilität, Fach-, Methoden- und Sozialkompetenz. Sportlehrpersonen sind immer auch Bewegungsvorbilder, was eine gute körperliche Konstitution und motorische Kompetenz voraussetzt. Im Gegensatz zu anderen Schulfächern findet der Sportunterricht in verschiedenen Lernsettings (Turnhalle, Hallenbad oder im Gelände) statt und verlangt entsprechende Sicherheitsvorkehrungen. Häufig übernehmen Sportlehrpersonen auch die Rolle von schulinternen Moderatoren für Sport-/Bewegungsprojekte. Diese besonderen Rahmenbedingungen stellen sehr hohe Ansprüche an die unterrichtenden Lehrpersonen und erfordern eine adäquate Berufsqualifizierung. Die heutige Fachausbildung in der Schweiz scheint diesen vielfältigen Ansprüchen leider nur ungenügend Rechnung zu tragen.

4 Aktuelle Bestrebungen auf nationaler Ebene

Auf bildungs- und sportpolitischer Ebene laufen mehrere Projekte, die auch den Schulsport tangieren. Neben der aktuellen Bildungsreform *HarmoS* sind in diesem Zusammenhang vor allem die Aktionsprogramme des Bundesamtes für Sport zur Bewegungsförderung im Schulalltag und Qualitätssicherung im Sportunterricht hervorzuheben.

4.1 Harmonisierung der obligatorischen Schule (*HarmoS*)

Ziel dieses interkantonalen Schulkonkordates ist die schweizweite Harmonisierung der obligatorischen Schule durch die Schaffung einheitlicher Strukturen und die Übernahme von nationalen Bildungszielen (www.edk.ch). Diese Vorgaben inkludieren u.a. die Schuldauer (zwei Jahre Kindergarten, sechs Jahre Primarschule, drei Jahre Sekundarschule), die Regelung des Sprachenunterrichts (Englisch und eine zweite Landessprache; erste Fremdsprache im 3. Schuljahr; zweite Fremdsprache spätestens ab 5. Schuljahr), die Erarbeitung sprachregionaler Lehrpläne sowie die Entwicklung von verbindlichen Bildungsstandards[2] (vorerst für die vier Fachbereiche Schulsprache, Fremdsprachen, Mathematik und Naturwissenschaften). In den 21 Deutschschweizer Kantonen wird bereits ein neuer gemeinsamer Lehrplan für die Volksschule erarbeitet (vgl.: www.lehrplan.ch). Im Fachbereich Bewegung und Sport soll die Gesundheitserziehung als überfachliches Thema künftig stärker verankert werden; ansonsten erfahren die bisherigen Rahmenvorgaben des Fachbereichs keine wesentlichen Änderungen.

4.2 Schulen in Bewegung bringen: *Schule.bewegt, J+S-Kids, qims*

Das Programm *schule.bewegt* will Schulen und Klassen in der Schweiz und Liechtenstein zu mehr Bewegung animieren und bietet für Lehrpersonen konkrete Umsetzungshilfen an (www.schulebewegt.ch). Seit Projektstart im Jahre 2005 haben sich bis heute (Stand 1.3.2010) 2733 Klassen beteiligt, mit dem Ziel sich täglich (ergänzend zum Schulsport) mindestens 20 Minuten zu bewegen. Diese Bewegung kann überall stattfinden: im Schulzimmer, auf dem Pausenplatz, vor oder nach dem Unterricht. Für die praktische Umsetzung stehen vier Bewegungsmodule (Seil+, Bewegungspausen, Footbag, Unterwegs) sowie

---

[2] Bildungsstandards beschreiben als normative Vorgaben einerseits den Erwerb von Grundkompetenzen und dienen im Sinne der Qualitätsentwicklung zugleich zur Überprüfung von Bildungszielen.

ein Zusatzmodul zum Thema Ernährung zur Verfügung. Mit der Ausdehnung des Jugend+Sport-Alters auf die 5- bis 10-Jährigen wird die Sportlandschaft zudem seit Kurzem durch ein weiteres Aktionsprogramm bereichert. *J+S-Kids* ist ein polysportiv ausgerichtetes Projekt, welches ergänzend zu bestehenden Schul- und Vereinssportangeboten dem Ausleben des Bewegungsdranges von Heranwachsenden und der Erfüllung allgemeiner Bewegungsempfehlungen mehr Rechnung tragen möchte. Zur Analyse und Sicherung der Qualität im Sport- und Bewegungsunterricht stehen durch das Projekt *qims* zudem praktische Grundlagen und Evaluationsinstrumente für alle Schulstufen zur Verfügung (www.qims.ch).

5 Fazit

Die Sportlehrerausbildung in der Schweiz befindet sich seit einigen Jahren im Umbruch. Dem Bedarf an gut qualifizierten Lehrpersonen stehen heute erweiterte Bildungsansprüche und heterogene Ausbildungsprofile gegenüber. Die universitäre Integration und interdisziplinäre Vernetzung haben einerseits zu einer Stärkung der sportwissenschaftlichen Forschung, der Fachanerkennung und klaren Positionierung der Sportinstitute, jedoch zugleich zu einer drastischen Reduktion von sportdidaktischen und -praktischen Ausbildungsinhalten geführt. Aufgrund der unterschiedlichen Studienausrichtung und Zugangsvoraussetzungen ist auch die mit der Bologna-Reform intendierte Mobilität erschwert. Auch an Pädagogischen Hochschulen fällt die heutige Dotierung der Sportausbildung aufgrund der Verteilkämpfe zwischen den einzelnen Fachdisziplinen teils sehr unbefriedigend, zuweilen sogar fragwürdig aus. Um das derzeitige Spannungsverhältnis aufzulösen, sind deshalb entsprechende Anpassungen der Studiengänge erforderlich, die vor allem eine national koordinierte Ausweitung der Sportdidaktik und berufsbezogenen Anteile in den Mittelpunkt stellen.

Literaturangaben

BRETTSCHNEIDER, W.-D., NAUL, R., BÜNNEMANN, A., HOFMANN, D.: Übergewicht und Adipositas bei Kindern und Jugendlichen. Ernährungsverhalten, Medienkonsum und körperliche (In-)Aktivität im europäischen Vergleich. Spectrum der Sportwissenschaften, 18/2006, 25-45.

BÖS, K.: Motorische Leistungsfähigkeit vom Kindern und Jugendlichen. In: SCHMIDT, W. HARTMANN-TEWS, I., BRETTSCHNEIDER W.-D. (Hg.): Erster Deutscher Kinder- und Jugendsportbericht. 85-107. -Schorndorf: Hofmann, 2003.

EIDG. SPORTKOMMISSION (ESK): Lehrmittel Sporterziehung. – Bern: EDMZ, 1997.

KUGELMANN, C. & KLUPSCH-SAHLMANN, R.: Sportlehrerinnen und Sportlehrer – heute und morgen. In: Sportpädagogik, 1/2000, 4-12.

KÜHNIS, J.: Trends im Bewegungs- und Gesundheitsstatus von Schulkindern und deren Implikation für die Lehrer-/Innenbildung. In: Pädagogische Hochschule Wien (Ed.) Neue Architekturen im europäischen Hochschulraum, 189-197. –Wien: LIT Verlag, 2009.

PÜHSE, U., GERBER, M., MENGISEN, W., REPOND, R.-M., LAUMANN, J., EICHENBERGER, L.: Zur aktuellen Situation des Sportunterrichts in der Schweiz. In: PÜHSE, U., FIRMIN, F., MENGISEN, W. (Hg.): Schulsportforschung im Spannungsfeld von Empirie und Hermeneutik. 17-55. – Magglingen: BASPO, 2005.

WEISS, O.: Zur Einführung: Entwicklungstendenzen im Sport. In: HILSCHER, P., NORDEN, G., RUSSO, M., WEISS, O. (Hg.): Entwicklungstendenzen im Sport. 9-11 – Wien: LIT Verlag, 2007.

ZIMMER, R.: Handbuch der Bewegungserziehung. Grundlagen für Ausbildung und pädagogische Praxis. – Freiburg: Herder, 2009.

Kontakt:
Prof. Dr. Jürgen KÜHNIS: juergen.kuehnis@phz.ch

BEITRÄGE AUS DEN ARBEITSGRUPPEN
PAPERS PRESENTED IN THE WORKING SESSIONS

LEHRERPROFESSION IN DER WISSENSGESELLSCHAFT

Josef Maňák, Masaryk Universität Brno, Tschechische Republik

Der Aufsatz analysiert die Funktionen der Lehrerprofession vom Standpunkt der historischen Entwicklung und den Funktionenwechsel dieses Berufs in der modernen Gesellschaft. Er zeigt, welche Anforderungen die Wissensgesellschaft an die Lehrerprofession und an die Erziehung überhaupt stellt. Der Autor befasst sich auch mit der Kritik der Lehrerprofession, sucht die Ursachen ihres Rückstandes und verweist auf seine Quellen, aber auch auf die Wege seiner Überwindung. Weiters skizziert er die Aufgaben der Lehrerprofession in der Wissensgesellschaft, die Möglichkeit der weiteren Professionalisierung und schlägt eine neue Konzeption der Lehrervorbereitung vor.

Schlüsselbegriffe: Lehrerprofession, Funktionenwechsel, Wissensgesellschaft, Kritik des Lehrerberufs, Lehrervorbereitung

1 Einleitung

Die Abhandlung über das gegebene Thema soll nicht eine Voraussage über die mögliche künftige Entwicklung der Lehrerprofession vorlegen, sondern eine Analyse des heutigen Zustandes sein, der allerdings wie das Residuum der Vergangenheit, so auch Elemente der künftigen Veränderungen in sich trägt. In diesem Sinne deuten wir auch den Begriff „Wissensgesellschaft", nämlich als soziale Veränderungen auf der Basis des aktuellen Informationszuwachses und der zuständigen Technologien, die sich im menschlichen Bewusstsein in Kenntnisse, Fertigkeiten und Kompetenzen verwandeln. In der neuen sozialen Realität gerät das Wissen in die Position des entscheidenden Elementes aller Aspekte des Lebens (Kopecký 2009, S. 35) und in diesem Zusammenhang muss man auch die Lehrerprofession betrachten.

Von den verschiedenen Lehrerkategorien werden wir uns auf den Lehrer der Primär- und Grundschule einstellen. Kurz werden wir die Entwicklung dieser

Lehrerkategorie skizzieren, die immer durch das Niveau der Gesellschaft markant beeinflusst wurde.

2 Funktionsveränderungen der Lehrerprofession

Die Lehrerprofession beginnt erst in den Kirchenschulen professionell orientiert zu sein, die Lehrerprofessionalität wird weiter gekräftigt durch die Einführung der Schulpflicht für die ganze Population (bei uns im Jahre 1774). Die Anforderungen an die Lehrerbildung waren niedrig, die Lehrervorbereitung dauerte nur einige Monate. Einen ziemlich großen Fortschritt bedeutete die Schulreform im Jahre 1869 – die Schulpflicht wurde auf acht Jahre verlängert und die Lehrer wurden in den Lehreranstalten vorbereitet. Dieser Zustand dauerte auch nach dem Jahr 1918 (Entstehung der Tschechoslowakischen Republik) an, aber der Lehrer war nicht mehr von der Kirche abhängig.

Die Anforderungen an die Fachkenntnisse wuchsen zunehmend, deshalb wurde im Jahr 1946 die Hochschulvorbereitung der Lehrer eingeführt. Die Betonung der fachlichen Seite der Lehrervorbereitung führte jedoch zur Schwächung des erzieherischen Wirkens des Lehrers. Diese Tendenz verstärkte sich noch im Zeitalter der sog. „Wissenschaftlichen Revolution"; infolge dessen hat sich in der Schule die Überforderung der Schüler geäußert.

Um die Mite des 20. Jahrhunderts sind die methodischen Funktionen des Lehrers in den Mittelpunkt getreten und unter dem Einfluss des „Programmierten Lernens" haben sich die modernen technologischen Mittel verbreitet. Die Unterrichtsuntersuchungen aus dieser Zeit haben bestätigt, dass unter dem Einfluss der modernen Technologien sich einige Lehrerfunktionen geändert haben. Schwächer wurden: die unmittelbare Vermittlung des Lehrstoffes an die Schüler, die Wiederholung und Kontrolle der Kenntnisse und Fertigkeiten und deren Bewertung. Dem entgegen traten folgende Funktionen stärker hervor: die Vorbereitung des Unterrichts, besonders des Lehrmaterials, die individuelle Arbeit mit den Schülern, die Operationen mit den technischen Mittlern. Es erschienen auch neue Funktionen: Manager des Unterrichtsprozesses, didaktischer Technologe usw. Mit der Ankunft der Computer sind auch die methodischen Fragen der Informationstechnologie mehr in den Vordergrund getreten. Die Wissensgesellschaft stellt jedoch an die Funktionen des Lehrers neue Ansprüche: intensive Arbeit mit den Informationen, d.h. den riesigen Fonds der Informationen zu bewältigen und die Schüler für die globale Zivilisation vorzubereiten.

3 Der Mensch in der Wissensgesellschaft

Der Terminus „Wissensgesellschaft" betont diejenigen Seiten, die sich durch die Erkenntnisentwicklung und die Lebensqualität charakterisieren. Dieser Entwicklungstrend der modernen Gesellschaft wurde schon früher bemerkt und auch benannt, wie z.B. Informationsgesellschaft, Erkenntnisgesellschaft, Zivilisation der drittem Welle (Toffler, Toffler, 1996) u.a. Zu den Hauptcharakteristika der Wissensgesellschaft gehört auch der internationale Aufschwung der Wissenserkenntnis, der auch die entscheidende Quelle der Ökonomie wird. Im Bereich der Politik kommt es zu Veränderungen in der Auffassung der traditionellen Demokratie dadurch, dass sich mehr die Interessen verschiedener Minderheiten durchsetzen. Es wird auch die Aufgabe der neuen Ethik, des kritischen Denkens und der entstehenden gesamtplanetarischen Kultur hervorgehoben (Abellán, Popper, Virilio, Dalajlama u. a.).

Die Wissensgesellschaft ist auch mit Recht mit der Forderung der „Edukativen Gesellschaft" vereinigt, d.h. mit Nachdruck auf die Bildungswerte, die Lebensbildung und auf die gesamte Kultivation des Menschen (Tondl 1999, S. 143). In diesem Zusammenhang wird auch die Ausbildung gegen verschiedene Formen der Demagogie und Desinformation hervorgehoben, die auf der Bildung parasitieren. Man muss auch mit den veränderten Normen des menschlichen Betragens, mit den inneren Veränderungen des Menschen *(metanoia)*, mit den neuen Beziehungen zur Natur rechnen. J. KRUPIČKA (2006, S. 157) fordert für diesen Zweck ein „Machtzentrum" zu bilden, ein gewisses Organ des „Weltwillens", das über die gemeinsamen Grundprobleme der Menschheit Entscheidungen treffen würde. In die Führung dieses Organs würden die hervorragendsten Persönlichkeiten ausgewählt.

Der Mensch bewegt sich schon jetzt auf der Szene der Wissensgesellschaft, obwohl sicher in einem provisorischen Zeitraum, wann die Informationsexplosion und die technologischen Innovationen in ihm Unsicherheit und Chaos hervorbringen. J. ŠAFAŘÍK (1969, S. 15) hat schon in der Hälfte des vorigen Jahrhunderts festgestellt, dass das Dilemma der Mensch – die Maschine fatal ist und dass es den schwersten Auftrag darstellt, der je auf die Schultern der Leute geladen wurde. Er hat jedoch auch richtig erkannt, dass die Gesellschaft nicht nur eine Maschinengesellschaft, sondern auch menschlich sein soll.

Ähnlich auch J. KOZIELECKI (1987, S. 8) hat begriffen, dass der aufgeklärte, einseitig rationalistische Mensch durch den schöpferischen Innovationsmenschen übertroffen wird. Die oben angeführte kurze Charakteristik der Wissensgesellschaft zeigt, dass es um eine historische Umwandlung geht, die einen neuen Menschen braucht, der sich durch ein neues Denken, Empfinden und durch reifere Moral charakterisiert. In dieser verwickelten Bewegung der Gesellschaft bekommen die Erziehung, die Pädagogik und auch der Lehrer, der sich allerdings auch ändern muss, große Chancen.

4 Die gegenwärtige Situation der Pädagogik als die Erziehungswissenschaft

Pädagogik wird als explorative Wissenschaft definiert (Průcha 2009, S. 19), die die Bedingungen und Mittel der Formierung des Menschen untersucht. Das Feld der Edukation ist sehr breit, diversifiziert und hängt nicht nur mit dem zu erziehenden Subjekt, sondern auch mit der Gesellschaftsordnung, mit der Familie und der gesamten Gesellschaftspraxis zusammen. Das ist einer der Gründe, warum sich die Pädagogik langsam und mit Schwierigkeiten gestaltet hat und warum sie noch heute zum Gegenstand verschiedener Vorurteile und sogar der Verachtung wird.

Die Gründe für die Verachtung der Pädagogik untersuchte W. BREZINKA (2001, S. 39) und als eine Lösung hat er drei Gebiete der Pädagogik zu unterscheiden vorgeschlagen, nämlich die Erziehungswissenschaft, die Philosophie der Erziehung und die praktische Pädagogik. Aber durch diese Gliederung würde sich die Wissenschaft der Erziehung ganz von der Erziehungspraxis entfernen und sie würde ein Kabinettfach, das sich nur mit theoretischen Problemen beschäftigt. Demgegenüber scheint es sinnvoller, die wissenschaftlichen Erkenntnisse über die Erziehung in die Praxis einzuführen und so die Verbindung der Theorie mit der Praxis zum Nutzen der Gesellschaft zu orientieren. Nach der Veröffentlichung der für die Schule ungünstigen Resultate der PISA-Untersuchungen hat sich in Deutschland die Kritik an der Pädagogik, an der Schule und an den Lehrern zugespitzt und man sucht die Ursachen dieser Situation (Ricken 2007). Die Lösung kann man jedoch nicht nur in der Pädagogik und in der Schule suchen, denn Schuld an diesem Zustand hat die Gesellschaftsatmosphäre, die mit der Unterschätzeng der Pädagogik zusammenhängt.

5 Die Anforderungen an die Lehrerprofession in der Wissensgesellschaft

Die Wissensgesellschaft schafft eine neue Situation für alle Professionen, jedoch besonders für die Lehrer, weil diese Profession sich speziell mit dem

Erwerb des Wissens beschäftigt. Der Lehrerprofession wird in der Gesellschaft große Aufmerksamkeit gewidmet. Es erscheinen wertvolle Monografien z. B. von J. PRŮCHA (2002) oder von F. KORTHAGEN (2001) über die Verbindung der pädagogischen Theorie mit der Praxis bei der Lehrervorbereitung, oder von R. SEEBAUER, die zahlreiche inspirative Studien über den europäischen Lehrer geschrieben hat. Versuchen wir, auf Grund der Beobachtungen, empirischen Untersuchungen und Analysen von vielen Studien, die Haupteigenschaften des progressiven Lehrers zu bestimmen, wie man sie bis heute identifizieren kann. Man kann feststellen, dass der Lehrer immer mehr und mehr der Zentralfaktor der Edukationsaktivitäten und der Fazilitator der Formierung der schöpferischen Persönlichkeit wird. Man muss jedoch auch zugeben, dass es noch ziemlich viele Lehrer gibt, die auch weiter in der Rolle eines Beamten agieren.

Ein wichtiger Auftrag für die Lehrerprofession folgt von der vertiefenden Globalisierung der Welt und der Internationalisierung der Bildung. W. KLAFKI (1992, S. 307-310) führt Hauptfaktoren der internationalen Erziehung ein, die er als einen unumstößlichen historischen Prozess versteht. In diesem Sinn sieht M. MCLEAN (1993, S. 261-270) die Notwendigkeit, ein gemeinsames, europäisches Curriculum zu konstruieren. Demgegenüber sollte der Lehrer auch ausdrucksvoll die Kompetenzen der Schüler für die Kommunikation mit der Umwelt äußern, in der die Schule tätig ist (R. Brockmeyer, 1993). Die Schule sollte deshalb nicht nur ein Zentrum des Lebensbildes sein, sondern auch Familienpartner werden (Kahl 2004). Mit diesen allgemeinen Schlüssen könnte man fortsetzen, aber man kann sie in zwei Linien zusammenfassen, und zwar in die Linie des Curriculums und des Unterrichtsprozesses und in die Linie des moralischen Charakters der Persönlichkeit und ihren Beziehungen zur Umwelt. Daraus folgt aber auch neue Funktion der Schule.

Der Lehrer in der Wissensgesellschaft muss einerseits die fortwährend schnell anwachsenden Erkenntnisse bewältigen, anderseits muss er auch neue psychologische Erkenntnisse über das Lernen und Erkennen beherrschen. V. KULIČ (1997) zeigt, dass die kognitive Psychologie eine Revolution in Bezug zur klassischen Psychologie (Assozianismus, Behaviorismus, Gestaltismus) bedeutete, und zwar in der Wendung zur Integration mit den Erkenntnissen anderer Fächer. Jedoch von Standpunkt der Personalisierung wird jetzt die Entwicklung des Menschen als aktive und autonome Persönlichkeit aufgehoben und deshalb muss der Lehrer auch die Erkenntnisse der humanistischen Psychologie in seine Arbeit eingliedern. V. SMÉKAL (2000) verweist auf die integrative Funktion der Persönlichkeit und im Unterrichtsprozess, er betont die Notwendigkeit die wesentlichen Zusammenhänge der Fakten aufzusuchen und einzelne Erscheinungen in höhere Gesamtheit einzureihen. Diese Funktion des Lehrers tritt in den Vordergrund besonders bei der Arbeit der Schüler mit der Überflutung an Informationen, was jedoch zuerst die Identifikation der Einzelheiten, dann ihre nachfolgende Komparation und resultierende Synthese voraussetzt. Diese Operationen organisiert und entfaltet der Lehrer mit Rücksicht auf die gesamte Situation des Schülers so, dass das Lernen für den Schüler angenehm und sinnfällig wird.

Auch die zweite Linie der professionellen Veränderungen des Lehrers ist nicht ganz neu, jedoch man muss sie jetzt markant stärken. Wie schon früher J. VANĚK (1960) darauf aufmerksam machte, die Schule sollte eine klinische Einrichtung werden, in welcher der Lehrer – ähnlich wie der Arzt – verschiedene Probleme der Erziehung löst. E. TERHART (2001) verlangt die Ausbreitung dieser Funktion des Lehrers im Sinne der Unterstützung des Schülers beim Lernen, bei der Überwindung verschiedener Lebensprobleme, bei der Einübung des kultivierten Benehmens usw. Die Lehrerkompetenzen sollten sich im größeren Maß in die Mitarbeit mit den außerschulischen Institutionen ausbreiten. Es zeigt sich, dass die geeignete Maßnahme zur Bewältigung aller dieser Funktionen die Ganztagschule werden könnte, die auch die Gelegenheit zur Entfaltung der Schülerinteressen bieten könnte. Allerdings kann der Lehrer alle angeführten Aktivitäten heute nicht selbst bewältigen, man braucht auch verschiedene Spezialisten, aber der Lehrer muss sein Mandat ausbreiten, um den Erziehungsprozess zu koordinieren und beeinflussen zu können.

Das Verbindungslied beider genannter Linien der Lehrerprofession und zugleich die profilierende Eigenschaft des Lehrers – wird das neue Lehrerethos sein. In der Wissensgesellschaft wird das Lehrerethos die unentbehrliche Ausrüstung jedes Lehrers, weil die Lehrerprofession viel größeres Engagement als zuvor verlangt, denn die Probleme, die die Edukation lösen muss, komplizierter und anspruchsvoller werden.

5 Die Lehrervorbereitung für die Wissensgesellschaft

Über die Problematik der Lehrervorbereitung stehen viele Publikationen zur Verfügung und es fanden auch viele Konferenzen statt, jedoch trotz mancher edelsinniger Vorhaben und verschiedener Verbesserungsvorschläge ist der Gesamtfortschritt klein. Versuchen wir wenigstens anzudeuten, worauf sich die erwünschte Wendung beziehen sollte:

- Die Voraussetzung der erfolgreichen Erfüllung der angedeuteten Probleme der Lehrerprofession ist eine solche Auswahl der Lehrerkandidaten, dass die Bewerber und die Lehrerprofession selbst die Ambition haben gute Lehrer zu werden.
- Die Gesellschaft muss dem Lehrer solche Materialbedingungen sichern, die mit anderen anspruchsvollen Professionen vergleichbar sind.
- Die Hochschulen, die die künftigen Lehrer vorbereiten, müssen sich konsequent an der Lehrerprofession orientieren, nicht andere Ziele verfolgen, ähnlich wie bei den Ärzten, Juristen u.a.
- Der Unterricht an Hochschulen, besonders in Pädagogik und Psychologie, muss seinen akademischen Stil ändern, d.h. mehr auf das Lösen der aktuellen Erziehungsprobleme sich orientieren.
- Es ist notwendig die praktische Ausübung der künftigen Lehrer zu ändern und zu stärken – am Anfang an den Fakultätsschulen, später durch die gesteuerte Praxis im Terrain.
- Unbedingt ist es notwendig die Karriereordnung einzuführen, dass schon der beginnende Lehrer eine Perspektive des professionellen Heranwachsens vor Augen hat.
- Die Vorbereitung der künftigen Lehrer sollte auch an der Hochschule das Lehrerethos durchringen.

Literaturangaben

BREZINKA, W.: Východiska k poznání výchovy. Brno: L. Marek, 2001.

BROCKMEYER, R.: Zukunft der Bildung – Schule der Zukunft. Pädagogik und Schule in Ost und West. 1993/4, 251-254.

KAHL, R.: Treibhäuser der Zukunft. Hamburg: Archiv der Zukunft, 2004.

KLAFKI, W.: Perspektivy vzdělání – základní rysy internacionální výchovy. Pedagogika, 1992, 3, S. 307-316.

KOPECKÝ, M.: Společnost vědění. In Průcha (ed.) Pedagogická encyklopedie. Praha: Portál, 2009, S. 31-38.

KORTHAGEN, F.A.J.: Linking practice and theory. London: Lawrence Erlbaum, 2001.

KOZIELECKI, J.: Czlowiek oświecony czy innowacyjny. Kwartalnik pedagogiczny, 1987, 1, 3-16.

KRUPIČKA, J.: Kosmický mozek. Praha – Litomyšl: Paseka, 2005.

KULIČ, V.: Učení a poznávání v současné psychologii. In Technologické otázky ve vzdělávání. Dobřichovice – Praha: Akademia Libroservo, 1997, 51-57.

MCLEAN, M.: Das europäische Curriculum. In K. Schleicher (Hg.): Zukunft der Bildung in Europa. Darmstadt: Wissenschaftliche Buchgesellschaft, 1993, S. 261-276.

PRŮCHA, J.: Učitel. Portál, Praha: 2002.

PRŮCHA, J. Edukační realita a pedagogika. Pedagogická encyklopedie. Praha: Portál, 2009, s. 16.

RICKEN, N. (Hg.): Über die Verachtung der Pädagogik. Wiesbaden: VS Verlag für Sozialwissenschaften, 2007, s. 15-40.

SEEBAUER, R.: Vom Europa-Projekt zum Projekt Europa. Wien: Mandelbaum, 2001.

SMÉKAL, V.: Fragmentárnost psychologie a integrita člověka. In Integrativní funkce osobnosti. Brno: MU, 2000, 11-21.

ŠAFAŘÍK, J.: Člověk ve věku stroje. Liberec: Severočeské nakladatelství, 1969.

TERHART, E.: Lehrerberuf und Lehrerbildung. Weinheim und Basel: Beltz Verlag, 2001.

TOFFLER, A., TOFLEROVÁ, H.: Utváranie novej civilizácie. Bratislava: Open Windows, 1996.

TONDL, L.: Hodnocení a hodnoty. Praha: Filosofia, 1999.

VANĚK, J.: Naše pedagogika a život. Jednotná škola, 1960, 4, 318-327.

Kontakt:
Univ. Prof. Dr. Josef MAŇÁK: manak@ped.muni.cz

PROFESSIONALISIERUNG? HISTORISCHE ANMERKUNGEN UND AKTUELLE TRENDS

Renate Seebauer, Pädagogische Hochschule Wien, Österreich

Im folgenden Beitrag wird den Merkmalen von Professionalität nachgegangen sowie der Frage, wie weit Lehrer/-in-Sein überhaupt als Profession und die damit verbundenen Tätigkeiten als professionell bezeichnet werden können. Einige historische Anmerkungen zeigen, dass Professionalität lediglich an Universitäten erreicht wurde und dass es bei Pflichtschullehrer/-inne/-n lediglich bei Bemühungen und Versuchen der Professionalisierung blieb. Die gegenwärtige Situation österreichischer Lehrer/-innen und die Ausbildung von Pflichtschullehrer/-inne/-n in Österreich muss aus vielfältigen Gründen eher als Ent-/Deprofessionalisierung betrachtet werden.

Schlüsselbegriffe: Professionalisierung, Deprofessionalisierung, Lehrerausbildung, Evaluation, Qualitätskontrolle, aktuelle Trends in der Ausbildung von Lehrer/-inne/-n

1 Professionelle Tätigkeiten von Lehrer/-inne/-n und Merkmale von Professionalität

„In den nächsten 15 Jahren werden in der Schweiz, in Österreich und in Deutschland insgesamt bis zu 600.000 Lehrerinnen und Lehrer in den Ruhestand treten. Diese gilt es hochwertig zu ersetzen, wenn negative Folgen für Bildung und Erziehung, Wirtschaft und Gesellschaft der drei deutschsprachigen Länder vermieden werden sollen" heißt es in einem am 20. November 2008 von der Gewerkschaft Öffentlicher Dienst (GÖD, Lehrer), vom Dachverband Schweizer Lehrerinnen und Lehrer (LCH) sowie vom Verband Bildung und Erziehung (VBE) in Wien verabschiedeten Papier „Qualifizierte Lehrerinnen und Lehrer – ein Eckpfeiler der Demokratie. Ein Leitbild für den Lehrerberuf heute".
Um welche professionellen Tätigkeiten handelt es sich bei Lehrerinnen und Lehrern? – Lehrerinnen und Lehrer

- … fördern und fordern ihre Schüler/-innen, sie gestalten fachlich und didaktisch ihren Unterricht und geben Anregungen zum selbstbestimmten Lernen. *Lehrer/-innen sind Fachleute für Lernen und Lehren.*
- … sind sich ihrer Vorbildfunktion bewusst, geben Orientierung und erziehen mit pädagogischer Kompetenz. *Lehrer/-innen haben einen Erziehungsauftrag.*

- … diagnostizieren mit pädagogisch-psychologischer und fachdidaktischer Kompetenz, um Schüler/-innen fördern, beraten und zertifizieren zu können. *Lehrer/-innen sind in der Lage kompetent zu urteilen.*
- … erkennen unterschiedliche Lernvoraussetzungen und reagieren mit individuellen Lernangeboten und Lernanforderungen. *Lehrer/-innen stellen Anforderungen an ihre Schüler/-innen.*
- … nutzen Fort- und Weiterbildungsangebote, um wissenschaftliche Erkenntnisse in ihrer beruflichen Tätigkeit berücksichtigen zu können. *Lehrer/-innen entwickeln ihre Kompetenzen ständig weiter.*
- … beteiligen sich an der inneren und äußeren Schulentwicklung und wirken an der Umsetzung des Schulprogramms mit. *Lehrer/-innen steuern die Schul- und Unterrichtsentwicklung maßgeblich mit* (vgl. GÖD, LCH, VBE, 2008, S. 1f.).

Vergleicht man die oben angeführten Tätigkeiten damit, was mit Modellen der Professionalisierung (z.B. „Attribute-Modell“ oder „Indikationstheoretisches Modell“) beschrieben wird, dann sollte sich der Begriff „Profession“ – primär angewandt auf Mediziner, Juristen und Theologen – in gleicher Weise auf Lehrer/-innen übertragen lassen. Folgende Charakteristika erscheinen – im Idealfall – kongruent:

- Sonderwissen, das wissenschaftlich fundiert ist und durch eine spezielle Fachterminologie charakterisiert ist;
- Ausbildungsgänge auf akademischem Niveau (staatl. Lizenz), lange Ausbildungsdauer und theoretische Fundierung;
- Existenz berufständischer Normen *(code of ethics)*; gesetzliche Beschränkung von Eigeninteressen *(non-profit)*;
- Existenz eines Handlungskompetenzmonopols, das exklusiv ist;
- Tätigkeitsbereich besteht aus gemeinnützigen Funktionen, Aufgaben von grundlegender Bedeutung;
- Autonomie bei der Berufsausübung (Fach- und Sachautorität);
- Selbstkontrolle durch Berufsverbände, Interessenvertretung …

HARTMANN (1968) und OEVERMANN (1996) verweisen im Bezug auf Lehrer/-innen darüber hinaus auf ein besonders lizenziertes Interventions- und Eingriffsrecht in die Lebenspraxis von Individuen (vgl. Hartmann 1968, Oevermann 1996).

Neuere Professionsmodelle versuchen, auf soziale und strukturelle Entwicklungen der Gesellschaft Bezug zu nehmen und betonen die *wissenschaftliche Begründungspflicht* sowie den *Berufskodex*.

2 Professionalisierung wird verdrängt von Evaluation und Qualitätskontrolle

In der aktuellen Bildungsdiskussion hat der Begriff der Professionalisierung zurzeit kaum Konjunktur. Fast erscheint er veraltet, verdrängt durch Begriffe wie *Qualitätskontrolle* oder *-management, Evaluation, Kompetenz, Mindeststandards und Wissensmanagement.*

Betrachtet man aktuelle Entwicklungen – hier im Besonderen in der österreichischen Ausbildung von Pflichtschullehrer/-innen – dann könnte man sogar von „Deprofessionalisierung" und einem Zurückfallen hinter das „Konzept des Lehrers als Experten für Lernen" sprechen. „Persönlichkeitsentwicklung" substituiert diagnostisches Wissen und methodische bzw. interventive Kompetenz. Bildungsdiskussionen – wiederbelebt durch die Ergebnisse der TIMSS- und/oder PISA-Studien – werden auch nicht von Lehrer/-inne/-n geleitet, viel häufiger jedoch von Politikern, und Medienmachern. Gleichzeitig wird von Lehrer/-inne/-n immer häufiger erwartet, dass sie sich nicht nur in vorgegebene institutionelle Strukturen eingliedern, Schüler/-inne/-n entsprechende Bildungsinhalte vermitteln und vorgegebenen Bildungsstandards gerecht werden, sondern dass sie auf Unterrichts-, Schul- und Professionsebene Entwicklungsarbeit leisten, und dass sie das, was die Erziehungsberechtigten nicht leisten können oder wollen kompensieren sollen.

Wissen ist im Lehrberuf nicht isoliert als Fachwissen zu sehen, sondern beinhaltet auch Wissen über die „Lehrbarkeit" von Fachwissen. Professionell agierende Lehrer/-innen verstehen die Strukturen ihres Faches auch hinsichtlich seiner Vermittlung. Des weiteren sind professionell handelnde Lehrer/-innen dadurch charakterisiert, dass sie Informationen rasch bzw. gleichzeitig wahrnehmen, sich an vergleichbare Situationen erinnern und bereits während des Unterrichts Modelle von/für Unterrichtssituationen entwickeln, die es ihnen ermöglichen, Entscheidungen zu treffen und entsprechend zu handeln. Das Berufsethos von Lehrer/-inne/-n wird letztlich im Berufsalltag wirksam – als Haltung, die von Verantwortung und Engagement gekennzeichnet ist.

3 Professionalisierung in der Ausbildung von Lehrer/-inne/-n

Lehrerinnen und Lehrer professionalisieren sich – um unterrichtlich und erziehlich „professionell“ handeln zu können – bereits im Zuge ihrer Ausbildung u.a. durch eigene, erfahrungsbezogene Erzeugung von Wahrnehmungsmustern und Wissenskomponenten in der Erprobung ihres ersten Könnens. Nach BAUER (1996, vgl. 2000) handelt eine Person dann „pädagogisch professionell“, wenn sie

- „gezielt ein berufliches Selbst aufbaut, das sich an berufstypischen Werten orientiert,
- sich eines umfassenden pädagogischen Handlungsrepertoires zur Bewältigung von Arbeitsaufgaben sicher ist (...),
- ihre Handlungen unter Bezug auf eine Berufswissenschaft begründen kann und
- persönlich die Verantwortung für Handlungsfolgen in ihrem Einflußbereich übernimmt“ (Bauer 1996, S. 15).

Auf dem Wege der Professionalisierung scheint die Konstellation, in welcher relevante Wahrnehmungsmuster erworben werden, von besonderer Bedeutung zu sein. Werden diese Wahrnehmungsmuster ohne wissenschaftliche Reflexion erworben, entsteht ein „Können“ und ein dazu gehöriges Wissen, das professionstypisch sein mag, aber im Bezug auf eine Berufswissenschaft nicht begründbar ist. Bei der Genese von Professionalität handelt es sich also u.a. um die Veränderung von Wahrnehmungsstrukturen (vgl. Seebauer 200 …).

- ihre Handlungen unter Bezug auf eine Berufswissenschaft begründen kann und
- persönlich die Verantwortung für Handlungsfolgen in ihrem Einflußbereich übernimmt“ (Bauer 1996, S. 15).

Auf dem Wege der Professionalisierung scheint die Konstellation, in welcher relevante Wahrnehmungsmuster erworben werden, von besonderer Bedeutung zu sein. Werden diese Wahrnehmungsmuster ohne wissenschaftliche Reflexion erworben, entsteht ein „Können“ und ein dazu gehöriges Wissen, das professionstypisch sein mag, aber im Bezug auf eine Berufswissenschaft nicht begründbar ist. Bei der Genese von Professionalität handelt es sich also u.a. um die Veränderung von Wahrnehmungsstrukturen (vgl. Seebauer 2007).

4 Das ewige Scheitern der Bemühungen um Professionalisierung bei Pflichtschullehrer/-inne/-n

Bemühungen um die Professionalisierung des Lehrberufs reichen zurück in die Mitte des 19. Jahrhunderts und lassen sich auf den einzelnen Bildungsebenen nach den folgenden Kriterien festmachen:

- Es handelt sich um Vollzeitberufe, die in der Regel „Ungeprüften" (Laien) nicht mehr zugänglich sind; der Beruf ist durch eine normierte Ausbildung und durch Fortbildung charakterisiert *(occupation)*;
- Steuerung durch normative Verhaltenserwartungen, nicht primär durch Erwerbsinteressen – im Sinne einer Berufung *(calling)*;
- Koordinierende Verbände *(organization)*;
- Existenz einer fachwissenschaftlichen Gesellschaft *(study association)* sowie einer Instanz zur Vermittlung von Wissen, Durchführen von Prüfungen, Lizensierung *(qualifying association);*
- Selbständigkeit *(autonomy)* (vgl. Engelbrecht 1986).

Für Grundschullehrer war das erste Merkmal bis weit ins 19. Jahrhundert hinein wenig zutreffend; zumeist verfügten sie selbst lediglich nur über eine Elementarbildung und bei den nach 1848 etwas umfassenderen Präparandenkursen stand die Beherrschung des „Methodenbuchs" – im Sinne einer Anleitung – im Vordergrund. Die Einkünfte der Lehrer setzten sich aus dem Schulgeld, aus Naturalien und aus Einkünften aus dem Mesnerdienst zusammen. Verbesserungen für die (professionelle) Stellung der Volks- und Bürgerschullehrer brachte das Reichsvolksschulgesetz von 1869, vor allem durch die Gründung von vierjährigen Lehrer- und Lehrerinnenbildungsanstalten und die Lehrbefähigungsprüfung als Anstellungserfordernis. Von Bürgerschullehrer/-inne/-n wurde ab 1883 eine zusätzliche – institutionell festgelegte – Ausbildung verlangt. Ferner erfolgte eine Besoldung nach einem Gehaltssystem und die Koppelung „Schul- und Mesnerdienst" fiel fortan weg.

Für weltliche Lehrer an Sekundarschulen („Gymnasiallehrer") eröffnete sich um die Mitte des 19. Jahrhunderts überhaupt erst ein neues Berufsfeld, denn geistliche Orden und Ordenslehrer führten bis in die Mitte des 19. Jahrhunderts den Unterricht an Gymnasien. Die 1856 definitiv eingeführte Lehrbefähigungsprüfung aus zwei Hauptfächern (oder einem Hauptfach und zwei Nebenfächern) verbunden mit Klausurarbeiten, kommissionellen mündlichen Prüfungen und einer Hausarbeit waren die Vorbedingungen für die Zulassung zum sog. „Probejahr", eine Einführung in das praktische Lehramt, während dieser Zeit bis zu sechs Stunden wöchentlich selbständig unterrichtet werden durften. In Folge Lehrermangels unterrichteten allerdings zahlreiche „ungeprüfte" Lehrer an den Gymnasien. Eine besoldungsrechtliche Besserstellung der Gymnasiallehrer erfolgte erst auf Grund des Gehaltsgesetzes von 1873; abgeschlagen blieben sie weiterhin gegenüber den Juristen, die in bessere Gehaltsklassen vorrücken konnten.

Im Jahr 1848 erfolgte eine Regelung des Zugangs zu den Hochschulen/Universitäten durch Einführung des Habilitationsverfahrens; ab den 70er Jahren des 19. Jahrhunderts war auch die Besoldung des Universitätspersonals soweit geregelt, dass Universitätsprofessoren nicht – wie früher so oft – in Beamtenstellen wechselten.

Das Reichsvolksschulgesetz des Jahres 1869 regelte die Fortbildung; es entstanden vermehrt Schulzeitschriften[3] und Lehrerbibliotheken; periodische Konferenzen und Fortbildungskurse wurden obligat. Das bereits 1868 durch die Stadt Wien geschaffene „Pädagogium" sollte vor allem der Entwicklung des städtischen Volksschulwesens dienen. Seit 1880 veranstaltete das Unterrichtsministerium „Ferial-Curse" für Lehrer an den gewerblichen Fortbildungsschulen[4].

Gymnasial- und Hochschullehrer bekamen schon im Jahr 1850 die Möglichkeit der Fernleihe von Büchern aus den Universitäts- und Studienbibliotheken, um die wissenschaftliche Tätigkeit zu heben. Aus den offiziösen bis offiziellen Organen („Zeitschrift für die österreichischen Gymnasien", „Zeitschrift für das Realschulwesen" ...) konnten wissenschaftliche Beiträge und wesentliche Informationen über das Berufsfeld bezogen werden. Ferial-Fortbildungskurse für Gymnasiallehrer gab es an Universitäten erst ab 1903.

Was die Berufung *(calling)* betrifft, war bei den Grundschullehrern am ehesten eine erwerbsorientierte Haltung anzutreffen, was allerdings aus ihrer äußerst bescheidenen materiellen Situation erklärt werden kann. Vor allem die philosophischen Fakultäten rekrutierten den wissenschaftlichen Nachwuchs für Forschung und Lehre aus dem Reservoir der Gymnasiallehrer, die zur Erreichung ihrer wissenschaftlichen Ziele auch bereit waren, materielle Nachteile in Kauf zu nehmen.

---

[3] Z.B. Gründung des „Österreichischen Schulboten" bereits im Jahr 1851 (Vorläufer der Zeitschrift „Erziehung und Unterricht").

[4] Der erste fand im Jahr 1880 in Reichenberg (heute: Liberec, CZ) statt; es folgten Graz und Wien.

Notwendige Zusammenschlüsse *(organization)* bestanden bei allen Lehrerkategorien; sie konnten vor allem den dienst- und besoldungsrechtlichen Forderungen Nachdruck verleihen, allerdings gelang es ihnen nicht Kontrollfunktion zu übernehmen, z.B. im Bezug auf den Berufszugang. Stark entwickelt – vor allem an den Universitäten – waren die fachwissenschaftlichen Gesellschaften.
Ein weiteres Merkmal von Profession, nämlich Selbständigkeit *(autonomy)* konnte von Lehrern im Grundschul- und Sekundarschulbereich nicht erreicht werden. Die „Unselbständigkeit" reichte weit in die Privatsphäre hinein, sodass provisorische Unterlehrer in Niederösterreich und Kärnten sowie provisorische Lehrer in Oberösterreich, Tirol und Vorarlberg eine Heiratsbewilligung benötigten; für Lehrerinnen galt – mit wenigen Ausnahmen – das Zölibat, sodass eine Verehelichung einer „freiwilligen Dienstentsagung" gleichkam und zum Verlust der Anstellung führte.
Selbständigkeit genoss nur die kleine Gruppe der Universitätsprofessoren.
Grundschul- und Sekundarschullehrer sind letztendlich über den seit Mitte des 19. Jahrhunderts in Gang gebrachten Prozess einer schrittweisen Professionalisierung nicht hinausgekommen. Der Versuch einer Annäherung an eine universitäre Ausbildung von Grundschullehr/-inne/-n blieb auf die sog. Wiener Schulreform der Zwanziger Jahre beschränkt.
Die merkwürdige Zweigleisigkeit in der Ausbildung von Lehrer/-inne/-n und in Österreich – Grundschul- und Hauptschullehrer werden an Pädagogischen Hochschulen ausgebildet, Lehrer für allgemeinbildende höhere Schulen an Universitäten – konnte auch durch die seit 2007 bestehenden Pädagogischen Hochschulen nicht aufgehoben werden.

5 Deprofessionalisierung unter aktuellen Arbeitsbedingungen

Die Ausbildung von Lehrer/-inne/-n war und ist immer wieder Systemänderungen und Reformen unterworfen. Gegenwärtige Bemühungen um Reformen orientieren sich an Entwicklungen, die die gesamte Wirtschaft und auch die Bildungssysteme im Allgemeinen betreffen. Diese Entwicklungen werden von Forderungen nach mehr Effizienz im Unterricht, nach Chancengleichheit und Bildungsqualität sowie nach Tertialisierung der Lehrer/-innenausbildung und internationaler Anerkennung der Abschlüsse geleitet.
Die erhoffte Professionalisierung scheint jedoch aus mehreren Gründen nicht erreicht zu werden, das Gegenteil – eine Ent- oder Deprofessionalisierung ist der Fall.

Die Gründe hierfür sind mannigfaltig:

- Die Arbeit von Lehrer/-inne/-n wurde vielfältiger und unspezifischer – sie/er ist nicht mehr nur „Expertin/Experte für Unterricht und Erziehung"; Lehrer/-inne/-n werden permanent und in zunehmend Tätigkeiten abverlangt, die mit ihrem professionellem Selbstverständnis nichts zu tun haben…
- Die von Lehrer/-inne/-n geleistete Arbeit gerät in eine funktional gedachte Beziehung zwischen Unterricht und der Erreichung von Bildungsstandards – Schlagwort vom *teaching to the test.*
- In Zeiten des Lehrermangels sickern mehr und mehr Personen in den „Lehrberuf" ein, die nicht stufen- oder fachgemäß ausgebildet sind, bzw. die keine pädagogisch-psychologische Ausbildung nachweisen können.
- „Bachelor-Lehrer/-innen" und „Master-Lehrer/-innen", die an zwei unterschiedlichen Institutionen ausgebildet werden (Pädagogische Hochschulen vs. Universitäten) und unterschiedlich besoldet werden, unterrichten beide im Bereich der Sekundarstufe I (im Schulversuch „Neue Mittelschule" sogar dieselben Kinder an ein und derselben Schule) – ein österreichisches Spezifikum.

Im Rahmen der Leipziger Erklärung vom 16. Juni 2007[5] forderte die Gewerkschaft Öffentlicher Dienst (GÖD) eine Ausbildung von Lehrer/-inne/-n auf mindestens Masterniveau, also die Absolvierung von „mindestens sechs plus vier Semestern bzw. 180 plus 120 ECTS-Credits – mit dem Ziel, dass die Lehrer/-innenausbildung europaweit und für Schüler/-innen aller Schulstufen auf einem einheitlichen hohen Qualifikationsniveau stattfindet.

Ein weiteres Kuriosum in Österreich stellt das „Gesetz über die Pädagogischen Hochschulen und ihre Studien (Hochschulgesetz 2005)" dar. In diesem wurde – entgegen den zwischen SPÖ und ÖVP akkordierten Intentionen des Akademiestudiengesetzes 1999, welche ein Magisterstudium für die Pflichtschullehrer/-innen in den zu schaffenden Hochschulen für Bildungsberufe vorgesehen hatten – ein Bachelorstudium für die Pflichtschullehrer/-innen aller Kategorien ohne Durchlässigkeit zu den Universitäten eingerichtet. Das Gesetz wurde in der letzten Phase der Kleinen Koalition gegen die Stimmen der SPÖ und

[5] Dreieinhalb Monate vor Beginn der sechssemestrigen Ausbildung von Pflichtschullehrer/-inne/-n an Pädagogischen Hochschulen im Oktober 2007.

der Grünen im Parlament durchgepeitscht. Die so geschaffenen Pädagogischen Hochschulen erreichen nicht einmal Fachhochschulniveau, da ihnen die akademische Autonomie (Selbstverwaltung) vorenthalten und die Grundlagen für eine hochschulische Lehr- und Forschungsfreiheit gem. Staatsgrundgesetz Artikel 17 nicht gewährt wurden (vgl. Seel, Internetpaper).

Als weitere Kennzeichen der Deprofessionalisierung sind zu nennen:

- Ein enges Curriculum, das auf Grund der Modularisierung eine Berücksichtigung fachimmanenter Strukturen nicht zulässt, und auch das Einbringen eigener aktueller Forschungsergebnisse nicht zulässt, fällt weit hinter die Lehrplanvorgaben der Pädagogischen Akademien (bis 2007) zurück.
- In der Organisationsstruktur der Pädagogischen Hochschulen sind Fachgruppen nicht vertreten. Die Fachgruppe hat daher auch auf die Erstellung einer Lehrfächerverteilung keinen Einfluss.
- Was von den Lehrer/-innenbildungsanstalten des Jahres 1869 in die Pädagogischen Akademien (1962 bis 2007) tradiert wurde, fand eine Perpetuierung in die sog. Pädagogischen Hochschulen: die abermalige Übernahme von nicht-akademischem Personal (sog. „Professoren"/Professorinnen") und ihr Einsatz in der Lehre.
- Ein weiteres, fatales österreichisches Spezifikum sind die zahlreichen Personen mit lediglich einem „Magister-Abschluss" in den höchsten Ebenen einer Pädagogischen Hochschule einerseits, und das völlige Ignorieren von hochqualifiziertem akademischem Personal („Habilitierte") andererseits. Dass Personen mit lediglich einem Magister-Abschluss unmittelbare Vorgesetzte von „Habilitierten" sind, und dass die Zugehörigkeit zu einer bestimmten politischen Partei oft vor Qualifikation geht, sei hier nur angemerkt.
- Am 18. Dezember 2009 erscheint ein im Auftrag des Bundesministeriums für Unterricht, Kunst und Kultur und des Bundesministeriums für Wissenschaft und Forschung in Auftrag gegebenes Papier – Empfehlungen einer Expert/-inn/-engruppe zur „LehrerInnenbildung NEU. Die Zukunft der pädagogischen Berufe". Dieses Papier sieht vor: „Jeder Bachelor-Abschluss bietet die Voraussetzung zu qualifizierter pädagogischer Berufstätigkeit. In allen Bereichen pädagogischer Professionen ist der Berufseinstieg mit dem Bachelor-Abschluss möglich ..." Ferner sieht dieses Papier einen Berufsstart als „Turnus-Kraft" vor, wobei auch „Tätigkeiten in bereichsüber-

greifenden pädagogischen Einsatzfeldern" angedacht sind (ExpertInnengruppe 2009, S. 6).

Im Klartext bedeutet dies:

- Die Ausbildung von Lehrer/-inne/-n für die gymnasiale Oberstufe fällt hinter jene von 1856 zurück.
- Der Einsatz von Lehrer/-inne/-n als Turnuskräfte steht unterschwellig für „Einsparungsmaßnahmen" und
- die Übernahme von Tätigkeiten in bereichsübergreifenden pädagogischen Einsatzfeldern ist einer weiterer Schritt zur Deprofessionalisierung!

Literaturangaben

BAUER, K.-O., KOPKA, A., BRINDT, S. (1996): Pädagogische Professionalität und Lehrerarbeit. Eine qualitativ empirische Studie über professionelles Handeln und Bewußtsein. Weinheim, München.

BAUER, K.-O. (2000): Pädagoge – Profession oder Nebenbeschäftigung? In: Jaumann-Graumann, O., Köhnlein, W. (Hg.): Lehrerprofessionalität – Lehrerprofessionalisierung. Jahrbuch Grundschulforschung Bd. 3. Bad Heilbrunn. S. 25-44.

ENGELBRECHT, H. (1986): Geschichte des österreichischen Bildungswesens. Erziehung und Unterricht auf dem Boden Wiens. Bd. 4 ÖBV Wien.

EXPERTINNENGRUPPE: LehrerInnenbildung NEU – Die Zukunft der pädagogischen Berufe. Arbeitspapier erstellt im Auftrag des Bundesministeriums für Unterricht, Kunst und Kultur und des Bundesministeriums für Wissenschaft und Forschung, datiert: 18.12.2009 (vgl. dazu auch „Die Presse" vom 22.11.2009).

GÖD/LCH/VBE (HG.) (2008): Qualifizierte Lehrerinnen und Lehrer – ein Eckpfeiler der Demokratie.
Abrufbar unter: http://www.lch.ch/dms-static/90fdc1de-54fe-49d9-b686-47320e5a3f27/081120_wiener_erklaerung.pdf. (zuletzt überprüft am 8/12/09).

HARTMANN, H. (1968): Arbeit, Beruf, Profession, in: Soziale Welt 19, 2, S. 193-216.

OEVERMANN, U. (1996): Theoretische Skizze einer revidierten Theorie professionalisierten Handelns. In: Combe, A./Helsper. W. (Hg.): Pädagogische Professionalität, Frankfurt am Main.

SEEBAUER, R. (2007): Verborgenes Praxiswissen und Professionalisierung. Studien zur schulpraktischen Ausbildung. VDM Verlag Dr. Müller, Saarbrücken.

SEEL, H. (2007): Vom „Schweigen im Walde“ bzw. in der GÖD. Abrufbar unter: http://www.bpag.at/pivot/entry.php?id=70#body (zuletzt überprüft am 8/12/09).

THIEL, F. (2007): Profession als Lebensform. Entwürfe des neuen Lehrers nach 1900. In: ZfPäd. 53. Jg. H.1, S. 74-91.

Kontakt:
Doz. Dr. hab. et Mag. Renate SEEBAUER, Prof. PH: renate.seebauer@phwien.ac.at

FABRIZIERTE FREIHEIT: NEOLIBERALE ASPEKTE DER PROFESSIONALISIERUNG VON LEHRERN

Ondrej Kaščák, Branislav Pupala, Trnavaer Universität in Trnava, Slowakische Republik

In der Studie werden die Auswirkungen des politisch und ökonomisch fundierten neoliberalen Diskurses auf die Debatte über Professionalisierung des Lehrerberufes rekonstruiert. Die neoliberalen Wurzeln des pädagogischen Diskurses über den sogenannten reflexiven Lehrer werden entlarvt, wobei dieser Diskurs Bestandteil einer neuen Normativität ist, die den Lehrerberuf eher entprofessionalisiert und die Lehrer unter größeren technokratischen Druck setzt – auch auf der Ebene der Subjektivierung.

Schlüsselbegriffe: der neoliberale Diskurs, der selbstreflexive Lehrer, Standardisierung der Autonomie, Entprofessionalisierung

Die Feststellung der „Betonung, ja der Feier und Absolutierung des Selbst“ (Brinkmann 2008, S. 3) auch im Rahmen des professionellen Diskurses ist heutzutage unbestritten. Auch die Professionalität der Lehrer bewertet (auch misst) man nach deren Fähigkeiten des Selbsterlernens, der Selbstbildung, der Selbstorganisation, der Selbstwirksamkeit, der Selbständigkeit, der Selbstkontrolle, der Selbstevaluation oder Selbstreflexion. Der professionelle Diskurs wird von solchen Bildern übersättigt, so dass man sogar von der Hervorbringung einer neuen Form von (Lehrer-)Subjektivität und Identität spricht. Subjekte werden dazu angehalten, produktiv ein neues Verhältnis zu ihrer Person einzunehmen. In der professionellen Sphäre heißt dies ein Verhältnis zu permanenter Selbstevaluation und -reflexion einzugehen.

1 Autonomie in neuen ideologischen Kontexten

Das Element der Autonomie, das diesem Selbstverständnis innewohnt, wird in natürlicher Weise mit dem humanistisch pädagogischen Diskurs, der sich in der slowakischen Lehrerkunde in Gestalt des Konzepts einer „reflexiven Lehrerbildung" manifestiert, verbunden (vgl. Kasáčová 2005). Die Gründe für die Stärkung der Reflexivität und der Selbstevaluation sieht man hier vor allem in der Humanisierung und Demokratisierung des Lehr- und Lernumfeldes, in der Herausbildung eines positiven Klimas sowie in der Intensivierung des Wohlgefühls aller Schulakteure. Permanente Selbstreflexion des Lehrers wird als ein Weg der permanent pädagogischen Gleichstellung gesehen.

Die Frage stellt sich, ob der humanistische Diskurs heutzutage spezifischen sozialen Zielen dient, die nicht mit seiner früheren emanzipatorischen Ausrichtung korrespondiert. BRINKMANN (2008, S. 3) führt dazu an: „Heute funktionieren die Begriffe Selbständigkeit, Kreativität oder Autonomie ... in einem neuen Kontext. Der emanzipatorisch-aufklärerische Gehalt dieser Begriffe ist verloren gegangen. Ihre weiterhin positive Konnotierung funktioniert nun, um im Regime der Effizienz die Individuen zu aktivieren und zu managen." Nicht das Regime der Emanzipation, sondern das Regime der Effizienz zählt. Autonomie und Selbstreflexion erwartet man vom Lehrer nicht wegen der eigenen Humanisierung und der Humanisierung der Schüler, sondern sie wird zum Instrument der effektiven Produktion eines bestimmten Subjekttypus.

Diese epistemologische Wende hängt mit dem Einbruch des politischen Neoliberalismus zusammen, der mit Hilfe einiger ökonomischer Theorien, z.B. des sogenannten Humankapitals, in die Sphäre der Professionen eindringen konnte. Die These lautet hier: Jeder trägt Verantwortung dafür, wie er sein Humankapital investiert. „Die Arbeitenden erscheinen in dieser Konzeption nicht mehr als abhängig Beschäftigte..., sondern werden zu autonomen Unternehmern, die eigenverantwortlich Investitionsentscheidungen fällen und auf die Produktion eines Mehrwertes abzielen: Unternehmer ihrer selbst" (Lemke 2001, S. 111).

Auch im Diskurs über Professionalisierung der Lehrer spricht man fortan vom „Unternehmen". Z. B. nach SLOTERDIJK (2005, S. 114) müssen wir „von einem gut verstandenen Unternehmer-Gedanken her, einem Lebensunternehmer-Gedanken, auch die öffentlichen Dienste reanimieren. Dann wird man vielleicht eine neue Generation von Lehrern entstehen sehen".

2 Selbstreflexion als Machtstrategie

Es ist aber nicht notwendig, solch allgemeine Individualisierung und professionelle Vereinsamung der Arbeitenden nur positiv zu reflektieren. Ihre Autonomie ist nämlich eine ökonomisch auferlegte Autonomie. In diesem Zusammenhang spricht man von einer „künstlich arrangierten Freiheit" (Lemke 2001) oder einer „eingeflüsterten Emanzipation" (Fach 2000). Nach ROSE (1996, S. 17) sind „die Formen der Freiheit, die wir heute wahrnehmen, ... unauflöslich auf ein Regime der Subjektivierung gebunden, in dem die Subjekte nicht nur ‚frei sind, zu wählen', sondern gezwungen sind, frei zu sein".

In diesem Sinne gewinnt auch die in zahlreichen gegenwärtigen Tugendkatalogen geforderte Selbstreflexion des Lehrers andere Konturen. Ihre Notwendigkeit erwächst aus dem Druck nach der Autonomie. Dieser Druck sieht man auch in den heutzutage populären neoliberalen Strategien der Schulevaluation. *Total Quality Management* (TQM) ist angesagt. Diese Evaluationstechnologie behandelt die Lehrer als aktive und selbstreflexive Mitglieder der Organisation, die für Mängelvermeidung verantwortlich sind. Selbstreflexivität sieht man als den Weg zur Risikobewältigung und Qualitätssicherung. „Die Qualitätsspezialisten kontrollieren nicht mehr die Produkte, sondern die Selbstkontrolle der Produzenten" (Brökling 2000, S. 136). Die Fähigkeit zur Selbsteinschätzung, Selbstbewertung und Selbsterkenntnis der Lehrer wird überprüft.

Wenn in der Evaluation solchen Merkmalen nachgegangen wird, dann werden sie auch im Diskurs über Professionalität der Lehrer akzentuiert. Inzwischen wurden zahlreiche manageriale Subjektivierungsstrategien geschaffen, die gerade diesen Typus des selbstreflexiven Arbeiters produzieren sollen. Erwähnt sei hier z. B. die Technologie D.A.T.A., im Rahmen derer der Lehrer bewusst und explizit seine Neigungen und Fähigkeiten in vier Bereiche zerlegen soll: persönliche Wünsche *(Desires)*, Fähigkeiten *(Abilities),* Temperament und persönliche Vorteile *(Assets)* (Bridges 1996). Zur effektiven Selbstreflexion sollen auch zahlreiche Feedback-Systeme beitragen, die den Ausgangspunkt einer methodischen Arbeit an sich selbst darstellen sollen.

3 Standardisierung der Lehrerautonomie

Obwohl der Reflexionsbegriff im Lehrerberuf in den letzten Jahrzehnten verschiedene Facetten gewonnen hat (vgl. Fendler 2003), wurde seine aktuelle Auffassung durch die neoliberale Bildungspolitik produziert, in der die Selbstkontrolle und Selbstreflexionspraktiken zu managerialen Orthodoxie wurden (Clegg 1999). Durch diese Politik werden auch Stützpunkte von massiv realisierten Bildungsreformen bestimmt. Sie wird durch drei miteinander verflochtenen politischen Technologien repräsentiert: Der Marktlogik, dem Managerialismus und der Performativität. Die Selbstreflexion des Lehrers wurde zum Bestandteil solcher Technologien. Er solle sich als Individualität mit einem „Mehrwert" wahrnehmen, die unaufhörlich ihre Produktivität steigert, die nach der Vorzüglichkeit strebt und ihre Karriere kalkuliert (Ball 2003). Selbstreflexion ist die Voraussetzung der „unternehmungslustigen Subjekte", die zum Prototyp des „neoliberalen Professionellen" wurden.

Diese pädagogischen Professionellen wurden durch die Maschinerie der Bildungsreformen zur Welt gebracht, die in unserem Kontext mit der Reglementierung seitens zentraler Strukturen der EU bzw. OECD zusammenhängt. Die erwähnten neoliberalen politischen Technologien werden hier protegiert mit dem Ziel, Bildungssysteme als ökonomische Werkzeuge im Sinne der Stärkung von Wettbewerbsfähigkeit und Wettbewerbslust der Nationalökonomien zu benutzen. Bildungssysteme als solche werden in dieser Logik zu Subjekten der Wettbewerbsfähigkeit, wenn sie z. B. durch Projekte wie PISA um die besten Ergebnisse in übernational festgelegten Kompetenzen ringen, die flexible und anpassungsfähige Arbeitskraft definieren sollen. Lehrer werden in dieser Maschinerie zu Instruktoren, deren Professionalität darin liegt, wie schnell und reibungslos sie Ziele erreichen, die in der neoliberalen Bildungspolitik als wertvoll gelten.

Die neoliberale Strategie des Managerialismus, die die Managementverantwortung bis zum Niveau des Selbstmanagements delegiert (wodurch der Eindruck einer Garantie der Organisations- und Individualautonomie entsteht), hat auch ihren komplementären Aspekt – die Stärkung einer zentralen Effektivitätsevaluation auf allen Ebenen des Bildungssystems: des Bildungssystems als solchem, der Schulen, der einzelnen Lehrer. Auf der Organisationsebene drückt sich dieser Aspekt z. B. in Konzepten der „Monitorsysteme" oder der „Informationsproduktion" aus (typische Rede der OECD), auf der Ebene der Evaluation von professionellen Profilen der Lehrer geht es um den Prozess der zentralisierten Festlegung von Lehrerberufsstandards nach dem Modell von Professionskompetenzen. Diese Standards sollen zu Referenzpunkten der Qualitätskontrolle des Professionsvollzugs sowie der Tendenzen zur Selbstinitiierung des professionellen Wachstums des Lehrers werden. Das Definieren im Kompetenzmodus bildet die Möglichkeit der wiederholbaren Evaluation und der messbaren Kontrolle nach dem Vorbild des Privatsektors. Die Organisationen und im Einzelnen auch die Lehrer sind dadurch auf das Präsentieren ihrer Leistungen im Regime von extern festgelegten Kriterien angewiesen. Im Falle der Lehrer bildet eine solche wiederholte und erzwungene Performativität die Grundlage eines Systems des professionellen Wachstums und der Weiterbildung.

In der neoliberalen Darstellung wird die proklamierte Professionsautonomie paradoxerweise zur „regulierten Autonomie" (Locke 2001), die versprochenen De-regulationsmechanismen werden in der Tat zu Prozessen der Re-regulation oder der weniger sichtbaren Regulation (Ball 2003). Deshalb bezeichnet man die neoliberalen Änderungen in der Lehrerprofessionalität auch mit strengeren Worten als Entprofessionalisierung oder als Erosion des Lehrerberufs. Auch wenn man den neoliberalen Professionellen nur als einen anderen Typus des Professionellen sehen will (Whitty 2000), wird bei diesem sogar auf dem Identitätsniveau ein enormer Grad an Selbstskepsis und persönlicher Beklemmung konstatiert (Ball 2003).

Literaturangaben

BALL, J. STEPHEN: The teacher's soul and the terrors of performativity. In: Journal of Educational Policy 2/2003, 215-228.

BRIDGES, WILLIAM: Ich & Co. Wie man sich auf dem neuen Arbeitsmarkt behauptet. - Hamburg: Hoffmann und Campe, 1996.

BRINKMANN, MALTE: „Lernen wie Onkel Dagobert". Humankapital und neues Lernen in Schule und Hochschule, 2008. [010-03-08].
URL: http://home.ph-freiburg.de/brinkmannfr/downloads/texte/Brinkmann_Humankapital%20und%20Neues%20Lernen.pdf

BRÖCKLING, ULRICH: Totale Mobilmachung. Menschenführung im Qualitäts- und Selbstmanagement. In: Bröckling, Ulrich, Krasmann, Susanne, Lemke, Zhomas (Hg.): Gouvernementalität der Gegenwart, 131-167. - Frankfurt am Main: Suhrkamp, 2000.

CLEGG, SUE: Professional education, reflective practice and feminism. In: International Journal of Inclusive Education 2/1999, 167-179.

FACH, WOLFGANG: Staatskörperkultur. Ein Traktat über den „schlanken Staat". In: Bröckling, Ulrich, Krasmann, Susanne, Lemke, Zhomas (Hg.): Gouvernementalität der Gegenwart, 110-130. - Frankfurt am Main: Suhrkamp, 2000.

FENDLER, LYNN: Teacher reflection in a hall of mirrors: Historical influences and political reverberations. In: Educational Researcher 3/2003, 16-25.

KASÁČOVÁ, BRONISLAVA: Reflexívna výučba a reflexia v učiteľskej príprave. - Banská Bystrica: PF UMB, 2005.

LEMKE, THOMAS: „Die Ungleichheit ist für alle gleich". Michel Foucaults Analyse der neoliberalen Gouvernementalität. In: Miszelle 2/2001, 99-115.

LOCKE, TARRY: Questions of professionalism: Erosion and reclamation. In: Change: Transformations in Education 2/2001, 30-50.

SLOTERDIJK, PETER: Lernen ist Vorfreude auf sich selbst. In: McK Wissen 14/2005, 110-117.

ROSE, NIKOLAS: Inventing ourselves. Psychology, Power, Personhood. - Cambridge: CUP, 1996.

WHITTY, GEOFF: Teacher professionalism in new times. In: Journal of In-Service Education, 2/2000, 281-295.

Kontakt:
Ondrej KAŠČÁK: okascak@truni.sk
Branislav PUPALA: bpupala@truni.sk

INTERGENERATIONALE UNTERSTÜTZUNG UNTER LEHRERN

Vladimír Jůva, Bohumíra Lazarová
Fakultät der Sportwissenschaft und Philosophische Fakultät
Masaryk Universität, Brno, Tschechische Republik

Der Beitrag fokussiert auf ausgewählte Aspekte der intergenerationalen Beziehungen unter den Grundschullehrer/-inne/-n. Der erste Textabschnitt fasst einige theoretische Ansätze zur Problematik der Lehrerposition in späteren Phasen deren Schulkarriere sowie zu erwarteten Aspekten deren Leistungen zugunsten der jüngeren Kollegen sowie der ganzen Schulanstalt zusammen. Der zweite Abschnitt präsentiert dann ausgewählte Daten einer Forschungserhebung, in der u. a. die Fragen nach Unterstützung älterer Lehrer und gegenseitiger Hilfe unter den Lehrergenerationen untersucht wurden.

Schlüsselbegriffe: intergenerationale Beziehungen bei Grundschullehrer/-inne/-n, Schulkarriere, Untersuchung zu gegenseitiger Unterstützung älterer und jüngerer Lehrer/-innen

1 Einleitung

Tschechische wie auch internationale Forschungen zeigen, dass man in den Schulen einen verhältnismäßig beträchtlichen Anteil an Lehrkräften höherer Alterskategorien finden kann. An ältere Lehrer werden hohe Anforderungen gestellt, sowohl in Verbindung mit der physischen und psychischen Intensität des Lehrerberufs als auch mit dem sich schnell ändernden Bild der gegenwärtigen Gesellschaft. Die schwierigere Situation der älteren Lehrer in der Tschechischen Republik – so wie in weiteren postkommunistischen Ländern – ist ferner auf das Faktum zurückzuführen, dass diese Altersgruppe der pädagogischen Mitarbeiter ihren Beruf unter ganz anderen Bedingungen, nämlich in der Zeit des realen Sozialismus studiert bzw. aufgenommen hat.

Theoretische Konzepte sowie die gegenwärtige Praxis unterstellen die Erwartung, dass ältere und erfahrene Lehrer ihren jüngeren Kollegen in professioneller Hinsicht behilflich sein und zur Entwicklung der ganzen Schulanstalt beitragen würden. Die anspruchsvolle Berufsposition der älteren Lehrkräfte setzt gleichzeitig voraus, dass ihnen seitens der Schulleitung und ihrer jüngeren Kollegen auch entsprechende Unterstützung zukommt. Einige konkrete Gebiete der intergenerationalen Beziehungen unter den Grundschullehrern werden durch Ergebnisse der Forschungsermittlung näher dargelegt, die im

Rahmen des von der *Czech Science Foundation* geförderten Projektes „Lehrer in späterer Karrierephase“ durchgeführt wurde (Projekt-Nr. 406/08/176).

2 Ältere Lehrer und intergenerationale Unterstützung in der Schule

Obwohl die älteren Lehrer an den Schulen eine große und bedeutende Gruppe darstellen, werden sie von der pädagogischen Forschung kaum erfasst. Die Erhebungen fokussieren vielmehr die Anfänge der Lehrerlaufbahn bzw. einzelne enger abgegrenzte Themen quer durch die Alterskategorien (näher dazu Lukas 2007, 2008). Fachstudien, welche direkt die Situation der älteren Lehrer aufnehmen, zielen insbesondere auf Möglichkeiten ab, ihre Motivation und Leistung aufrecht zu erhalten und ihre Erfahrungen für die Schulentwicklung zu nutzen (Hanson, Moir 2008; McCreight 2000; McCann, Johannessen 2005). Die Autoren weisen auf eine Reihe von Änderungen hin, welche die Karriere älterer Lehrer begleiten. Dazu zählen z.B. zunehmende Gesundheitsbeschwerden, das Burnout-Syndrom, subjektive Gefühle körperlicher und geistiger Abnutzung, vermindertes Selbstbewusstsein, erhöhte Reflektivität, Verlust an Ambitionen und persönlichem Einsatzwillen, zunehmender Abstand der älteren Lehrer von den Schülern durch wachsende Generationsunterschiede, weniger Toleranz zu anderen Verhaltensweisen jüngerer Lehrkräfte und Schüler etc. Die Studien erinnern gleichzeitig daran, dass ältere Lehrer keinesfalls als schlechtere Lehrer einzustufen sind (Huberman 1989). Im Gegenteil, älteren Lehrkräften werden mehr Vertrauenswürdigkeit, Effektivität und Gelassenheit (Huberman (1989) sowie eine höhere Sicherheit zugeschrieben, z.B. bei Konfliktregelung oder in der Kommunikation mit den Eltern (Melnick, Meister 2008).

Für die Problematik der intergenerationalen Lehrerkooperation sind Studien zur Einbindung von emeritierten Lehrern in Mentoring-Programme und weitere Formen der Schulhilfe nutzbringend (Botwinik, Rothman Press 2006). Durch Forschungen wurde auch belegt, dass es mehrere Themen gibt, z.B. Klassenführung, Elternkommunikation oder Konfliktregelung, welche die älteren Lehrer effektiver bewältigen als ihre jüngeren Kollegen und für sie in diesen Bereichen inspirierend sein können (Melnick, Meister 2008). McCann und Johannessen (2005) weisen sogar auf die professionelle Verantwortung der älteren Lehrer gegenüber ihren jüngeren Kollegen hin. Die Schaffung eines Klimas von gegenseitiger Lehrerunterstützung und -zusammenarbeit sowie deren Erfahrungsaustausch und -teilung gehören derzeit zu den Grund-anforderungen an eine erfolgreiche Schule. In diesem Prozess können sich die ältere und die jüngere Generation, d.h. Lehrernovizen und erfahrene Lehrer in ihrer letzten Karrierephase einander bereichern und inspirieren und somit zur Entwicklung einer „guten Schule" ihren gemeinsamen Beitrag leisten.

3 Forschungsmethodik

Das Forschungsprojekt „Lehrer in späterer Karrierephase" setzt sich zum Ziel, die spezifischen Effekte der Berufsausübung bei älteren Lehrkräften auf der zweiten Grundschulstufe zu erkennen und zu beschreiben. Unter dem Begriff „Lehrer in späterer Karrierephase" versteht man in unserer Auffassung die letzte Phase der Berufslaufbahn eines Lehrers (Huberman 1989), d.h. Lehrer/-innen mit mehr als 20 Jahren Unterrichtserfahrung und über 50 Jahre alt. In dem vorliegenden Beitrag verkürzt „ältere Lehrer" genannt. Als partielles Ziel dieses breit angelegten Forschungsprojektes gilt die Schwerpunktsetzung auf Analyse von Umfeld, Entwicklungsmöglichkeiten und Umsetzung des pädagogischen und Persönlichkeitspotenzials der älteren Lehrer für die Weiterentwicklung der Schule als Institution. Im Hinblick auf dieses Teilziel treten mehrere Anregungen in Erscheinung, die mit der Problematik der generationsübergreifenden Lehrerhilfe zusammenhängen.

In unserem 2008 aufgenommenen Forschungsprojekt wird eine Kombination qualitativer und quantitativer Ansätze herangezogen. In der ersten Erhebungsphase gewannen wir mit der Focus-Group-Methode eine tiefere Einsicht in die untersuchte Problematik. In dieser Ermittlungsphase erhoben wir Unterlagen für die Gestaltung von zwei Fragebögen.

Die Bögen enthielten geschlossene Fragen (vor allem in Feldern für personenbezogene Angaben), halbgeschlossene (z.B. nähere Angaben zum beruflichen Werdegang) und offene Positionen (z.B. Möglichkeit für themenbezogene Anmerkungen und Ergänzungen). Zur Messung der Einstellungen der untersuchten Schuldirektoren und älteren Lehrer wurde die Likert-Skala eingesetzt, indem wir eine Reihe von Aussagen und Behauptungen vorgelegt hatten, denen die Befragten den Grad ihrer (Nicht-)Zustimmung durch eine Fünf-Grad-Skala mit der zusätzlichen Option „0 – kann ich nicht beurteilen" zuordneten. Insgesamt wurden 217 ausgefüllte Fragebögen aus 53 tschechischen Grundschulen ausgewertet. 173 Fragebögen wurden von Lehrer/-inne/-n ausgefüllt und 44 Bögen von Schuldirektor/innen (25 männlich, 19 weiblich) beantwortet. Im Unterschied zu der relativ ausgeglichenen Geschlechtsverteilung bei den Direktoren war im Fall der Lehrer/-innen eine ausgeprägte Feminisierung dieses Berufs offensichtlich. Lediglich ein Fünftel der Befragten waren Männer, die restlichen 80 % Frauen. Das Durchschnittsalter der Lehrer/-innen betrug 55 Jahre, was in unserer Probe ebenfalls den Median darstellte. Die längste pädagogische Berufserfahrung wurde mit 46 Jahren erfasst.

4 Von den Forschungsergebnissen

In der ersten qualitätsorientierten Phase der Forschungsuntersuchung wurden mehrere Aspekte zur Problematik der intergenerationalen Lehrerhilfe augenscheinlich. Nebst der vorausgesetzten Unterstützung der jüngeren Lehrer durch ihre erfahrenen Kollegen (z.B. bez. der Unterrichtsmethodik oder bei der Regelung von Erziehungsproblemen mit Schülern) profilierte sich auch der Bedarf an einer spezifischen Unterstützung der älteren Lehrer, um ihnen den Schuldienst leichter zu machen (z.B. Mithilfe von vorwiegend jüngeren Kollegen der bei Nutzung und dem Einsatz von Informationstechnologien). Durch die daran knüpfenden Fragebögen konnte eine relativ große Datenmenge erhoben werden. Angesichts des Umfangs dieses Beitrags ist es uns möglich, nur ausgewählte Aspekte der intergenerationalen Zusammenarbeit herauszugreifen.

Der Fragebogen für die Grundschuldirektoren war auf das Berufsleben der älteren Lehrer ausgerichtet – auf ihr berufliches Selbstverständnis, ihren Kummer und ihre Sorgen im Beruf sowie auf ihre Weiterbildung. Das intergenerationale Thema wurde vor allem durch Items zu konkreter Zusammenarbeit, Erfahrungsweitergabe durch die älteren Lehrer und zur erwarteten Unterstützung für dieselben behandelt. 70 % der Grundschuldirektoren sind der Meinung, dass ältere Lehrer mit den jüngeren Schulkollegen gerne zusammenarbeiten und die jüngeren Kollegen die Erfahrungen der älteren gerne nutzen. Diese hilfsorientierte Beziehung betrifft am häufigsten methodische Unterrichtsfragen, die Beilegung von Erziehungsproblemen (z.B. Aufrechterhaltung der Unterrichtsdisziplin, Umgang mit Problemschülern) und Anregungen zur Kommunikation mit den Schuleltern. Die Hälfte der Schuldirektoren glaubt, dass die älteren Lehrer ihre Erfahrungen an jüngere Kollegen gerne weitergeben. 57 % der befragten Direktoren geben an, dass in ihrer Schule ein organisierter Erfahrungsaustausch zwischen den älteren und jüngeren Lehrern laufe. In Bezug auf die in wissenschaftlichen Studien oft erwähnte Tendenz, erfahrene Lehrer in Mentoring-Programme einzubinden, ist eine derartige Inanspruchnahme der älteren Lehrer bei uns nicht all zu hoch. Zu Konflikten und Missverständnissen zwischen jüngeren und älteren Kollegen kommt es eher sporadisch. Ihre Ursachen können in den unterschiedlichen Ansätzen zum Schülerverhalten („die Jüngeren tolerieren vieles"), in der ungleichen Intensität des Arbeitseinsatzes oder zu viel Assertivität und Rücksichtslosigkeit der jüngeren Kollegen liegen.

Durch den Fragebogen für ältere Lehrer wurden neben personenbezogenen Angaben und Informationen zum Verlauf ihrer Berufslaufbahn insbesondere Meinungen zu ihrem beruflichen Selbstverständnis und zu Kummer und Freuden des Lehrerberufs erhoben. Mit den Aspekten des intergenerationalen Zusammenlebens hingen vor allem die Items mit den Schwerpunkten Zusammenarbeit mit Kollegen und Schulleitung, Erfahrungsaustausch und Wahrnehmung einer Unterstützung zusammen. Die älteren Lehrer äußerten sich vergleichbar mit den Direktoren, ihre Erfahrungen gerne an jüngere Kollegen weiter zu geben (75 %), und meinen zugleich zu 73 %, diese Erfahrungen würden in der Schule positiv geschätzt. Jedoch nur eine beträchtlich kleinere Gruppe der Befragten (44 %) gab an, von ihren jüngeren Kollegen oft um Rat gebeten zu werden. 58 % der älteren Lehrer haben das Gefühl, dass die Schulleitung ihre Autorität unterstützt und sich gleichzeitig ihrer Erfahrungen bedient. Dagegen nur 7 % der älteren Lehrer meinen, die Schulleitung setze mehr auf das Potenzial der jüngeren Kollegen. Inhaltlich betrifft die Hilfe an jüngere Kollegen – entsprechend den Direktorenmeinungen – meistens methodische und erziehungstechnische Probleme.

5 Schlussfolgerung

Ältere Lehrer geraten in der Schule in eine Position, die einerseits durch Erfahrungsweitergabe und Unterstützung an jüngere Kollegen geprägt ist, in der sie aber auch einen sozialen Rückhalt seitens der Schulleitung und der jüngeren Kollegen brauchen. Diese notwendige und für die Schulentwicklung kostbare intergenerationale Zusammenarbeit kann jedoch auf Kommunikationsbarrieren stoßen. Diese können bei den älteren Lehrern durch allfällige Überheblichkeit, Direktivität und eventuell mangelnde Bereitschaft zu einer „Know-how-Weitergabe" aufgestellt werden, bei den jüngeren Kollegen dann mit dem Risiko verbunden sein, die Leistungen und Berufserfahrungen der Älteren zu unterschätzen. In der intergenerationalen Kooperation scheint die Reziprozität eine wichtige Rolle zu spielen: Wenn der junge Lehrer in der Lage ist, um Hilfe zu bitten und mit seiner Offenheit als erster zu kommen, kann dies zur Gelegenheit werden, sich gegenseitig kennen zu lernen und demnach auch gegenseitiges Vertrauen aufzubauen, das der ältere Kollege zu seiner Selbstöffnung braucht.

Literaturangaben

BOTWINIK, RUTH: Rothman Press, Marlyn: Career Option for Retired Teachers. In: The clearing house 3/2006, S. 145-146.

HANSON, SUSAN/MOIR, ELLEN: Beyond mentoring: Influencing the professional practice and careers of experienced teachers. In: Phi Delta Kappan, 6/2008, S. 453-458.

HUBERMAN, MICHAEL: The Professional Life Cycle of Teachers. In: Teachers College Record 1/1989, S. 31-57.

LUKAS, JOSEF: Vývoj učitele: přehled relevantních teorií a výzkumů. In: Pedagogika 4/2007, S. 364-379; 1/2008, S. 36-49.

MCCANN, THOMAS/JOHANNESSEN, LARRY, R.: The Role and Responsibility of the Experienced Teacher. In: English Journal 2/2005, S. 52–57.

MCCREIGHT, CAROLYN: Teacher Attrition, Shortage, and Strategies for Teacher Retention. – Texas: A&M University, 2000.

MELNICK, STEVEN, A./ MEISTER, DENISE, G.: A Comparison of Beginning and Experienced Teachers' Concerns. In: Educational Research Quarterly 3/2008, S. 39-56.

Kontakt:
Vladimír JŮVA: juva@fsps.muni.cz
Bohumíra LAZAROVÁ: lazarova@phil.muni.cz

WIE (LANGE) WIRKT FORTBILDUNG?

Stefan Zehetmeier, Universität Klagenfurt, Österreich

Der vorliegende Beitrag fasst Forschungsbefunde zum Thema „Nachhaltige Wirkungen von Lehrerfortbildung" zusammen. Die zentralen Fragen dabei sind: Auf welchen Ebenen kann Fortbildung wirksam werden? Anhand welcher Elemente lassen sich Fortbildungsinitiativen kategorisieren? Wie kann Nachhaltigkeit definiert und charakterisiert werden? Welche Faktoren fördern oder hemmen die Wirkungen von Fortbildungsmaßnahmen, und wie können diese Faktoren kategorisiert werden? Der Beitrag erörtert die theoretischen und begrifflichen Zugänge sowie die empirischen Arbeiten zu diesen Themenbereichen und fasst diese schließlich in einem Wirkungsmodell zusammen.

Schlüsselbegriffe: Lehrerfortbildung, Nachhaltigkeit, Wirkung von Fortbildungsmaßnahmen, Wirkungsmodell zur Lehrerfortbildung

1 Einleitung

Die Fragen *wie* und *wie lange* Veranstaltungen zur Lehrerfortbildung wirken, sind sowohl für die teilnehmenden Lehrkräfte, als auch für die Anbieter/-innen von großer Bedeutung (Ingvarson, Meiers, & Beavis 2005). Evaluationsmaßnahmen, welche die Wirkungen von Lehrerfortbildung erfassen (sollen), werden meist während oder am Ende solcher Veranstaltungen durchgeführt und liefern ausschließlich Ergebnisse über unmittelbare Wirkungen. *Langfristige und nachhaltige Wirkungen* werden oftmals aufgrund mangelnder zeitlicher, finanzieller oder personeller Ressourcen nicht untersucht (Datnow 2006, McLaughlin & Mitra 2001). HARGREAVES (2002) stellt dazu fest:

"The sustainability of educational change has (...) become one of the key priorities in the field" (S. 120).

Die folgenden Abschnitte fassen Forschungsergebnisse zu diesem Themenbereich zusammen.

2 Wirkungsebenen

Bei der Analyse möglicher Wirkungen von Fortbildungsmaßnahmen stellt sich die zentrale Frage, auf welchen Ebenen diese Wirkungen überhaupt erwartet werden können.

Die Ebenen *Wissen, Einstellungen* und *Praxis* der Lehrkräfte scheinen gut geeignet, um die Wirkungen von Lehrerfortbildung zu kategorisieren (Ingvarson et

al., 2005; Lipowsky 2004, 2010; Meiers 2007). Auch das Wissen, die Einstellungen und das Unterrichtsverhalten der Schüler/-innen kann und soll – zumindest mittelbar – von den Wirkungen der Lehrerfortbildung betroffen sein. Darüber hinaus kann diese Dreiteilung in Wissen, Einstellungen und Praxis auch auf weitere *innerschulische* (etwa Kolleg/-inn/-en, Direktion oder Eltern) und *außerschulische Ebenen* (wie etwa andere Schulen, Medien, Politik oder Wissenschaft) angewendet werden (Zehetmeier 2008). Daraus ergibt sich ein allgemeiner Raster möglicher Wirkungsebenen, welcher in Abbildung 1 dargestellt ist. Die Felder des Rasters in Abbildung 1 sind exemplarisch mit Schlagworten möglicher Wirkungen gefüllt, etwa *Hospitation* (auf der Ebene „Praxis des Kollegiums"), *evidence-based policy* (auf der Ebene „Wissen der Politik") oder *Vertrauen* (auf der Ebene „Einstellungen der Eltern").
Eine Wirkung auf diesen Ebenen bedeutet, dass die Fortbildung einen Unterschied im Bereich dieser Schlagworte bewirkt[6]: etwa *vermehrte Hospitation, verstärkte evidence-based policy* oder *verbessertes Vertrauen.*

	Innerschulische Ebenen					Außerschulische Ebenen			
	Lehrkräfte	Schülerinnen und Schüler	Kollegium	Direktion	Eltern	Schulen	Medien	Politik	Wissenschaft
Wissen	Kompetenz	Leistung	Learning Community	Führungskompetenz	Erziehungskompetenz	Lernen am Modell	Öffentlichkeitsarbeit	Evidence-based policy	Grundlagenwissen
Einstellungen	Beliefs	Eigenverantwortung	Wertschätzung	Rollendefinition	Vertrauen	Bereitschaft zur Schulpartnerschaft	Image der Lehrkräfte	Bewusstsein für Bildungsthemen	Paradigmenwechsel
Praxis	Berufspraxis	Selbstständigkeit	Hospitation	Gewährung von Autonomie	Engagement	Schulkooperation	Berichterstattung	Strukturmaßnahmen	Forschungs-Bildungs-Kooperation

Abb. 1: Raster möglicher Wirkungsebenen (Zehetmeier 2008, S. 197)

3 Nachhaltigkeit

Im Rahmen einer Wirkungsanalyse sind zwei Arten von Wirkungen von besonderem Interesse: *unmittelbare* Wirkungen, welche während oder am Ende der Fortbildungsmaßnahme auftreten, und *langfristige* Wirkungen, welche (eine zu

[6] Vergleiche WILLKE (1999): Intervention bedeutet das Bewirken eines bedeutsamen Unterschiedes.

definierende Zeit) nach Abschluss der Fortbildung auftreten. Dabei können Wirkungen ausschließlich unmittelbar, ausschließlich langfristig, oder beides zugleich sein. In diesem Sinne lassen sich jene Wirkungen, welche sowohl unmittelbar als auch langfristig sind, als *nachhaltig* definieren.

Der Begriff *Nachhaltigkeit* findet in verschiedenen Disziplinen und Kontexten Verwendung, wird dort jeweils unterschiedlich eingesetzt und erfährt dadurch sowohl eine inflationäre Verwendungshäufigkeit als auch einen unklaren Bedeutungsgehalt: Aus ökologischer Perspektive wird damit Versöhnung mit der Natur, Ressourcenschonung, Artenschutz oder Energieverbrauch assoziiert; Personen aus dem Bereich der Wirtschaft verbinden damit Wachstum, umweltschonende Produktion, volkswirtschaftliche Gesamtrechnungen, Technikfolgenabschätzungen und Kostenwahrheiten, und aus sozialer Sicht geht es dabei um bessere Verteilungsgerechtigkeit, Abkehr von Konsumzwang sowie Arbeits- und Einkommenssicherung (Glotz, 2001). Kurz und drastisch formuliert von Lucke: „Nachhaltigkeit ist längst zum Plastikwort verkommen – unendlich dehnbar und unendlich nichts sagend“ (2004, S. 15). Umso wichtiger ist es daher, den Begriff im jeweiligen Kontext klar zu definieren. Dabei ist es hilfreich, die historische Entwicklung des Begriffes zu kennen. Im Folgenden werden verschiedene Auffassungen und Definitionen vorgestellt, welche im Laufe der Zeit versuchten, einen Begriff im Bereich Schule und Bildung zu fassen, welcher in seinem Kern die Dauerhaftigkeit, Kontinuität und Verlässlichkeit langfristiger Wirkungen von Ursachen verschiedenster Art umfasst.

Ohne den Begriff Nachhaltigkeit explizit zu verwenden, hatte bereits Johann Amos Comenius 1657 in seinem Werk *„Didactica Magna“* ein Kapitel dem Thema „Grundsätze zum dauerhaften Lehren und Lernen“ gewidmet. Darin sieht er die Ursachen von nicht dauerhaften Lernergebnissen vor allem auf Seiten der Schulen, welche sich mit Nebensächlichem und Wertlosem abgeben und das Dauerhafte vernachlässigen würden (Flitner 1970).

In jüngerer Zeit wurde zunächst der Begriff *Institutionalisierung* verwendet, um zeitlich stabile Veränderungen zu beschreiben. Institutionalisierung stellte in den 1970er und zu Beginn der 1980er Jahre die dritte von drei Phasen von Veränderungsprozessen in Schulen dar: (1) Mobilisierung, (2) Implementierung und (3) Institutionalisierung (Anderson & Stiegelbauer, 1994, S. 280). ANDERSON UND STIEGELBAUER (1994) definieren Institutionalisierung als: *“a phase after initial implementation when an innovation either got ‘built in’ to ongoing use and organizational structures or was discontinued due to such factors as the loss of funding, staff turnover, competing practices, and low administrator or teacher commitment"* (S. 280).

Die in den letzten Jahren zunehmende Verwendung des Begriffes *Nachhaltigkeit* bedingt zahlreiche, teils konkurrierende Auffassungen und Definitionen dieses Begriffes: Das deutsche Bundesinstitut für Berufsbildung (BIBB, 2002) analysiert die Nachhaltigkeit von Projekten, indem untersucht wird, ob die mit den jeweiligen Projekten erreichten Innovationen ohne fremde Hilfe dauerhaft weitergeführt werden. Ähnlich definiert FISCHER (2006) Nachhaltigkeit als Folgewirksamkeit in der Zukunft, als dauerhaften und anhaltenden Erfolg von Maßnahmen und Vorhaben. Dabei unterscheidet er zeitliche und systemische Komponenten von Nachhaltigkeit: Während sich die zeitlichen Komponenten im Rahmen der Schule auf die Dauerhaftigkeit von Lehren und Lernen beziehen, stehen bei den systemischen Komponenten Partizipation und Kooperation aller beteiligten Personen (etwa Eltern, Lehrkräfte, Schülerinnen und Schüler) im Mittelpunkt. Ebenso betonen SEUFERT und EULER (2003) eine differenzierte Sichtweise von Nachhaltigkeit und unterscheiden dabei Langfristigkeit (zeitliche Ebene) und Nachhaltigkeit auf Ebene der beteiligten Institutionen und Projekte (systemische Ebene). Insbesondere wird dabei die Funktion von Nachhaltigkeit als ein Gradmesser des Erfolges der Implementierung von Innovationen betont. FULLAN (2006) definiert *„sustainability"* im Rahmen seiner Erörterungen zum Thema *„educational change"* als *"the capacity of a system to engage in the complexities of continuous improvement consistent with deep values of human purpose"* (Fullan 2006, S. 114).

4 Förderliche Faktoren

Im Folgenden wird eine Auswahl von Faktoren vorgestellt, welche für die Nachhaltigkeit der Wirkungen von Lehrerfortbildung förderlich sind (vgl. Zehetmeier 2010):

Passung bedeutet, dass die Fortbildungsmaßnahme die Bedürfnisse der Lehrkräfte trifft und diesbezüglich Auswahlmöglichkeiten bereitstellt (Peter 1996), die lokalen Rahmenbedingungen berücksichtigt (Anderson & Stiegelbauer 1994), die Arbeitskontexte und Lehrpläne der Lehrkräfte beachtet (Mundry 2005) sowie mit anderen Lerngelegenheiten der Lehrkräfte abgestimmt ist (Garet, Porter, Desimone, Birman, & Yoon 2001).

Ownership weist darauf hin, die Lehrkräfte bei Planung und Durchführung der Fortbildungsmaßnahme mit einzubeziehen (Peter, 1996), sie in ihrer Rolle als

Multiplikatorinnen und Multiplikatoren zu unterstützen (Loucks-Horsley, Stiles & Hewson 1996) und die *„innovation champions"* zu fördern (Owston, 2007). Ebenso stellt HAYES (1995) fest, dass die Beteiligung von Lehrkräften an innovativen Prozessen deren Bereitschaft fördert, diese Innovation auch langfristig umzusetzen. HARVEY und GREEN (2000) benutzen dafür den Begriff *„empowerment"*, welcher auf die Möglichkeit hinweist, dass die teilnehmenden Lehrkräfte ihre Entwicklung selbst beeinflussen können.

Vernetzung bedeutet, dass die Fortbildungsmaßnahme sowohl die Kooperation der beteiligten Lehrkräfte einer Schule unterstützt, als auch den Austausch und die Zusammenarbeit mit Lehrkräften anderer Schulen fördert (Ingvarson et al. 2005, Lerman & Zehetmeier 2008, Maldonado 2002, McLaughlin & Mitra 2001, Mundry 2005, Peter 1996). Darüber hinaus ist die Beteiligung von Fachgruppen statt Einzelpersonen einer Schule besonders förderlich (Anderson & Stiegelbauer 1994, Garet et al. 2001, Peter 1996). Damit wird eine Gruppenbildung gefördert, welche als *learning community* (Loucks-Horsley et al. 1996, Maldonado 2002) oder *community of practice* (McLaughlin & Mitra 2001) oder *professional community* (Ingvarson et al. 2005) bezeichnet wird.

Reflexion umfasst Diskussionen und Reflexionen unter den teilnehmenden Lehrkräften (Farmer, Gerretson, & Lassak 2003, Maldonado 2002, Peter 1996) sowie die Auswertung von Artefakten wie etwa Unterrichtsvideos oder Arbeiten der Schülerinnen und Schüler (Ingvarson et al. 2005). Der Begriff *„inquiry as stance"* wird bereits 1999 von COCHRAN-SMITH und LYTLE verwendet und be-schreibt die reflexive Haltung von Lehrkräften gegenüber dem Verhältnis von Wissen und Praxis. Auch FARMER ET AL. (2003) bezeichnen die Haltung von Lehrkräften, welche den eigenen Unterricht als Quelle für Reflexion und Ler-nen sehen, als *„inquiry stance"* (S. 343).

Weitere förderliche und hemmende Faktoren finden sich etwa in ZEHETMEIER (2008, 2010).

5 Zusammenfassung

Einen theoretischen Rahmen für den hier vorgestellten Themenkomplex bietet das *IPROD-model* (*Impact of Professional Development model;* Zehetmeier, 2008). Darin werden verschiedene Wirkungsebenen von Lehrerfortbildung unterschieden. Das *IPROD-model* beinhaltet darüber hinaus eine Kategorisierung der charakteristischen Elemente von Fortbildungsmaßnahmen und jener Faktoren, welche das Auftreten von Wirkungen fördern oder hemmen.

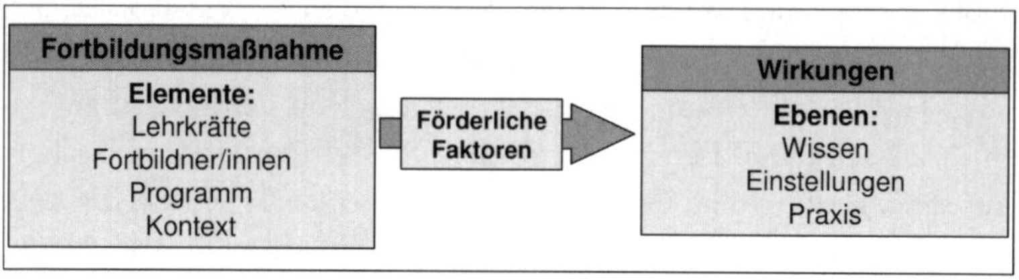

Abb. 2: (Vereinfachtes) IPROD-model

6 Ausblick

Breit angelegte Wirkungsanalysen, insbesondere (internationale) Vergleiche verschiedener Methoden und Inhalte von Fortbildungsmaßnahmen, scheinen geeignet, um folgende Fragen zu bearbeiten:

- Gibt es Muster von Wirkungen, welche bei vielen oder allen Lehrkräften (nicht) nachhaltig auftreten?
- Gibt es hierarchische Strukturen innerhalb der Elemente der Fortbildung oder der Wirkungsebenen?
- Gibt es Faktoren, welche bestimmte Wirkungsebenen besonders fördern oder hemmen?
- Gibt es quantifizierbare Unterschiede zwischen den einzelnen förderlichen oder hemmenden Faktoren?
- Gibt es allgemeingültige förderliche oder hemmende Faktoren?

Weitergehende, breitere und gleichzeitig vertiefte Untersuchungen dieser und ähnlicher Fragen zum Thema Nachhaltigkeit von Lehrerfortbildung erscheinen sowohl aus wissenschaftlicher als auch aus praktischer Perspektive notwendig und viel versprechend.

Literaturangaben

ANDERSON, S., & STIEGELBAUER, S. (1994): Institutionalization and renewal in a restructured secondary school. School Organization, 14(3), 279-293.

BUNDESINSTITUT FÜR BERUFSBILDUNG (BIBB) (2002): Weiterentwicklung von Instrumenten für Berufsbildungsberatung im Ausland auf der Grundlage einer Nachhaltigkeitsanalyse von TRANSFORM-Projekten. In BIBB (Hg.), Arbeitsprogramm 2002 (S. 76-78). Bonn: BIBB.

COCHRAN-SMITH, M., & LYTLE, S. (1999): Relationships of knowledge and practice: Teacher learning in communities. Review of Research in Education, 24, 249-305.

DIREKTION FÜR ENTWICKLUNGSHILFE UND ZUSAMMENARBEIT/DEZA (2002): Glossar deutsch. Bern: DEZA.

FARMER, J., GERRETSON, H., & LASSAK, M. (2003): What teachers take from professional development: cases and implications. In Journal of Mathematics Teacher Education, 6, 331-360.

FISCHER, A. (2006): Offenbar schöpfen wir Wasser mit einem Siebe. PAradigma, 1, 6-10.

FLITNER, W. (1970): Johann Amos Comenius. Große Didaktik. Düsseldorf, München: Helmut Küpper.

FULLAN, M. (2006): The future of educational change: system thinkers in action. Journal of Educational Change, 7, 113-122.

GARET, M./PORTER, A./ DESIMONE, L./ BIRMAN, B. & YOON, K. (2001): What makes professional development effective? Results from a national sample of teachers. American Educational Research Journal, 38(4), 915-945.

GLOTZ, P. (2001): Von Analog nach Digital. Unsere Gesellschaft auf dem Weg zur digitalen Kultur. Stuttgart, Wien: Huber.

HARGREAVES, A. (2002): Sustainability of educational change: the role of social geographies. Journal of Educational Change, 3, 189-214.

HARVEY, L., & GREEN, D. (2000): Qualität definieren. Zeitschrift für Pädagogik, 41. Beiheft, 17-37.

HAYES, D. (1995): In-service teacher development: some basic principles. ELT Journal, 49(3), 252-261.

INGVARSON, L./MEIERS, M. & BEAVIS, A. (2005): Factors affecting the impact of professional development programs on teachers' knowledge, practice, student outcomes & efficacy. Education Policy Analysis Archives, 13(10), 1-28.

LERMAN, S. & ZEHETMEIER, S. (2008): Face-to-face communites and networks of practising mathematics teachers. In: K. Krainer (Hg.), International handbook of mathematics teacher education: Vol. 3. Participants in mathematics teacher education: individuals, teams, communities, and networks (S. 133-154). Rotterdam: Sense Publishers.

LIPOWSKY, F. (2004): Was macht Fortbildungen für Lehrkräfte erfolgreich? Die deutsche Schule, 96, 462-479.

LIPOWSKY, F. (2010): Lernen im Beruf. Empirische Befunde zur Wirksamkeit von Lehrerfortbildung. In: F. H. Müller, A. Eichenberger, M. Lüders, & J. Mayr (Hg.), Lehrerinnen und Lehrer lernen. Konzepte und Befunde zur Lehrerfort-bildung (S. 51-72). Münster: Waxmann.

LOUCKS-HORSLEY, S./ STILES, K. & HEWSON, P. (1996): Principles of effective professional development for mathematics and science education: A synthesis of standards. NISE Brief, 1(1), 1-6.

MALDONADO, L. (2002): Effective professional development. Findings from research. Abgerufen am 8.3.2010 von http://apcentral.collegeboard.com.

MCLAUGHLIN, M. & MITRA, D. (2001): Theory-based change and change-based theory: going deeper, going broader. Journal of Educational Change, 2, 301-323.

MEIERS, M. (2007): Teacher professional learning, teaching practice, and student learning outcomes: important issues. In: T. Townsend & R. Bates (Hg.), Handbook of Teacher Education (S. 409-414). Dordrecht: Springer.

MUNDRY, S. (2005): What experience has taught us about professional development. National Network of Eisenhower Regional Consortia and Clearinghouse.

OWSTON, R. (2007): Contextual factors that sustain innovative pedagogical practice using technology: an international study. Journal of Educational Change, 8(1), 61-77.

PETER, A. (1996): Aktion und Reflexion – Lehrer/innenfortbildung aus international vergleichender Perspektive. Weinheim: Deutscher Studienverlag.

ROGERS, E. (2003): Diffusion of innovations. New York: Free Press.

SEUFERT, S. & EULER, D. (2003): Nachhaltigkeit von eLearning-Innovationen. Ergebnisse einer Delphi-Studie. St. Gallen: Swiss Centre for Innovations in Learning.

VON LUCKE, A. (2004): Vorwärts in die Vergangenheit! Zur Zukunft der Grünen. Die Kommune – Forum für Politik Ökonomie Kultur, 1(2004), 14-15.

ZEHETMEIER, S. (2008): Zur Nachhaltigkeit von Lehrer/innenfortbildung. Dissertation. Klagenfurt: University of Klagenfurt.

ZEHETMEIER, S. (2010): Aktionsforschung in der Lehrerfortbildung: Was bleibt? In F. H. Müller, A. Eichenberger, M. Lüders, & J. Mayr (Hrsg.), Lehrerinnen und Lehrer lernen. Konzepte und Befunde zur Lehrerfortbildung (S. 197-212). Münster: Waxmann.

Kontakt:
Ass.Prof. Dr. Stefan ZEHETMEIER: stefan.zehetmeier@uni-klu.ac.at

DER REFLEKTIERTE PRAKTIKER – EIN NEUES LEITBILD IN DER LEHRERAUSBILDUNG ?

Herbert Zoglowek, Høgskolen in Finnmark, Alta, Norwegen

Der „reflektierte Praktiker" erscheint als ein neues Leitbild in der Lehrerausbildung. Was ist darunter zu verstehen, was ist daran neu, und welche möglichen Implikationen sind damit verbunden? Nach der Diskussion dieser grundsätzlichen Fragen wird versucht, das Konzept des „professionellen Selbst" (Bauer, u.a. 1999, 2005) als Kern des reflektierten Praktikers zu verorten. Hierzu werden zunächst die Komponenten und Kriterien pädagogischer Professionalität diskutiert und das Konzept des professionellen Selbst eingehend dargestellt. Wesentliches Element ist die Herausarbeitung und Weiterentwicklung eines professionellen Bewusstseins, welches als Voraussetzung für eine reflektierte Praxis angesehen werden kann. Bei dieser Fragestellung lässt sich schließlich auch die Theorie-Praxis-Problematik in der Lehrerausbildung neu ausleuchten.

Schlüsselbegriffe: der reflektierte Praktiker, professionelles Selbst, Kriterien pädagogischer Professionalität, professionelles Bewusstsein

1 Einleitung

Die berufliche Arbeit des Lehrers sei komplexer als die eines Arztes, hat der amerikanische Professionsforscher LEE SHULMAN (1986) einmal behauptet. Ich möchte dem zustimmen, ist sie doch in weiten Teilen geprägt durch *Unerreichbares* und *Unplanbares.*

Unerreichbar müssen die Zielvorhaben des Lehrers erscheinen, wenn sie so ambivalent und widersprüchlich, ja paradox sind wie zur Entwicklung von selbstständiger und unabhängig denkender Persönlichkeit beizutragen, aber auch zu Gemeinschaft und Zusammenarbeit; egozentrisches Denken aufzubrechen, aber auch ein Selbstbewusstsein für eigene Meinungen, Querdenken und gegen den *mainstream* aufzubauen; eine solide Wissens- und Fertigkeitsbasis zu vermitteln, aber auch zu Neugier, Kreativität, neues Wissen und neuen Fertigkeiten zu motivieren, um nur einige zu nennen (vgl. auch Meyer 2005; Zoglowek 2008). Fachlichen Ansprüchen und gesellschaftlichen Anforderungen soll in gleichem Maße entsprochen werden wie den individuellen Anforderungen der Schüler und nicht zuletzt auch den eigenen Ansprüchen.

Zu dieser Quadratur des Zielkreises kommt die in vielen Bereichen Unplanbarkeit komplexer Unterrichts- und Lernsituationen. Wenn auch vieles vorausschaubar und somit planbar ist, ebenso viele Momente, die den Unterricht bestimmen, sind nicht vorhersehbar und quasi unplanbar. Zudem sind die sozialen und kommunikativen Strukturen, auf denen Unterricht aufbaut, äußerst komplex, anfällig und heterogen, und können durch äußere Einflüsse immer wieder gestört oder verändert werden. Das Unterrichten entwickelt häufig eine Eigendynamik, die das ganze Geschehen unvorhersehbar und die Weiterentwicklung unvoraussagbar macht.
Aber trotzdem gibt es immer wieder und genügend Beispiele für guten und gelingenden Unterricht. Wie ist das möglich? Hier möchte ich antworten: durch die speziell dem Lehrer zuzuschreibenden Kompetenzen der Handlungskompetenz und besonders der Reflexionskompetenz. Diese Erkenntnis ist nicht neu, und auch das in jüngster Zeit aufgekommene Leitbild des „reflektierten Praktikers" ist nicht neu, doch macht es auf eine wichtige, speziell für die Lehrerausbildung relevante Pointierung aufmerksam: den reflektierende Umgang mit theoretischem Wissen und praktischem Handeln.

2 Der reflektierende und reflektierte Praktiker

Hat nicht J.F. HERBART bereits 1802 in seinen „Ersten pädagogischen Vorlesungen" den reflektierenden Praktiker im Blick gehabt, wenn er zwischen Theorie und Praxis ein „Mittelglied" schiebt, welches er „pädagogischer Takt" nannte? „Nun schiebt sich aber bei jedem noch so guten Theoretiker, wenn er seine Theorie ausübt, ... zwischen die Theorie und die Praxis ganz unwillkürlich ein Mittelglied ein, ein gewisser Takt nämlich, eine schnelle Beurteilung und Entscheidung, die nicht wie der Schlendrian ewig gleichförmig verfährt, aber auch nicht, wie eine vollkommen durchgeführte Theorie wenigstens sollte, sich rühmen darf, ... die wahre Forderung des individuellen Falles ganz und gerade zu treffen" (Herbart 1806/1965, Bd.2, 126). Dieser *pädagogische Takt* wird heute u.a. als *Berufswissen* (Meyer 2005) oder *subjektive Theorie* (Zoglowek 1995) beschrieben. Das „im berufspraktischen Handeln gewachsene, aus vielen unterschiedlichen Quellen schöpfende Handlungs- und Reflexionswissen zur Gestaltung und reflektierenden Verarbeitung von Lehr-Lern-Situationen" (Meyer 2005, S. 211).
Zum Aufbau dieses Berufswissens benötigt der (zukünftige) Lehrer Reflexionsfähigkeit, um sich erstens theoretisches Wissen kritisch-reflexiv anzueignen

und zweitens, dieses in seine eigene subjektive Theorie von Unterrichten und Lernen zu transformieren und zu integrieren. Zum anderen braucht der Lehrer ein Handlungsrepertoire, um dieses Berufswissen praktisch-reflexiv umsetzen zu können. Diese beiden Kompetenzen bilden das Grundgerüst des professionellen Lehrers als eines „reflektierenden Praktikers“ (Schön 1991).
Die Betonung der Reflexionskompetenz setzt nun diese für die Lehrerausbildung in ein neues Licht. Vielfalt und Komplexität der Aufgaben des Lehrerberufs erlauben keine Rezept- oder Standardlösungen, auch wenn Leitfäden und Unterrichtshilfen nützlich und hilfreich sind – besonders in der Ausbildung von zukünftigen Lehrern. Diese dürfen jedoch nicht unreflektiert übernommen und auf jedwelche Situation angewendet werden. Unterrichten erfordert ein reflektiertes Vorgehen, d.h., die Inhalte oder Aktivitäten und das pädagogisch-didaktische Handlungsrepertoire müssen auf die stets wechselnden Situationen und die unterschiedlichen Schüler hin überdacht, variiert, angepasst werden. Die Forderung für die Lehrerausbildung – wie auch für die Lehrerfort- und -weiterbildung – muss daher sein, die Reflexion über das eigene Wissen und die eigenen beruflichen Erfahrungen, somit die Reflexionskompetenz, in den Mittelpunkt zu stellen, um bewusster an einer *professionellen Selbst-Entwicklung* arbeiten zu können.

3 Das professionelle Selbst

Diese reflektierende Art von Berufsaneignung, Berufsausübung und Berufsauffassung wird als *professionell* bezeichnet. Die eigene Rolle, das eigene Handeln, und dessen Bedeutung für die jeweilige Lehr-Lern-Situation zu hinterfragen, sich ‚Selbst zum Thema zu machen’ ist ein äußerst wichtiger Aspekt des Berufsverständnisses, und macht einen wichtigen Teil des professionellen Lehrerselbst aus. Zum Schlüsselbegriff für pädagogisch professionelles, d.h. in sich stimmiges und authentisches Handeln wird damit das „professionelle Selbst“.

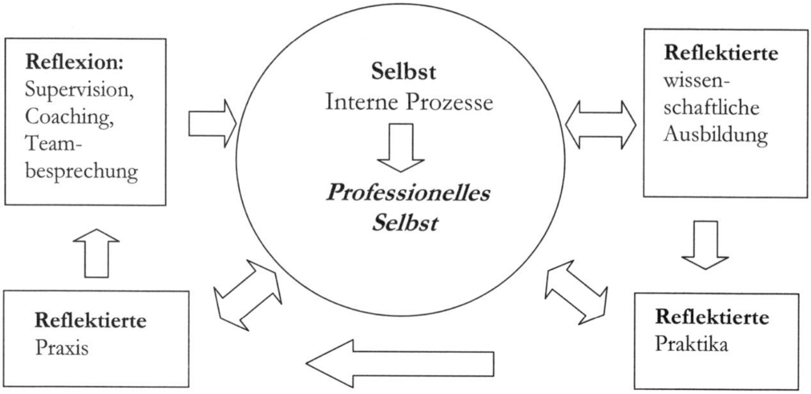

Abb.1: Das professionelle Selbst (Weiterentwicklung nach Bauer 2005, S. 82)

Das professionelle Selbst lässt sich beschreiben als das organisierende Zentrum, von dem aus Ziele, Handlungen, Fähigkeiten und Erfahrungen miteinander zu einem Ganzen verknüpft, d.h. gedacht und in Handlungen umgesetzt werden. Es basiert auf dem Vertrauen in die eigenen Möglichkeiten und garantiert eine gewisse Beständigkeit. Das professionelle Selbst ist dynamisch, d.h. es ist im Kern konsistent, verändert sich aber ständig durch Erfahrung. BAUER (2005, S. 81) beschreibt das pädagogische professionelle Handeln wie folgt: „Pädagogisch professionell handelt eine Person, die gezielt ein berufliches Selbst aufbaut, das sich an berufstypischen Werten orientiert. Sie ist sich eines umfassenden pädagogischen Handlungsrepertoires zur Bewältigung von Arbeitsaufgaben sicher, kann sich mit sich selbst (innerlich) und anderen Angehörigen der Berufsgruppe Pädagogen in einer nichtalltäglichen Berufssprache verständigen, ihre Handlungen aus einem empirisch-wissenschaftlichen Habitus heraus unter Bezug auf eine Berufswissenschaft begründen und übernimmt persönlich die Verantwortung für Handlungsfolgen in ihrem Einflussbereich“. In dieser Definition werden einige professionelle Kriterien und Komponenten genannt, die es gezielt zu entwickeln gilt, so dass das subjektive professionelle Selbst zum Ausdruck und zur Wirkung kommen kann.

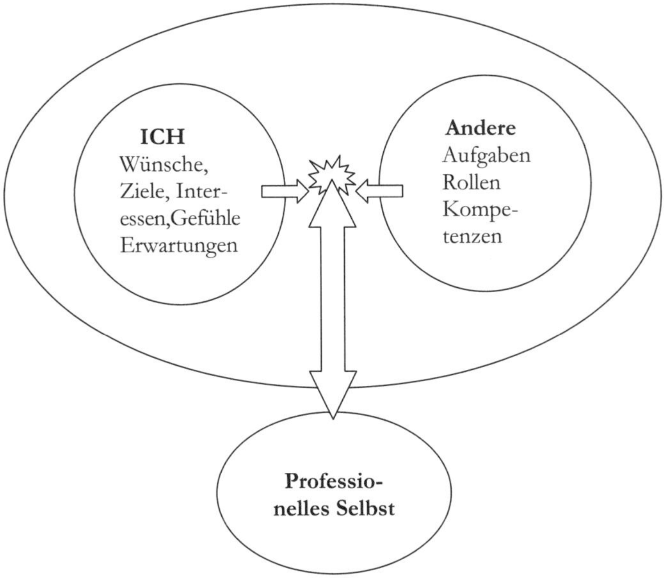

Abb.2: Entstehung des professionellen Selbst
(Weiterentwicklung nach Bauer 2000, S. 65)

Als Teil des gesamten Selbst beginnt die Entwicklung des beruflichen Selbst nicht erst mit Eintritt ins Berufsleben, sondern bereits im Studium, manchmal sogar schon früher, in der eigenen Schulzeit. Von daher ist es wichtig, die Entwicklung des professionellen Selbst auch stärker in den Mittelpunkt der Lehrerausbildung zu stellen. Abb. 2 zeigt die entscheidende Schnittstelle zur Entwicklung des subjektiven professionellen Selbst. In einem inneren reflexiven Prozess muss das Subjekt (der Lehrer) eine Balance zwischen eigenen Wünschen, Zielen und Ansprüchen und den verinnerlichten Erwartungen anderer finden (vgl. Bauer 2000). Dies lässt sich nur in Verbindung mit Erfahrungssituationen, d.h. Schulpraktika, eigene Praxis, und kollegialen Beratungs-/Supervisionssituationen angehen, indem dort Stärken und Schwächen erfahren, und somit im professionellen Selbstbild verortet werden. Die das professionellen Selbst ausmachenden Elemente sind das *wissenschaftliche Wissen*, d.h. das Fachstudium und das erziehungswissenschaftliche Studium, das eigene *Erfahrungswissen*, das in der Praxis und im Schulalltag gewonnen wird, und das *reflexive Wissen*. Die Entwicklung und Ausweitung des reflexiven Wissens dient dabei der subjektiven Verknüpfung des wissenschaftlichen und des Erfahrungswissens.

Um dies zu gewährleisten, müssen die auf die Aufgaben des Lehrers bezogenen Schlüsselkategorien reflexiv entwickelt und angeeignet werden. Diese Schlüsselkategorien sind nach BAUER (1999, 26) soziale Strukturenbildung, Interaktion, Kommunikation/Information, Gestaltung und Hintergrundarbeit. In der Lehrerausbildung müssen diese Schlüsselkategorien theoretisch-praktisch vermittelt und immer wieder in Praxissituationen erfahren werden. Nur so können sie subjektiv reflexiv zur individuellen subjektiven Theorie, dem individuellen professionellen Selbst, verinnerlicht werden.
Damit ist der reflektierte Praktiker, gemäß dem professionellen Anspruch, in der Lage, seine berufliche Arbeit selbstständig und auf wissenschaftlicher Grundlage, in Kooperation mit anderen, unter Beachtung der widersprüchlichen Ziele, und seiner Berufsethik folgend, aus zuführen und zu begründen (vgl. auch Meyer 2005, 232).

Literaturangaben

BASTIAN, J./HELSPER, W./REH, S./SCHELLE, C. (Hg.): Professionalisierung im Lehrerberuf. Opladen, 2000.

BAUER, K.O./KOPKA, A./BRINDT, S.: Pädagogische Professionalität und Lehrerarbeit. Weinheim/München, 1999.

BAUER, K.O.: Konzepte pädagogischer Professionalität und ihre Bedeutung für die Lehrerarbeit. In: Bastian, J., u.a. Professionalisierung im Lehrerberuf. Opladen, 2000.

BAUER, K.-O.: Pädagogische Basiskompetenzen. Weinheim und München, 2005.

HERBART, J.F.: Allgemeine Pädagogik, aus dem Zweck der Erziehung abgeleitet, 1806. In: Pädagogische Schriften, Bd.2. Hrsg. von W. Asmus. Düsseldorf/ München, 1965.

MEYER, H.: Türklinkendidaktik. Berlin, 2005.

SCHÖN, D.: The Reflective Practitioner. How professionals think in action. Vermont, 1991.

SHULMAN, L.S.: Those Who Understand: Knowledge Growth in Teaching. In: Educational Researcher 15 (1986), 4-14; dt. Übersetzung in Terhart, E. (1991).

TERHART, E.: Unterrichten als Beruf. Köln/Wien, 1991.

ZOGLOWEK, H.: Zum beruflichen Selbstkonzept des Sportlehrers. Frankfurt a.M., 1995.

ZOGLOWEK, H.: Lehrer und Sportunterricht. In: Lange, H./Sinning, S. (Hg.): Handbuch Sportdidaktik. Balingen, 2008.

Kontakt:
Herbert ZOGLOWEK, Dr.phil., Dipl. Päd.: herbert@hifm.no

DIAGNOSTISCHE KOMPETENZ VON LEHRER/-INNE/-N: ERFASSUNG UND ENTWICKLUNG IM RAHMEN EINER VIDEOBASIERTEN LERNUMGEBUNG

Tomáš Janík, Petr Knecht, Päd. Fakultät der Masaryk Universität, Brno,
Marcela Janíková, Eva Valkounová, Fakultät für Sportwissenschaften,
Masaryk Universität, Tschechische Republik

Im Beitrag werden die Begriffe berufliche Kompetenz und diagnostische Kompetenz von Lehrer/-inne/-n diskutiert. Es wird nachgedacht, wie die diagnostische Kompetenz von Lehrer/-inne/-n über die kasuistische Arbeit mit Videoaufzeichnungen des Unterrichts entwickelt werden kann. In diesem Zusammenhang werden ausgewählte theoretische Ausgangspunkte für die Entwicklung der videobasierten Lernumgebung CPV Videoweb präsentiert.

Schlüsselbegriffe: Diagnostische Kompetenz, Kasuistische Arbeit mit Videoaufzeichnungen, vidoebasierte Lernumgebung

1 Zur Einleitung

Im Zentrum für pädagogische Forschung an der Pädagogischen Fakultät der Masaryk-Universität in Brno (in der Folge „CPV") läuft seit 2004 das Forschungsprojekt *„CPV Videostudien"*. Ziel ist es, die inhaltsbezogenen Lehr- und Lernprozesse in verschiedenen Unterrichtsfächern auf der Sekundarstufe I zu dokumentieren, zu beschreiben und zu analysieren.

Im Rahmen der *CPV Videostudien* wird u.a. auch der Frage nachgegangen, wie Videoaufzeichnungen von Unterrichtssequenzen in der Lehrer/-innenbildung benutzt werden könnten (vgl. Janíková, Janík & Mužík 2008). Eine videobasierte Lernumgebung *CPV Vidoeweb* wird entwickelt (Janík et al. 2009). Im Beitrag wird gezeigt, wie die *diagnostische Kompetenz* von Lehrer/-inne/-n über die kasuistische Arbeit mit Videoaufzeichnungen des Unterrichts erfasst und entwickelt werden kann.

2 Berufliche Kompetenz von Lehrer/-inne/-n

Es ist die Aufgabe der Lehrer/-innenbildung, die professionelle, bzw. berufliche Kompetenz von Lehrer/-inne/-n zu entwickeln. Unter dem Begriff *berufliche Kompetenz* wird in Anlehnung an FREY (2004, S. 904) „ein Bündel von körperlichen und geistigen Fähigkeiten bezeichnet, das jemand benötigt, um anstehende berufliche Aufgaben oder Probleme zielorientiert und verantwortungsvoll zu lösen, die Lösungen zu bewerten und das eigene Repertoire an Handlungsmustern weiterzuentwickeln." FREY (2006) legt ein hierarchisches Strukturmodell von Handlungskompetenz vor, das für die Analyse der beruflichen Kompetenz von Lehrer/-inne/-n brauchbar ist. Im Modell werden vier Ebenen unterschieden: einzelne Fertigkeiten (Ebene I), gebündelte Fertigkeiten (Ebene II), Fähigkeiten (Ebene III), Gesamtkompetenz (Ebene IV). In unserem Ansatz gehen wir von der Annahme aus, dass eine wichtige Komponente der gesamten beruflichen Kompetenz von Lehrer/-inne/-n (Ebene IV) die *diagnostische Kompetenz* (Ebene III) ist. Diese umfasst mehrere gebündelte Fertigkeiten (Ebene II), die sich in die einzelnen Fertigkeiten zerlegen lassen (Ebene I).

Gesamtkompetenz (Ebene IV).

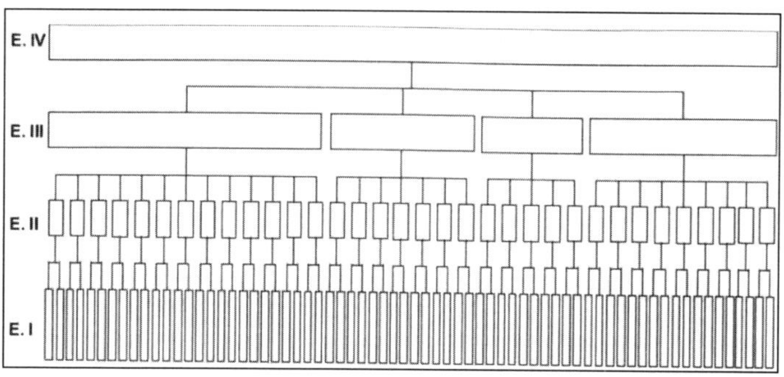

Abb. 1: Hierarchisches Strukturmodell von Handlungskompetenz (Frey 2006)

3 Diagnostische Kompetenz von Lehrer/-inne/-n

Ein wichtiger Kompetenzbereich betrifft die Diagnostik. Warum sollen Lehrer/-innen über diagnostische Kompetenz verfügen? Lehrer/-innen gehören zur Gruppe der *people processing professions* – sie verfügen über „ein besonders lizenziertes Interventions- und Eingriffsrecht in die Lebenspraxis von Individuen" und sie müssen „die Folgen ihrer Handlungen/Eingriffe abschätzen

und sie zu verantworten wissen" (Radtke 2000, S. 1). Weiters „... bedarf es [dazu] neben ethischer Selbstbindungen und institutionell gestützter Handlungssicherheit in erster Linie eines besonderen Beobachtungs-, Wahrnehmungs- und Beurteilungsvermögens, aber auch eines systematisierten Reflexionswissens, daß die eigenen Entscheidungen zu begründen und zu legitimieren, zu kontrollieren und gegebenenfalls zu korrigieren vermag" (Radtke 2000, S. 2).
Die von RADTKE erwähnten Anforderungen auf das Lehrerhandeln stehen nahe zum Begriff der *diagnostischen Kompetenz*.
Es werden zahlreiche Konzeptualisierungen der *diagnostischen Kompetenz* vorgelegt. In der Auffassung von HELMKE und HOSENFELD (2004) wird *diagnostische Kompetenz* als *Diagnosegenauigkeit* konzipiert, wobei hier die Übereinstimmung von Schülerleistungseinschätzungen durch die Lehrperson mit den Ergebnissen standardisierter Tests als Referenzpunkt gilt. Wie ABS (2007, S. 64) anführt, bleibt bei dieser Auffassung diagnostischer Kompetenz die didaktische Relevanz der diagnostischen Kompetenz unklar. „Eine Konzeptualisierung diagnostischer Kompetenz, die didaktische Relevanz beanspruchen will, muss die didaktische Einbettung der Beurteilungssituation einbeziehen" (Abs 2007, S. 64). Unter dieser Perspektive wird die Definition von EDELENBOS und KUBANEK-GERMAN (2004, S. 260) aufgeführt – die Autoren bestimmen *diagnostische Kompetenz* im Fremdsprachenunterricht als *„the ability to interpret students' foreign language growth, to skilfully deal with assessment material and to provide students with appropriate help in response to this diagnosis"*.
Nach dem Abwägen von oben angeführten Definitionen wird in unserem Ansatz unter dem Begriff *diagnostische Kompetenz* Folgendes verstanden: *„the ability to identify and describe relevant components of teaching and learning processes; to explain an observed situation by applying scientific theories; to predict possible effects of a given situation with regard to future teaching and learning processes"* (Seidel et al. 2009, S. 245).
Weiters gehen wir der Frage nach, wie die diagnostische Kompetenz von Lehrer/-inne/-n über die kasuistische Arbeit mit Videoaufzeichnungen des Unterrichts entwickelt werden kann. Es werden theoretische Grundlagen für kasuistisches Lernen in einer videobasierten Lernumgebung präsentiert.

4 CPV Videoweb – wie eine videobasierte Lernumgebung für Lehrer/-innen entwickelt wird

Im Rahmen der innovativen Konzepte und Methoden der Lehrer/-innenbildung setzen sich in letzter Zeit die videobasierten Lernumgebungen (z.B.

LessonLab Viewer™, MILE, LUV, IMST²) durch. Diese werden vor allem für die Erfassung und Entwicklung der *diagnostischen Kompetenz* der Lehrer/inne/-n eingesetzt. Im Zentrum für pädagogische Forschung an der Pädagogischen Fakultät der Masaryk-Universität in Brno wird vom Jahr 2008 an die videobasierte Lernumgebung für Lehrer/-innen – *CPV Videoweb* – entwickelt (mehr siehe Janík et al. 2009; Minaříková in diesem Band).
Den Ausgangspunkt für die Entwicklung des *CPV Videoweb* bilden Videoaufzeichnungen von 260 Unterrichtsstunden (Physik, Geografie, Englisch, Sportunterricht), die im Rahmen der *CPV Videostudie* aufgenommen wurden. Das *CPV Videoweb* ist modular aufgebaut und fokussiert auf thematische Bereiche (z.B. die Rolle der Muttersprache im Englischunterricht, die Rolle der Experimente im Physikunterricht). Aus den Unterrichtsvideos werden kurze Videoclips extrahiert. Zu jedem Videoclip werden Fragen und Aufgaben formuliert – so entstehen Videobeispiele. Sie werden in das *CPV Videoweb* eingebettet. Ähnlich wie in der Lernumgebung *LUV* (Seidel et al. 2009) betrachten die Lehrer/-innen im *CPV Videoweb* eine Reihe von kurzen Videoclips und an Hand von vorgegebenen Fragen und Aufgaben schätzen sie diese ein. Das *CPV Videoweb* wird als Instrument für die Erfassung und Entwicklung der diagnostischen Kompetenz der Lehrer/-innen verwendet. Die analytische Arbeit mit Videobeispielen ermöglicht den Lehrer/-inne/-n die unterrichtliche Praxis aus kritischer Distanz zu betrachten und auf der kognitiven Ebene zu reflektieren. Die Videobeispiele betreffen drei Komponenten der *diagnostischen Kompetenz: the ability (a) to identify and describe relevant components of teaching and learning processes; (b) to explain an observed situation by applying scientific theories; (c) to predict possible effects of a given situation with regard to future teaching and learning processes* (mehr siehe Seidel et al. 2009). Anhand von Videobeispielen sollen die einzelnen Fertigkeiten (Ebene I) und gebündelten Fertigkeiten (Ebene II), die die diagnostische Kompetenz (Ebene III) bilden, erfasst und entwickelt werden (vgl. Frey 2006).

5 Entwicklung und Erfassung der diagnostischen Kompetenz

Geht es um die Entwicklung der *diagnostischen Kompetenz* von Lehrer/-inne/-n, ist der Gedanke des kasuistischen Lernens an/durch Fälle/-n von Bedeutung. Sie steht nahe zu dem, was die Lehrer/-innen tagtäglich tun. Radtke (2000, S. 2) weist darauf hin, dass die Lehrer/-innen als Professionelle ihre Aufgaben in einer besonderen, doppelt verankerten Handlungslogik vornehmen: „Sie müssen (a) situativ (und intuitiv) in der Lage sein zu individuellem Fallverstehen und können dies (b) in hermeneutischer Haltung auf der Basis universellen Regelwissens, also wissenschaftlicher Theorien. Sie applizieren ihr theoretisches, situationsunabhängiges Wissen bei der Interpretation von Situationen, bei der stellvertretenden Deutung von Problemen ihrer Klienten und bei der Formulierung des Angebots von Therapie/Lösungsstrategien in einer ‚klinisch' zu nennenden Weise".

Damit eröffnet sich die Frage nach dem Potenzial des Lernens mit Videobeispielen. Im Kontext der kasuistischen Didaktik wird die Frage gestellt, wie die didaktischen Begriffe mit unterrichtlichen Ereignissen verknüpft werden können (vgl. Schierz 2000). Nach SCHIERZ (2000, S. 61) geht es um *konzeptionelle Begriffe,* d.h. um eine Sorte von Begriffen, die ihre Bedeutung erst durch Beispiele erhalten, was in der didaktischen Verständigung über unterrichtliche Erfahrung eine wesentliche Rolle spielt. „Sie umfasst Begriffe, die recht vage und unexakt – aber keineswegs unnütz sind. Sie sind nicht in der Absicht der Eindeutigkeit wie Begriffe der Mathematik methodisch erzeugt und kontrolliert. Ihre Funktionstüchtigkeit liegt gerade darin, jener Mannigfaltigkeit auch in der Begriffsbedeutung gerecht zu werden, in der wir einer Sache im Umgang immer schon begegnen. Umgangserfahrungen bringen wir alltagssprachlich auf Begriffe, die eine ungefähre Bedeutung haben, aber erst in der Verständigung durch Beispiele in dieser oder jener Hinsicht schärfer werden". Um zu erfassen, ob und wie die Entwicklung der diagnostischen Kompetenz der Lehrer/-inne/-n stattfindet, muss ein *Kompetenzmodell der diagnostischen Kompetenz* entwickelt werden. Die Arbeiten zur Modellierung von Kompetenzen sind in diesem Zusammenhang relevant (z.B. Hartig, Klieme et al. 2007; Abs 2007).

Bei der Entwicklung von Kompetenzmodellen geht es prinzipiell darum, die äußere („objektive") Aufgabenstruktur einerseits und die innere („subjektive") Fähigkeitsstruktur andererseits in Beziehung zu setzen (siehe Terhart 2007, S. 45). Bei der Erfassung der *diagnostischen Kompetenz* kommen die Videobeispiele wieder ins Spiel. Den untersuchten Personen werden die Videobeispiele vorgelegt mit der Aufforderung, diese zu kommentieren, zu analysieren und Handlungsalternativen zu generieren und dies zu begründen.

Die Videobeispiele, die den untersuchten Personen zum Bearbeiten vorgelegt werden, sind nach Schwierigkeitsgraden geordnet, damit verschiedene Stufen diagnostischer Kompetenz unterschieden werden können. Die Kompetenzstufen werden anhand von *Post-Hoc*-Definitionen konstruiert (s. Abs 2007).

Das Prinzip besteht in der Entwicklung eines empirischen Kompetenzkontinuums, das sich anhand der Lösungshäufigkeiten konstruieren lässt. Häufig gelöste Aufgaben werden als leicht kategorisiert und als Indikatoren für Kompetenzen auf einer unteren Stufe behandelt; selten gelöste Aufgaben werden als schwierig kategorisiert und höheren Kompetenzen zugeordnet (Abs 2000, S. 79f.).
Die Lösungen von Aufgaben und die schriftlichen Reflexionen der Lehrer/-innen werden anhand diverser Kategorien- oder Ratingsysteme analysiert, bzw. ausgewertet. Diese betreffen sowohl fachliche (z.B. physikalische, sportwissenschaftliche), als auch didaktische (z.B. physikdidaktische, sportdidaktische) Aspekte der *diagnostischen Kompetenz* der Lehrer/-innen. Es wird eine Interventionsstudie geplant, die die Effekte des Lernens in einer videobasierten Lernumgebung auf die diagnostische Kompetenz von Lehrer/-innen untersuchen soll.

Literaturangaben

ABS, H. J.: Überlegungen zur Modellierung diagnostischer Kompetenz bei Lehrerinnen und Lehrern. In: Lüders, M. & Wissinger, J. (Hg.): Forschung zur Lehrerbildung: Kompetenzentwicklung und Programmevaluation. Münster: Waxmann, 2007, S. 63-84.

EDELENBOS, P. & KUBANEK-GERMAN: A. Teacher Assessment. The concept of "diagnostic competence". In: Language Testing, 2004, 21 (3), S. 259-283.

FREY, A.: Die Kompetenzstruktur von Studierenden des Lehrerberufs. Eine internationale Studie. In: Zeitschrift für Pädagogik, 2004, 50, S. 903-925.

FREY, A.: Methoden und Instrumente zur Diagnose beruflicher Kompetenz von Lehrkräften – eine erste Standortbestimmung zu bereits publizierten Instrumenten. In: Allemann-Gionda, C. & Terhart, E. (Hg.) Kompetenzen und Kompetenzentwicklung im Lehrerberuf: Ausbildung und Beruf. 51. Beiheft der Zeitschrift für Pädagogik. Weinheim : Beltz, 2006, S. 30-64.

HARTIG, J. & KLIEME, E. (Hg.): Möglichkeiten und Voraussetzungen technologiebasierter Kompetenzdiagnostik. Berlin: BMBF, 2007.

HELMKE, A. & HOSENFELD, I.: Vergleichsarbeiten als Instrument zur Verbesserung der Diagnosekompetenz von Lehrkräften. In Arnold, R. & Griese, C. (Hg.) Schulleitung und Schulentwicklung. Voraussetzungen, Bedingungen, Erfahrungen. Baltmanssweiler: Schneider Verlag, 2004, S. 119-144.

JANÍK, T., JANÍKOVÁ, M., KNECHT, P., KUBIATKO, M., NAJVAR, P., NAJVAROVÁ, V. & ŠEBESTOVÁ, S.: Exploring Different Ways of Using Video in Teacher Education: Examples from CPV Video Web. In: Janík, T. & Seidel, T. et al. The Power of Video Studies in Investigating Teaching and Learning in Classroom. Münster: Waxmann Verlag, 2009, S. 207-224.

JANÍKOVÁ, M., JANÍK, T., MUŽÍK, V.: Nutzen von Videobeispielen in der LehrerInnenbildung. In Pädagogische Hochschule Wien (Hg.) Lehrer/-innenbildung in Europa. Konferenzband. Berlin: LIT, 2008, S. 188–193.

RADTKE, F.-O.: Professionalisierung der Lehrerbildung durch Autonomisierung, Entstaatlichung, Modularisierung. Sowi On-line Journal, 2000, S. 1-8.

SEIDEL, T., PRENZEL, M., SCHWINDT, K., STÜRMER, K., BLOMBERG, G. & KOBARG, M.: LUV and Observe: Two Projects Using Video to Diagnose Teachers' Competence. In: Janík, T. & Seidel, T. et al. The Power of Video Studies in Investigating Teaching and Learning in Classroom. Münster: Waxmann Verlag, 2009, S. 243-258.

SCHIERZ, M.: Narrative Didaktik als Beispieldidaktik im Medium von „Geschichten" der Sportlehrerausbildung und des Sportunterrichts. In: Voigt, H.-F. & Jednrusch, G. (Hg.) Sportlehrerausbildung wofür? Hamburg: Czwalina Verlag, 2000, S. 57-66.

TERHART, E.: Erfassung und Beurteilung der beruflichen Kompetenz von Lehrkräften. In: Lüders, M. & Wissinger, J. (Hg.) Forschung zur Lehrerbildung: Kompetenzentwicklung und Programmevaluation. Münster: Waxmann, 2007, S. 37-62.

Die Studie wird gefördert aus Mitteln des MŠMT ČR im Rahmen des Projektes LC 06046 Centrum základního výzkumu školního vzdělávání.
Für die sprachliche Unterstützung danken die Autoren Frau Renate Seebauer.

Kontakt:
Doc. PhDr. Tomáš JANÍK, Ph.D., M.Ed.: tjanik@ped.muni.cz
Mgr. Petr KNECHT, Ph.D.,: knecht@ped.muni.cz
PhDr. Marcela JANIKOVA, Ph.D.: janikova@fsps.muni.cz
Mgr. Eva VALKOUNOVÁ: valkev@seznam.cz

ERFASSUNG VON LEHRERVORSTELLUNGEN: PEDAGOGICAL CONTENT KNOWLEDGE UND SUBJEKTIVE THEORIEN

Patrícia Jelemenská, Martin Scheuch & Franz Radits
Austrian Educational Competence Centre of Biology (AECC-Bio), Universität Wien, Österreich

Die angloamerikanische Forschung beschäftigt sich seit 25 Jahren mit dem Lehrerwissen im Fokus des Pedagogical Content Knowledge (z.B. Shulmann 1986). In der deutschsprachigen Forschung entwickelte sich zeitgleich aus einer Kritik an vorherigen psychologischen Ansätzen der Zugang der Subjektiven Theorien (Groeben et al. 1988). Dieser spielt in der (Fach)Didaktik eine wichtige Rolle in der Lehrervorstellungsforschung (z.B. Fischler & Schröder 2003). Subjektive Theorien von Lehrern wie auch deren Pedagogical Content Knowledge wurden durch qualitative Inhaltsanalyse von Aktionsforschungsberichten herausgearbeitet (Jelemenská et al. 2009). Das Ziel des Beitrags ist eine Darstellung von methodologischen Ansätzen zur Erforschung von Lehrervorstellungen.

Schlüsselbegriffe: Pedagogical Content Knowledge, subjektive Theorien, Lehrervorstellungsforschung,

1 Einleitung

In Österreich hat das zuständige Bildungsministerium als Reaktion auf unzureichende Schülerleistungen in der TIMS-Studie 1995 das Forschungs- und Entwicklungsprojekt *„Innovations in Mathematics, Science and Technology Teaching"* (IMST) in Auftrag gegeben. Lehrer/-innen werden eingeladen, über ein Jahr Unterrichtsinnovationen zu verschiedenen Themen zu formulieren, unter fachdidaktischer Betreuung der Lehrer/-innenfortbildner/-innen umzusetzen und mit dem Paradigma der Aktionsforschung zu evaluieren (Krainer 2008). Diese Aktionsforschungsberichte der Lehrer/-innen sind die Datenbasis für die explorative Studie *Impressions of Biology Teaching in Austria* (BiTe), deren methodischer Umgang mit den Daten hier thematisiert wird.

Die Vorstellungen der Lehrer/-inne/-n werden zuerst im Sinne von Subjektiven Theorien (ST) (s.u. Groeben et al. 1988) betrachtet. In der Literatur wird darüber hinaus darauf hingewiesen, dass sich weitgehend Übereinstimmungen zwischen (fach)didaktischen (deutschen) Modellen und den Komponenten von *Pedagogical Content Knowledge* (PCK) zeigen (z.B. van Dijk & Kattmann 2007). So ist es nahe liegend, dass Komponenten in den Subjektiven Theorien eine Übereinstimmung zu bestimmten PCK-Komponenten zeigen können (Jelemenská et al. eingereicht). Inwiefern sich jedoch die methodischen Vorgangsweisen für die Erfassung der Lehrervorstellungen von ST und PCK ergänzen können, soll hier behandelt werden.

2 Ziele der BiTe-Studie

- Herausstellen des methodologischen Zugangs für das Erfassen der Lehrervorstellungen aus den Aktionsforschungsberichten.
- Übergeordnetes Ziel von BiTe war es, aus Aktionsforschungsberichten (AFB) von erfahrenen Lehrer/-inne/-n ihre Vorstellungen zum Biologieunterricht zu analysieren und anhand der Ergebnisse Vorschläge für die Verbesserung des Ökologieunterrichts durch Lehrer/-innenprofessionalisierung zu formulieren.

3 Theoretischer Rahmen für die Analyse der Lehrervorstellungen

Die Untersuchung der Aktionsforschungsberichte orientiert sich an dem Grundgedanken des Modells der Didaktischen Rekonstruktion zur Erfassung von Vorstellungen (Kattmann et al. 1997). Das Modell wurde bereits in der Analyse von Lehrerwissen im Bereich Evolution von VAN DIJK (2009; ERTE-Modell) angewendet. Die Lehrervorstellungen werden in der vorliegenden Arbeit zunächst nicht in ihrer fachlichen Korrektheit beurteilt, sondern sie werden in ihren Sinnzusammenhängen betrachtet, wie sie die Lehrer/-innen berichten. Die Vorstellungen der Lehrer/-innen werden als ST (Groeben et al. 1988) verstanden, d.h. als komplexe Aggregate von Kognitionen der Selbst- und Weltsicht, die eine entsprechende implizite Argumentationsstruktur besitzen und somit ähnlich wie wissenschaftliche Theorien aufgebaut und fassbar sind (Helmke 2007). Dem Herausstellen der inhaltlichen und strukturellen Zusammenhänge in den Vorstellungen der Lehrer/-innen liegt somit zunächst keine Norm zugrunde, sondern ist rein deskriptiv. Erst dann, wenn die Vorstellungen der Lehrer/-innen und ihre Argumentation für die Gestaltung des Unterrichts verstanden worden sind, werden die lernförderlichen und lernhinderlichen Aspekte analytisch herausgestellt. Die Basis dafür sind die Grundannahmen und Ergebnisse der Grundlageforschung der DR, die im Sinne von fachdidaktisch geklärtem Theoriewissen auf die ST der Lehrer bezogen werden (s. n. Jelemenská et al. 2009).

4 Material und Methoden

Die AFB der Lehrer/-innen entstehen nicht im Zuge systematischer theoriegeleiteter Datenerhebung von Fachdidaktik-Forschern, sondern unabhängig davon zu einem anderen Zweck: Sie sind ein non-reaktives Datenmaterial (Mayring 2003). Den Fokus bestimmt jeder Berichtschreiber autonom. Die im IMST Fonds bis 2006 entstandenen 66 AFB von Biologie-Lehrer/-inne/-n wurden in BiTe zuerst quantitativ kategorisiert. Zusätzlich wurden neun Berichte vertiefend qualitativ analysiert und die zentralen Ergebnisse des jeweiligen Berichts validiert. Aus zeitökonomischen Gründen fand die Validierung per E-Mail statt. Die wesentlichen Aspekte der Lehrervorstellungen im Sinne der ST (Groeben et al. 1988) wurden mit der qualitativen Inhaltsanalyse (Mayring 2003, modifiziert nach Gropengießer 2005) und computergestützt (MAXQDA 2007) herausgearbeitet und im Sinne von Fallstudien dargestellt.

Darüber hinaus wurden Ergebnisse von vier Aktionsforschungsberichten (zu Ökologieunterricht) mit dem Theoriehintergrund der PCK betrachtet. Aus diesen Ergebnissen wird hier auf die ST und das PCK eines erfahrenen Biologie-Gymnasiallehrers kurz eingegangen.

5 Diskussion der ausgewählten Ergebnisse zu ST im Hinblick auf PCK

PCK ist professionelles Wissen von Lehrer/-inne/-n, das bei der Integration von anderen Wissensbereichen (Fachwissen & pädagogisches Wissen) hilft, wobei es selbst auch aus einer Schnittmenge von beiden hervorgeht (s. Abell 2008). Es stellt sich die Frage, wie die Integration der PCK-Bereiche erreicht wird und was sie bewirkt (vgl. Kind 2009). Ausgehend von der ST des Gymnasiallehrers wird hier auf Integration der PCK-Bereiche eingegangen.

Authentizität ist ein wesentlicher Gedanke der ST des Gymnasiallehrers. Die Unterrichtsgestaltung ist durch die Authentizität (Echtheit) der Erfahrungen mit der Natur und die damit verbundene Angemessenheit der Naturbetrachtung charakterisiert und in seinem Fall für die Integration folgender PCK-Bereiche verantwortlich: *„orientation to teaching science"*, *„knowledge of students' understanding in science"* und *„knowledge of instructional strategies for teaching science"* (die PCK-Bereiche orientieren sich an Park & Oliver 2008). Für den Gymnasiallehrer ist dabei folgende Argumentation zentral: *Das Defizit in direkten Erfahrungen mit der Natur in der modernen Gesellschaft führt dazu, dass die Schüler/-innen Defizite im Wissen aufweisen und nicht angemessene Einstellungen (negative Haltung gegenüber der Jagd) entwickeln.* Mit den Defiziten der Schüler/-innen verdeutlicht der Gymnasiallehrer einerseits die Relevanz des Biologieunterrichts für die Gesellschaft, andererseits zeigt er die schwierige Aufgabe des Biologieunterrichts auf, solche anthropomorphen Einstellungen zu ändern. Für das Lernen der Schüler/-innen werden dementsprechend authentische Situationen gefordert. Durch eigene Erfahrungen an authentischen Lernorten (z.B. im Wald), wie auch durch die authentische Vermittlung über entsprechende Personen (Förster, Jäger, Tierschützer etc.) wird angenommen, dass die emotionalen Einstellungen der Schüler/-innen weitgehend einer objektiven und kritischen Betrachtungsweise wiechen. Diese angemessenen Einstellungen sind dann eine Voraussetzung für die Schüler/-innen, die in der Gesellschaft vorherrschende Meinungen aufgrund des Biologieunterrichts kritisch beurteilen können. Der Schwerpunkt im konkret erfahrbaren Erkenntnisgewinn in der Natur ist auch damit zu erklären, dass der Gymnasiallehrer selber als Jäger tätig ist. Die ST des Lehrers – hier am Verständnis von Erkenntnisgewinn dargestellt – hat eine handlungsleitende Funktion für die Gestaltung des Unterrichts (vgl. Helmke 2007).

Im Vergleich eines Aspekts der ST des Gymnasiallehrers zu dem fachdidaktisch geklärten Theoriewissen der DR kann die Wirksamkeit des Unterrichts und eine Integration von PCK-Bereichen angesprochen werden: Am Ende des eigenen Projekts betrachtet der Gymnasiallehrer seine Wirksamkeit. Eine wesentliche Veränderung wird in den Schülermeinungen beim *„Zuwachs am Detailwissen"* geortet. Re-analysiert man jedoch die von dem Gymnasiallehrer angeführten Zitate der Schüler/-innen aus der Perspektive der fachdidaktischen Forschung zur Ökologie (z.B. Jelemenská 2006) zeigen sich zwar bei den Schüler/-inne/-n die Gemeinsamkeiten mit der vom Gymnasiallehrer angenommenen korrekten Argumentation, das fachliche Verständnis von Änderungen in der Population wird jedoch noch immer normativ betrachtet: Beim *„Abschießen von Tieren, weil es zu viele sind"* (vor dem Unterricht) wird ebenso eine für einen Lebensraums angemessene Anzahl von Tieren gefordert wie bei der neuen Formulierung (nach dem Unterricht) *„Reduktion des Schalenwildbestandes auf ein dem Biotop angepasstes Maß"*. Diese Schwierigkeiten deuten darauf hin, dass von dem Gymnasiallehrer mit der Objektivität des Erkennens auch eine überholte wissenschaftliche Position angenommen wurde. Die Bedeutung der Integration der PCK-Bereiche – *„orientation to teaching science"* und *„knowledge of students' understanding in science"* wird hier sichtbar.

Die Integration von PCK-Bereichen ist aus unterschiedlichen Perspektiven zu behandeln. Ausgehend von der ST können handlungsleitende Aspekte in den Lehrervorstellungen herausgearbeitet werden. Die Gegenüberstellung der ST und des PCK zu fachdidaktisch geklärtem Theoriewissen hilft Ansatzpunkte für die Unterstützung von Lehrerfortbildung zu finden (s. z. B. Jelemenská in diesem Band). PCK-Modelle sind ein unterstützendes Konstrukt, die beim Fokussieren von Lehrerwissensforschung helfen können. Eine stärkere Integration durch den Ansatz der ST kann so die Lehrerwissensforschung sinnvoll ergänzen.

Literaturangaben

ABELL, S. K.: Twenty Years Later: Does pedagogical content knowledge remain a useful idea? IJSE 10/2008, 1405-1416.

DIJK, E. M. V. & KATTMANN, U.: A research model for the study of science teachers' PCK and improving teacher education. Teaching and Teacher Education, 23/2007, 885-897.

DIJK, E. M. V.: Teachers' views on understanding evolutionary theory: A PCK-study in the framework of the ERTE-model. Teaching and Teacher Education 25/2009, 259–267.

FISCHLER, H. & SCHRÖDER, H.-J.: Fachdidaktisches Coaching für Lehrende in der Physik. ZfDN 9/2003, 43-62.

GROEBEN, N. ET AL. (Hg.): Das Forschungsprogramm Subjektive Theorien. Eine Einführung in die Psychologie des reflexiven Subjekts. – Tübingen: Francke, 1988.

GROPENGIEßER, H.: Qualitative Inhaltsanalyse in der fachdidaktischen Lehr-Lern-Forschung. In: Mayring, P. & Gläser-Zikuda M. (Hg.). Die Praxis der Qualitativen Inhaltsanalyse. – Weinheim und Basel: Beltz, 2005.

HELMKE, A.: Unterrichtsqualität erfassen – bewerten – verbessern. – Seelze: Kallmeyer, 2007.

JELEMENSKÁ, P.: Biologie verstehen: ökologische Einheiten. Beiträge zur Didaktischen Rekonstruktion 12. – Oldenburg: Didaktisches Zentrum, 2006.

JELEMENSKÁ, P. ET AL.: Wie kann man Ökologieunterricht verbessern? Eine qualitative Analyse von LehrerInnen-Aktionsforschungsberichten zum Ökologieunterricht, Vortrag auf der Tagung FdDB: Kiel, 2009.

KATTMANN, U. ET AL.: Das Modell der Didaktischen Rekonstruktion. Ein Rahmen für naturwissenschaftliche Forschung und Entwicklung. In: ZfDN 3/1997, 3-18.

KIND, V.: Pedagogical content knowledge in science education: perspectives and potential for progress. In: Stud Sci Educ 2/2009, 169-204.

KRAINER, K.: Genese, Ansatz und Wirkungen des Projekts IMST. In F. Hofmann et al. (Hg.), Qualitative und quantitative Aspekte. Zu ihrer Komplementarität in der erziehungswissenschaftlichen Forschung. – Münster: Waxmann, 2008.

PARK, S., & OLIVER, J. S.: Revisiting the Conceptualisation of Pedagogical Content Knowledge: PCK as a Conceptual Tool to Understand Teachers as Professionals. RiSE 3/2008, 261-284.

SHULMAN, L. S.: Those Who Understand: Knowledge Growth in Teaching. ER 2/1986, 4-14.

Datenquelle (IMST Aktionsforschungsberichte der Lehrer/-innen): http://imst.uni-klu.ac.at/imst-wiki/index.php/Kategorie:Biologie

Kontakt: Patricia JELEMENSKÁ: patricia.jelemenska@univie.ac.at; Martin SCHEUCH: martin.scheuch@univie.ac.at; Franz RADITS: franz.radits@univie.ac.at

WIE BEWERTEN LEHRER/-INNEN DIE INTEGRATION VON UNTERRICHTSPRAXIS IN DIE FORTBILDUNG UND DIE WIRKUNG DER FORTBILDUNG AUF IHREN UNTERRICHT?

Erika Keller, Martin Scheuch
AECC-Bio Austrian Educational Competence Centre of Biology,
Universität Wien, Österreich

Das Lehrer/-innenfortbildungsmodell des AECC-Bio hat das Ziel Lehrer/-innen in ihrer Professionalitätsentwicklung und hier vor allem die Entwicklung ihres fachdidaktischen Handlungswissens (Pedagogical Content Knowledge – PCK) zu unterstützen. Da diese Entwicklung vor allem durch reflexive Praxis erfolgt, ist die Integration der Schulpraxis in die Fortbildung ein zentraler Teil des Fortbildungskonzepts. Das Fortbildungsmodell besteht aus drei Modulen und erstreckt sich über den Zeitraum von einem Jahr. Im zweiten Modul entwickeln die Teilnehmer/-innen ein Unterrichtsprojekt und setzten dieses mit ihrer Schulklasse um. Im Rahmen der vorliegenden Evaluationsstudie wurden eineinhalb Jahre nach Abschluss des Pilotkurses „Highschools" – mit dem fachbiologischen Inhalt „Ökologie der Alpen" – qualitative Interviews mit Teilnehmer/-innen geführt. Ziel der Studie war es, die Bewertung der Lehrer/-innen im Bezug auf die Wechselwirkungen von Fortbildung und Unterricht zu untersuchen.

Die Entwicklung und Durchführung der Alpenprojekte im Rahmen der Fortbildung wurde von den Teilnehmer/-innen als wesentlich für die Entwicklung von Aspekten ihres Biologie Unterrichtens gesehen. Sie berichteten auch zwei Jahre nach Abschluss der Fortbildung über aktuelle Wirkungen im Unterricht. Für etliche Kursteilnehmer/-innen schien allerdings die Konzeption der Fortbildung mit inkludierter Unterrichtspraxis eine Hürde darzustellen. Einige wesentliche Evaluationsergebnisse werden im Beitrag analysiert und ihre Auswirkungen für die weitere Fortbildungskonzeption diskutiert.

Schlüsselbegriffe: Fachdidaktische Professionalitätsentwicklung, Evaluation, Fortbildungskonzept

1 Zielsetzung

Ein Ziel unserer Fortbildung ist die fachdidaktische Professionalitätsentwicklung der LehrerInnen (*Pedagogical Content Knowledge* – PCK; Park & Oliver 2008), für die eine reflexive Unterrichtspraxis notwendig ist. Ein zentrales Element unseres Fortbildungsmodells ist daher die konzeptionelle Verankerung von Unterrichtspraxis und der Reflexion darüber im Kurs. Im Rahmen der Evaluationsstudie beleuchten wir diesen Aspekt der Unterrichtsbezüge genauer. Auf Basis des Theoriehintergrundes werden einige zentrale Ergebnisse aus den Interviews vorgestellt und im Bezug auf die Weiterentwicklung unseres Fortbildungsmodells diskutiert.

2 Theoriehintergrund

In der Wirkungsforschung zu Lehrer/-innenfortbildung (siehe Hewson 2007, Lipowsky 2010) wird nahe gelegt, dass Lehrer/-innenfortbildung im Sinne einer Professionalisierung dann erfolgreich ist, wenn sie eine Integration in den Unterricht erfährt und eine Reflexion über die Unterrichtspraxis in der Fortbildung stattfindet. Ähnliche Forderungen stellen ALTRICHTER & KRAINER (1996), die „Aktion“ (im Unterricht) & „Reflexion“ (über den Unterricht) als sich ergänzende Aktivitäten von Lehrer/-innenprofessionalisierung ansehen. Bezogen auf die Entwicklung von Handlungswissen der Lehrer/-innen beschreiben PARK & OLIVER (2008) in ihrem Konzept des *Pedagogical Content Knowledge* (PCK) *"reflection in action"* und *"reflection on action"* als wesentliche Triebfedern. Ein weiteres Element für die Wirksamkeit von Fortbildung ist der Austausch der Lehrer/-innen über ihre Unterrichtsplanung und die gemachten Erfahrungen im Unterricht (Altrichter & Krainer 1996, Hewson 2007, Lipowsky 2010) sowie das Arbeiten in Lerngemeinschaften (Reinmann & Mandl 2006).

3 Modell & Kurs „Highschools"

Bei dem hier beschriebenen Kurs zur Ökologie der Alpen, handelt es sich um einen dreimodularen Pilotkurs unserer Modellentwicklung. Für eine detaillierte Modellbeschreibung siehe SCHEUCH ET AL. (in diesem Buch). Sowohl Modul I als auch Modul III erstreckten sich über einen Zeitraum von mehreren Tagen und fanden direkt am „Lernort Alpen" statt. In Modul II planten und entwickelten die Lehrer/-innen eigenständig ein Alpenprojekt und führten es mit ihrer Klasse durch. Das Design der Lehrer/-innenfortbildung sollte es den Lehrer/-innen im Sinne eines *„community-centered learning environments"* (Reinmann & Mandl 2006) erleichtern, Unterricht gemeinsam zu planen und sich auszutauschen, um die in der Fortbildung gewonnenen Erkenntnisse und Erfahrungen in den eigenen Unterricht zu integrieren und zu reflektieren. Hier stand das vergleichende Lernen durch Feedback der Kolleg/-inn/-en im Vordergrund. In Modul II und Modul III, in welchen die Lehrer/-innen ihre Alpenprojekte planten, umsetzten bzw. reflektiert haben, ist die Lernumgebung vorwiegend teilnehmer/-innenzentriert (*„learner-centered environment"* – Reinmann & Mandl 2006).

4 Fragestellung und Methode

Der Forschungsfokus liegt in diesem Beitrag auf der Einschätzung der Lehrer/-innen zu den Wirkungen der Fortbildung im Unterricht.
Folgende Fragestellungen stehen daher im Zentrum:

- Welche Rückmeldungen geben Lehrer/-innen zu den Unterrichtsbezügen in der Fortbildung und zur Integration der Lehrer/-innenfortbildung in die Schulpraxis?
- Welche Bedeutung haben Austausch und Vernetzung mit Kolleg/-inn/-en in der Fortbildung im Bezug auf den eigenen Unterricht?

Für die Untersuchung wurden mit vier Kursteilnehmer/-innen halbstrukturierte leitfadengestützten Interviews geführt. Die Analyse der Daten erfolgte mit der Qualitativen Inhaltsanalyse (Mayring 2003) nach einem vorwiegend deduktiven Kategoriensystem, das aus dem Modell der AECC-Biologie Lehrer/-innenfortbildung abgeleitet wurde. Zur Illustration der Ergebnisse werden paraphrasierte Zitate der Lehrer/-innen verwendet.

5 Ergebnisse

Der Bezug zum Unterricht (Projektentwicklung und Durchführung in Modul II) wurde von den Teilnehmer/-inne/-n als zentral an der Fortbildung angesehen. Die Lehrer/-innen erlebten es als wesentlich, interessensgeleitet ein individuelles Projekt zu entwickeln und sich die Umsetzung im Unterricht zuzutrauen.

...Für mich war das Wichtigste, dass ich mich an das Thema im Unterricht herangewagt habe... (A 30-36).

Der Druck ein Projekt umzusetzen, der durch die Konzeption der Fortbildung entstand, wurde von den Teilnehmer/-innen, die den Kurs abgeschlossen hatten, als förderlich beschrieben (z.B. B 24). Allerdings wurde er auch als möglichen Beweggrund für etliche Teilnehmer/-innen gesehen, den Kurs abzubrechen.

... Ein Stolperstein war, dass nach dem Modul 1 die Teilnehmer/-innen geglaubt haben, sie müssen ein Riesenprojekt machen... (D 195-202)

Als langfristige Wirkungen des Alpenkurses im Unterricht wurden unter anderem genannt:

- dass bei Freilandprojekten die Schüler/-innen seither verstärkt eingebunden wurden und dass die Aktivitäten jetzt vermehrt erlebnispädagogisch orientiert sind sowie einen höheren Anteil an Gelegenheiten und Zeit zum Experimentieren und Forschen aufweisen (C 101-102);
- dass in den Folgejahren häufig thematische bzw. methodische Bezüge zum Alpenprojekt mit den Klassen hergestellt werden konnten und es die Möglichkeit gab, auf den gemachten Erfahrungen und dem Gelernten aufzubauen.

...In der 6. Klasse haben die Schüler/-innen die Bedeutung noch nicht nachvollziehen können, aber in der 7. Klasse habe ich das Thema in einer anderen Form – unter „Nachhaltigem Tourismus in den Alpen" weiter bearbeitet. Da habe ich immer wieder auf das Alpenprojekt zurückgreifen können... (A 41-50) *...es ist den Schüler/-inne/-n einfach hängen geblieben, auch wenn sie am Anfang nicht verstanden haben, warum das eigentlich wichtig ist. Heute in der achten Klasse wissen sie es...*(A39-40).

- dass methodische Anregungen (A14-17, D 40, 240) zu Natursensibilisierung, dem naturwissenschaftlichen Forschungszyklus, Erlebnis- & Spielpädagogik (C14), Freilandbiologie etc. aus der Fortbildung und Materialien (Fotos, Kursunterlagen, Präsentationen … A 1-4) für verschiedene Klassen und unterschiedliche Unterrichtskontexte genutzt werden konnten (D 40):

…Ich habe mit meiner ersten Klasse das Alpen-Herbar gemacht, das hat sich dann in der zweiten und dritten Klasse weiterentwickelt. Dann habe ich den Alpenkurs für den Oberstufenkurs „Wissenschaftliches Arbeiten" nutzen können. Von einem Kollegen habe ich Tipps zu außerschulischen Lernorten zum Thema Nutzung der Alpen erhalten. Das habe ich in der Folge für meinen Lebensmitteltechnologie Kurs nutzen können (D 134-150).

Die Bedeutung des Austausches mit Kolleg/-inn/-en für die eigene Unterrichtspraxis wird sehr hoch bewertet. Allerdings findet der Austausch vor allem auf der Ebene des vergleichenden Lernens über die Präsentationen und Rückmeldungen zu den Ideen für die Alpenprojekte (Modul II) und die Präsentationen und Reflexionen der durchgeführten Alpenprojekte (Modul III) statt und nicht im Sinne von gemeinsamer Unterrichtsplanung und echter Kooperation.

… es war wichtig, dass man von den Anderen erfahren hat, was sie für ein Projekt gemacht haben und wie es ihnen ergangen ist um selber etwas in diese Richtung ausprobieren zu können… (B30.)

Ein Teilnehmer hebt besonders die Bedeutung des Erfahrungsaustausches mit den KollegInnen für das Überdenken der eigenen Einstellung zum Biologie Unterrichten hervor:

… es war viel Zeit dem Gedankenaustausch zwischen Lehrern verschiedener Schulsysteme gewidmet und das war sehr wertvoll. Mich hat fasziniert, wie Andere den gleichen Inhalt vermitteln. Man bekommt dadurch ein weites Land präsentiert und denkt darüber nach, was man selber macht und kann sich wieder neu orientieren: was ist wirklich wichtig, was ist weniger wichtig, worauf kommt es überhaupt in der Vermittlung von Wissen an…(C 24).

6 Diskussion

Die Rückmeldungen der Lehrer/-innen bestärken uns, an unserem dreimodularen Modell mit integrierter Unterrichtspraxis weiterzuarbeiten, da diese Art der Fortbildung eine langfristige Wirkung auf die Umsetzung im Unterricht zeigt. Dies wird auch dadurch bestätigt, dass zwei Jahre nach Abschluss des Kurses noch so viel über die Wirkung des Alpenkurses im (aktuellen) Unterricht berichtet wird. Aufgrund der Interviewdaten vermuten wir weiters, dass die Fortbildung Auswirkungen auf mehrere Aspekte der Professionalitätsentwicklung und hier vor allem auf die PCK Entwicklung der Teilnehmer/-innen hat. So finden sich z.B. Hinweise auf Änderungen zu verschiedenen PCK Kategorien die bei PARK & OLIVER (2008) beschrieben werden, wie Selbstwirksamkeit (A 30-36), der Einstellung zum Biologie Unterrichten (C24), dem Wissen um Schüler/-innenperspektiven (C 101-102) oder den Bezügen zu Unterrichtsstruktur und Lehrplan (D 134-150). Diese ersten Ergebnisse müssen aber noch durch die Tiefenanalysen der Interviews überprüft werden. Zu überlegen ist weiters, wie wir zukünftig die Hemmschwelle für die Lehrer/-innen senken können, damit sie sich aktiv mit einem eigenen Projekt an Modul II und III beteiligen können.

Literaturangaben

ALTRICHTER, HERBERT & KRAINER KONRAD: Wandel von Lehrerarbeit und Lehrerfortbildung. In Krainer, Konrad & Posch Peter: Lehrerfortbildung zwischen Prozessen und Produkten, 33-51. Verlag Julius Klinkhardt, 1996.

HEWSON, PETER: Teacher Professional Development in Science. In Abell, Sandra & Ledermann Norman: Handbook of Research on Science Education, 1177-1202. Mahwah, New Jersey: Lawrence Erlbaum Associates, 2007.

KELLER, ERIKA, SCHEUCH, MARTIN & RADITS FRANZ: Förderung der Professionalitätsentwicklung von BiologielehrerInnen durch Fortbildung. Weiterentwicklung eines Arbeitsmodells mit den Konzepten der Communities of Practice und des Pedagogical Content Knowledge. In: Erkenntnisweg Biologie 7/ 2008, 183-197.

LIPOWSKY, FRANK: Lernen im Beruf. Empirische Befunde zur Wirksamkeit von Lehrerfortbildung. In: Müller, Florian H., Eichenberger, Astrid, Lüders, Manfred, Mayr, Johannes (Hg.): Lehrerinnen und Lehrer lernen. Konzepte und Befunde zur Lehrerfortbildung, 51-72. – Münster: Waxmann, 2010.

MAYRING, PHILIPP: Qualitative Inhaltsanalyse. Grundlagen und Techniken. 8. Auflage. - Weinheim & Basel: Beltz Verlag, 2003.

PARK, SOONHYE & OLIVER J. STEVE: Revisiting the Conceptualisation of Pedagogical Content Knowledge (PCK). PCK as a Conceptual Tool to Understand Teachers as Professionals. In: Research in Science Education 38 (2) / 2008, 127-147.

REINMANN, GABI & MANDL HEINZ: Unterrichten und Lernumgebungen gestalten. In: Krapp Andreas & Weidenmann Bernd (Hg.): Pädagogische Psychologie, 615-658 – Basel: Beltz, 2006.

Kontakt:
Erika KELLER: erika.keller@univie.ac.at
Martin SCHEUCH: martin.scheuch@univie.ac.at

PROFESSIONALISIERUNG VON BIOLOGIELEHRER/-INNE/-N DURCH SYSTEMATISCHE REFLEXION IN FORSCHUNGS-BILDUNGS-KOOPERATIONEN

Franz Radits, Christine Heidinger, Austrian Educational Competence Centre Biology (AECC-Bio), Universität Wien, Österreich

Im Pilotprojekt KiP (Kids Participation in Research) wurden in der Pilotphase zehn Lehrer/-innen von fünf Wissenschaftler/-inne/-n eingeladen, gemeinsam mit ihren Schüler/-innen in biologischen Forschungsprojekten zu partizipieren. Labors werden so zu anspruchsvollen komplexen Lernumgebungen. Lehrer/-innen werden bei deren Aufbau durch gezielte Fortbildungsmaßnahmen (Inputs, Community of Practice, Aktionsforschung) unterstützt. Die ersten Ergebnisse der formativen Evaluation zeigen, dass Lehrer/-innen sehr unterschiedliche Rollenmuster in der Kooperation einnehmen. In der Wahrnehmung der Lehrer/-innen schwinden die Barrieren für die Kooperation im Projektverlauf zunehmend. Erste Hypothesen über die Ursachen dieser Veränderungen werden dargelegt.

Schlüsselbegriffe: Komplexe Lernumgebung, Fortbildungsmaßnahme, Aktionsforschung

1 Einleitung: KiP – "what goes on"

In Österreich und in vielen anderen europäischen Staaten wirbt das Wissenschaftssystem um Wissenschaftler/-innen, die Schulen und Lehrer/-innen in ihre Institute zur gemeinsamen Forschung einladen (Forschungs-Bildungs-Kooperationen, FBK). Es geht um Nachwuchsförderung und um Wissenschaftskooperation (www.sparklingscience.at). In diesem Kontext entwickelten Biologiedidaktiker/-innen der Universität Wien das Pilotprojekt *„Kids Participation in Research"* („KiP": http://aeccbio.univie.ac.at/kip) mit dem Ziel, diese neuen Lernumgebungen evidenzbasiert zu modellieren und fachdidaktisch zu beforschen (Laufzeit: 2008 bis 2010). Dazu wurde auf Basis breiter Theoriebestände das sogenannte KiP-Arbeitsmodell 2008 formuliert (s. Grafik): Wissenschaftler/-innen der Fakultät für Lebenswissenschaften der Universität Wien luden zehn Lehrer/-innen und ihre Schüler/-innen (5.-11. Schulstufe) ein, in ihren fachlichen Forschungsprojekten der Neurobiologie, Landschaftsökologie, Meeresbiologie, forensischen Palynologie oder Evolutionsbiologie forschend zu lernen (*Inquiry Learning*). In diesen Arbeitsgruppen („Bio-KiPs"; s. Grafik) variieren Inhalte (z.B. Pollenforschung, *Nature of Science*), Intensität (Frequenz der Treffen) und Form (Rolle der Akteure/Akteurinnen) der Zusammenarbeit stark. Die Lehrer/-innen übernehmen die Aufgabe, diese Arbeit im Regelunterricht zu unterstützen (s. Grafik). Sie werden durch spezifische fachdidaktische Workshops, die dem Muster von *Communities of Practice* (Wenger 2004) folgen, durch Einzelcoaching und durch themenbezogene Papers („Fachdidaktische Briefe") von Fachdidaktiker/-inne/-n unterstützt. Drei Lehrerinnen reflektieren systematisch in Aktionsforschungsprojekten (Altrichter & Posch 2007) ihre Lernerfahrungen in den Bio-KiPs. Zentraler Ort der gemeinsamen Reflexion aller Akteursgruppen sind die Reflexionswerkstätten (s. Grafik). Sie dauern ein bis zwei Tage und finden ein Mal pro Semester statt.

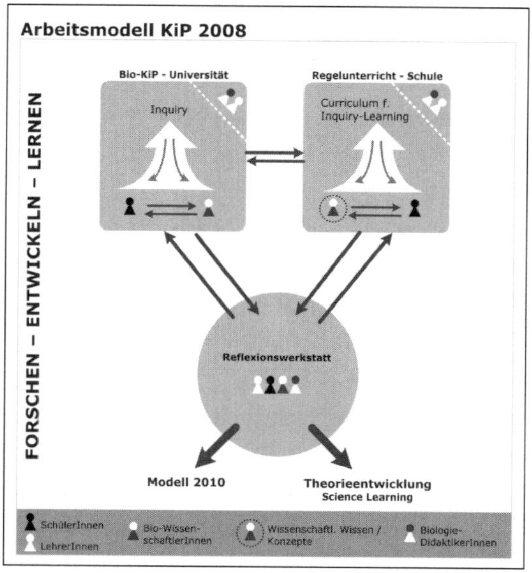

2 Lernen in komplexen Aktivitätssystemen – zum theoretischen Rahmen der Lehrer/-innenfortbildung in KiP

Lehrer/-innen entwickeln in KiP kollaborativ mit Wissenschaftler/-inne/-n (Fachwissenschaft, Fachdidaktik) Lösungen für das Problem des *Inquiry Learnings* in außerschulischen Labors, die längerfristig im Unterricht implementiert werden sollen. GERSTENMAIER & MANDL (2001) beschreiben in ihrem Forschungsbericht über „situiertes Lernen" solche Systeme in Anlehnung an GREENO,

COLLINS UND RESNICK (1996) als „implementierende Aktivitätssysteme". Diese zeichnen sich durch einen hohen Grad an Partizipation und kollaborativem Lernen in *Communities of Practice* aus. Neben der Implementierung des *Inquiry Learnings* sieht das KiP-Modell die Lehrer/-innen auch als Gestalter/-innen der Kooperation von Schüler/-inne/-n und Wissenschaftler/-inne/-n. Der Wissensaufbau in den Bio-KiPs wird in Anlehnung an die Konzeption der „Didaktischen Rekonstruktion" (Kattmann et al. 1997) als aktiver konstruktiver Prozess, der in erster Linie zwischen dem/der Wissenschaftler/-in und den Schüler/-inne/-n ausgehandelt wird, gedeutet. Der/die Lehrer/-in wird dabei moderierend, unterstützend oder als Mitlernende/-r gesehen. In der klassischen Lehrer/-innenrolle kontrollieren die Lehrenden das für den Lernprozess vorgesehene Wissen. Der Wechsel zur moderierenden, planenden und unterstützenden Rolle fällt in der Praxis schwer, wie empirische Studien zeigen (Windschitl 2002). Lehrer/-innen bei diesem Rollenwechsel zu unterstützen, setzt ein wirkungsvolles System von Lehrer/-innenfortbildung voraus. Fachdidaktisches Coaching (Fischler & Schröder 2003), *Communities of Practice* (Wenger 2004), Langfristigkeit und Einbeziehung der eigenen Praxis fördern den Konzeptwechsel, wie LIPOWSKY (2004) und GOODNOUGH (2008) zeigen.

Dieses Paper exploriert die Wirkung der Interventionen des KiP-Modells zunächst mit folgenden Forschungsfragen:

- Wie verläuft die Entwicklung von projektbezogenen Einstellungen? Welche Chancen und Befürchtungen äußern Lehrer/-innen am Beginn des Projekts? Wie verändert sich die Sicht auf das Aktivitätssystem während des Projekts?
- Welche Akteursrollen besetzen Lehrer/-innen in den Arbeitsgruppen (Bio-KiPs)?

3 Methode

Die KiP-Begleitforschung folgt dem Muster einer formativen Evaluation (Flick 2006). Erkenntnisse aus der Evaluation werden zum einen als Steuerungswissen in den Prozess zurückgespielt und zum anderen zur Überarbeitung des Modells eingesetzt. Die Beantwortung der Frage nach dem Entwicklungsverlauf von projektbezogenen Einstellungen der Lehrer/-innen in KiP erfolgt über die Analyse der Daten aus der Evaluation: Es wurden im Projektverlauf durch teilnehmende Beobachtung bei Zusammenkünften der *Community of Practice* Daten gesammelt (z.T. transkribierte Audiofiles aber auch Feldnotizen) und diese mittels inhaltsanalytischer Techniken auf Basis deduktiver und induktiver Kategorien (Mayring 2007) ausgewertet. Zur Beantwortung der Frage nach den Rollen der Lehrer/-innen in den Bio-KiPs wurden für die hier vorgelegte Untersuchung die Transkripte zu den Gesprächen in drei von zehn Bio-KiPs ausgewertet. Der Fokus lag dabei auf einer Beschreibung des Lehrer/-innen-Handelns in der Interaktion mit Wissenschaftler/-inne/-n und Schüler/-inne/-n. Aus der Analyse der Gesprächsprotokolle lassen sich Akteursmuster von Lehrer/-inne/-n identifizieren.

4 Erste Ergebnisse und theoretische Anbindung

4.1 Entwicklung der Einstellungen zur Kooperation in KiP

Lehrer/-innen betonen am Beginn des Projekts drei Barrieren (Restriktionen) für ihre künftigen Aktivitäten: Die Motivationslage der Schüler/-innen und Wissenschaftler/-nnen, Zeit und Differenz des Wissens. Die beiden letztgenannten betreffen zentrale Problemfelder jedes transdisziplinären Aktivitätssystems vom Typ einer Forschungs-Bildungs-Kooperation (Weingart 1997; Radits & Rauch 2008).

Zeit: Als Expert/-inn/-en für das Schulsystem kennen Lehrer/-innen genau ihr Zeitsystem und wissen um Schwierigkeiten, die aus ihnen erwachsen, wenn sie versuchen, dieses an andere Systeme anzupassen. Sie antizipieren dabei das Zeitsystem der Wissenschaftler/-innen. Aus dem Empfinden der Differenz erwächst das Gefühl einer unüberwindlichen Barriere (Radits 2000).

Wissen/Nichtwissen und Sozialisation: neun der zehn Lehrer/-innen des KiP-Projekts wurden an einer Universität für ihren Beruf als Biologielehrer/-innen sozialisiert. Kern des Sozialisationsprozesses ist es „außeruniversitäre Erfahrungen“, biologische Alltagserfahrungen, Alltagswissen und „biologisches Schulwissen“ scharf vom wissenschaftlichen Wissen abzugrenzen (Arnold 2004). Es ist anzunehmen, dass diese Sozialisationserfahrungen die Eingangsängste der Lehrer/-innen in Bezug auf „Wissensdefizite“ beförderten. Die am Beginn des Projekts geäußerten Barrieren (Restriktionen) für ihre künftigen Aktivitäten sind zur Halbzeit des Projekts verblasst, wie die erste Auswertung der Daten zeigt. Zwei Problembereiche transdisziplinärer Aktivitätssysteme werden in der Mitte des Projekts nicht mehr als Barrieren empfunden: Motivationslage der anderen Akteure und die Unsicherheit bezügliche des eigenen Wissens. Das Zeit-Problem persistiert.

4.2 Rollenverständnis

Drei Handlungsmuster konnten bislang identifiziert werden: *„Lehrer/-in und Wissenschaftler/-in als Fachwissenschaftler/-innen"*, *„Lehrer/-in als Moderator/-in des Dialogs Schüler/-innen – Wissenschaftler/-in"* und *„Lehrer/-in als passiver Facilitator"*. Diese Muster sind stark kontextabhängig. Sie zeigen aber die erwarteten Schwierigkeiten (Windschitl 2002) eine für die jeweilige Lehrer/-in stimmige Rolle in den BioKiPs zu besetzen.

5 Resümee und Ausblick

Von einem Aktivitätssystem, das wie KiP, auf situatives Lernen, Reflexion und Partizipation baut, kann erwartet werden, dass anfänglich aus dem Wissen über das eigene System entwickelte Befürchtungen über die Kooperation im Verlauf des Prozesses zurücktreten. Diese in den Daten klar abgebildete Entwicklung kann nach GREENO, COLLINS & RESNICK (1996) als „Passung" verstanden werden. Die unterschiedlichen Akteure lernen sich durch fortschreitende Partizipation in der komplexen Lernumgebung von KiP zu bewegen (Gerstenmaier & Mandl 2001). Aus diesen Überlegungen ist weiters zu folgern, dass mit zunehmender Projektdauer die Lehrer/-innen mehr Rollensicherheit gewinnen. In den weiteren Analysen der Prozessdaten wird zu klären sein, welche Anteile an der Passung den verschiedenen Elementen des KiP-Modells zukommen.

Literaturangaben

ALTRICHER, H. & POSCH, P.: Lehrerinnen und Lehrer erforschen ihren Unterricht. – Bad Heilbrunn: Klinkhardt, 2007.

ARNOLD, M.: Disziplin und Initiation. Die kulturellen Praktiken der Wissenschaft. In: Arnold M. & Fischer, R. (Hrsg.): Disziplinierungen. Kulturen der Wissenschaft im Vergleich, S. 18-52. - Wien: Turia + Kant, 2004.

FISCHLER, H. & SCHRÖDER, H.J.: Fachdidaktisches Coaching für Lehrende in der Physik. Zeitschrift für Didaktik der Naturwissenschaften, 9/2003, S. 43-62.

FLICK, U. (Hg.): Qualitative Evaluationsforschung: Konzepte, Methoden, Umsetzungen. – Reinbek bei Hamburg: Rowohlt Taschenbuch Verlag, 2006.

GERSTENMAIER, J. & MANDL, H.: Methodologie und Empirie zum Situierten Lernen (Forschungsbericht Nr. 137). – München: Ludwig-Maximilians-Universität, Lehrstuhl für Empirische Pädagogik und Pädagogische Psychologie, 2001.

GOODNOUGH, K.: Moving Science Off the "Back Burner": Meaning Making Within an Action Research Community of Practice. Journal of Science Teacher Education, 19/2008, S. 15-39.

GREENO, J. G., COLLINS, A. M. & RESNICK, L. B.: Cognition and learning. In: Calfee, R. C. (Ed.): Handbook of Educational Psychology, S. 15-46. - New York: MacMillan Co, 1996.

KATTMANN, U., DUIT, R. ET AL.: Das Modell der Didaktischen Rekonstruktion - Ein Rahmen für naturwissenschaftsdidaktische Forschung und Entwicklung. Zeitschrift für Didaktik der Naturwissenschaften, 3(3)/1997, S. 3-18.

LIPOWSKY, F.: Was macht Fortbildungen für Lehrkräfte erfolgreich? Befunde der Forschung und mögliche Konsequenzen für die Praxis. Die Deutsche Schule, 96(4)/2004, S. 462-479.

MAYRING, P.: Qualitative Inhaltsanalyse. Grundlagen und Techniken. – Weinheim und Basel: Beltz Verlag, 2007.

RADITS, F.: Umweltbildung rund um den Bauernhof: Integration von Fachausbildung, Schulpraxis und Forschendem Lernen. In: Posch, P., Rauch, F. & Kreis, I: Bildung für Nachhaltigkeit, S. 189-212. – Innsbruck: Studienverlag, 2000.

RADITS, F. & RAUCH, F.: Wissenschaft ruft Schule. Forschungs-Bildungs-Kooperationen als Forschungsfeld – Explorationen aus der Perspektive von Science Education. In: Eder, F. & Hörl, G.: Gerechtigkeit und Effizienz im Bildungswesen: Unterricht, Schulentwicklung und LehrerInnenbildung als professionelle Handlungsfelder. – Wien: Lit Verlag, 2008.

WEINGART, P.: From „Finalization" to „Mode 2": old wine in new bottles? In: Social Science Information, 36(4)/1997, S. 591-613.

WENGER, E.: Communities of practice: a brief introduction. 2004. http://www.ewenger.com/theory/communities_of_practice_intro_WRD.doc) 29.9.2008.

WINDSCHITL, M.: Framing Constructivism in Practice as the Negotiation of Dilemmas: An Analysis of the Conceptual, Pedagogical, Cultural, and Political Challenges Facing Teachers. Review of Educational Research Summer, 72(2)/2002, S. 131-175.

Kontakt:
Franz RADITS: franz.radits@univie.ac.at
Christine HEIDINGER: christine.heidinger@univie.ac.at

Der Lehrer als *Spiritus movens* des Fremdsprachenunterrichts

Mirjana Pehar, Universität Zadar, Kroatien

Das Grundziel des Fremdsprachenunterrichts ist die Aneignung der Kommunikationsfähigkeit auf pragmatischer Ebene. Dies schließt sowohl Kenntnisse von sprachlichen Inhalten als auch Wissen über die kulturellen Gegebenheiten des Zielsprachenlandes ein. Um den Unterricht so erfolgreich wie möglich zu gestalten, sollte der sprachlich kompetente und selbstbewusste Lehrer allen Neuerungen im Fremdsprachenunterricht gegenüber Offenheit und einen inneren Beweggrund zeigen, sich mit neuen Ideen auseinander setzen zu wollen, ihre positiven Seiten zu schätzen wissen und sie, soweit es die Umstände erlauben, zur Anwendung zu bringen. Er soll bei der Fremdsprachenvermittlung die kognitiven und affektiven Bedürfnisse sowie die unterschiedliche Leistungsfähigkeit der Schüler berücksichtigen, womit er jedem ermöglicht, sich im Rahmen seiner Fähigkeiten mit Freude und Erfolg die von ihm ausgewählte Fremdsprache anzueignen, die zur Erweiterung seines Wissenshorizonts und zur Persönlichkeitsbildung beiträgt. Der Lehrer sollte motivationsfördernd wirken und versuchen, durch Lob und Unterstützung ein Vertrauensverhältnis zu seiner Gruppe aufzubauen und für ein positives Klima sorgen: seine Schüler ermutigen und ihren Erfolg bestätigen, in ihnen den Geist der Zusammenarbeit wecken, kurz gesagt, er soll der spiritus[7] movens[8] im Fremdsprachenunterricht sein und jede angstverursachende Situation vermeiden. Dabei sollte er ständig über neue Lehr- und Lernformen nachdenken und sich das bisherige Lehrer-Schüler-Verhältnis bewusst machen und gegebenenfalls ändern. Um aktuellen Diskussionen in der heutigen schülerorientierten Pädagogik gerecht zu werden, müssen in der Lehrerausbildung viele Lücken geschlossen werden, vor allem fehlende oder unzureichende Kenntnisse der Kultur des Zielsprachenlandes und neuerer Arbeitsformen (Gruppendynamik u.ä) sowie mangelndes Wissen darüber, wie die Bedürfnisse der Schüler geweckt werden können, wie sie animiert werden sollen und vieles mehr.

Schlüsselbegriffe: Fremdsprachenunterricht, Kommunikation, Zielsprache, Persönlichkeitsbildung

---

[7] *Spiritus*, der; -, -; aus lat. *spiritus* „(Luft)hauch, Atem, Leben, Seele, Geist" zu *spirare* „(be)hauchen, atmen": Hauch, Atem, [Lebens]geist; Spiritus Rector: belebender Geist, treibende Kraft, Seele (z.B. eines Betriebes, Vorhabens), In: Duden, Das große Fremdwörterbuch, 3., überarbeitete Auflage 2003, S. 1269.

[8] *Movens,* das; -; zu lat. *movens,* Part. Präs. von *movere* ...: Beweggrund, Antriebskraft. In: ibidem, S. 901.

1 Die Lehrerrolle in der Geschichte des Fremdsprachenunterrichts

In der Geschichte des Fremdsprachenunterrichts waren dem Lehrer jeweils unterschiedliche Rollen zugeteilt. Erst seit der zweiten Hälfte des 19. Jahrhunderts kann man von systematischem bzw. institutionalisiertem Fremdsprachenunterricht sprechen, in dem es oft zu einem Wechsel in der Methodologie kam: Fremdsprachenlehrer musste sich stets aufs Neue den veränderten Anforderungen anpassen. Man schätzt, dass im 19. Jh. weniger als ein Prozent der Bevölkerung Fremdsprachen kannte (vgl. Mair/Meter 1981, S. 17). Im Unterricht dominierten die klassischen Sprachen, da das Lernziel die Herausbildung des logischen Denkens und die Disziplinierung des Geistes war. Es war wichtig, die Kultur- und Geistesgeschichte eines Volkes darzustellen, und im Mittelpunkt des Unterrichts stand die Lektüre. Die Rolle des Lehrers bestand darin, die Schüler für die Übersetzung von Texten ausgewählter literarischer Werke aus der Fremdsprache in die Muttersprache und umgekehrt zu befähigen. Das methodische Verfahren, nach welchem damals gearbeitet wurde, war die *klassische, traditionelle* bzw. *Grammatik-Übersetzungs-Methode.*

Ende des 19. Jahrhunderts kam es zu Veränderungen in der Methodologie des Fremdsprachenunterrichts und damit verbunden zur Entwicklung der *direkten Methode.* Ziel war nun die Befähigung der Schüler für die praktische Anwendung der Sprache. Das Erlernen der Fremdsprache sollte wie das Erlernen der Muttersprache im Wesentlichen durch Zuhören und strikte Durchführung des Prinzips der Einsprachigkeit verlaufen. Der Lehrer diente als Sprachmodell, welches die Schüler nachzuahmen hatten, wobei er fließend und akzentfrei sprechen können musste.

Unter Einfluss der strukturalistischen Linguistik und der behavioristischen Lernpsychologie entstand nach dem 2. Weltkrieg die *audiolinguale Methode*, die durch Strukturübungen und das Skinnersche Konzept charakterisiert ist. Die Rolle des Lehrers bestand darin, die in den Satzmusterübungen *(pattern drill)* eingebettete Grammatik zu präsentieren und die Schüler vor allem zum Hören und Sprechen, weniger zum Lesen und Schreiben zu befähigen.

Als Weiterentwicklung der audiolingualen Methode entwickelte sich die *audiovisuelle Methode*, in der die Medien als integraler Bestandteil der Methode selbst sind. Als typisches Beispiel für die Technisierung des Unterrichts wäre die von P. GUBERINA entwickelte *audiovisuelle-strukturo-globale Methode* zu nennen. Der Lehrer musste die technischen Hilfsmittel gut bedienen und den vorprogrammierten Ablauf des Unterrichts überwachen können, während der Schüler dagegen mehr oder weniger inaktiv war (vgl. Mair/Meter 1981, S. 59). Der Lernprozess gestaltete sich nicht mehr als Interaktion zwischen Lernenden und Lehrer, sondern beschränkte sich auf die einseitige Relation Maschine-Mensch.

In den 70er Jahren spielte die Pragmalinguistik eine derart entscheidende Rolle, dass es zu einer Neuorientierung in der Fremdsprachendidaktik und -methodik kam, was sich unumgänglich auch auf die Lehrerolle auswirkte. Pragmalinguistik betrachtet die Sprache nicht als System sprachlicher Formen, sondern als einen Aspekt menschlichen Handelns, als zwischenmenschliche Kommunikation. Da in jeder Kommunikation eine Beziehung enthalten ist, d.h. jeder Beziehungspartner sie auf seine Weise zu gestalten sucht, reagiert der andere in seiner eigenen Art und bestätigt oder verwirft sie (vgl. Watzlavick/ Beavin/Jackson 1982, S. 127). Sprache kann man nicht als Verhaltensprogrammierung betrachten, wie dies die behavioristische Lerntheorie betrieb, sondern sie ist ein bewusster, kognitiver und kreativer Vorgang. Das Ziel des Unterrichts war nicht nur die Befähigung zur alltäglichen Kommunikation, sondern auch die Entwicklung von fremdsprachlichen Fertigkeiten (Hören, Sprechen, Lesen und Schreiben) in der Fremdsprache.

Die Begegnung mit einer fremden Sprache ist zugleich die Begegnung mit einer fremden Welt, was zur Persönlichkeitsbildung des Schülers und zur Erweiterung seines Erfahrungshorizonts beiträgt, gerade so, wie dies HUMBOLDT in seinen Schriften betonte: „Die Sprache ist gleichsam die äußerliche Erscheinung des Geistes der Völker; ihre Sprache ist ihr Geist, und ihr Geist ist ihre Sprache; man kann sich beide nie identisch genug denken (...).“ (vgl. Humboldt 1973, S. 33ff.). Dieses so wichtige von Humboldt aufgestellte Prinzip der inneren Sprachform wurde im Fremdsprachenunterricht erst ein Jahrhundert später anerkannt. Mit seiner Verwirklichung begann man in den 70er Jahren, und zwar zunächst mit dem pragmatisch-funktionalen und später vor allem mit dem interkulturellen Konzept, das sich seit der Mitte der 80er Jahre wesentlich weiterentwickelte. Man war bestrebt, die enge Beziehung der inneren und der äußeren Sprachform zum Ausdruck zu bringen. Die innere Form zeigt sich im Wortschatz, in seinem etymologischen Aufbau und seiner Semantik, der auch die Kulturbedeutung innewohnt; und das alles widerspiegelt sich in der äußeren Form.

Damit ist das didaktische Problem umrissen und es kommt auf die Durchführung an, wie der Lehrer den Schülern auf jeder Stufe der Spracherlernung das Sichtbare (die Form) und das Geistige (den Inhalt) angemessen vermittelt, damit sie dies als eine Einheit empfinden können. Die Einprägung des Wortschatzes bietet den Schülern die Möglichkeit, dem Wirken des Sprachgeistes nachzuspüren und zugleich das Vokabellernen, welches als Rückgrat des Fremdsprachenunterrichts zu betrachten ist, anregend zu gestalten (vgl. Bohlen 1966, S. 175).

Um all diesen neu gesetzten Forderungen im Fremdsprachenunterricht gerecht zu werden, muss der Fremdsprachenlehrer solche Vermittlungsmethoden anwenden, die ihm ermöglichen, das gesetzte Ziel zu erreichen. Das erweiterte Konzept des kommunikativen Unterrichts hält den Schüler an, sich mit Gegebenheiten der fremden Kultur auseinanderzusetzen, die als ein wichtiger Faktor für lerner- bzw. schülerzentrierten Fremdsprachenunterricht erkannt wurde (vgl. Krumm 1986, S. 124). Die angemessene Auseinandersetzung mit den Schülern muss im schülerzentrierten Unterricht ihren Platz auf verschiedenen Ebenen finden und der Fremdsprachenlehrer muss sich dessen bewusst sein, dass der Schüler *ganzheitlich*, d.h. im *kognitiven, affektiven* und *motorischen Bereich* in den Lernprozess einbezogen werden muss, was sagen will, dass jeder *Kopf, Herz* und *Hände* hat, um seine Fähigkeit im *Denken, Fühlen* und *Schaffen* bestätigen zu können und zu wollen, jeder nach seinen Fähigkeiten und Möglichkeiten. Ihre eigenen Erfahrungen sollen sie in den Unterricht einbringen und lernen, aufeinander einzugehen, miteinander zu arbeiten, kooperativ zu sein, die Verantwortung für die Arbeit zu übernehmen, und all das soll der Lehrer fördern und aus seinem inneren Beweggrund her in ihnen den Lebensgeist und Freude für das Andersartige, Fremde und Neue wecken, kurz er soll sich seiner Rolle als *spiritus movens* des Fremdsprachenunterrichts stets bewusst sein. All dies werden die Schüler erreichen können, wenn es dem Lehrer gelingt, sie zu motivieren, im Unterricht mitzumachen, denn das verstärkte Interesse am Lernen äußert sich im Einbezug wissenschaftlicher Erkenntnisse zur Motivation, zu Lernstrategien, zu Lernersprache und zu Fragen bestimmter Lernertypen (vgl. Düwell 1995, S. 167). Deshalb erscheint es angebracht, etwas mehr über den Einfluss des Lehrers auf die Schülermotivation zu sagen.

2 Der motivationale Einfluss des Lehrers auf die Schülermotivation

Die Motivation stellt den entscheidendsten Faktor bei der Fremdsprachenvermittlung dar. Sie ist ein wesentliches und bestimmendes Element bei der Erlernung einer Fremdsprache. Gelingt es dem Lehrer nicht, seine Schüler zu motivieren, ist sein Bemühen zum Scheitern verurteilt, auch wenn er die besten Methoden anwendet. Obwohl unterschiedliche Motivationstheorien zu unterscheiden sind, sind sie in der Praxis miteinander verwoben und gehen ineinander über (vgl. Maier 1991, S. 51). Entscheidend für die Motivation ist der Schüler selbst, die ehrliche Überzeugung des Lehrers und sein persönlicher Einsatz, so dass auch die beste Technik kein Ersatz für einen guten Lehrer und echten Pädagogen sein kann. Als wichtigste Motive, die für die Motivation im Fremdsprachenunterricht eine Rolle spielen, sind folgende zu nennen:

- das Gesellschaftsmotiv – Das Lernen einer Fremdsprache wird als gesellschaftliche Notwendigkeit im engeren und weiteren Sinne verstanden.
- das Elternmotiv – Man lernt eine Fremdsprache, um den Eltern eine Freude zu machen.
- das Nützlichkeitsmotiv – Das Lernen von Fremdsprachen wird mit dem Nutzen für das spätere Leben und den Beruf begründet.
- das Lehrermotiv – Man lernt eine Fremdsprache, um dem Lehrer zu gefallen oder sich mit ihm zu identifizieren.
- das Wissensmotiv – beinhaltet das Streben nach neuem Wissen, neuen Erfahrungen und Erkenntnissen.
- das Kommunikationsmotiv – stellt das Bedürfnis zu kommunizieren dar.
- das Geltungsmotiv – stellt das Streben nach Anerkennung und Achtung in der Gemeinschaft dar (vgl. ibidem, S. 52).

Die hier aufgezählten Motive werden nach Gardner und Lambert in zwei gegensätzliche Motivationspaare geordnet, die sie als *integrative* und *instrumentale Motivation* bezeichnen. Der Schüler ist integrativ motiviert, wenn er sich mit den Angehörigen der fremden Kultur identifizieren kann und wenn er deren Sprache als ein Tor zu ihrer Kultur und Gesellschaft betrachtet. Instrumentell motiviert ist derjenige, der größeren beruflichen Erfolg erreichen will.

Wenn man davon ausgeht, dass die in der Schule erworbenen Einstellungen und Verhaltensmuster das Verhalten der Schüler oft bis in das Erwachsenenalter bestimmen können, fällt dem Lehrer eine sehr ernst zu nehmende Rolle im Unterricht zu. Der Schüler versucht den Lehrer als sprachliches Vorbild zu imitieren und sich mit ihm zu identifizieren. Je positiver sich die Beziehung zwischen Lehrer und Schüler gestaltet, umso ausgeprägter wird die Identifikation sein. All dies hängt vom Lehrer und seiner Motivation ab, seiner Einstellung zur betreffenden Fremdsprache und Kultur sowie von seiner fremdsprachlichen Kompetenz. Um den Erfordernissen nachzukommen, sollte der Lehrer sich selbst bewerten und hinsichtlich seines Erziehungsstils einordnen können. Dazu helfen ihm einige von Schiffler angeführte Kriterien.

Dominativer (autokratischer) Erziehungsstil	*Integrativer – sozialorientierter Erziehungsstil*
1. Unfreundliche, verständnislose ungeduldige Äußerungen 2. Persönlich gehaltene Verbote 3. Direkt abschlägige Antworten 4. Aufforderung zur Aufmerksamkeit 5. Willkürliche Strafen 6. Aufforderung, begonnene Sätze zu wiederholen 7. Drohung 8. Setzen von Bedingungen 9. Demütigende Äußerungen 10. Aufforderungen und Befehle	1. Freundliche, verständnisvolle geduldige Äußerungen 2. Unpersönlich gehaltene Verbote 3. Nützliche Hinweise 4. Anregung zum Selbsttun 5. Strafen als natürliche Konsequenz 6. Hilfen beim Formulieren 7. Sachliche und konstruktive Kritik 8. Lobende Äußerungen 9. Alle übrigen Bestätigungen 10. Verbalisierung kindlicher Vorgänge

(vgl. Schiffler, in: Maier 1991, S. 61).

Diese für die Motivation entscheidenden Kriterien sind für den Lehrer sehr wichtig, weil sie ihm helfen, Einblick in seine pädagogischen und methodisch-didaktischen Fortschritte zu bekommen. Da davon auszugehen ist, dass nicht jeder Schüler von seinem Elternhaus die gleiche Einstellung zur Fremdsprache mitbekommt, muss der Lehrer differenziert auf die individuelle Wesensart jedes Einzelnen achten und ihn nach seinen Fähigkeiten sprachlich fordern. Die unmittelbare Erfolgsbestätigung erleichtert den Lernprozess und wirkt besonders bei den jüngeren Schülern sehr motivierend.

3 Das Idealbild des professionellen Fremdsprachenlehrers von heute

Um einen guten Fremdsprachenunterricht auf allen Stufen zu erreichen, müssen einige wichtige Bedingungen erfüllt werden. Die Grundvoraussetzung dafür ist eine gute sprachliche, fachliche und pädagogische Ausbildung des Lehrers, der die wichtigste Rolle im Unterricht spielt. Seiner aktiven Sprachkompetenz kommt besondere Achtung zu, denn er agiert und bewegt die Schüler zur Aktion, er ist diejenige Antriebskraft, der Spiritus Movens, der in keinem Unterricht fehlen kann. Im Idealbild des professionellen Fremdsprachenlehrers vereinigen sich wesentliche Elemente der vorangegangenen Lehrerbilder. Seine Ausbildung soll immer *berufsorientiert* (lehrend, erziehend, beratend, beurteilend, innovierend), *wissenschaftsorientiert* (studierend, sich informierend und weiterbildend) und *gesellschaftsorientiert* sein (vgl. Sauer 1995, S. 174). In der produktiven Phase der Spracherlernung soll der Schüler die Initiative ergreifen; der Lehrer tritt in den Hintergrund, gibt klare Anweisungen und stimuliert die Ausdrucksfähigkeit der Sprechenden. Er sorgt für eine entspannte Lernatmosphäre, in der die Schüler ihre sprachlichen Hemmungen verlieren und lernen, selbstständig und spontan die Fremdsprache zu gebrauchen. Das Lernen soll als angenehme und befriedigende Tätigkeit empfunden werden. Zugleich bewegt er die anderen Schüler dazu nachzudenken, zu zweifeln, ihre Meinung zu äußern, zu diskutieren; er weckt das Interesse und sorgt dafür, dass sprachlich schwächere und fortgeschrittenere Schüler gemeinsam lernen, weil dadurch emotionales und intellektuelles Verhalten gefördert wird (vgl. Baur 1990, S. 144). Für wichtig halten wir an dem idealen Bild des professionellen Fremdsprachenlehrers alles, was sich im Rahmen der persönlichen Beziehungen abspielt. Um ein gutes Klima in der Klasse zu begünstigen, vermeidet der Lehrer Frontalunterricht, regt die Schüler zu wechselnden Interaktionsformen an, organisiert Partner- und Gruppenarbeit und steuert gruppendynamische Prozesse. In der Gruppenarbeit bekommen die Schüler das Gefühl, von der Gruppe unterstützt und angenommen zu werden. Das gesteuerte Lernen in der Gruppe ermöglicht den Schülern, durch die Hilfe des Lehrers oder durch andere Mitschüler schnell und leicht zu fehlenden Bedeutungen zu kommen, da es für den Fremdsprachenunterricht unökonomisch ist, den Schüler über längere Zeit nach einer möglichen Sprachstruktur suchen zu lassen, statt zu erlauben, dass dies entweder ein anderer Mitschüler sagt oder er das Gewünschte in der Muttersprache äußert.

4 Schlussfolgerung und Perspektiven

Der Lehrer sollte allen Neuerungen im Fremdsprachenunterricht gegenüber Offenheit zeigen, sich mit neuen Ideen auseinander setzen, ihre positiven Seiten zu schätzen wissen und sie zur Anwendung bringen. Derjenige Lehrer, der seinen Unterricht anders gestalten will, verändert dabei auch sein eigenes Lehrverhalten und versucht aus dem ‚herkömmlichen Verhalten' (vgl. Baur

1990, S. 106) auszubrechen und die Schüler zur Selbstständigkeit und zum autonomen Lernen zu befähigen. Effektiv ist der Unterricht erst dann, wenn der Lehrer die Schüler dazu befähigt, selbstständig ihre Kenntnisse in der Fremdsprache zu erweitern und sich mit der Zielsprachenkultur auseinander zu setzen.

Die Beschleunigung der Wissensvermehrung und des sozialen Wandels führt heute dazu, dass ein Hochschulstudium nicht mehr für einen lebenslang ausgeübten Beruf vorbilden kann, sondern auf viele Berufsfelder vorbereiten muss. Deshalb sollte die Frage der Weiterbildung unentbehrlicher Gegenstand der gesellschaftlichen Verantwortung sein, da nur wenige Lehrer einen längeren Auslandsaufenthalt im Zielsprachenland verbracht haben, der sie sprachlich und landeskundlich-interkulturell auszubilden vermag. Sich lebenslang weiterzubilden sollte der Lehrer als Notwendigkeit und als Aufgabe verstehen, um sich stets als diejenige Antriebskraft, als *spiritus movens* im Fremdsprachenunterricht beweisen zu können. Darunter ist gemeint, dass der Lehrer sich dessen stets bewusst sein sollte, dass seine Spracharbeit gleichzeitig auch Kulturarbeit ist, denn der Fremdsprachenunterricht ist heute kulturwissenschaftlich und interkulturell orientiert, und er dazu noch viele Erfahrungen aus dem Bereich der Gruppenpädagogik, Gesprächsführung, Menschenkenntnisse sowie eine hohe Eigenmotivation in den Unterricht mitbringen muss.

Die an den Hochschulen ausgebildeten Fremdsprachenlehrer sollen nicht glauben, dass sie mit beendetem Studium ihre Ausbildung tatsächlich abgeschlossen haben. Vielmehr dient das Studium als Wegbereiter für ihren künftigen Beruf und später dann als Wegweiser zur Weiterbildung und Vorbereitung auf das lebenslange begleitende Lernen, vor allem im didaktisch-methodischen Bereich, in dem sich vieles so schnell ändert. Deshalb ist es wichtig, den Lehrern mehrere kurzfristigere Weiterbildungsmöglichkeiten anzubieten, damit sie sich in ihrem Lehrbereich autonom und sicher bewegen können. Das Ziel ist also die Förderung der Fachkompetenz und deren Fähigkeiten und Fertigkeiten sowohl für den beruflichen Alltag als auch zu kreativem Denken und Arbeiten (vgl. Fries 1996, S. 38). Die Rolle des Lehrers in der Klasse muss deshalb neu bestimmt und definiert werden, wobei die Lehrerweiterbildung als gesamtgesellschaftliche, gesetzlich festgelegte Verantwortung angesehen werden soll, damit er seine Rolle als diejenige im Fremdsprachenunterrichts so nötige treibende Kraft, als *spiritus movens* auch bestätigen kann.

Literaturangaben

BAUR, RUPPRECHT S. (1990): Superlearning und Suggestopädie, Langenscheidt, Berlin/ München.

BOHLEN, ADOLF (1966): Methodik des neusprachlichen Unterrichts, Heidelberg.

DUDEN (2003): Das große Fremdwörterbuch, 3. überarbeitete Auflage.

DÜWELL, HENNING (1995): „Der Fremdsprachenlerner", In: Handbuch Fremdsprachenunterricht, Tübingen/Basel, S. 166-171.

FRIES, MARLENE (1996): „Probleme wissenschaftlicher Weiterbildung", In: Jahrbuch DaF, Bd. 22, München, iudicium, S. 29-55.

HUMBOLDT, VON WILHELM (1974): „Über die Verschiedenheit des menschlichen Sprachbaues", In. Documenta Semiotika, Hildesheim, Georg Olms Verlag.

KRUMM, HANS JÜRGEN (1986): Lehrerfortbildung im Bereich DaF, München, Goethe-Institut.

KRUMM, HANS JÜRGEN (1995): „Der Fremdsprachenlehrer", In: Handbuch Fremdsprachenunterricht, Tübingen /Basel, S. 475-480.

MAIER, WOLFGANG (1991): Fremdsprachen in der Grundschule, Berlin/ München, Langenscheidt.

MAIR, W./METTER, H. (1981): Fremdsprachenunterricht wozu?, Tübingen, Gunter Narr.

NEUNER, G./ HUNFELD, H. (1993): Methoden des fremdsprachlichen Deutschunterrichts, Berlin/ München/ Wien/ Zürich/ NewYork, Langenscheidt.

SAUER, HELMUT (1995): „Der Fremdsprachenlehrer", In: Handbuch Fremdsprachenunterricht, Tübingen/ Basel, S. 171-175.

WATZLAWICK, P./BEAVIN, J./JACKSON, D. (1982): Menschliche Kommunikation, Bonn/ Stuttgart/ Wien.

Kontakt:

Dr. Mirjana PEHAR: mpehar@unizd.hr

Unterrichtsqualität und Professionalisierung von Fremdsprachenlehrern

Věra Janíková, Pavel Zlatníček, Masaryk-Universität Brno,
Tschechische Republik

Sowohl in den Fachdiskussionen, als auch in der Öffentlichkeit herrscht Übereinstimmung, dass unter dem Gesichtspunkt der Qualitätssicherung des unterrichtlichen Geschehens die Lehrer/-innen mit ihren fachlichen und persönlichen Qualifikationen eine entscheidende Rolle spielen. Die Qualitätssicherung im fremdsprachlichen Unterricht gehört heutzutage zu den Mainstreams der europäischen Sprachenpolitik und fordert nachdrücklich professionell ausgebildete Lehrkräfte, deren Qualifikationen den gegenwärtigen sowie den künftigen Anforderungen der modernen Gesellschaft bezüglich der Sprachkenntnisse ihrer Bürger entsprechen. Im Beitrag wird in Bezug auf die Förderung der Professionalisierung der Fremdsprachenlehrer/-innen anhand der theoretischen Ausgangssituation sowie empirischer Befunde nach den Antworten auf mehrere Fragen gesucht. Die zentralen Fragestellungen lauten: Was kann die Aus- und Fortbildung dazu beitragen? Wie charakterisieren die Lehramtstudierenden einen guten und professionell ausgebildeten Fremdsprachenlehrer? Finden wir in der Praxis eine Lehrkraft, die dem Idealbild entspricht?
Anm: im Text werden Lehrerinnen und Lehrer als „Lehrer" bezeichnet.

Schlüsselbegriffe: Unterrichtsqualität, Qualitätssicherung, Professionaliierung von Fremdsprachenlehrern

1 Zur Unterrichtsqualität

Der Begriff *Qualität* (aus dem Lateinischen: *qualitas*) wurde früher eher mit dem Wirtschaftsmanagement verbunden. In den letzten Jahren setzt er sich in erhöhtem Ausmaß auch in der Bildung durch. Die Fragen über Unterrichtsqualität werden zu zentralen Themen der bildungspolitischen, fachwissenschaftlichen sowie schulinternen Diskussionen, wobei aber immer betont werden muss, dass der Prozess der Qualitätssicherung im Unterricht mit der Wirtschaft kaum zu vergleichen ist, denn „für viele im pädagogischen Bereich Tätige unterliegt Bildung nicht denselben Gesetzen wie irgendeine Handelsware" (Handt 2003, S. 390). Helmke (2003) fügt dazu, dass der Begriff Qualität in Bildungskontexten sehr unterschiedliche Bedeutungen hat, die dann sehr differenzierte Analysen der Qualitätssicherung und -entwicklung forcieren:

- „Qualität als *Beschaffenheit* eines Gegenstandes (z.B. des unterrichtlichen Angebots) oder Phänomens; etwa im Sinne von *qualitativen Merkmalen*, also beschreibend und nicht wertend),
- Qualität im Sinne von *Exzellenz*, als Bezeichnung für die Güte. Damit liegt ein (wenn er auch implizit sein kann) Maßstab zugrunde, es handelt sich um eine normative Aussage; der Begriff wird also „zur einschätzenden, objektivierten Bewertung der Güte, des Wertes oder des allgemeinen Niveaus eines Objektes verwendet" (Helmke 2003, S. 40).

In den fachlichen Diskussionen über die Unterrichtsqualität wird im Allgemeinen u.a. betont, dass man der Gefahr der Vereinfachung und Trivialisierung des relevanten Wissens entgehen sollte. In der unten angeführten Graphik *Angebots-Nutzungs-Modell des Unterrichts* (siehe Grafik 1) bietet HELMKE ein Rahmenmodell an, „das unser gegenwärtiges Wissen über Bedingungen, Vernetztheit und Konsequenzen des Unterrichts darstellt und dadurch eine Hilfe leistet, das Thema *guter Unterricht* kurzschlüssig auf nur wenige Elemente im gesamten Wirkungsprozess zu beschränken" (Helmke 2006, S. 2).

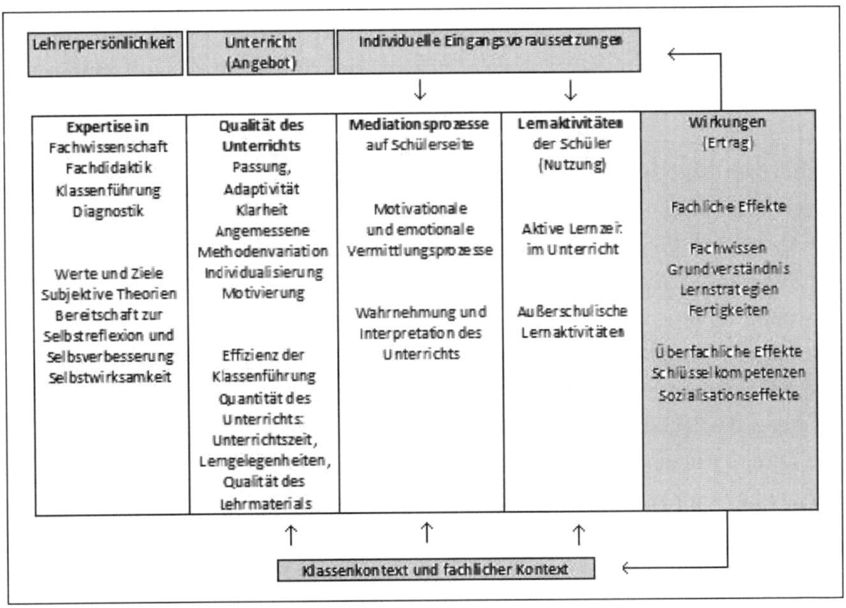

Grafik 1: Angebots-Nutzungs-Modell des Unterrichts

Grafik 1 macht transparent, dass die Unterrichtsqualität von mehreren Faktoren beeinflusst wird, die ein unterschiedliches Ausmaß an Wechselwirkung aufweisen. Die Faktoren lassen sich für ihre präzisere Abgrenzung sowie eine überschaubare Orientierung in der ganzen Problematik in drei Gruppen aufteilen:

Ein Faktorenkomplex, der sich auf

- die *Lehrenden* bezieht (ihre persönlichen, fachlichen und fachdidaktischen Qualifikationen),
- den *Unterricht* bezieht,
- wechselseitige *Wirkungen* von beiden oben angeführten Faktoren bezieht.

Auf die Unterrichtsqualität können allerdings auch andere Faktoren einen wichtigen Einfluss haben, die sich als *unterrichtsexterne Faktoren* bezeichnen lassen können, wie z. B. der allgemeine bildungspolitische sowie der institutionelle Rahmen. Eine ausführlichere Auflistung von solchen Faktoren, die die Unterrichtsqualität beeinflussen, führen wir am Beispiel des fremdsprachlichen Unterrichts an.

2 Fremdsprachenunterricht und Qualität

„Stellt man die Frage, warum der Qualität des fremdsprachlichen Unterrichts in den letzten Jahren eine so hohe Aufmerksamkeit gewidmet wird, kann man sie in Kürze folgendermaßen beantworten: In der heutigen *enger* werdenden Welt spielen die sprachlichen Kenntnisse eine besonders wichtige Rolle. Die Tatsache, dass Englisch schon heutzutage als *lingua franca* verstanden und auch in steigendem Maße verwendet wird, kann man aus sprachökonomischen und pragmatischen Gründen teilweise positiv sehen. Wenn man aber die kulturelle Vielfalt und die Bildungsfunktion des Fremdsprachenlernens in Bezug auf die Erweiterung des persönlichen Horizonts und die Teilhabe an anderen Kulturen betrachtet, scheint die Forderung der europäischen Sprachenpolitik nach der Beherrschung von mindestens drei Sprachen durchaus logisch zu sein. Und nur das Unterrichtsgeschehen, das das Fremdsprachenlernen effizient sowie attraktiv macht, kann die Chance aufgreifen, den sich veränderten Anforderung an den Fremdsprachenunterricht gerecht zu werden“ (Janíková 2009a, S. 35).

Was kommt in Bezug auf die Qualität des fremdsprachlichen Unterrichts in Frage? Es zeigt sich, „dass es sich um mehrere Bereiche der Prozesse von Fremdsprachenlehren und -lernen handelt: seien es besonders effiziente Methoden, das Herausfinden der Bedürfnisse des Sprachlerners, die professionelle Aus- und Fortbildung, der Sprachlehrer – überall sieht man Bemühungen das Erlernen einer Sprache so einfach, angemessen und gut wie möglich zu machen. Die Qualitätssicherung betrifft heutzutage auch bisher ziemlich getrennte Bereiche in einem System" (Janíková 2009a, S. 35), die als eher unterrichtsexterne und eher unterrichtsinterne zu bezeichnen sind. In Bezug auf den Fremdsprachenunterricht spricht LIEBALD (2000, zit. in Handt 2003, S. 391) von der:

- *Einrichtungsqualität* (Schulorganisation, Personal, Arbeitszufriedenheit, Arbeitsklima, Kommunikation und Kooperation, Unterrichtsräume, Recht und Finanzierung, Entwicklung und Qualitätssicherung),
- *Programmqualität* (Konzeption der Aus- und Weiterbildungseinrichtung; curriculare Planung, curriculare Grundlagen),
- *Planungsqualität* (sog. Input-Output im Hinblick auf die eingesetzten Ressourcen: institutioneller Rahmen, Personal, Organisation, Technik),
- *Erfolgsqualität* (Effektivität, Zufriedenheit, Wirkungen im gesellschaftlichen Umfeld),
- *pädagogischen Qualität* (Kompetenz der Unterrichtenden, Begleitung der Lehrenden und Lernenden, Lernprozess, Lern- und Lehrziele, Lehr- und Lernmaterialien, Unterrichtsmethoden, Lernerzentriertheit, Evaluation, Feedback),
- *Durchführungs-Qualität* (sog. Prozess-Qualität oder Lernereignis).

Zu eher *unterrichtsexternen Faktoren* gehören: Einrichtungsqualität, Programmqualität, Planungsqualität und Erfolgsqualität. Als eher *unterrichtsinterne Faktoren* sind die pädagogische Qualität und die Durchführungs-Qualität zu bezeichnen.

2.1 Ein professioneller Fremdsprachenlehrer

Die Diskussion um die Qualität des fremdsprachlichen Unterrichts kann nicht von der Professionalität der Lehrer losgelöst werden. Sowohl in den Fachdiskussionen als auch in der Öffentlichkeit herrscht Übereinstimmung darüber, dass der kompetente und professionell ausgebildete Fremdsprachenlehrer einen entscheidenden Einfluss auf den Unterricht hat. ALLWRIGHT und BALLEY (1991, zit. in Krumm 2003, S. 357) sagen dazu: „Unter dem Gesichtspunkt der Qualitätssicherung spielen Lehrer, ihre Ausbildung, ihre fachlichen und persönlichen Qualifikationen sowie ihr Verhalten eine zentrale Rolle."

Die Konzepte der Fremdsprachenlehrerausbildung setzen im 21. Jahrhundert gute *Traditionen* fort, wobei hier die Unterrichtsqualität und Lehrerprofessionalisierung zu zentralen Themen werden. Von den Fremdsprachenlehrern werden neue Qualifikationen verlangt, die u.a. mit Veränderungen in der Auffassung vom Fremdsprachenlehren und -lernen im Einklang stehen, die sich wiederum im Fremdsprachenunterricht widerspiegeln. Zu nennen sind insbesondere die unten aufgelisteten Entwicklungen, aus denen sich neu formulierte Fremdsprachenlehrerkompetenzen ableiten lassen (vgl. Christ 2002, Krumm 2003, Helmke 2006):

- das „lebensbegleitende" Lernen fremder Sprachen,
- der unverkennbare Wandel der Formen des Fremdsprachenlehrens und -lernens,
- offenes Methodenkonzept und offene Unterrichtsformen,
- die Förderung des autonomen (selbstständigen) Fremdsprachenlernens,
- die Individualisierung/Lernerorientierung,
- die Förderung der Qualitätssicherung.

2.2 Professionalisierung von Fremdsprachenlehrern aus der Sicht der Lehramtsstudierenden

Auf der Suche nach effizienten Modellen der modernen und auf Qualität orientierten Fremdsprachenlehrerausbildung entsteht allmählich eine breite Palette von unterschiedlichen Konzepten, die mittlerweile auch intensiv analysiert und aktualisiert werden. Unser Anliegen liegt aber nicht darin, eine weitere Analyse von diesen Konzepten vorzunehmen, sondern die Kompetenz zur Reflexion über den Fremdsprachenlehrer-Beruf bei den Lehramtsstudierenden zu entwickeln, die einen relevanten Impuls für die Organisation, Inhalte sowie Methoden eines fachdidaktischen Curriculums in der hochschulischen Fremdsprachenlehrerausbildung mitbringen können.

Im Folgenden werden einige Aussagen der Befragten aus einer Pilotuntersuchung vorgestellt, die darauf abzielte, die Vorstellungen der angehenden Fremdsprachenlehrer über die Kompetenzen bzw. Qualifikationen guter/professioneller Lehrer zum Vorschein zu bringen sowie ihre eigenen Schülererfahrungen mit dem Unterricht und konkreten Lehrpersonen zu verknüpfen. Für die Datenerhebung wurde die Inhaltsanalyse als eine der qualitativen Forschungsmethoden verwendet, indem die von den Studierenden geschaffenen Essays analysiert und im Nachhinein dann mit den Befragten diskutiert wurden. Es wurden zwei Aspekte herausgegriffen und zwar die Reflexionen der angehenden Fremdsprachenlehrer über ihre positiv bzw. negativ bewerteten *Lehrerbilder* und Erfahrungen mit dem Fremdsprachenlernen in der Schule sowie ihre Vorstellungen über die guten Fremdsprachenlehrer (vgl. Janíková 2009b).

Positive und negative *Lehrerbilder* und Erfahrungen

- *Der Lehrer erniedrigte die Schüler durch bissige Bemerkungen. Dadurch unterstützte er die Atmosphäre der Angst und der Lernunlust.*
- *Vor jeder Stunde mit Frau Professorin A hatte ich Bauchschmerzen.*
- *Die Stunden bestanden aus den Gereden darüber, was passiert, wenn Herr Professor der Direktor wird.*
- *Ich erinnere mich an verschiedene langweilige Übungen aus den Lernbüchern.*
- *Der Lehrer schimpfte mich fast aus, als ich nach etwas fragen wollte.*
- *Der Deutschkurs sah ungefähr so aus: wir lasen einen Artikel im Lehrbuch. Wir übersetzten den Artikel ins Tschechische. Dann las der Lehrer die Phrasen und Wörter vor, die im Text vorkamen. Aus diesen Phrasen und Wörtern schrieben wir nächste Stunde einen Test. Dann machten wir die Übungen aus dem Lehrbuch. Auf das Sprechen oder das Hören nahm er keine Rücksicht.*
- *Ich hatte eine Lehrerin, die für mich ein Vorbild darstellt und dank ihr studiere ich die Fremdsprache.*
- *Die Englischlehrerin schätzte ich als Menschen. Das war der Hauptgrund dazu, warum ich sie bewunderte. Das führte mich dazu, dass ich ihr Freude machen wollte.*

Erwünschte Qualifikationen guter Fremdsprachenlehrer

- *Für die wichtigsten Voraussetzungen halte ich die Voraussetzungen, die uns an der Uni nicht beigebracht werden können: z.B. Wie man Verhältnis zu den Kindern aufbauen kann? Wie man Konfliktsituationen in der Klasse lösen kann? etc.*
- *Der Lehrer sollte vor allem ein Mensch sein. Der Mensch ist keine Maschine. Er ist also nicht in der Lage, alles perfekt zu machen.*
- *Ich glaube, dass für die Lehrer nicht die Informationsmenge, die sich im Gedächtnis speichern müssen, wichtig ist, sondern das, wie er in der Lage ist, diese Informationsmenge den Schülern zu „verkaufen" oder beizubringen.*
- *Der Fremdsprachenlehrer sollte in der Lage sein, eine Methodenvielfalt zu benutzen, die allgemeine Übersicht zu haben, Kontakt mit den neuen Erkenntnissen in seiner Disziplin zu halten und mit dem Internet umzugehen.*
- *Der Fremdsprachenlehrer sollte die Fremdsprache gut beherrschen und den Unterricht in der Fremdsprache führen.*

- *Der Fremdsprachenlehrer sollte den Schülern den genügenden Raum bieten und er sollte den Schülern die Selbstreflexionsfähigkeit beibringen.*
- *Der Fremdsprachenlehrer braucht Toleranz, Humor, Phantasie und Empathie.*
- *Der Fremdsprachenlehrer sollte auch fähig sein, sich zu eigenen Schwächen zu bekennen.*

3 Schlusswort

Die Qualität des Fremdsprachenunterrichts muss in der Zeit, wo die sprachlichen Grenzen in persönlichen sowie beruflichen Domänen abgeschafft werden, hoch sein. Ein guter (Fremdsprachen)Unterricht ist ein Unterricht mit hohem Wohlbefinden und hohen Lernleistungen. Zu den bedeutsamen Merkmalen für einen solchen Unterricht gehören vor allem: Schülerorientierung, aktives selbstständiges Lernen, Berücksichtigung der Wirkungen, lernförderliche Klassenatmosphäre, bewusster Umgang mit der Heterogenität, Förderung der Schülerkompetenzen sowie Methodenvielfalt. Einen entscheidenden Einfluss auf die Unterrichtsqualität hat eine professionell ausgebildete Lehrerperson. Es besteht kein Zweifel daran, dass es kaum einen idealen Fremdsprachenlehrer gibt. Trotzdem sollten wir uns aber darum bemühen, die Konzepte zur Ausbildung von Fremdsprachenlehrern so zu gestalten, dass die künftigen Unterrichtenden sich diesem Lehrerideal soweit wie möglich annähern können.

Literaturangaben

CHRIST, HERBERT: Fremdsprachenunterricht in neuen Dimensionen im 21. Jahrhundert. In: Neveling, Christiane (Hg.): Perspektiven für die zukünftige Fremdsprachendidaktik. – Tübingen: Gunter Narr Verlag, 2002.

HANDT, GERHARDT, VON DER: Qualitätssicherung und -entwicklung. In: Bausch, Karl-Richard; Christ, Herbert; Krumm, Hans-Jürgen (Hg.): Handbuch Fremdsprachenunterricht, S. 390-394. – Tübingen und Basel: A.Francke Verlag, 2003.

HELMKE, ANDREAS: Unterrichtsqualität erfassen, bewerten, verbessern. – Seelze: Kallmeyersche Verlagsbuchhandlung, 2003.

HELMKE, ANDREAS: Was wissen wir über guten Unterricht? In: Pädagogik Heft 2/2006, S.42-45.

JANÍKOVÁ, VĚRA: Qualität des fremdsprachlichen Unterrichts: ein facettenreicher Begriff. In: JANEBOVÁ, EVA (ed.): Dosahování a hodnocení kvality ve výuce cizích jazyků, S. 33-46. – Praha: Metropolitní univerzita, 2009a.

JANÍKOVÁ, VĚRA: Možnosti a limity oborové didkatiky při kultivaci profesních i lidských kvalit učitele cizích jazyků. In: Rybičková, M.; Hladík, J. (ed.): Škola v proměnách. Učitel a učivo, S. 196-206. – Zlín: Universita Tomáše Bati ve Zlíně, 2009b.

KRUMM, HANS-JÜRGEN: Fremdsprachenlehrer. In: Bausch, Karl-Richard; Christ, Herbert; Krumm, Hans-Jürgen (Hg.): Handbuch Fremdsprachenunterricht, S. 352-358. - Tübingen und Basel: A.Francke Verlag, 2003.

Kontakt:
Doc. PhDr. Věra JANÍKOVÁ, Ph.D.: janikova@ped.muni.cz
Mgr. Pavel ZLATNÍČEK: 160506@muni.cz

MEHRSPRACHIGKEITSKONZEPT UND DESSEN STELLENWERT IN DER AUS- UND FORTBILDUNG VON FREMDSPRACHENLEHRER/-INNE/-N

Alice Brychová, Pädagogische Fakultät MU, Brünn, Tschechische Republik

Seit der Formulierung der neuen curricularen Standards für die Schulen in Tschechien wurde der in Europa bereits viel diskutierte Begriff der Mehrsprachigkeit auch bei uns zu einem aktuellen Thema. Dieses Konzept sollte nicht nur in die schulische Praxis, sondern auch in die Aus- und Fortbildung von Fremdsprachenlehrer/-inne/-n implementiert werden. In dem Beitrag versuchen wir den Begriff Mehrsprachigkeitskonzept abzugrenzen, bildungspolitische Merkmale des Konzeptes vorzustellen und methodisch-didaktische Umsetzungsmöglichkeiten zu beschreiben.

Schlüsselbegriffe: Mehrsprachigkeit, vereintes Europa, Gemeinsamer europäischer Referenzrahmen, kommunikative Kompetenz

1 Mehrsprachigkeit als Erziehungs- und Bildungskonzept in der Theorie und Praxis des Fremdsprachenlernens

In der Theorie des Fremdsprachenunterrichts wurde in den letzten Jahren das Thema Mehrsprachigkeit – einer Forderung, die der Europarat formuliert hat – zu einer neuen Herausforderung im Bereich der Methodik und Didaktik des DaF-Unterrichts. Den Begriff der Mehrsprachigkeit verbinden Lerner und Unterrichtende mit noch nicht ganz klar abgegrenzten Bedeutungen, weil sich viele unter Fremdsprachenunterricht traditionellerweise die Vermittlung nur *einer* Fremdsprache vorstellen. Mit der Entwicklung der Mehrsprachigkeit der

Europäer stellen sich verschiedene Fragen. In welchem Verhältnis steht die europäische Mehrsprachigkeit zur Etablierung einer *Lingua franca*? Wie fördert man Mehrsprachigkeit? In welchem Zusammenhang stehen Sprachenpolitik und Mehrsprachigkeit? Wie sieht Mehrsprachigkeit als erlebte Realität in Schule, Beruf oder Familie aus? Was bedeutet Mehrsprachigkeit als Teil der kulturellen Identität? Welches Potenzial birgt eine Sprachenvielfalt in sich? Natürlich handelt es sich hier um eine vieldimensionale Problematik, die wir im folgenden Text versuchen näher zu beschreiben, wobei der Akzent besonders auf der Aus- und Weiterbildung von Lehrkräften für den DaF-Unterricht in Tschechien liegen wird.

1.1 Begriffsbestimmung

Ein vereintes Europa kann es nur geben, wenn die Kommunikation der Europäer untereinander verbessert wird. Damit die Kommunikation funktioniert, müssen alle Europäer sich miteinander verständigen können. Somit kommt dem Sprachenlernen, aber auch der Zusammenarbeit der Bildungseinrichtungen auf europäischer Ebene eine Schlüsselrolle zu. Der Europäische Rat für kulturelle Zusammenarbeit (CDCC) hat daher im Jahr 2001 auf Weisung des Europarates den Gemeinsamen Europäischen Referenzrahmen für das Sprachenlernen *(CEF = Common European Framework of Reference for Language Learning and Teaching*, 2001) entwickelt. Dieser Rahmen (im Folgenden abgekürzt als „Rahmen") bildet mittlerweile sowohl methodisch als auch im Bereich der Bildungspolitik eine gemeinsame Basis für die Entwicklung des Fremdsprachenunterrichts. Damit bildet er die Grundlage für die Entwicklung von Curricula und deren Aktualisierung.

Eine der wichtigen Forderungen, die im Rahmen formuliert sind, ist die allgemeine Ausbildung der Bevölkerung zu Mehrsprachigkeit. Explizit wird der Begriff Mehrsprachigkeit dabei in vier der neun Kapitel des Rahmens erwähnt. Kapitel 1, das die Funktion und Ziel des Rahmens beschreibt, enthält einen programmatisch formulierten Abschnitt, der eine Definition von Mehrsprachigkeit gibt:

- Mehrsprachigkeit wird von der Vielsprachigkeit unterschieden, wobei die Vielsprachigkeit ein bloßes Nebeneinander von Sprachkenntnissen bedeutet.
- Mehrsprachigkeit bedeutet eine komplexe kommunikative Kompetenz.
- In der mehrsprachigen kommunikativen Kompetenz sind die Sprachkenntnisse integriert und unterstützen sich gegenseitig (vgl. GERR, S. 17).

Mehrsprachigkeit ist ein relativ neuer Begriff in der Fremdsprachendidaktik, der aber in der aktuellen schulischen Praxis umzusetzen ist. Die Empfehlungen des Weißbuches, neben der Muttersprache zwei weitere Fremdsprachen zu lernen, im Idealfall eine Nachbar- oder Minderheitensprache und eine überregionale Verständigungssprache (Weißbuch, 1995), scheinen vor dem Hintergrund der tatsächlichen Entwicklungen realistisch zu sein. Immer mehr Länder, sofern sie überhaupt mehr als eine Fremdsprache im Curriculum hatten, gehen dazu über, Englisch als erste – obligatorische – Fremdsprache anzubieten. Die weiteren Fremdsprachen verlegt man oft in den Bereich von Wahlpflicht- oder gar Wahlfächern. In der Tschechischen Republik wird dieses Modell beispielsweise ab dem Schuljahr 2011/12 obligatorisch realisiert. Bis jetzt scheint in vielen Ländern Europas die Stellung des Englischen als chronologisch gesehen erster Fremdsprache nicht infrage gestellt. Die anderen Sprachen können, wie zahlreiche Ergebnisse der Spracherwerbsforschung andeuten, nach dem Motto „mehr Sprachen – mehr Leistung“ beworben werden. Mit Hilfe mehrsprachigkeitsdidaktischer Verfahren bekommt man Folgefremdsprachen sozusagen günstig gleich mitgeliefert. Außerdem zeigt die Erfahrung, dass mehr Sprachen die Chancen bei der Stellensuche verbessern, das Beherrschen mehrerer Sprachen (v.a. der Sprache der Kundinnen und Kunden) mehr Absatz versprechen.

2 Deutsch als zweite Fremdsprache, Tertiärsprachenerwerb

Deutsch kann als eine attraktive zweite oder weitere Fremdsprache angeboten werden um das Konzept der mehrsprachigen Sprachhandlungskompetenz gesellschaftsfähig zu machen. Dieses Konzept besagt, dass eine Fremdsprache nicht in allen Bereichen beherrscht werden muss, sondern nur in denen, die für bestimmte Situationen, Sachverhalte und Gesprächspartner (in spezifischen Domänen) benötigt werden. Diese geänderte Sichtweise sollte von Lehrer/-inne/-n wahrgenommen und methodisch bearbeitet werden. In der Tschechischen Republik handelt es sich bei dieser zweiten, funktional ggf. auf gewisse Domänen eingeschränkten Fremdsprache um die Sprache der Nachbarländer, also um Deutsch. Die deutsche Sprache könnte dabei das Verständigungsmittel im Bereich der Touristik, der Zusammenarbeit in der Wirtschaft und bei der Anknüpfung von Partnerschaften zwischen Schulen oder auch im privaten Bereich sein. Die deutsche Sprache ermöglicht zudem das Kennenlernen der Kultur der Nachbarländer, kann also zu einem Mittel für den Abbau von Ethnozentrismus werden.

Für das Lernen des Deutschen als L3 (als zweite Fremdsprache nach der Muttersprache und der ersten Fremdsprache) erweist sich als günstig, dass diese zweite Fremdsprache (L3) in der Regel in einem Alter gelernt wird, in dem aus lernpsychologischer Sicht alle kognitiven Fähigkeiten schon voll entwickelt sind und beim Lerner die Fähigkeit zur Analyse sprachlicher Formen und der Wunsch nach Bewusstmachung der Regularitäten der Fremdsprache zu erwarten sind. Wenn es sich bereits um die dritte Sprache handelt, mit der der Lerner Erfahrungen macht, ist auch zu vermuten, dass er bereits über strategisches Wissen im Bereich Fremdsprachenlernen verfügt, das er beim Lernen einer weiteren Sprache weiterentwickeln kann und will.

Außerdem handelt es sich bei Deutsch und Englisch um zwei verwandte Sprachen (vgl. Spiropoulou, 2003, S. 2), was beim aufeinanderfolgenden Lernen mehr Vorteile als Nachteile verspricht: Bereits vorhandene Englischkenntnisse können das Verstehen des Deutschen erleichtern. So führt SPIROPOULOU für Englisch und Deutsch über 600 „gemeinsame“ Wörter an, wobei im heutigen Deutsch noch zahllose Anglizismen und Internationalismen hinzukommen, die ebenfalls den Zugang zur zweiten Fremdsprache erleichtern (vgl. Hufeisen/ Neuner 2000, S. 15).

3 Mehrsprachigkeitsdidaktik

Die Fragen, wie der DaF-Unterricht auf die gewandelte Stellung des Deutschen als nunmehr häufig zweiter Fremdsprache reagieren sollte, haben sich schon mehrere DaF-Theoretiker und Praktiker gestellt. Als besonders wichtige Arbeit im europäischen Kontext wäre z.B. HUFEISEN (2003) zu nennen, wo eine detaillierte Übersicht über die Forschung auf diesem Bereich vorgelegt wird. In einer weiteren Arbeit (Hufeisen 1991) befasst sich die Autorin dann mit der Frage, wie das schon beim Lernen der ersten Fremdsprache gewonnene, geistige Potenzial weiter entwickelt werden könnte. Gerhard NEUNER (2003), einer der wichtigsten Experten im Bereich Deutsch als Fremsprache, spezialisiert sich auf die Fragen, wie die Problematik der Tertiärsprachen in verschiedenen Lehrwerken bearbeitet wird. Ulrike GRUBE (1998) wiederum untersucht, ob das Lernen mehrerer Sprachen den Lernern zusätzliche Hilfestellungen bietet oder sie eher verwirrt. Auch in Polen (Targonska, Joanna, 2004), Bulgarien (Groseva, Maria, 1998), Griechenland (Spiropoulou,

Paulina, 2000) und Schweden (Kjär, Uwe, 2000) wurde die hier behandelte Problematik bereits untersucht. Zu internationalen Projekten im Bereich der Untersuchung und Unterstützung der Mehrsprachigkeit gehört z.B. das Projekt *Creating Synergy in the Learning of Subsequent Languages*, das am Sprachenzentrum für moderne Sprachen in Graz durchgeführt wurde, oder auch das am EFZS realisierte vierjährige Projekt Mehrsprachigkeitskonzept-Tertiärsprachenlernen-Deutsch nach Englisch (2000-2003). Einerseits heben die Autoren den positiven Einfluss der Erfahrungen mit der ersten Fremdsprache und mit dem Erwerb der Muttersprache und dessen Transfer auf das Tertiärsprachenlernen hervor, andererseits machen sie aber auch darauf aufmerksam, dass es in der dritten Sprache unter dem Einfluss der L1(der Muttersprache) und L2 (der ersten Fremdsprache) zu Interferenzfehlern kommen kann.

Auch an der Pädagogischen Fakultät der Masaryk-Universität beginnen in diesem Jahr Didaktikerinnen des Lehrstuhls für Deutsche Sprache und Literatur sich mit diesem aktuellen Thema zu beschäftigen. Zurzeit werden die bereits vorhandenen Forschungsergebnisse gesichtet, um ein eigenes Konzept zur Lösung von Fragen, die sich im Zusammenhang mit dem Bildungsziel Mehrsprachigkeit bei den Lernern in Theorie und Praxis ergeben, zu entwickeln. Damit möchten wir an das internationale Netz der Forschung im Bereich Mehrsprachigkeitsdidaktik anknüpfen und die spezifisch tschechischen Erfahrungen in diesem Bereich in die Fachdiskussion einbringen. Die Ergebnisse dieser Forschung sollen später in theoretischen Publikationen vorgelegt werden, auf Konferenzen präsentiert und in die Aus- und Fortbildung von Deutschlehrern implementiert werden.

2.1 Mehrsprachigkeitsdidaktik als Bestandteil des DaF-Lehramtstudiums

Unser Ziel ist es, empirisch zu untersuchen, welche Aspekte die Mehrsprachigkeitsdidaktik von der Fremdsprachendidaktik für eine Sprache unterscheiden, wie die Erfahrungen im Lernen einer ersten Fremdsprache bei dem Lernen jeder weiteren benutzt werden können. Im Prinzip geht es nicht darum, eine völlig neue Lehrmethode oder Didaktik zu erarbeiten, vielmehr sollen bereits vorhandene Sprachkenntnisse, Lernerfahrungen und -strategien beim Lernen von L1 oder L2 aktiviert und weiterentwickelt werden. Es sollte überprüft werden, in wieweit man in Tschechien beim Erlernen des Deutschen als zweiter Fremdsprache an das Lernen der Muttersprache und der ersten Fremdsprache (in den meisten Fällen Englisch) anknüpfen kann. Wir glauben, dass es vorrangig notwendig ist auf folgende Fragen Antworten zu suchen:

- Welche methodischen Verfahren sind geeignet, das Ziel *Mehrsprachigkeit* zu erreichen?
- Wie können Unterrichtende verschiedener Fremdsprachen an Schulen kooperieren?
- Wie kann die Entwicklung und Erweiterung von Lern- und Kommunikationsstrategien (Janíková 2004/2005) und von allgemeinen Strategien der Schüler im Rahmen des Fremdsprachenunterrichts unterstützt werden?
- Welche sind die Spezifika des Lernens und Lehrens von Tertiärsprachen?
- Wie und in wie weit unterscheidet sich die Motivation der Schüler für das Lernen der L2 und L3 im Falle Deutsch nach Englisch? Wie unterscheiden sich die Lernziele?
- Welche sind die negativen und positiven Interferenzen zwischen L1 (Tschechisch), L2 (Englisch) und L3 (Deutsch)?
- Wie werden die Kenntnisse aus L1 und L2 in den Lehrwerken für Deutsch berücksichtigt?
- Wie stark ist die kontrastive und interkulturelle Dimension im fremdsprachlichen Unterricht vertreten?

Die theoretisch bearbeiteten Themen werden anschließend in das Rahmencurriculum der Deutschlehrerausbildung implementiert und sollen auf diese Weise auch für die Unterrichtspraxis nutzbar gemacht werden. Die Ergebnisse dieser empirischen Untersuchungen sollen zusammengefasst werden und in der Form von praktischen methodischen Empfehlungen formuliert werden und in einer methodischen Publikation (einer „Handreichung") herausgegeben werden. Geplant ist die Zusammenstellung von Mehrsprachigkeitsmaterialien für die Fächer Didaktik und evtl. Sprachpraktische Übungen. Für die Deutschlehrer und -lehrerinnen sollte in Zukunft eine Reihe von Workshops und Seminaren mit dem Thema Mehrsprachigkeitsdidaktik veranstaltet werden. Wir hoffen, dass auf diese Weise das Fremdsprachenlernen effizienter wird und eine wirkliche Mehrsprachigkeit der Lerner in Tschechien in Zukunft erreicht werden kann.

Literaturangaben

EUROPARAT: Common European Framework of Reference for Language Learning and Teaching, 2001.

GROSEVA, M.: Deutsch als L3 bei bulgarischen Lernern. Wichtige Herangehensweisen und Strategien. In: Hufeisen, B./Lindemann, B. (Hg.): Tertiärsprachen. Theorien, Modelle, Methoden. Tübingen, Stauffenburg, 1998.

GRUBE, U.: Fremdsprachliche Interaktion im Bereich der Ostslavistik – Hilfe oder Verwirrung? In: Hufeisen, B./Lindemann, B. (Hg.): Tertiärsprachen. Theorien, Modelle, Methoden. Tübingen: Stauffenburg, 1998.

HUFEISEN, B.: Englisch als erste und Deutsch als zweite Fremdsprache. Empirische Untersuchung zur fremdsprachlichen Interaktion. Europäische Hochschulschriften, Reihe 21: Linguistik Bd. 95 Frankfurt/Main: Peter Lang Verlag, 1991.

HUFEISEN, B./NEUNER, G.: Mehr als eine Sprache effizient lernen: Tertiärsprachen lehren und lernen in Europa. Beispiel: Deutsch als Folgefremdsprache nach Englisch. Graz: Council of Europe/Goethe Institut, 2000.

JANÍKOVÁ, VĚRA: Osvojování slovní zásoby a učební strategie. In: Cizí jazyky 2004/2005, 48/2., S. 42-44.

NEUNER, G.: Mehrsprachigkeitskonzept und Tertiärdidaktik. In: Hufeisen, B. Neuner, G.: Mehrsprachigkeitskonzept – Tertiärsprachen – Deutsch nach Englisch. Europäisches Fremdsprachenzentrum. Strasbourg: Council of Europe Publishing, 2003.

KJÄR, U.: Deutsch als L3. Zur Interimsprache schwedischer Deutschlerner (unter Berücksichtigung des Einflusses des Englischen als L2). In: Dentler, S./ Hufeisen, B./Lindemann, B. (Hg.): Tertiär- und Drittsprachen: Projekte und empirische Untersuchungen. Tübingen, Stauffenburg, 2000.

KOLLEKTIV: Weißbuch zur allgemeinen und beruflichen Bildung. Lehren und Lernen. Auf dem Weg zur kognitiven Gesellschaft, Europäische Kommission, 1995.

SPIROPOULOU, P.: Fehler im Tertiärsprachenunterricht. Beitrag im Rahmen eines Forschungsstipendiums am Europäischen Fremdsprachenzentrum (EFSZ) im Rahmen des Projekts „Mehrsprachigkeitskonzept – Tertiärsprachenlernen – Deutsch nach Englisch“ (2000-2003), 2003.
Zugänglich auch: http://www.ecml.at/documents/relresearch/Spiropoulou.pdf

TARGOSKA, J.: Zur Nutzung von Englischkenntnissen beim Erwerb des deutschen Wortschatzes. Eine empirische Untersuchung an polnischen Schülern. In:

Hufeisen, B./Marx, N. (Hg.): „Beim Schwedischlernen sind Englisch und Deutsch ganz hilfsvoll“. Untersuchungen zum multiplen Sprachenlernen. Frankfurt/M. u.a., Lang, 2004.

Kontakt:
PhDr. Alice BRYCHOVÁ, Ph.D.: brychova@ped.muni.cz

GESTALTPÄDAGOGISCHE ANSÄTZE IM FREMDSPRACHENUNTERRICHT

Ivica Lenčová, Lehrstuhl für Germanistik, Matej-Bel-Universität
Banská Bystrica, Slowakei

Die humanistische Orientierung der Schule schuf Bedingungen für neue methodische Ansätze im Fremdsprachenunterricht. Vor diesem Hintergrund vereint Gestaltpädagogik dementsprechende Methoden und Arbeitsformen. Im Sinne der ganzheitlichen Entwicklung der Schülerpersönlichkeit werden der Lehrkraft Möglichkeiten geboten, das Individuelle unter der Berücksichtigung der Vielfalt der Sinneswahrnehmung mit dem persönlich bedeutenden Lerninhalt zu verbinden. Dadurch werden den Lernenden gleiche Chancen eröffnet zu experimentieren, sich selbst auszudrücken sowie produktiv und kreativ zu sein. Verschiedene Kommunikationsformen (verbale, nonverbale, aktives Zuhören) in Verbindung mit passenden Verfahren (z. B. Identifikation, szenische Bearbeitung, Phantasiereise) gewährleisten eine freundliche Arbeitsatmosphäre unter der Berücksichtigung der Persönlichkeit des Lernenden.

Schlüsselbegriffe: Gestaltpädagogik, humanistische Orientierung der Schule, Persönlichkeit des Lernenden

1 Einleitung

Die derzeitige dynamische Entwicklung der Gesellschaft, historische Veränderungen und laufende Innovationen verlangen die Vertiefung von demokratischen Beziehungen, eine Zivilisation, in der die Meinungspluralität akzeptiert wird, Vielfältigkeit von Kulturen, Vielgestaltigkeit der Welt, die nicht ohne Toleranz, Empatie und Kulturbewusstheit zu realisieren sind.

1.1 Humanistische Orientierung der Schule

In dem oben geschilderten Kontext müssen in der heutigen Gesellschaft die Fragen der Erziehung überall dort im Vordergrund stehen, wo es möglich ist. In der edukativen Umgebung der modernen Schule bedeutet dies, Bedingungen für die Entwicklung des Kreativen, Produktiven und damit auch des Moalischen und des Ästhetischen zu schaffen.

Bildung und Erziehung sollen anthropologische Konstanten sein, die Edukation zum *„Wesensmerkmal des Menschen in seiner humanen Identität"* (Ries 2001, S. 151). Auf die Aktualität und das Bedürfnis einer Erziehung für das Leben unter der Voraussetzung einer Qualitätsarbeit des Lehrenden wird in zahlreichen pädagogischen und didaktischen Schriften hingewiesen. Eine qualitativ neue Erziehung stellt die Entwicklung der Metakognition (Selbsterkennung, Selbstregulation etc.), der Emotionalität, der Sozialisation, der Kommunikation, Autoregulation und der Kreativität in den Vordergrund. Für ein vollwertiges Leben ist *die emotionale Intelligenz*, der an den Schulen kaum genug Aufmerksamkeit gewidmet wird, sehr wichtig. In dieser Hinsicht verdient die Erziehung eine größere Aufmerksamkeit. Primäre Voraussetzungen für die Änderungen zum Vorteil von Erziehung sind Transformation des Schulsystems und der Erziehungsphilosophie, curriculare Transformation und Änderungen in der Aus- und Weiterbildung von Lehrenden. In Anlehnung an ZELINA (1999) „ist die Erziehung wichtiger als die Bildung – dieses erste Axiom negiert keinesfalls Bildung, es betont bloß die Tatsache, dass es nötig ist, überflüssige uneffektive Bildung zu eliminieren und mehr Erziehungsmethoden zu stärken, mehr den Erlebnissen, Wertsystemen und der Motivation und den Gefühlen der Kinder zu folgen" (Zelina 1999, S. 11).

Durch die gesellschaftlich-ökonomischen Veränderungen wurden in der Slowakei neue Bedingungen für eine neue Philosophie der Schule geschaffen – die traditionelle, auf die Leistungen orientierte Zielsetzung wird durch die humanistische Orientierung ersetzt, in der Erziehungswerte, Erlebnissphäre des Schülers und Interessantheit des Unterrichts einen festen Platz haben. In der pädagogischen Praxis spielen Aktivität, Selbstständigkeit, Selbstverantwortung und Kreativität der Lernenden deutlich eine wichtige Rolle. Diese werden von den Arbeitsformen und Methoden des Lehrenden abgeleitet und sind sehr eng an seine Persönlichkeit gebunden. Funktionen des Lehrenden wie Wissensvermittler oder Kontrolleur werden durch andere wichtige Funktionen (Partner, Berater, Helfer) ergänzt. Das transmissive edukative Modell wird durch das kommunikative interaktive Modell ersetzt (vgl. Homolová 2004, Storch 1999, Turek 2004).

Neben der Fachkompetenz tritt auch die psychodidaktische Kompetenz in den Vordergrund (geeignete Bedingungen für den Lernenden zu schaffen, sein kreatives Denken zu aktivieren,...), kommunikative Kompetenz gegenüber den Lernenden und Kollegen, Kompetenz der Selbstreflexion (auf Grund der Selbstreflexion zu Schlußfolgerungen zu kommen, seine Arbeit innovieren, modifizieren zu können). Nur das Ausführen von Funktionen, Kompetenzen oder Kriterien selbst reicht nicht, wichtiger ist ihre Applikation in den konkreten pädagogischen Situationen als Ausdruck von neuen Beziehungen zwischen dem Lehrenden und dem Lernenden in Form der humanen Unterrichtsverfahren und Interaktionen (Janíková 2009, S. 314). Dominierend sind die Lernenden mit ihren Interessen, Fähigkeiten und Wünschen unter der Bedingung des gegenseitigen Ver-ständnisses und des Respekts zwischen ihnen und dem Lehrenden. Die Vision der Schule der Zukunft ist die kreative Schule, in der „das Gedächtnisparadigma durch das Paradigma des kreativen Denkens und des verantwortlichen Tuns – mit dem Akzent auf der emotionalen und moralischen Entfaltung der Schülerpersönlichkeit ersetzt wird. Statt des Enzyklopedismus wird die Kreativität, Humanismus, Freude am Lernen präferiert" (Petlák 2000, S. 105). Die traditionelle leistungsorientierte Schule soll durch die humanistisch orien-tierte Schule ersetzt werden, in der Erziehungswerte, Erlebnissphäre des Lernenden und Interessantheit der Edukation einen festen Platz haben werden. Heutige Philosophie, Richtung und fachliche Überzeugung über die Sinnhaftigkeit der neuen Orientierung charakterisiert nach KOSOVÁ (2006) „der Akzent auf die Aktivität und Freiheit der Persönlichkeit und ihre Kraft, ihre eigene progressive, kreative Lebensweise für das Leben im neuen Jahrtausend" (Kosová 2006, S. 10).

Im Jahre 2002 wurde durch den Nationalrat und die Regierung der Slowakischen Republik. Das Nationalprogramm der Erziehung und Bildung in der Slowakischen Republik für die nächsten 15-20 Jahre, bekannt als Projekt *Milénium* eingeführt. In diesem Projekt sind Wege und Ziele der Schule angeführt – im Einklang mit der kreativ-humanistischen Pädagogik unter der Berücksichtigung der transformativen und zukünftigen Aufgaben unseres Schulwesens und der neuen Trends im Bereich Bildung und Erziehung. Die zentrale Idee ist gerade die Humanisierung der Schule, die parallele Innovationen im ganzen Schulsystem und in der Arbeit der Lehrkräfte konkret voraussetzt. Im Teil Allgemeine Ziele und Prinzipien des Projekts *Milénium* wird dargelegt, dass man neue Methoden, u.a. Methoden der Entwicklung der emotionalen Intelligenz, Metamotivation, Prosozialisation, Kreativität und der hohen ethischen Verantwortung anwenden soll.

1.2 Neue Verfahren im Fremdsprachenunterricht

Die aktuellen pädagogischen Fragen und didaktisch-methodischen Fragen der Fremdsprachendidaktik, die zusammenhängen, knüpfen an die Umgestaltung der Bildung und der Erziehung in Richtung Humanisierung und Förderung der Kreativität und Emotionalität an. Die Fremdsprachendidaktik spiegelt in jeder Zeit die gesellschaftlich-politischen Forderungen wider, die die Gesellschaft in den legislativen Dokumenten zum Ausdruck bringt, sie steht in enger Verbindung mit Bezugsdisziplinen wie Neurowissenschaften, Psycholinguistik und kognitive Psychologie, deren neueste Erkenntnisse in die edukative Realität einzubauen sind. Theoretische Konsequenzen sollen in ihrer transformierten Form (als methodisch-didaktische Implikationen) in die schulische Praxis zurückkommen, denn „die beste Theorie ist eine gute Praxis und das pratischste Ding ist eine gute Theorie" (Zelinová 2007, S. 8). Das Ideal, dem im modernen Fremdsprachenlernen gefolgt wird ist die ganzheitliche Entwicklung der Schülerpersönlichkeit, die ausgeglichene Wirkung der informativ-bildenden und der formativ-entwickelnden Sphären. „Eine der Aufgaben des Lehrers der humanistisch orientierten Schule ist es, offenherzig gegenüber den Schülerbedürfnissen zu sein und die Schüler möglichst zur Orientierung an den höheren Bedürfnissen anzuregen“ (Lenčová 2006, S. 51). In einem so orientierten Unterricht fällt den künstlerischen Medien (Literatur, bildende Kunst etc.) dank ihres Reichtums an Werten, die die einfache Darstellung der Realität überschreiten, eine spezifische Funktion zu. Kunstwerke mit ihren Botschaften und Signalen geben dem Lehrer ein wirkungsvolles Medium in die Hand, den Lernenden zu aktivieren, seine emotionalen Sphären zu fördern und dadurch den Unterricht um die Qualitäten der kreativ-humanistischen Pädagogik zu bereichern (Lenčová 2006).

Der direkte Kontakt mit Kunst findet in *Form des interkulturellen Dialogs als Erlebnistreffen* des Lernenden mit dem Kunstwerk statt, das an die Wahrnehmung und das Erlebnis als Grundbedingungen der Selbstreflexion und –identifikation des Lernenden anknüpft und ihm die authentische Erfahrung auf dem Such- und Entdeckungsweg gewährleistet. Durch den Kontakt mit Kunst werden Wertprozesse, kreatives Denken, nonkognitive Charakteristiken der Per-

sönlichkeit (Gefühle, Motivation, progressive Affinität zu den Werten) unterstützt. In diesem Kontext scheinen uns gestaltpädagogische Arbeitsformen und Methoden geeignet zu sein, dem Lernenden viele Möglichkeiten für den Selbstausdruck und die Identitätsdarstellung zu bieten (Lenčová 2007).
Die Gestaltpädagogik als eines der humanistischen reformpädagogischen Konzepte verbindet die persönlichkeitsfördernden Ansätze und Methoden der humanistischen Pädagogik und Psychologie, der Gestalttherapie, des Psychodramas und der Gruppendynamik. Mit ihrem Blickpunkt auf den Lehrenden, seine persönliche Entwicklung und berufliche Identität, seinen kritischen Kontakt zu sich selbst ermöglicht die Gestaltpädagogik ihm und dem Lernenden, Lerninhalte mit persönlichen Bedeutungen zu füllen, individuelle Lebensgeschichten in den Unterricht einzubeziehen, möglichst multiplex Sinnesebenen zu berücksichtigen, das aktive Zuhören, Kritik und Selbstkritik einzuüben. Durch die Verwendung von Spielen, Identifikationsübungen, Phantasiereisen und Experimentieren wird eine positive lernanregende Atmosphäre aufgebaut. Das Nonverbale wird mit dem Verbalen eng verbunden.
Zu den wichtigen Methoden der Gestaltpädagogik gehört die Identifikation – man geht von der Voraussetzung aus, dass alles (Informationen, Probleme etc.) eine persönliche Bedeutsamkeit beinhaltet. Diese „affektive Aufladung" als Methode fördert die Gedächtnisleistung und bietet dadurch vielfältige Anwendungsmöglichkeiten. Der Lernende kann aus einem neuen Blickwinkel das ihn Umgebende wahrnehmen und reflektieren. Phantasieübungen oder Phantasiereisen ermöglichen den Lernenden zusammen mit ihrem Lehrer Begegnungen zu erleben, bei denen die affektive Seite des Lernens betont wird, wobei das Erlebte durch szenische Darstellungen ergänzt und bereichert wird. Die Lernenden können sich gegenseitig besser kennen lernen, sind aktiv, die Leistungsschwächeren fühlen sich nicht diskriminiert. Im sprachlichen Bereich werden besonders stark die sprachliche Interaktion, Argumentationsfähigkeit und die Fähigkeit, eigene Gefühle zu äußern geübt. Nicht zuletzt werden bei den Lernenden Phantasie, Imaginationskraft und Erfindungsreichtum gefördert. Die Methode des Körperkontakts und der Bewegung tragen dazu bei, dass in den Fachunterricht die körperliche Dimension einbezogen wird und dadurch das Körperbewusstsein beim Lernenden gefördert wird (Lenčová 2007).

2 Fazit

Fremdsprachenlehrkräfte können mittels gestaltpädagogischer Seminare bzw. Kurse ihre Qualifikation in mehrerlei Hinsicht erhöhen: Durch eine stärkere Selbstwahrnehmung und -reflexion werden sie geschult, ihre Aufmerksamkeit auf die Vielfalt und Verschiedenheit der Lernenden zu schärfen und können sie dadurch objektiver einschätzen. Durch das Angebot von Freiräumen zum Selbstausdruck werden sie ihre Schüler ganzheitlich, d.h. im kognitiven Bereich und ebenso im affektiven und emotionalen Bereich unterrichten. Wir sind überzeugt, dass die ausgewählten gestaltpädagogischen Arbeitsformen und Methoden in Verbindung mit fremdsprachlichen Inhalten aus der künstlerischen Welt dazu beitragen können, humane Komponenten im Fremdsprachenunterricht stärker einzubinden.

Literaturangaben

BUROW, OLAF-AXEL/GUDJONS, HERBERT: Gestaltpädagogik in der Schule. 2. Auflage. – Hamburg: Bergmann & Helbig Verlag, 1998.

BÜRMANN, J./HEINEL, J.: Wege zu verändertem Unterricht. Bad Heilbrunn: Klinkhardt, 1997.

HOMOLOVÁ, EVA: Učiteľské a žiacke roly na hodine cudzieho jazyka. Banská Bystrica: UMB, 2004.

JANÍKOVÁ, VĚRA. Efektivita využívání metod dramatické výchovy u žáků se specifickými poruchami učení ve výuce němčiny. In Vítková, Marie/ Bartoňová, Miroslava. Vzdělávání žáků se speciálními vzdělávacími potřebami III. Education of Pupils with Special Educational Needs *III*. Brno: MU, 2009, S. 311-320.

RIES, LUMÍR/KOLLÁROVÁ, EVA: Svet cudzích jazykov dnes. Bratislava: SPN, 2004.

KOSOVÁ, B: Teoretické východiská vytvárania koncepcie odbornej učiteľskej praxe. In: Doušková, A. – Porubský, Š. Vedenie študentov na odbornej učiteľskej praxi. Banská Bystrica:PF UMB, 2006.

LENČOVÁ, IVICA: Imagination und Emotion als Unterrichtsziel. Förderung des kreativen Potentials und der Emotionalität des Schülers durch Bild, Text und Musik. In: Zeitschrift für Gestaltpädagogik 17. Jahrgang, Heft 1, 2006, S. 50-57.

LENČOVÁ, IVICA: Celostná pedagogika ako cesta k humanizácii vyučovania. Banská Bystrica: FHV UMB, 2007.

PETLÁK, ERICH: Pedagogicko-didaktická práca učiteľa. Bratislava: IRIS, 2000.

TUREK, IVAN: Inovácie v didaktike. Bratislava: Metodicko-pedagogické centrum, 2004.

ZELINA, MIRON: Stratégie a metódy rozvoja dieťaťa. Bratislava: Práca, 1999.

ZELINOVÁ, MILOTA: Hry pro rozvoj emocí a komunikace. Praha: Portál 2007.

Kontakt:
Ivica LENČOVÁ: lencova@fhv.umb.sk

PERSÖNLICHKEITSARBEIT UND LEHRER/INNEN - PROFESSIONALISIERUNG

Eva Unterweger, Pädagogische Hochschule Wien, Österreich

Vor dem theoretischen Hintergrund einschlägiger aktueller Forschungsergebnisse und den Ergebnissen eigener Untersuchungen werden Zusammenhänge zwischen Persönlichkeitsarbeit und Lehrer/-innen-Professionalität diskutiert. Ein Modell zur Persönlichkeitsarbeit an der PH Wien wird vorgestellt und die Umsetzung in Aus- und Fortbildung dargestellt.

Schlüsselbegriffe: Persönlichkeitsarbeit, Lehrer/-innenbildung, Professionalisierung

1 Lehrer/innen-Persönlichkeit und Professionalisierung

Hartmut von HENTIG bezeichnet die Person als „das wichtigste Curriculum des Lehrers“ (von Hentig, 1984, S.112). Tatsächlich ist gerade die Professionalisierung von Lehrer/-inne/-n in der subjekt- und personorientierten Annäherung an die Lehrerinnenaus- und fortbildung eine besondere Herausforderung für Hochschulen und Universitäten. Als Konsequenz fordert MESSNER „ [...] auch Arbeits- und Inszenierungsformen, welche die für die Lehrertätigkeit so wichtige *Person der Handelnden* schon in der Ausbildung in Szene setzen und präsent werden lassen“, denn „Lehrerinnen und Lehrer wirken mit ihrer ganzen Persönlichkeit.“ (Messner, 2001, S. 12). TERHART beschreibt die Professionalisierung von Lehrer/innen als biografischen Prozess (vgl. Terhart 1994), der mit der Ausbildung beginnt und sich im weiteren Verlauf als ein das Berufsleben begleitender (vgl. Seitz 2008), andauernden Entwicklungsprozess ausprägt. Dieser aktiv gestaltete Prozess der Professionalisierung ist im optimalen Fall auf Mündigkeit ausgerichtet; unreflektierte berufliche Erfahrung allein kann dagegen auch „de-professionalisierend“ wirken, wie BAUER ausführt: „Das berufliche Selbst wandelt sich durch Erfahrung, nicht immer und nicht notwendig zum Besseren. Gerade bei Lehrkräften besteht ein hohes Risiko des Kompetenzverlustes in der Berufsbiographie [...]“ (Bauer, K.-O. 2006, S.17). Forschungsergebnisse zur Wirksamkeit der Lehrer/-innenbildung lassen vermuten, dass ein großer Teil des Professionalisierungsprozesses in einem „Sich-Selbst-Professionalisieren“ im Laufe der Berufspraxis erfolgt (vgl. Blömeke 2004) und zwar in Interaktion mit den jeweils individuellen, situativen und systemischen Gegebenheiten vor Ort. Daraus entwickelt sich die Frage, welche spezifischen Aspekte der Curricula, welche Rahmenbedingungen des Studiums und welche Organisationsstrukturen seitens der Institutionen der Lehrer/-innenaus- und -fortbildung angeboten werden können, dass dieser personale Aspekt der Selbst-Professionalisierung von Lehrer/-inne/-n unterstützt und gefördert werden kann. Von der jeweiligen Schulleitung am Schulstandort bis zum Staat als Arbeitgeber zieht sich die Verpflichtung adäquate institutionelle Strukturen und Personalentwicklungsmaßnahmen zur Verfügung zu stellen, um die berufsbegleitende Selbstprofessionalisierung von Lehrer/-inne/-n systemisch zu stützen, zu fördern und zu gewährleisten.

2 Persönlichkeitsarbeit an der Pädagogischen Hochschule Wien

2.1 Persönlichkeitsarbeit an der Vorgängerinstitution der Pädagogischen Hochschule

Seit 1995 gab es an der Pädagogischen Akademie Wien eigene Veranstaltungen zur Persönlichkeitsentwicklung, die auch evaluiert wurden. Zwei Drittel der befragten Studierenden schätzten Persönlichkeitsarbeit in der Lehrer/-innenbildung für grundlegend notwendig ein (vgl. Boltz, Unterweger, Weiss 1998). Es kristallisierten sich vier didaktische Prinzipien heraus, die die Prozesse der Persönlichkeitsentwicklung besonders unterstützen: Selbsterfahrungsorientierung, Orientierung an den personalen Ressourcen der Studierenden, Orientierung an biografischen Aspekten und Berufsfokussierung (vgl. Unterweger, Weiss 2004).

2.2 Die drei SSS - Kompetenzen

Auf der Kompetenzebene erfolgt die Persönlichkeitsarbeit in den Bereichen Selbst-, Sozial- und Systemkompetenz; sie sind in weiten Bereichen miteinander verknüpft oder stehen in Wechselwirkung zueinander. Die in der Tabelle angeführten Bildungsinhalte werden in der Persönlichkeitsarbeit der Erstausbildung bearbeitet und finden auch in den Angeboten Fortbildung Berücksichtigung.

Selbstkompetenz	*Sozialkompetenz*	*Systemkompetenz*
• Bewusstheit o der eigenen Visionen, o der Facetten (Rollen) des Berufsbildes, o der Werte, o der Ressourcen, o von subjektiven Theorien und Wahrnehmungs-mustern, • Emotionale Kompetenz, • Stressmanagement und professionelle Psychohygiene, • Selbstpräsentation, • Empowerment als Burnout Prävention,...	• Beziehungskompetenz, • Grenzen, Nähe und Distanz, • emotionale Kompetenz • verbale und nonverbale Kommunikationskompetenz • Konfliktmanagement und Mediation, • professionstypische Kommunikationskompetenz (Beratungskompetenz, Teamarbeit, kollegiale Intervision, Moderation,...) • Sozialdidaktische Kompetenz, um konstruktive Gruppenentwicklungen und die sozial-emotionale Entwicklung der Schüler/-innen zu fördern,...	• Bewusstheit über die Arbeit in Systemen, o systemische Perspektiven auf Schule, o Vernetzungen und Abhängigkeiten in der Gesellschaft, o das eigene Eingebundensein in organisatorische und politische Zusammenhänge im Berufsfeld erkennen und reflektieren. • In der Arbeit mit Einzelnen und der Gruppe eine lösungsorientierte, systemische Haltung einnehmen,...

Abb.1: Bildungsziele der Persönlichkeitsarbeit im engeren Sinne (vgl. Unterweger 2009)

2.2.2 Die Persönlichkeitsarbeit mit den drei SSS-Kompetenzen

Die Persönlichkeitsarbeit an der Pädagogischen Hochschule orientiert sich an den oben genannten didaktischen Prinzipien und an den Bildungsinhalten der 3SSS Kompetenzen (Abb1). In den Seminaren zur Persönlichkeitsarbeit liegt der Fokus teilweise stark auf der Selbstreflexions- und Selbsterfahrungsarbeit sowie der Arbeit mit professionellen Handlungsstrategien; diese Aspekte erhalten in Veranstaltungen zur Persönlichkeitsarbeit oft mehr Gewicht als die

Aneignung von reinem Wissen. Das aus den Prozessen der Selbstreflexion und Selbsterfahrungsarbeit entwickelte Bewusstsein für das sich entwickelnde „professionellen Selbst" ist die Basis, auf der Lehrer/innen ihren eigenen Weg der Professionalisierung finden und für sich selbst Lernpfade entwickeln. Die Arbeit mit professionellen Handlungsstrategien wiederum erweitert das individuelle Handlungsrepertoire und erhöht damit die Chance eines situationsadäquaten Einsatzes von professionellen Handlungsmustern.

2.3 Lehrveranstaltungen, die die Förderung der Persönlichkeitsarbeit fokussieren

2.3.1 In der Ausbildung (Grundstufe und Sekundarstufe 1)

In der Lehrveranstaltung *„Einführung in die personalen Aspekte des Berufs"* (im ersten Semester, Anfangsmodul) erleben Student/-inn/-en gerade zu Beginn ihres Studiums, wie entlastend und unterstützend es ist, die anderen Mitglieder in der neuen Gruppe kennen zu lernen und bewusst selbst zu erleben, wie sich dadurch soziale Sicherheit in einer Gruppe entwickeln kann. Der Fokus der Erkundung der Individuen in der Gruppe liegt auf den Ressourcen und ihrer Umsetzung im Lehrer/-innen-Beruf, was oft für Menschen, deren Lernerfahrungen aus einer traditionell stark defizitorientierten Schulsozialisation resultieren, als überraschend persönlichkeitsstärkend erlebt wird. Das Sichtbarmachen der systemischen Gruppenstrukturen (z.B. Geschwisterpositionen, Altersstruktur, Männer-Frauen, Wohnorte, Herkunfts-(bundes)länder etc.) und die Reflexion ihrer Auswirkungen auf die Entwicklung und Dynamik der Gruppe ist für die Teilnehmer/innen eine vorerst neue und ungewöhnliche Perspektive. Schließlich setzt die Arbeit mit der Berufsmotivation und besonders die „Reise zur individuellen Vision" vom Beruf für die meisten Teilnehmer/-innen einen Schwerpunkt des Seminars und trägt gleichzeitig zur Klärung eines Orientierungsparameters für den weiteren individuellen Professionalisierungsprozess bei. Ein Studierender schreibt in seinem Portfolio über diese Erfahrung: „Mir hat dieser Tag enorm viel gebracht. Im Laufe eines Lebens entscheidet man sich zu vielen Dingen ohne wirklich zu wissen warum. Nachdem man aber das „Ziel" gefühlt hat, geht man wesentlich motivierter und ausdauernder an die Verwirklichung eines Traumes heran. Für mich ist der Wunsch Lehrer zu werden durch diese Reise nun haptisch geworden, da ich etwas gefühlt habe. Jedoch macht mir dieses Gefühl auch etwas Angst. Ich habe mir bereits die Frage gestellt „Was, wenn ich dieses Gefühl nie wieder erlebe?" Habe ich dann versagt? Ist mein Ziel, dieses Gefühl wieder erleben zu können oder eben „nur" Lehrer zu werden? Ich für meinen Teil weiß nun die Antwort. Mein Ziel ist es beides zu erreichen. Ich möchte ein Lehrer werden, der nicht unbedingt tagtäglich dieses Gefühl empfindet, aber doch einige Male in seinem Leben" (Stud., m., 1. Sem. WS 09/10). Bemerkenswert in dieser Passage ist auch noch die Ergänzung und Relativierung des Idealbildes durch ein unspezifisches Realbild und eine ansatzweise Integration beider.

Im Weiteren konstituieren die Erstausbildung noch folgende persönlichkeitsspezifische Veranstaltungen:

Das *Seminar „Wirkungsvoll auftreten, klar sprechen"* im zweiten Semester unterstützt die Selbstpräsentation, das sichere Sprechen und Auftreten und die Entwicklung der Präsenz im Allgemeinen.

Im dritten Semester werden *Kommunikationsseminare* angeboten, in denen das Thema „Kommunikation" sowohl theoretisch als auch handlungsorientiert bearbeitet wird. Verbale und nonverbale Handlungsstrategien werden in den Schulpraktischen Studien ausprobiert und umgesetzt; anhand von Videografien der eigenen Unterrichtskommunikation entwickeln die Studierenden die Kompetenz, eigenes unterrichtliches Kommunikationshandeln zu analysieren und zu reflektieren.

Das *Seminar „Professionelles Selbstmanagement"* kann im vierten und fünften Semester gewählt werden; Strategien des Zeit- und Stressmanagements werden hier reflektiert und erweitert, ebenso wie der bewusste Einsatz von Ressourcen und persönlichen Kraftquellen. Die Arbeit mit den eigenen Grenzen und das bewusste Experimentieren mit Distanz und Nähe bringen vielen Studierenden wesentliche Erfahrungen für ihren professionellen Umgang mit schulischen Alltagsinteraktionen. Im *Seminar „Soziales Lernen als Gewaltprävention"* setzen sich die Studierenden mit ihren eigenen Strategien der Emotionsregulation, ihren Konfliktlösungsstrategien, aber auch mit dem didaktischen Aufbau und der Förderung der Sozialen Kompetenz von Schüler/-inne/-n auseinander.

2.3.2 Persönlichkeitsarbeit in der Fortbildung

Neben einzelnen Veranstaltungsangeboten in der Fortbildung von im Dienst stehenden Lehrer/-inne/-n ist der *Lehrgang „Selbst-Professionalisierung und Persönlichkeitsarbeit"* besonders zu erwähnen, der Angebote zur Weiterentwicklung von Selbst-, Sozial- und Systemkompetenz vor allem für Berufseinsteiger/-innen des ersten bis dritten Berufsjahres anbietet.

Auch *Supervisionsangebote* als Einzel- und Gruppensupervision fördern die Professionalisierung durch die Arbeit an den personalen Kompetenzen.

2.3.3 Seminar- und hochschuldidaktische Maßnahmen zur Förderung der personalen Kompetenz

Persönlichkeitsarbeit kann nicht nur auf einzelne Veranstaltungen beschränkt bleiben, personorientierte Studienkonzepte erfordern daher eine Lernkultur und Lernformen, die den Lernenden/die Lernende als ganze Person ansprechen (vgl. Teml/Unterweger 2002).

In Seminar- und Praxistagebüchern beispielsweise setzen sich Studierende mit ihren persönlichen Lernprozessen auseinander und verwenden ihre Eintragungen auch als Grundlage für resümierende Selbstreflexionen für die jeweiligen Semesterabschlüsse. Anstelle von traditionellen Prüfungsarbeiten können im Rahmen von Portfolio-Arbeiten starke Impulse zur Selbstreflexion eigener Professionalisierungsprozesse gesetzt werden.

Die Seminardidaktik an sich braucht Strukturen, die Zeit, Raum und Impulse für die personorientierte Arbeit anbieten. Entsprechende Aufträge für die Einzelarbeit, den Dialog mit Studienkolleg/inn/en, aber auch in Peergruppen erweisen sich als effiziente und ertragreiche Anregungen für personale Reflexionsprozesse. In den Beratungsstunden der Schulpraktischen Studien lässt eine personorientierte Haltung des/der Betreuer/in den Studierenden genügend Raum zu eigenen Lösungen zu kommen; anregende Fragen und Impulse führen wiederum zu selbstreflektierenden Auseinandersetzungen der Studierenden mit den Erfahrungen aus eigenen Handlungen und Entscheidungen, aber auch mit den jeweils zu Grunde liegenden subjektiven Theorien der unterrichtenden Student/inn/en.

2.3.5 Institutionelle Maßnahmen zur Förderung der personalen Kompetenz der Lehrenden und deren Vernetzung

Im vergangenen Jahr wurden an der PH Wien Arbeitskreise für Persönlichkeitsentwicklung an den einzelnen Instituten der Aus- und Fortbildung gebildet. Sie dienen einerseits der Evaluierung der Ziel- und Leistungspläne im Bereich „Persönlichkeitsentwicklung", andererseits der kollegialen Vernetzung und dem fachlichen Austausch. Langsam entwickelt sich auch ein institutsübergreifendes Netzwerk, in dem sich alle Personen der PH, die sich mit Persönlichkeitsarbeit beschäftigen, miteinander vernetzen und fachliche Inform-

tionen austauschen, sowie Weiterbildungsmöglichkeiten im Sinn von *„Train the Trainer"* entwickeln.
Abschließend ist noch das österreichweite Institut für „Persönlichkeitsentwicklung und Soziales Lernen" (ÖZEPS) zu erwähnen, das vom Bundesministerium für Unterricht, Kunst und Kulturelle Angelegenheiten ins Leben gerufen wurde. Es hat einen Pool an Trainer/-inne/-n für spezielle Bereiche, wie Soziales Lernen, Peer-Mediation, stärkende und förderliche Leistungsbeurteilung, Gewaltprävention und betreibt ein Netzwerk mit Partner/-inne/-n von jeder Pädagogischen Hochschule in Österreich.
Den berufslebenslangen Selbstprofessionalisierungsprozess von Lehrer/-inne/-n im Blick wird für die Persönlichkeitsarbeit von Studierenden in der Erstausbildung im Bereich der personalen Kompetenzen (Selbst-, Sozial- und Systemkompetenz) mit spezifischen Lehrveranstaltungen, mit adäquater Seminar- und Hochschuldidaktik und mit unterstützenden organisatorischen Strukturen eine nachhaltige Basis geschaffen. Darauf aufbauend brauchen Lehrer/-innen für ihre Selbstprofessionalisierung im Beruf – ganz besonders in ihren ersten Dienstjahren – institutionelle Unterstützung durch Schulleiter und Kolleg/-inn/-en am Schulstandort, förderliche bildungspolitische Rahmenbedingungen und schließlich adäquate personorientierte Fortbildungsangebote.

Literaturangaben

BAUER, Karl-Oswald: Das professionelle Selbst (mit einem Exkurs über die glückliche Lehrkraft). In: Mergner, B./Schoof-Wetzig, D./Stiller, E. (Hg.): Lehrerfortbildung als Personalentwicklung – Persönliches Lernen begleiten. Bad Berka: ThILLM-Publikation, 2006 Forum Lehrerfortbildung, Heft 40, S. 15-25.

BLÖMEKE, Sigrid: Empirische Befunde zur Wirksamkeit der Lehrerbildung. In: Blömeke, S. u.a. (Hg.): Handbuch Lehrerbildung. Bad Heilbrunn, Klinkhardt, 2004, S.59-91.

BOLZ, Martin/UNTERWEGER, Eva / WEISS, Waltraud: Sich als Persönlichkeit weiter entwickeln. Eine Evaluationsstudie über Persönlichkeitsentwicklung in der Lehrer/-innen-Ausbildung. Wien: Pädagogische Akademie des Bundes in Wien, 1998.

HENTIG, Hartmut von: Vom Verkäufer zum Darsteller. Absagen an die Lehrerbildung. In: Becker,H./Hentig, H.v (Hrsg.): Der Lehrer und seine Bildung. Beiträge zur Überwindung einer Resignation (s. 99-146). Frankfurt: Ullstein, 1984.

MESSNER, Rudolf: Szenarien zur Bearbeitung des Theorie-Praxis-Problems in der Lehrerbildung. In: Journal für Lehrerinnen- und Lehrerbildung 1(2), 2001, S.10-19.

TERHART, Ewald u. a.: Berufsbiographien von Lehrern und Lehrerinnen. Frankfurt/M., Lang, 1994.

TEML, Hubert /UNTERWEGER, Eva: Persönlichkeitsförderung in der LehrerInnenbildung. Journal für LehrerInnenbildung, 2/2002, S. 7-21. Innsbruck: Studienverlag, 2002.

UNTERWEGER, Eva/WEISS, Waltraud: forum paedak 3 – sich als persönlichkeit weiter entwickeln. Evaluationsstudie „Persönlichkeitsentwicklung 2000" an der Pädagogischen Akademie des Bundes in Wien. – Wien: Eigenverlag der Pädagogischen Akademie des Bundes, 2004.

UNTERWEGER, Eva: Selbstprofessionalisierung und Persönlichkeitsarbeit in der Ausbildung. In: Erziehung und Unterricht, 1-2/2009, S. 95 -103.

Kontakt:
Dr. Eva UNTERWEGER: eva.unterweger@phwien.ac.at

ZWEI MODELLE DES SCHULPRAKTIKUMS IN DER LEHRERAUSBILDUNG AN DER TARTUER UNIVERISTÄT (ESTLAND)

Meeli Väljaots & Esta Sikkal, Univeristät Tartu, Estland

Man strebt in der europäischen Lehrerausbildung nach einem gewissen einheitlichen Modell, aber sogar an einer Universität (am Beispiel der Universität Tartu, Estland) werden die Lehrer immer noch nach zwei unterschiedlichen Modellen ausgebildet. So studiert ein/-e Klassenlehrer/-in nach einem integrierten Curriculum fünf Jahre und beendet ihr Studium mit einer Magisterarbeit. Ein/e Grund-/Hauptschullehrer/-in dagegen erwirbt ihre Hochschulbildung dagegen in zwei Schritten (3 + 2 Ausbildungsmodell). Auch das Schulpraktikum spielt in diesen beiden Lehramtstudien eine ganz unterschiedliche Rolle. Diese Rolle wird vor dem Hintergrund der anderen Bestandteile beider Curricula beschrieben.

Schlüsselbegriffe: Schulpraktikum, schulpraktische Ausbildung, Curriculum

Seit der Unterzeichnung der Bologna-Erklärung im Jahr 1999 bewegen sich alle beteiligten europäischen Staaten in einem immer einheitlicher werdenden Hochschul(bildungs)raum. Man muss nicht mehr erklären, was ein Bakkalaureat oder Masterstudium ist, was ECTS oder „3+2 Ausbildungssystem" bedeuten. Wenn man sich aber heute nach einem einheitlichen europäischen Lehrerausbildungsmodell umsieht, ist so etwas nicht leicht zu finden. Das behaupten Friedrich BUCHBERGER und Irina BUCHBERGER (2002) anhand ihrer Untersuchung und ähnliches kann man auch in den EU-Dokumenten, z.B. in der Zusammenfassung der Lehrerbildungsanalyse der EU (2008) lesen. So ist es auch an der zu den ältesten Universitäten Europas gehörenden Tartuer Univerität, obwohl hier seit 1999 viele organisatorische und curriculare Neuerungen und Reformen in dem Bereich der Lehrerausbildung durchgeführt worden sind. Heute existieren zwei Modelle, nach denen die Lehrer für die Grund-/Primarschule und Hauptschule ausgebildet werden. (Die Ausbildung der Gymnasiallehrer wird im Folgenden nicht unter die Lupe genommen, denn diese vollzieht sich im Prinzip so wie die der Hauptschullehrer.)

Die Klassenlehrer sind in Estland die Lehrer/-innen, die in der Grundschule (Klasse 1-4) in einer Klasse alle Hauptfächer (Estnisch, Mathematik, Naturkunde, Kunst usw.) unterrichten. An der Tartuer Universität haben die Student/-inn/-en die Möglichkeit, ein Nebenfach (Englisch, Deutsch oder Kunst und Handarbeit) zu wählen. Zusätzlich erhalten sie in einigen Fächern, die vertieft studiert werden, das Recht, in der Schulstufe II (bis Klasse 7) zu unterrichten.

Die Klassenlehrer/-innen werden aufgrund eines integrierten Curriculums ausgebildet, das ein einheitliches fünfjähriges Magisterstudium vorsieht und mit dem Verfassen einer wissenschaftlichen Magisterarbeit (30 ECTS) endet. Von den unterschiedlichen Modulen, aus denen dieses Curriculum besteht, sind außerdem folgende zu nennen:

- allgemeinbildende Fächer (24 ECTS);
- die zu unterrichtenden Fächer und Fachdidaktiken (96 ECTS);
- erziehungswissenschaftliche und psychologische Fächer und ein Schulpraktikum (39 + 30 ECTS);
- Nebenfach (Englisch, Deutsch, Kunst und Handarbeit) (pro Fach 45 ECTS);
- Wahlfächer (18 ECTS);
- freie Fächer (18 ECTS).

Insgesamt umfasst das Curriculum 300 ECTS.

Während des Studiums werden die allgemein pädagogischen und fachdidaktischen Fächer ab dem viertem Semester konstant mit dem Schulpraktikum verbunden. Es gibt sechs unterschiedliche Schulpraktika, mit einem Gesamtumfang von 30 ECTS , die von den Fachdidaktiker/-inne/-n begleitet werden. Es ist wichtig zu erwähnen, dass jedes Praktikum ganz unterschiedliche Ziele hat und dass sie auch immer als eine Bedingung für ein weiteres Praktikum gelten. Die freiwilligen staatlichen, aber manchmal auch privaten Schulen, in denen das Praktikum stattfindet, leisten eine ausgezeichnete Zusammenarbeit mit der Universität. Die Lehrer/-innen arbeiten mit den Fachdidaktiker/-inne/-n zusammen, um die künftigen Klassenlehrer/-innen auf ihren Beruf vorzubereiten. Wie schon erwähnt, findet das erste Praktikum im 4. Semester statt und dauert in der Praxisschule zwei Wochen. In dieser Zeit werden die Stunden in unterschiedlichen Klassen (Klassen 1-3/4) bei unterschiedlichen Lehrern beobachtet und reflektiert. Eine erfolgreiche Reflexion kann nur dann zustande kommen, wenn in jeder Stunde auch die entsprechende Fachdidaktiker/-in dabei ist und sie in enger Zusammenarbeit mit der Lehrerin, die die Stunde durchgeführt hat, die Schlussreflexion durchführt. Nur so kann die in den Vorlesungen und Seminaren erarbeitete und angeeignete Theorie in der Praxis gesehen und beobachtet werden. Die Beobachtungsergebnisse werden alle dokumentiert und in einem gemeinsamen Schlussseminar nochmals systematisiert. Im fünften Semester gehen die Student/-inn/-en für vier Wochen in die Schule, wo sie am Anfang noch gewisse Hospitationen durchführen, dann aber allmählich schon Teile des Unterrichts, am Ende des Praktikums volle Unterrichtseinheiten (45 Minuten) erteilen. Von den Praxisschulen wird für jede Studentin eine Betreuerin – Klassenlehrerin bestimmt, deren Aufgabe es ist, der Studentin bei der Planung des eigenen Unterrichts zu helfen, die durchgeführte Stunde zu beobachten und gemeinsam zu reflektieren. Die Universitätsmethodiker/-inn/-en versuchen die Student/-innen während dieser Zeit auch wenigstens ein- bis zweimal zu beobachten und dann entweder eine mündliche oder schriftliche Rückmeldung zu geben. Im siebten Semester haben die Student/-inn/-en ein einwöchiges Hospitationspraktikum in der Schulstufe II. Dabei wird ähnlich vorgegangen wie bei dem ersten Beobachtungspraktikum, nur die Ziele des Praktikums variieren. Unter anderem muss man auch wenigstens ein Fach wählen, in dem man sich so stark fühlt, dass man selbst bereit ist, dieses in der II Schulstufe zu unterrichten. Im achten Semester findet das nächste Praktikum statt, wo die künftigen Lehrer/-innen dann einige Fächer nach ihrer Wahl (meistens sind es Estnisch, Mathematik, Naturkunde) und ihr Nebenfach (Englisch, Deutsch oder Kunst und Handarbeit) in der Schulstufe II unterrichten. Dieses Mal hat man in der Schule meistens mehrere Betreuer/-innen, die die Studenten in ihrem Fach begleiten. Im letzten Studienjahr müssen die Student/-inn/-en ihre Magisterarbeit schreiben und drei umfangreiche Praktika absolvieren. Das erste Praktikum findet in der ersten Schulwoche statt. In der ständigen Begleitung einer Fachmethodikerin wird von der Gruppe der Student/-inn/-en eine erste Klasse ab dem ersten Schultag Stunde für Stunde beobachtet. Ziel dieses Beobachtungspraktikums ist zu erfahren, was ein/-e Klassenlehrer/-in schon vor dem Schulanfang alles tun muss, wie der erste Schultag in der Schule sich gestaltet (meistens ein Fest und die erste Stunde mit oder ohne Eltern), welche Methoden in der ersten Woche genutzt werden, um den Übergang vom Kindergarten oder von zu Hause zu erleichtern usw. Da ist schon gelegentlich auch die Erlaubnis der Eltern nötig, denn die erste Schulwoche ist wirklich etwas Einmaliges und fast Intimes. Dieses Mal jedoch sitzt eine Gruppe von Studenten dabei. Obwohl die Lehrer/-innen in den Praxisschulen immer bereit sind, ihre Erfahrungen zu teilen, muss man auch die Wünsche der Eltern akzeptieren. Im neunten Semester muss auch das Diplompraktikum absolviert werden. Dieses dauert zwei Monate und wird meistens an unterschiedlichen Schulen Estlands durchgeführt. In dieser Zeit müssen die Studierenden schon so selbständig und auch so gut auf ihren künftigen Beruf vorbereitet sein, dass sie ohne alltägliche Unterstützung der Fachmethodiker/-innen in allen beruflichen Situationen zurechtkommen. An den Schulen werden sie von den dortigen Betreuer/-inne/-n begleitet. Ihre Aufgabe in diesem Praktikum ist es, den gesamten Unterricht ihrer Betreuer/-innen vorzubereiten und zu gestalten, Zensuren zu geben, Veranstaltungen durchzuführen usw. Die Praxisschulen geben nach den vorgegebenen Kriterien auch eine Zensur auf dem Niveau A-F.

Die Student/-inn/-en selbst schätzen ein solches Praktikumssystem sehr hoch ein, denn so gewinnen sie schon während des Studiums einen guten Überblick über den Lehrerberuf und erwerben nicht nur theoretische Kenntnisse. Eine kurze Befragung der Studenten des 8. und 9. Semesters ergab, dass die vier bzw. fünf Schulpraktika, die sie bereits absolviert haben, ihre bisherige berufliche/professionelle Entwicklung stark beeinflusst haben. Alle Befragten antworteten (100 %), dass sie gelernt haben, die theoretischen Kenntnisse in die Praxis umzusetzen, wodurch sie den Sinn ihres Studiums auch besser verstanden haben. 90 % der Befragten betonen, dass ihre Motivation, Lehrer/-in zu werden, während des Schulpraktikums weiter gestiegen ist. Nur 10 % mein-

ten, dass sie auch die Nachteile dieses Berufes erlebt haben und noch überlegen, ob sie nach dem Abschluss des Studiums als Lehrer/-innen arbeiten werden.
Die Haupt-/Grundschullehrer/-innen sind Lehrer/-innen, die darauf vorbereitet werden, in der Grund-/Hauptschule mehrere Fächer (z.B Englisch, Deutsch und/oder Geschichte; Physik, Chemie und/oder Geographie) zu unterrichten. Im Vergleich zu den Klassenlehrer/-inne/-n werden sie nach einem anderen Modell ausgebildet. Die Studierenden absolvieren zuerst ein dreijähriges Bakkalaureatsstudium und bewerben sich danach um einen Magisterstudienplatz. Insgesamt können die Student/-inn/-en zwischen drei Hauptzweigen wählen: 1. Lehrer für humanwissenschaftliche Fächer; 2. Lehrer für naturwissenschaftliche Fächer; 3. Lehrer für realwissenschaftliche Fächer. Das Bakkalaureatstudium umfasst 180 ECTS und besteht aus folgenden Modulen: 1) pädagogische Fächer (24 ECTS) 2) humanwissenschaftliche, naturwissenschaftliche oder realwissenschaftliche Fächer (24 ECTS). 3) Richtungsmodule I und II (48 ECTS), 4) Fachmodule I und II (48 ECTS); Wahlfächer (12 ECTS); Freifächer (18 ECTS); 5) und der Bachelorarbeit (6 ECTS). Während des ganzen Bakkalaureatsstudiums gibt es im sechsten Semester ein einwöchiges Schulpraktikum das sogenannte Einstiegspraktikum (3 ECTS), wo die Studierenden die Schule als Organisation kennen lernen und auch Stunden in ihren Wahlfächern beobachten und reflektieren sollen. Das Einstiegspraktikum wird mit einem kurzen theoretischen Seminar eingeleitet.
Das darauffolgende Magisterstudium für Grund-/Hauptschullehrer, die bis zur 9. Klasse mehrere Fächer unterrichten werden, umfasst 120 ECTS (Magisterarbeit 30 ECTS, das Schulpraktikum 18 ECTS). In der Regel wird dieses Praktikum im zweiten Studienjahr durchgeführt und die Studierenden erhalten im Rahmen dieses Praktikums die Möglichkeit, in den Praxisschulen diese Fächer zu unterrichten, die sie während des Bakkalaureats- und Magisterstudiums gewählt haben. Wie die Analyse der Lehrerausbildungscurricula (2006) zeigte, bildet das Schulpraktikum 7 % des gesamten Studienumfangs. Dieselbe Analyse zeigt auch, dass man im Studium zu Grund-/Hauptschullehrer/-inne/-n mehr Möglichkeiten finden sollte, die Theorie mit der Praxis (mit dem Schulpraktikum) zu verbinden. Leider gibt es zu viele Studierende, die sich mit dem Bachelordiplom zufrieden geben und nicht nach dem Bakkalaureat das Magisterstu-

dium aufnehmen. Für sie gibt es keine Möglichkeiten, die angeeigneten theoretischen Kenntnisse in der Schulrealität auszuprobieren.

Bis heute wurden angesichts dieser Curriculumentwicklung schon zahlreiche Verbesserungsmaßnahmen implementiert und eine Befragung in Form des e-Formulars zwecks möglichen Erneuerungen des Schulpraktikums durchgeführt. Die befragten Masterstudenten haben ihre Antworten gegeben und Vorschläge signalisiert. Die Befragung hat viele Aspekte berührt, z.B. den Inhalt der Module, die Integration der didaktischen Fächer mit den Fachmodulen und natürlich mit dem Schulpraktikum. Gleichzeitig wurden auch Arbeitgeber, Absolventen und Lehrkräfte befragt.

Die Befragung unter Studenten vom Februar 2010 zeigt, dass 67 % der befragten Studenten mit dem Studium im Allgemeinen zufrieden ist. Die Zufriedenheitsgrad mit dem Gesamtcurriculum (inwiefern kann das Curriculum die Anforderungen an die angehenden Lehrer/-innen erfüllen?) wurde mir 3,6 von 5 Punkten ermittelt.

Jedoch war der Zufriedenheitsgrad mit dem Schulpraktikum erheblich niedriger: nur 35 % haben sich mit der Organisation und den Grundprinzipien des Schulpraktikums zufrieden gegeben.

Interessant war auch, dass die Probleme mit dem Schulpraktikum für Studenten wichtiger waren als die für Lehrkräfte. Die Student/-inn/-en haben selbst das Einstiegspraktikum als sehr wichtig eingeschätzt, jedoch haben sie den Wunsch nach einem extra Fach geäußert, damit der Nutzen dieses Praktikums maximiert werden kann. Genauso wichtig sei die darauf folgende Reflexion in Kleingruppen.

Zusammenfassend kann man feststellen, dass an der Universität Tartu, wie oben schon erwähnt, nebeneinander zwei Modelle der Lehrerausbildnug existieren, nach denen die Lehrer für die Grund-/Primarschule und Hauptschule ausgebildet werden. Jedes Modell hat Vor- und Nachteile, immerhin gilt das Modell für Klassenlehrer heute als ein gutes Beispiel, das sowohl von den Studierenden als auch von Dozenten, Schulen und Experten hoch geschätzt wird.

Das Modell der Hauptschullehrer ermöglicht die Mobilität und Flexibilität im Studium sowie im Schulpraktikum, aber die allgemeine übergreifende Integration zwischen Theorie und Praxis soll noch erheblich verbessert werden.

Literaturangaben

OTS, AIVAR/JAANI, JUTA/SEPPA, ANU: Ülevaade Tartu Ülikooli õpetajakoolituse õppekavadest, Tartu Ülikooli õppekava arenduskeskus, Tartu, 2006.

SISEPOLIITIKA PEADIREKTORAAT: Struktuuri- ja ühtekuuluvuspoliitika osakond Kultuur ja haridus. Õpetajahariduse sisu ja kvaliteet Euroopa Liidus, Brüssel, Euroopa Parlament, 2008.

BUCHBERGER, FRIEDRICH & BUCHBERGER, IRINA: Europäische Lehrerausbildung zwischen Finnland und England; in: B. Laudenbach (Hg.): Reform der Lehrerbildung. Bremen: LSI 2002
http://www.so.ut.ee/

FACULTY OF SOCIAL SCIENCES AND EDUCATION, CURRICULA: Educational Science (Humanities); Educational Science (Sciences); Educational Science (Math and Sciences); Primary School Teacher (5-year BA and MA combined); Teacher of Several Subjects in Basic School.

Kontakt:
Meeli VÄLJAOTS: meeli.valjaots@ut.ee   Esta SIKKAL: esta.sikkal@ut.ee

MUSIK-METHODIK ALS BESTANDTEIL DER VORBREITUNG DER VORSCHULLEHRER/-INNEN IN LETTLAND

Ligita Stramkale, Universität Lettlands, Lettland

In diesem Artikel werden die Formen der musikalischen Tätigkeiten im Vorbereitungsprozess der zukünftigen Vorschullehrer-/innen analysiert.
Durch eine Befragung der Studierenden des Studienganges Vorschulpädagogik werden die musikalischen Fertigkeiten, die während des Studium schwer zu erwerben sind, festgestellt; dazu wird die Meinung der Studierenden über die Notwendigkeit der Aneignung der Musik-Methodik im Vorbereitungsprozess der Vorschullehrer/-innen aufgeklärt.

Schlüsselbegriffe: Musikmethodik, musikalische Tätigkeiten, Vorschulpädagogik, Selbstbewertung musikalischer Tätigkeiten

1 Einführung

Die Vorschulausbildung hat große Bedeutung für Land, Gesellschaft, Eltern und Kinder. Die Fakultät für Pädagogik und Psychologie an der Universität Lettlands ist eine von mehreren Hochschulen, die ihren Studierenden die Mög-

lichkeit bieten, eine Ausbildung zum Beruf der Vorschullehrer/-innen zu bekommen. Die Studierenden sollen während des Studiums die beruflichen Kompetenzen der Vorschulehrer/-innen erwerben, um die Ausbildung der Vorschulkinder durch das Spiel als Grundmethode zu verwenden, die pädagogischen Theorien mit der Ausbildungspraxis verbinden zu können und die individuelle Entwicklung des Kindes zu fördern.
Die zukünftigen Vorschullehrer/-innen werden nicht nur durch Lehrgänge für Pädagogik und Psychologie, sondern auch durch verschiedene Unterrichtsmethodiken ausgebildet. Es ist eine Pflicht, dass alle Studierenden unabhängig von ihren musikalischen Fähigkeiten am Studienkurs *„Musik-Methodik in der Vorschule"* im Ausmaß von 4 Kreditpunkten teilnehmen müssen.
Ziel der Forschung ist es, die Spezifik der Formen von musikalischen Tätigkeiten theoretisch zu analysieren und die Meinung der Studierenden zur Frage der Notwendigkeit der Aneignung der Musik-Methodik in der Vorbereitung der Vorschullehrer/-innen zu erheben.

2 Die Formen der musikalischen Tätigkeiten im Vorbereitungsprozess der zukünftigen Vorschullehrer/-innen

Die pädagogischen Tätigkeiten in der Lettischen Vorschule werden durch ein vom Bildungs- und Wissenschaftsministerium erarbeitetes Ausbildungsprogramm bestimmt. In diesem Programm werden Ziele, Aufgaben und Inhalte der Ausbildung festgelegt, dazu ist es vorgesehen, „dass *das Milieu, die Tätigkeiten des Kindes und die Spiele große Bedeutung haben, um dieses Programm zu realisieren"* (*Pirmskolas izglītības programma*, 1998, S.3).
Nach GOLUBINA (2007) müssen die Vorschullehrer/-innen in Zusammenarbeit mit Musiklehrer/-inne/-n *„Feste, lustige Momente und andere Unterhaltungsformen organisieren"* (Golubina 2007, S. 139). Die Vorschullehrer/-innen helfen Kindern und Musiklehrer/-inne/-n bei der Durchführung der im Ausbildungsprogramm festgelegten Forderungen. Im Ausbildungsprogramm werden 3 mögliche Entwicklungsniveaus für jede Form der musikalischen Tätigkeiten festgelegt, die nicht vom Alter der Kinder abhängig sind, sondern durch die Individualität und das erreichte musikalische Niveau des Kindes bestimmt werden.
Die zukünftigen Vorschullehrer/-innen können sich während des Studiums alle Formen der musikalischen Tätigkeiten, die im Ausbildungsprogramm festgelegt sind, wie Gesang, Musikhören, Spielen auf den Rhythmus- und Musikinstrumenten und rhythmische Bewegungen aneignen.

Gesang ist eine der Hauptformen der musikalischen Tätigkeiten in der Vorschule. Nach BÄßLER, Vizepräsident des Deutschen Musikrats ist *„die Stimme ... das erste Instrument des Menschen überhaupt, die gleichzeitig am stärksten mit dem eigenen Körper zu tun hat"* (Kopitze, 2009). Im Laufe des Studienkurses *„Musik-Methodik in der Vorschule"* beschäftigen sich die zukünftigen Vorschullehrer/-innen vertieft mit den Stimmumfängen der Kinderstimme und stellten fest, warum Kinder singen müssen und warum sie intonativ nicht richtig singen können; dazu werden sie die Gesangsfähigkeiten der Kinder entsprechend ihren Altersbesonderheiten charakterisieren und erwerben die Fähigkeit, den Kindern beizubringen, wie sie einfache Lieder nach dem Gehör singen können. Kinder können Musikstücke nicht nur im Musikunterricht, sondern auch in ihrer Freizeit hören. Die zukünftigen Vorschullehrer/-innen erwerben die Methodik des Musikhörens und beherrschen die Methoden zur Entwicklung der Musikauffassung.

In der Vorschule werden verschiedene Rhythmus- und Musikinstrumente genutzt, um das Rhythmusgefühl zu entwickeln und die gelernten Lieder zu variieren. Um die Lieder begleiten zu können, müssen die zukünftigen Vorschullehrer/-innen die Nutzung von Körperinstrumenten, Schlaginstrumenten (Trommel, Tamburin, Triangel, Kastagnetten, Maracas und verschiedene Glocken), sowie melodische Musikinstrumente (Xylophon und Metallophon) beherrschen. Die Studierenden lernen während des Studiums verschiedene Methoden zur Aneignung der Rhythmus- und Musikinstrumente kennen, um innerhalb und auch außerhalb des Musikunterrichtes die Kinder beim Spielen eines Instruments unterstützen zu können.

Durch rhythmische Körperbewegungen werden der Rhythmus- und Metrenwechsel sowie die musikalische Gestalt erkannt und dazu können verschiedene Tanzschritte ausgeführt werden.

3 Empirische Forschungsmethodologie und Messinstrumente

Um die Wichtigkeit der Aneignung einer musikalischen Ausbildung für die Vorbereitung der Vorschullehrer/-innen durch den Studienkurs *„Musik-Methodik in der Vorschule"* zu bestimmen, wurde eine Befragung durchgeführt, an der 43 Vollzeit-Studierende teilgenommen haben, davon sind 25 Studierende im 2. Studienjahr und 18 sind im 3. Studienjahr, darunter waren zufällig an dieser Befragung keine männlichen Studierenden beteiligt.

Mehrere Bedingungen wurden bei der Vorbereitung des Fragebogens beachtet. Erstens, zu Beginn des Fragebogens wurde kurz das Ziel der Forschung geklärt und darauf hingewiesen, dass vollständige Anonymität der Befragten gewährleistet ist. Zweitens, es wurde darauf geachtet, dass der Schwierigkeitsgrad der Fragen ansteigt. Drittens, die Fragen und die vorgegebenen Antwortmöglichkeiten wurden so formuliert, dass die Resultate durch die Verwendung mathematischer statistischer Datenbearbeitungsmethoden in möglichst kurzer Zeit analysiert werden können.
In Anbetracht der Meinung, dass *„die Respondenten nur inhaltsreiche, vollständige Antworten geben können, wenn die Fragen im Fragebogen nicht mehr als zehn sind"* (Образцов, 2004, S. 86), wurden eben zehn Fragen im Fragebogen gestellt. Durch die ersten zwei Fragen konnten Informationen über Alter und Geschlecht der Respondenten gesammelt werden. Es wurde durch die im Fragebogen gestellten Fragen aufgeklärt, ob die Studierenden des Studienganges *„Vorschulpädagogik"* bereits zuvor eine Ausbildung in Musik erhalten hatten – ob sie Musikinstrumente spielen können.
Der Fragebogen enthält geschlossene Fragen mit vorformulierten Antwortmöglichkeiten und daneben wurden auch teilweise offene Fragen formuliert, damit die Studierenden außerhalb der vorgegebenen Antwortmöglichkeiten andere Antworten geben können. Drei von zehn Fragen sind auf einer Ratingskala zu beantworten. Die Respondenten bewerteten auf einer fünfteiligen Skala das Niveau ihrer musikalischen Fähigkeiten, die Wichtigkeit der Aneignung verschiedener Formen der musikalischen Tätigkeiten und gaben an, welche davon die größten Schwierigkeiten im Studium bereiten.
Im Fragebogen wurde auch eine offene Frage gestellt, um festzustellen, wie die Aneignung der Musik-Methodik in der Vorbereitung der zukünftigen Vorschullehrer/-innen verbessert werden kann.
Die Resultate der Befragung wurden durch Verwendung des arithmetischen Mittels berechnet und analysiert. Der Korrelationskoeffizient nach Pearson wurde verwendet, um festzustellen, ob es einen Zusammenhang gibt zwischen dem Niveau der musikalischen Fähigkeiten und den Formen der musikalischen Tätigkeiten, die nach der Meinung der Studierenden Schwierigkeiten darstellen. Beim einem Wert von +1 (bzw. -1) besteht ein vollständig positiver (bzw. negativer) Zusammenhang zwischen den betreffenden Merkmalen. Wenn der Korrelationskoeffizient den Wert (r=0) aufweist, besteht zwischen

beiden Merkmalen kein Zusammenhang. Als Maß des Zusammenhangs gilt bis 0,2 ist als „sehr schwach", von 0,2 bis 0,4 als „schwach", von 0,4 bis 0,7 als „eher eng" und über 0,7 als „eng". Die Daten wurden mit SPSS 16 erarbeitet.

4 Die Resultate der Forschung

Die Resultate zeigen, dass die Mehrheit der Studierenden (88 %) im Studiengang *„Vorschulpädagogik"* keine vorherige musikalische Ausbildung erhalten haben. Nur eine der Befragten ist Absolventin einer Musikschule und zwei davon haben schon damals an der Musikschule studiert, ihr Studium aber nicht abgeschlossen. Nur 28 % der Befragten können melodische Musikinstrumente spielen, davon spielen drei Studierende ein bisschen Klavier, zwei spielen Gitarre und zwei spielen sowohl Geige als auch Klavier.

Die Studierenden sollten ihre musikalischen Fähigkeiten wie Rhythmusgefühl, musikalisches Gehör, Gesangsqualität, musikalisches Gedächtnis und musikalisches Denken selbst einschätzen. Durch die Zusammenfassung der Resultate wurde festgestellt, dass die Mehrheit der Studierenden des 2. Studienjahres (54 %) nach ihrer Meinung ein gutes Rhythmusgefühl haben, nur 39 % der Studierenden des 3. Studienjahres haben die gleiche Einschätzung geäußert (alle Angaben in Prozenten).

Musikalische Fähigkeiten	*Gut*		*Eher gut*		*Eher schlecht*		*Schlecht*		*Schwer zu sagen*	
	2. SJ	3. SJ	2. SJ	3. SJ	2. SJ	3. SJ	2. SJ	3. SJ	2. SJ	3. SJ
Rhythmusgefühl	54	39	38	50	8	6	0	0	0	5
Musikalisches Gehör	28	17	40	33	20	28	12	11	0	11
Gesangsqualität	12	22	50	28	23	28	15	5	0	17
Musikalisches Gedächtnis	19	11	38	50	31	22	4	6	8	11
Musikalisches Denken	12	6	31	33	38	22	12	11	8	28

Selbstbewertung der musikalischen Fähigkeiten

Der größte Teil der Studierenden des 2. Studienjahres sind der Meinung, dass sie ihr musikalisches Gehör als eher gut (40 %) und als gut (28 %) beurteilen können. Gleichfalls haben die Mehrheit der Studierenden des 3. Studienjahres ihr musikalisches Gehör mit eher gut (33 %) bewertet, aber 28 % der Befragten haben gesagt, dass ihr musikalisches Gehör eher schlecht ist, und sogar 11 % davon denken, dass es schlecht ist.
12 % der Studierenden des 2. Studienjahres haben ihre Gesangsqualität als gut bewertet, aber 15 % der zukünftigen Vorschulehrerinnen denken, dass es schlecht ist. 17 % der Studierenden des 3. Studienjahres konnten ihre Gesangsqualität nicht bewerten, ihrerseits haben sich 22 % der Befragten für gut entschieden.
Die Mehrheit der Studierenden des 2. und 3. Studienjahres haben ihr musikalisches Gedächtnis als eher gut (38 %, 50 %) bzw. die Minderheit als eher schlecht (31 %, 22 %) bewertet.
Die zukünftigen Vorschullehrerinnen haben ihr musikalisches Denken am kritischesten bewertet, denn 38 % der Studierenden des 2. Studienjahres sind der Meinung, dass das Niveau ihres musikalischen Denkens eher schlecht ist, und 12 % der Befragten haben zugesagt, dass es sogar schlecht ist. Einer der Gründe für die von Studierenden über ihr musikalisches Denken so kritische gegebene Bewertung liegt darin, dass das Verständnis für das Wesen dieser musikalischen Fähigkeit bei manchen Studierenden ungenügend ist. Dafür ist die Antwort der Studierenden des 3. Studienjahres der beste Beweis, denn 28 % davon konnten ihr musikalisches Denken überhaupt nicht bewerten.
Die Mehrheit der Studierenden des 2. und 3. Studienjahres (56 %, 72 %) sind der Meinung, dass der Studienkurs „*Musik-Methodik in der Vorschule*“ wichtig für die Vorbereitung der Vorschullehrer/-innen ist, 24 % und 11 % der Befragten denken, dass es sehr wichtig ist, 20 % und 17 % der Studierenden halten es für wenig wichtig, dazu glaubt kein einziger der Befragten, dass dieser Studienkurs unwichtig oder unnötig ist (s. Angaben in der Tabelle in Prozenten):

Form der musikalischen Tätigkeiten	*Sehr wichtig*		*Wichtig*		*Wenig wichtig*		*Unwichtig*		*Schwer zu sagen*	
	2. SJ	3. SJ	2. SJ	3. SJ	2. SJ	3. SJ	2. SJ	3. SJ	2. SJ	3. SJ
Gesang	32	44	56	56	12	0	0	0	0	0
Musikhören	32	22	64	78	4	0	0	0	0	0
Rhythmische Bewegungen	44	72	56	28	0	0	0	0	0	0
Musikalische Spiele	68	78	28	22	4	0	0	0	0	0
Spielen auf den Rhythmus- und Musikinstrumenten	20	39	52	50	28	6	0	0	0	5

Bewertung der Wichtigkeit der Aneignung der Formen musikalischer Tätigkeiten

Der größte Teil der Studierenden denkt, dass Musikhören (64 %, 78 %), Gesang (56 %) und Spielen auf den Rhythmus- und Musikinstrumenten (52 %, 50 %) die wichtigsten Formen der musikalischen Tätigkeiten in der Vorbereitung der zukünftigen Vorschullehrer/-innen sind. 56 % der Studierenden des 2. Studienjahres bewerten die rhythmischen Bewegungen als wichtig, aber nur 28 % der Studierenden des 3. Studienjahres haben die gleiche Meinung geäußert. Die größte Zahl der Befragten haben die Aneignung von Methodik zur Organisierung musikalischer Spiele als sehr wichtig beurteilt. Es ist interessant zu bemerken, dass viele der Studierenden des 2. Studienjahres (28 %) im Gegensatz zu den Studierenden des 3. Studienjahres (6 %) die Aneignung der Methodik zum Spielen auf einem Rhythmus- oder Musikinstrument als unwichtig bewertet haben. Keine der befragten Studierenden denkt, dass die Formen der musikalischen Tätigkeiten unwichtig sind.

Die Studierenden haben keine Schwierigkeiten bei der Aneignung mancher Formen der musikalischen Tätigkeiten wie Musikhören (76 %, 89 %) und musikalische Spiele (64 %, 61 %) gehabt, aber Gesang (24 %, 11 %) sowie Spielen der Rhythmus- und Musikinstrumente (24 %, 22 %) bereiten mehr oder weniger Schwierigkeiten (s. Tabelle; Angaben in Porzenten):

Form der musikalischen Tätigkeiten	*Nicht schwierig*		*Eher nicht schwierig*		*Eher schwierig*		*Schwierig*		*Schwer zu sagen*	
	2. SJ	3. SJ	2. SJ	3. SJ	2. SJ	3. SJ	2. SJ	3. SJ	2. SJ	3. SJ
Gesang	24	44	40	28	24	11	12	17	0	0
Musikhören	76	89	20	11	4	0	0	0	0	0
Rhythmische Bewegungen	40	44	40	50	16	6	4	0	0	0
Musikalische Spiele	64	61	32	39	4	0	0	0	0	0
Spielen der Rhythmus- und Musikinstrumente	20	22	48	28	28	22	4	17	0	11

Formen der musikalischen Tätigkeiten, die am meisten Schwierigkeiten für die Studierenden darstellen

Die Studierenden haben Schwierigkeiten mit dem Gesang, weil sie keine vorherige Vorbereitung im diesen Bereich bekommen haben, dazu spielt die Schüchternheit und Aufregung, die beim Singen sehr deutlich zu spüren sind, eine große Rolle. Manche Studierende haben zugesagt, dass sie Gesang einfach nicht mögen. Die unzureichende Entwicklung des musikalischen Gehörs ist der Grund dafür, warum Gesang Schwierigkeiten bereitet. Die Studierenden können Kinderlieder intonativ nicht richtig singen, deswegen sind sie von ihrer Gesangsfähigkeit nicht überzeugt. Spielen auf einem Rhythmusinstrument ist schwierig, weil die Studierenden die Pulsation des Rhythmus zeitweise nicht fühlen können, aber Spielen auf einem Musikinstrument ist so kompliziert, um damit ein Lied angemessen und überzeugend begleiten zu können.
Um die Aneignung einer Form der musikalischen Tätigkeiten zu vereinfachen, sollen die Studierenden mehr Zeit für praktische Betätigungen und weniger für die Theorie im Bereich Musik geben.
Die Studierenden haben anerkennt, dass es sehr wichtig ist, sich Kenntnisse im Studienkurs Musik-Methodik über alle Formen der musikalischen Tätigkeiten (musikalische Spiele, Musikhören, Gesang, Rhythmische Bewegungen und Spielen der Rhythmus- und Musikinstrumente) anzueignen sowie die Methoden zur Entwicklung des Rhythmusgefühls und des musikalischen Gehörs anwen-

den zu können. Genau so wichtig ist die Fähigkeit, ein Musikstück zu analysieren, weil die Vorschullehrer/-innen mit den Kindern ihre Meinung über ein Musikstück ausdrücken und begründen sollen.
Die Studierenden denken, dass eine Form der musikalischen Tätigkeiten entsprechend dem Alter der Kinder richtig methodisch geleitet werden muss. Es ist wichtig zu wissen, welche Formen für welche Altersgruppe passen, damit die musikalische Tätigkeit für die Kinder interessant sein kann.
Die Studierenden sind der Meinung, dass die Vorschullehrer/-innen eine Zusammenstellung von Musikstücken und Kinderliedern zweckmäßig nutzen können. Die Aneignung der musikalischen Spiele und ihre Didaktik fördert die Lehrer/-innen; dadurch kann die Attraktivität des Musikunterrichts erhöht werden, der die Vorstellungskraft und Ausdrucksfähigkeit der Vorschulkinder anregen soll.
Durch die Analyse der Forschungsresultate wurde festgestellt, dass es einen relativ engen Zusammenhang zwischen dem – von Studierenden selbstbewerteten – Rhythmusgefühl und den dargestellten Schwierigkeiten der Ausführung rhythmischer Bewegungen ($r=0,67$) bzw. Gesang ($r=0,50$) gibt. In gleicher Zeit ist die Korrelation zwischen dem Rhythmusgefühl und der musikalischen Spiele schwach ($r=0,30$). Das heißt, dass der Mangel an Rhythmusgefühl die Organisation musikalischer Spiele nicht beeinflussen kann. Ebenso wurde ein Zusammenhang zwischen Rhythmusgefühl und Spielen auf den Musikinstrumenten nicht festgestellt. Die Studierenden geben zu, dass eher die unzureichende Entwicklung ihrer Fähigkeit und auf keinen Fall das mangelhafte Rhythmusgefühl der Grund dafür ist, warum sie Schwierigkeiten bei der Aneignung von Spielen eines Musikinstruments haben. Es besteht ein relativ enger Zusammenhang zwischen der Selbstbewertung der Studierenden in Bezug auf ihr musikalisches Gehör und den Schwierigkeiten, die beim Gesang auftreten können ($r=0,59$). In der Forschungsarbeit wurde nicht festgestellt, dass musikalisches Gehör und Gesangsqualität die Einführung der musikalischen Spiele in der Vorschule beeinflussen können.

5 Schlussfolgerung und Diskussion

„*Warum müssen sich die Vorschullehrer/-innen Musik- Methodik aneignen, wenn sie Musik in der Vorschule nicht unterrichten werden?*“ Es ist richtig, dass die Vorschullehrer/-innen an der Vorschule nicht als Musiklehrer/-innen arbeiten werden, aber immer wird Musik für die Vorschulkinder unterrichtet. Aus diesem Grund muss den Musiklehrer/-inne/-n von den Vorschullehrer/-innen bei der Arbeit mit den Kindern geholfen werden. Nur durch eine erfolgreiche Zusammenarbeit kann die vollwertige Entwicklung der musikalischen Fähigkeiten der Kinder gefördert werden und damit können erfolgreiche musikalische Veranstaltungen in der Vorschule durchgeführt werden.

Durch die Forschungsresultate wurde festgestellt, dass die Studierenden trotz ihrer Schwierigkeiten mit Gesang bzw. Spielen auf den Rhythmus- und Musikinstrumenten die Wichtigkeit der Aneignung der Musik-Methodik verstehen können, unabhängig davon, ob sie Vorkenntnisse über Musik haben.

Die Studierenden denken, dass sie ein ziemlich gutes Rhythmusgefühl besitzen, dazu haben sie ihr musikalisches Gehör und die Gesangsqualität als eher gut bewertet. Die Respondenten beurteilten ihr musikalisches Denken am kritischesten, denn eine große Anzahl der Studierenden (8 % des 2. Studienjahrs bzw. 28 % des 3. Studienjahrs) konnten diese musikalische Fähigkeit überhaupt nicht bewerten. Der Grund dafür sind die mangelhaften Kenntnisse über das Wesen dieser musikalischen Fähigkeit.

Die Studierenden erkennen, dass alle Formen der musikalischen Tätigkeiten im Rahmen ihrer Ausbildung zu Vorschullehrer/-innen wichtig sind. Nach ihrer Meinung ist die Aneignung der Methodik zur Organisation der musikalischen Spiele sehr wichtig. Genau so wichtig ist es, ein methodisch richtiges Musikhören durchzuführen und den Kindern das Singen beibringen zu können.

Literaturangaben

GOLUMBINA, V: Pirmskolas pedagoga rokasgrāmata. Rīga: Izglītības soļi, 2007. 308 lpp.

KOPITZKE, O.: Erziehung beginnt mit dem Abendritual.
In: http://www.zeit.de/kultur/musik/2009-11/hans-baessler-wiegenlieder?page=all

Pirmskolas izglītības programma. R.: Mācību apgāds, 1998. 40 lpp.

ОБРАЗЦОВ, П.И.: Методы и методология психолого – педагогического исследования. СПб: Питер, 2004. 268 стр.

Kontakt:
Dr. paed. doc. Ligita STRAMKALE: ligita.stramkale@lu.lv

Die neue Lehrerausbildung im Sekundarbereich in Spanien am Beispiel der DaF-Lehrer an der UCM

Luisa Schilling, Irene Szumlakowski,
Universidad Complutense de Madrid, Spanien

In den letzten fünf Jahren hat die Lehrerausbildung für die Sekundarstufe in Spanien eine grundlegende Reform erfahren. Im Studienjahr 2009/10 haben die ersten Masterstudiengänge „zur Ausbildung von Sekundarlehrern, Lehrern in Berufsschulen und Fremdsprachenlehrern" begonnen. Die Lehrerausbildung wird nicht mehr mit einem einfachen pädagogischen Zertifikat abgeschlossen, sondern mit einem einjährigen Masterstudiengang, der ein Praktikum von drei Monaten einschließt. Das Beispiel der DaF-Lehrer an der Universität Complutense zeigt, wie in der Reform neueste Wege des autonomen Lernens, des lebenslangen Lernens und des kooperativen Lernens integriert und gefördert werden können.

Schlüsselbegriffe: Lehrerausbildung in Spanien, DaF-Lehrerausbildung, Lehrerfortbildung

1 Vorgeschichte

1.1 Wie die Ausbildung der Lehrkräfte im Sekundarbereich früher organisiert war

Vom Jahre 1970 bis Oktober 2009 war der *Certificado de Aptitud Pedagógica* (CAP, Zertifikat zur pädagogischen Eignung) die einzige offizielle Ausbildung für Lehrkräfte im Sekundarbereich in Spanien. Um Lehrer im Sekundarbereich zu werden, benötigte man zunächst ein abgeschlossenes Hochschulstudium und danach die bestandene schriftliche Prüfung über pädagogische und fachspezifische Inhalte als Zugang zu den offiziellen Beamtenauswahlprüfungen *(oposiciones)*. Lehrerstellen für Philosophie, Erdkunde und Geschichte, spanische Sprache und Literatur, Englisch oder Französisch durften von Absolventen der Fächer Geographie, Geschichte, Philologie, Philosophie, Jura oder Publizistik, das heißt aus dem Bereich der Humanwissenschaften, besetzt werden. Es wurden einige pädagogische Seminare angeboten, die in den jeweiligen Instituten der Erziehungswissenschaften (ICEs) erteilt wurden. Die Studenten mussten selber die Inhalte mit hauseigenen Lehrbüchern vorbereiten, nach der schriftlichen Prüfung musste außerdem ein Praktikum absolviert werden. Jede Universität bot in ihrer CAP-Prüfung beliebige Fachrichtungen an, aber in keiner von ihnen Deutsch, obwohl in Spanien in einer kleinen Auswahl von Gymnasien Deutsch als (erste oder zweite) Fremdsprache unterrichtet wird.

1.2 Andere Fortbildungsmaßnahmen

Im Jahr 2000 wurde an der Universität Complutense Madrid in Zusammenarbeit mit dem Goethe-Institut Madrid ein Postgraduiertenkurs *(Renovación y adecuación metodológicas aplicadas a la enseñanza del alemán como lengua extranjera)* nach dem Modell der Germanisten in Barcelona veranstaltet. In zwei Jahren konnten die Teilnehmer (zukünftige und fortzubildende Deutschlehrer) in zwei 14-tägigen Präsenzseminaren und fünf Folgeseminaren pro Jahr unterschiedliche Module belegen. Die dort erworbenen Kenntnisse und Fähigkeiten wurden auf der Basis der Fernstudieneinheiten dann in der nachfolgenden Lehrtätigkeit angewandt. Im Kurs standen die Kooperation, die berufliche Reflexion und die autonome Fortbildung der Teilnehmer im Vordergrund. Die Themen wurden den Bedürfnissen der Teilnehmer entsprechend ausgewählt. Die Eigenarbeitsphasen der Teilnehmer wurden mit 30 % der Kreditpunkte anerkannt.

Die Lerner des Postgraduiertenkurses stellten ein Lehrerportfolio vor, das sowohl als Abschlussevaluation wie als Nachweis des Lernprozesses und Werkzeug des lebenslanges Lernens diente.

Dieser Postgraduiertenkurs, der nicht offiziell, aber doch für einen Teil des CAPs anerkannt wurde, fand bis zum Jahr 2006 statt.

2 Vom CAP zum Master

Im Jahr 2003 wurden von staatlicher Seite die ersten Verhandlungen aufgenommen, um das System des CAP als Zugang für Sekundarschullehrer zu reformieren. Aber erst im Jahre 2008 trat die neue Regelung in Kraft. Im Erlass vom 8. November 2008 wird bestimmt:

"Para ejercer la docencia en la educación secundaria obligatoria, el bachillerato, la formación profesional y la enseñanza de idiomas, será necesario estar en posesión de un título oficial de máster que acredite la formación pedagógica y didáctica." (Um eine Lehrtätigkeit in der Sekundarstufe, in Berufschulen und in Sprachschulen auszuüben, muss man einen offiziellen Masterstudiengang belegen, der die pädagogische und didaktische Ausbildung des Kandidaten akkreditiert.)

Im Studienjahr 2009-2010 haben die Universitäten zum ersten Mal Masterstudiengänge zur Ausbildung von Sekundarlehrern, Lehrern in Berufschulen und

an staatlichen Sprachenschulen angeboten. Dieser 60 ECTS umfassende Master besteht aus drei Modulen (pädagogische, didaktische und fachspezifische Kurse), einem dreimonatigen Praktikum und einer schriftlichen Abschlussarbeit.
In allen Fachrichtungen wird eine gemäß dem Gemeinsamen Europäischem Referenzrahmen B1-Kompetenz in einer Fremdsprache verlangt. In Madrid kann man einen solchen Master an vier von sechs öffentlichen Universitäten sowie an drei privaten Universitäten absolvieren.

3 Erste Erfahrungen mit der DaF-Lehrerausbildung an der UCM

Die einzige Universität in Madrid und fast in ganz Spanien, die einen Master für Deutschlehrer in der Sekundarstufe und an staatlichen Sprachenschulen anbietet, ist die Universität Complutense.

3.1 Struktur

Die Grundstruktur für alle Fachrichtungen des Masters wurde vom Institut für Erziehungswissenschaften vorgegeben. Sie besteht aus 60 ECTS, die sich auf die folgenden drei Module verteilen: 1. fachübergreifendes Modul, 2. fachspezifisches Modul und 3. Praktikum mit Abschlussarbeit. Die Lehrveranstaltungen der zwei ersten Module finden im Wintersemester statt. Für Praktikum und Abschlussarbeit ist das Sommersemester geplant. Für das fachspezifische Modul der vier möglichen Fremdsprachen Englisch, Französisch, Deutsch oder Italienisch wurde eine gemeinsame Struktur entworfen.
Die Verteilung der ECTS in den verschiedenen Modulen ist wie folgt:

Module		
Allgemein	Fachspezifisch	Praktikum + Abschlussarbeit
12 ECTS	30 ECTS	18 ECTS
Kurse	Kurse	
Aprendizaje y desarrollo de la personalidad 4 ECTS	*Diseño y evaluación de unidades docentes. Innovación docente y tecnológica* 5 ECTS	Praktikum 12 ECTS

<table>
<tr><td></td><td>Didáctica de las competencias comunicativas literarias y culturales 5 ECTS</td><td></td></tr>
<tr><td rowspan="2">Procesos y contextos educativos
4 ECTS</td><td>Fundamentación didáctica del alemán como lengua extranjera 5 ECTS</td><td rowspan="2">Abschlussarbeit
6 ECTS</td></tr>
<tr><td>Lingüística alemana aplicada a la enseñanza y aprendizaje de la lengua alemana
5 ECTS</td></tr>
<tr><td rowspan="2">Sociedad, familia y educación
4 ECTS</td><td>Tipología y variedad textual de la lengua alemana
5 ECTS</td><td rowspan="2"></td></tr>
<tr><td>Manifestaciones literarias e interculturalidad en la lengua alemana 5 ECTS</td></tr>
</table>

Das Praktikum an einem Gymnasium oder an einer offiziellen Sprachschule dauert zweieinhalb Monate. Die Praktikanten werden in dieser Zeit von einem Gymnasiallehrer zusammen mit einem Masterdozenten betreut. Sie werden nicht nur in die Praxis der Lehrtätigkeit eingeführt, sondern auch in die Umgebung der jeweiligen Institution. Sie sollen die offiziellen Regelungen, Dokumente und Sitzungen kennen lernen. Als Abschluss sollen sie einen Praktikumsbericht verfassen, dessen Kern die Bearbeitung und Durchführung einer mindestens zweiwöchigen didaktischen Einheit bildet.

In der Master-Abschlussarbeit soll die theoretisch begründete Bearbeitung eines Themas in enger Beziehung mit der Lehrerfahrung erfolgen; dazu gehört eine Zusammenstellung ausgewählter authentischer Materialien aus der Unterrichtspraxis. Diese Arbeit wird vor einem Prüfungsausschuss vorgestellt und verteidigt.

3.2 Eigener Vorschlag

Unsere Erfahrungen mit dem Postgraduiertenkurs ermöglichten es, innerhalb dieses strengen Programms neue Vorschläge und Arbeitsweisen zu integrieren. Die sechs Kurse aus dem fachspezifischen Modul werden exklusiv in deutscher Sprache erteilt, was zur Befestigung der kommunikativen Sprachkompetenz der Teilnehmer beiträgt. Unter anderem werden die Studieneinheiten des Fernstudienprojekts DIFF-GHK-GI (Universität Tübingen, Universität Kassel und Goethe-Institut München) eingesetzt, die von den Teilnehmern im Selbststudium bearbeitet werden. Unsere kontinuierliche Zusamenarbeit mit dem Goethe-Institut Madrid öffnet diesen Master auch für die Entwicklung des Projekts „Schule im Wandel".

Innerhalb des ersten Semesters werden fünf vierstündige Workshops veranstaltet. In diesen Workshops besprechen die Teilnehmer in Gruppen unter Anwesenheit aller Dozentinnen des fachsprachlichen Moduls ihre Bearbeitungen der Fernstudieneinheiten, präsentieren ihre Unterrichtsentwürfe, rahmen eine Aktionsforschung (*action research*) ein und fokussieren die möglichen Themen der Abschlussarbeit. Dadurch werden die unterschiedlichen Bereiche der jeweiligen Fächer vertieft und vereinheitlicht. Darüber hinaus sollen diese gemeinsamen Arbeitsphasen die Bildung einer Lerngemeinschaft unter den Teilnehmer/-inne/-n unterstützen.

Wir arbeiten nach dem Modell Barcelona das in dem Comenius-Projekt „Aus der Praxis lernen" entwickelt wurde, da wir die Auffassung der Autoren teilen, dass in der Lehrerausbildung der „Ausgangspunkt ist, dass (angehende) Lehrer in hohem Maße selbstverantwortlich für ihre eigene Entwicklung sein sollten. Die Lehrerausbildung sollte u.E. dabei Reflexion als eine der zentralen Tätigkeiten lehren und unterstützen. Ein zentraler Begriff unserer Arbeit ist: ‚reflexives Erfahrungslernen' ".

Als Evaluationswerkzeug ziehen wir das Lehrerportfolio vor, das nicht nur die Reflexion über den Unterrichtsverlauf im Master beinhaltet, sondern auch die Lehrerfahrung unserer Student/-inn/-en in dem zweieinhalbmonatigen Praktikum widerspiegeln soll. Für jeden Kurs werden unterschiedliche Evaluationsmethoden angewandt, die den Lernprozess belegen und unterstützen sollen: Hausarbeit, Ideenmarkt, Posterpräsentation, PowerPoint-Präsentation, Unterrichtsentwürfe, Unterrichtssimulationen, Rezension von Fachliteratur, etc. Teil unseres Portfolios ist sowohl der Praktikumsbericht wie die vorgegebene Abschlussarbeit des Masters. Eine wichtige Bedingung dabei ist die gelungene Verknüpfung von Theorie und Praxis. Damit wollen wir die angehenden Lehrer/-innen darin unterstützen, autonom zu lernen, prozessorientiert zu arbeiten und Reflexion und Selbstbeobachtung als wichtige Werkzeuge ihrer Fortbildung zu verstehen. Kurz gesagt: aus der Praxis ständig für das Leben lernen.

4 Wege in die Zukunft: neue Herausforderungen

Nur aus der Erfahrung aus diesem Jahr können wir noch nicht sagen, ob diese neue Fortbildung die gewünschten Ergebnisse bringen wird. Aber auf Grund unserer Erfahrung in anderen Fortbildungen sind wir davon überzeugt, dass die Eigenverantwortung und die ständige Reflexion der zukünftigen Lehrerinnen und Lehrer der beste Weg für ihre Ausbildung ist.

Vielversprechend ist auch die Zusammenarbeit von Universitätsdozenten und Sekundarlehrern in der Ausbildung der neuen Lehrer der Sekundarstufe, die zum ersten Mal in diesem Master verwirklicht wird.

Wünschenswert wäre, dass alle Fachrichtungen die Ausbildung ihrer Lehrer auch nach diesen reflexiven Voraussetzungen organisieren würden. Die DaF-Student/-inn/-en des Masters werden schon von ihren Mitstudenten wegen der engen, koordinierten Zusammenarbeit mit ihren Dozentinnen beneidet. Denn die Arbeit aus reiner Überzeugung ist spürbar.

Literaturangaben

REAL DECRETO 1834/2008, de 8 de noviembre, por el que se definen las condiciones de formación para el ejercicio de la docencia en la educación secundaria obligatoria, el bachillerato, la formación profesional y las enseñanzas de régimen especial y se establecen las especialidades de los cuerpos docentes de enseñanza secundaria. (BOE num. 287, viernes 28 de noviembre de 2008)

http://www.ucm.es/centros/webs/m5057/index.php: Master de Formación del Profesorado de Educación Secundaria Obligatoria y Bachillerato, Formación Profesional y Enseñanza de Idiomas (25. Februar 2010).

http://www2.ivlos.uu.nl/comenius/information.htm: Aus der Praxis lernen. Comenius Projekt: Lehrerbildung (25. Februar 2010).

Kontakt:
Prof. Dr. Mª Luisa SCHILLING: mlschill@filol.ucm.es
Dr. Irene SZUMLAKOWSKI: ireneszm@filol.ucm.es

Phonetik-Unterricht als Teil der Deutschlehrerausbildung: Methodisch-didaktische Aspekte

Alena Kovářová, Masaryk Universität Brno, Tschechien

Der Phonetikunterricht ist ein wichtiger Bestandteil der Ausbildung künftiger Deutschlehrer. Aus dem Vergleich der Lautsysteme der deutschen und der tschechischen Sprache können Phoneme ermittelt werden, die im Tschechischen nicht vorkommen und den tschechischen Muttersprachlern Schwierigkeiten in der Aussprache auf der segmentalen Ebene bereiten. Eine besondere Aufmerksamkeit muss jedoch den Unterschieden in der suprasegmentalen Ebene gewidmet werden, da das Deutsche eine akzentzählende, das Tschechische eine silbenzählende Sprache ist. Der Lehrer muss nicht nur die korrekte Standardaussprache des Deutschen gut beherrschen, sondern gleichzeitig auch die entsprechende und gezielte Methodik zur Behebung möglicher Aussprachefehler kennen.

Schlüsselbegriffe: Vergleich der Lautsysteme, Phoneme, Schwierigkeiten in der Aussprache, Standardaussprache

1 Das Fach *Deutsche Phonetik und Phonologie*

Das Fach *Deutsche Phonetik und Phonologie* wird im Rahmen der Deutschlehrerausbildung an der Pädagogischen Fakultät in Brno im 1. Studienjahr unterrichtet und ist für Studenten in allen Studienformen obligatorisch. Von Anfang an hat der Phonetik-Unterricht seine spezifischen Probleme, die aus dem vorherigen Deutschunterricht resultieren, den die Studenten vor ihrem Hochschulstudium absolviert haben. Ihre Einstellung zum Deutschen und zur Aussprache einer Fremdsprache überhaupt wurde dadurch wesentlich vorgeformt, wobei es sich nicht nur um alle möglichen Aussprachefehler handelt, die tschechische Muttersprachler typischerweise machen, sondern v. a. auch um eine falsche Vorstellung von der Aussprache des Deutschen und deren Gesetzmäßigkeiten allgemein.

Aus ihrem bisherigen Deutschunterricht an den Grund- und Mittelschulen bzw. aus den verschiedenen Sprachkursen an Sprachschulen bringen die Studenten keine ausreichenden Kenntnisse der richtigen deutschen Aussprache mit. Die Aussprache bereitet ihnen nicht selten große Schwierigkeiten, und zwar auch dann, wenn sie eine Abiturprüfung in Deutsch oder ein Staatsexamen an einer Sprachschule mit Erfolg bestanden haben. Die meisten Studenten erhalten erst an der Pädagogischen Fakultät eine systematische Ausspracheschulung sowie weiterreichende Informationen über die Aussprache des Deutschen. In Gesprächen mit Unterrichtenden an der Pädagogischen Fakultät geben sie zu, dass sie den Grundsätzen der richtigen deutschen Aussprache bis dahin keine größere Beachtung widmen mussten.

Aus solchen und ähnlichen Reaktionen der Studenten ist zunächst eine Überraschung darüber zu spüren, was alles mit der Problematik der richtigen Aussprache einer Fremdsprache verbunden ist. Manchmal resultiert daraus sogar das unangenehme Gefühl, bisher eine Sprache gelernt zu haben, deren gesprochene Form vom richtigen Deutsch ziemlich stark abweicht. Ähnliche Schwierigkeiten haben die Studenten auch in sprachpraktischen Übungen mit deutschsprachigen Lektoren, wo die Studenten nicht selten Probleme beim Verstehen der gesprochenen Sprache haben.

An der Pädagogischen Fakultät stehen dem Fach *Deutsche Phonetik und Phonologie* im ersten Studienjahr zwei Unterrichtsstunden zur Verfügung. Die Grundlagen der Theorie werden in einer einstündigen Vorlesung vermittelt. Die praktische Einübung der Aussprache erfolgt dann in einer Stunde Seminar pro Woche. Es ist zu beobachten, dass sich die Studenten bald dessen bewusst werden, dass ihre Beherrschung der deutschen Aussprache mangelhaft ist und dass sie an der Verbesserung ihrer Aussprache noch intensiv arbeiten müssen.

2 Methodische Aspekte

Methodisch ist es sehr wichtig, die optimale Reihenfolge festzulegen, in der die phonetischen Erscheinungen im Laufe der beiden Semester behandelt werden. Es hat sich bewährt, dabei vom Vergleich des Sprachtyps des Deutschen und des Tschechischen auszugehen. Der Sprachtypologie nach gehören Tschechisch und Deutsch zu unterschiedlichen Sprachtypen. Tschechisch, wie andere slawische Sprachen (mit Ausnahme des Bulgarischen und Makedonischen), ist eine synthetische Sprache. Deutsch dagegen gehört zu den germanischen Sprachen, die in ihrem Sprachbau viel mehr analytische Merkmale aufweisen. Der unterschiedliche Sprachbau hat nicht nur Unterschiede im Bereich der Grammatik zur Folge, sondern bewirkt auch gravierende Unterschiede in der Aussprache.

Deutsch wird als eine akzentzählende Sprache charakterisiert, Tschechisch ist eine typisch silbenzählende Sprache. Deshalb ist Deutsch eine Sprache, in der die Akzentverhältnisse den Gesamtcharakter der gesprochenen Sprache bestimmen. Der deutsche Wortakzent macht den wichtigsten Unterschied in der Aussprache der beiden Sprachen aus, auf den sich demnach der DaF-Unterricht für tschechische Muttersprachler von Anfang an konzentrieren muss. Es geht vor allem um folgende Erscheinungen, in denen sich die beiden Sprachen grundsätzlich unterscheiden:

Deutsch:

- der Akzent ist sehr stark,
- der starke Akzent (die starke Silbe) hat eine Abschwächung der unbetonten Silben zur Folge,
- es gibt einen wesentlichen Unterschied zwischen der starken und schwachen Silbe,
- der Akzent liegt meistens auf der Stammsilbe, d. h. er ist mit der Semantik der Wörter verbunden,
- der deutsche Akzent hat eine distinktive Funktion (*Au*gust x Au*gust*, *über*setzen x über*set*zen).

Tschechisch:

- der Akzent ist relativ schwach,
- die unbetonten Silben unterliegen keiner Abschwächung, auch in den Endsilben bleiben die vollen Vokale immer erhalten,
- der Unterschied zwischen der starken und schwachen Silbe ist gering,
- der Akzent liegt auf der ersten Silbe, auch in allen Fremdwörtern wird immer die erste Silbe betont; in Verbindungen von Nomina mit einsilbigen Präpositionen verschiebt sich der Akzent auf diese Präposition (*ško*la x *ve* škole),
- der tschechische Akzent ist fest und nie bedeutungsunterscheidend.

Die angeführten typischen Unterschiede zwischen dem deutschen und tschechischen Akzent sind für tschechische Schüler und Studenten in der Regel völlig neu, und deshalb ist es notwendig, dass sie von der ersten Unterrichtsstunde an auf diese Unterschiede aufmerksam gemacht werden und sie in ihrer Artikulation des Deutschen beachten.

Mit der distinktiven Funktion des deutschen Akzents hängen auch seine enge Verbindung mit dem grammatischen Bau des Deutschen und sein Einfluss auf die Strukturierung der deutschen Sprache zusammen. Auch dies ist für tschechische Studenten eine unbekannte Erscheinung. Es handelt sich vor allem um die unterschiedliche Bildung grammatischer Formen bei den Verben mit betonten und unbetonten Präfixen (durch-, über-, unter-, wieder-/wider-, hin-

ter-, miss-), wobei bei der Konjugation der häufig gebrauchten Verben auf Grund der falschen Akzentuierung häufig semantische Fehler entstehen.
Mit dem starken Charakter des deutschen Akzents hängt noch ein anderes, den Studenten häufig ebenfalls unbekanntes Merkmal der deutschen Artikulation zusammen, und zwar der erhöhte Tonus, die erhöhte Spannung der Sprechmuskulatur bei der Aussprache. Das Tschechische unterscheidet nicht zwischen gespannter und ungespannter Artikulation.

3 Die Unterschiede im Bereich der Vokale

Was die Unterschiede im Bereich der Vokale betrifft, besteht das vokalische System des Deutschen aus 17 Vokalen, das Tschechische dagegen nur aus 10 Vokalen. Beide Sprachen unterscheiden zwischen langen und kurzen Vokalen, wenn auch mit gewissen Unterschieden.
Im Deutschen gibt es also 7 bzw. 8 Vokale, die im Tschechischen nicht vorkommen. Diese Vokale sind für tschechische Lerner ungewohnt und verursachen bei ihnen daher zahlreiche Aussprachefehler. Da sie alle als Phoneme fungieren, führt die falsche, „tschechische" Artikulation in bestimmten Minimalpaaren unausweichlich zu Missverständnissen, beispielsweise bei der falschen Aussprache der gerundeten Vorderzungenvokale (*Tür* x *Tier, können* x *kennen, Mähren* x *Möhren* usw.). Bei langen Vokalen ist außerdem noch auf die gespannte deutsche Aussprache zu achten.
Aus dem Vergleich ergeben sich dann deutlich die typischen tschechischen Aussprachefehler (der im Tschechischen fehlenden Phoneme), die in drei Problemgruppen zusammengefasst werden können:

- Artikulation der langen geschlossenen Vokale E und O.

Bei der Bildung dieser Phoneme muss auf einen kleineren Kieferwinkel als im Tschechischen geachtet werden.

- Artikulation der labialisierten langen und kurzen Vorderzungenvokale Ü und Ö.

Im Tschechischen gibt es nur gerundete Hinterzungenvokale U und O.

- Artikulation der reduzierten Vokale - des reduzierten E und des vokalisierten R.

Die richtige abgeschwächte Aussprache dieser Vokale, die nur in unbetonten Silben vorkommen, wird im Zusammenhang mit der starken Akzentuierung der betonten Silben erzielt.

Meinen Erfahrungen nach ist es gerade die letzte Gruppe, die die größte Aufmerksamkeit bei der Ausspracheschulung erfordert, da das Tschechische keine Reduktion kennt und alle Silben voll ausgesprochen werden. Die abgeschwächten Vokale sind in deutschem Sprachmaterial die häufigsten. Als sehr schwierig erweist sich für tschechische Lerner die Einübung des vokalisierten R, was wahrscheinlich auch durch das grafische Bild (Buchstabe <r> im Wort- und Silbenauslaut) erschwert wird und zur Aussprache des vokalisierten R als Konsonant (Zungenspitzen-R) verleitet, und dies in so häufigen Wörtern wie *er*, d*er*, *sehr, wer, wir, nur, vor, für, Jahr, verstehen* u.v.a.m.
Auch die Aussprache der drei deutschen Diphthonge unterscheidet sich von der Aussprache des einzigen tschechischen Diphthongs OU. Die korrekte deutsche Artikulation wird durch die oben erwähnten Akzentverhältnisse beeinflusst, wobei der erste Teil des Diphthongs stärker artikuliert und der zweite abgeschwächt wird. Bei der Aussprache des tschechischen OU ist die Aussprache der beiden Komponenten dagegen fast gleich stark.
Der typische Unterschied bei der Artikulation der in beiden Sprachen vorkommenden Konsonanten besteht in der Opposition *gespannt – ungespannt* und betrifft die Aussprache der Verschlusslaute P – B, T – D und K – G. Während im Deutschen die Aussprache dieser Laute entweder gespannt oder ungespannt ist, ist für die tschechische Aussprache die Opposition *stimmlos – stimmhaft* ausschlaggebend. Der häufigste Fehler von tschechischen Muttersprachlern ist daher die ungespannte und unbehauchte Aussprache des P, T, K. Zur Einübung der korrekten Aussprache sollte unbedingt auch die Behauchung mit einbezogen werden, die es im Tschechischen ebenfalls nicht gibt, die aber relativ leicht eingeübt werden kann. Besonders geeignet sind hier Übungen mit Minimalpaaren wie z.B. *packen x backen, tanken* x *danken, Karten* x *Garten* usw.
Schwierig für tschechische Lerner ist auch das velare N, das im Deutschen nicht nur eine positionsbedingte Variante des N vor K oder G ist, sondern auch als selbständiges Phonem fungiert. Durch die orthographische Wiedergabe des velaren N als <ng> werden die Lerner dazu verleitet, dass sie hinter dem velaren N noch ein K bzw. G aussprechen.
Zu weiteren Konsonanten, deren Artikulation im Deutschen anders ist als im Tschechischen, gehört der Unterschied zwischen dem Ich-Laut und dem Ach-Laut. Auch das deutsche L wird anders als das tschechische L artikuliert.

Das deutsche stimmlose H muss ebenfalls eingeübt werden, da das H im Tschechischen immer stimmhaft ist. Das R wird im Tschechischen immer als Zungenspitzen-R realisiert. Deutschlernende müssen jedoch darauf hingewiesen werden, dass die Zunge bei der Artikulation des deutschen Zungenspitzen-R nicht so stark vibriert, wie dies im Tschechischen der Fall ist. Fehler in der Artikulation dieser Laute führen jedoch zu keinen Verständigungsschwierigkeiten. Aus dem oben Genannten geht eindeutig hervor, dass ständig auf den Einfluss des starken deutschen Akzents auf die Aussprache vieler Segmente hingewiesen werden muss und dass die Studierenden diese Zusammenhänge auch erkennen sollten. Dies zeigt auch das Wesen der Artikulation als Ganzes: Die Aussprache ist ein geschlossenes System, in dem alle Bestandteile innerlich zusammenhängen und aufeinander abgestimmt sind.

4 Lehrmaterialien

Stellt man sich die Frage, wie die Phonetik in Tschechien unterrichtet wird und ob auch geeignete Unterrichtsmaterialien für die Ausspracheschulung zur Verfügung stehen, kommt man zu dem eindeutigen Schluss, dass es an solchen Lehrmaterialien allgemein mangelt.

Dennoch stehen den Studierenden an der Pädagogischen Fakultät der MU einige Lehrmaterialien für dieses Fach zur Verfügung, die hier in Auswahl kurz genannt werden sollen. Für den theoretischen Teil der Lehrveranstaltung wurde das Lehrheft *Einführung in die deutsche Phonetik und Phonologie* erarbeitet. Dieses Heft enthält auch geeignete Ausspracheübungen, die gezielt für tschechische Muttersprachler konzipiert sind.

Zusätzlich führen die Studenten ein sog. *phonetisches Vokabelheft*, das sie selbst schrittweise während ihres Studiums erarbeiten. Hier werden von der ersten Seminarstunde an die behandelten problematischen Erscheinungen der deutschen Aussprache anhand von konkreten Beispielen eingetragen. Die Aufgabe der Studenten besteht darin, bei der Lektüre eines deutschsprachigen Textes Wörter mit den für sie schwierigen phonetischen Erscheinungen herauszusuchen und sie dem entsprechenden Stichwort in ihrem phonetischen Vokabelheft zuzuordnen. Das phonetische Vokabelheft entsteht im Verlauf der beiden Semester des Phonetik-Unterrichts und enthält dann etwa 25 Stichwörter, die den typischen Aussprachefehlern tschechischer Muttersprachler entsprechen. Bei jedem Stichwort wird anfangs eine Charakteristik des betreffenden Phonems angeführt, das Zeichen für seine phonetische Umschrift sowie eine kurze Anleitung zu seiner richtigen Aussprache, die sich von der tschechischen Aussprache unterscheidet. Die Wörter, die das jeweilige Aussprachephänomen enthalten, suchen die Studenten bei ihrer Arbeit mit geschriebenen Texten (einerseits in den Phonetikseminaren, aber auch in ihren sprachpraktischen Übungen) selbst heraus. In beiden Fällen können sie sich auf ihre eigenen Fehler konzentrieren, d. h. genau auf die Wörter, die ihnen bei der Aussprache die größten Schwierigkeiten bereiten. Die eingetragenen Ausdrücke können sie dann jederzeit wiederholen und auf diese Weise relativ schnell und gezielt ihre Aussprachefehler und falschen Gewohnheiten korrigieren. Ein weiterer Vorteil dieses phonetischen Vokabelheftes besteht darin, dass die Studenten es auch bei ihrer eigenen selbständigen Vorbereitung für die Phonetikseminare benutzen können, wenn sie einen neuen Text analysieren und die einzelnen Wörter den entsprechenden Stichwörtern zuordnen.

Ein weiterer Bestandteil des Unterrichts im Fach *Deutsche Phonetik und Phonologie* sind dann die Seminararbeiten, die im zweiten Semester erarbeitet werden. Die Studenten wählen sich einen kurzen, zusammenhängenden deutschsprachigen Text aus (Mindestumfang 100 Wörter) und analysieren ihn aus phonetischer Sicht. Es handelt sich in der Regel um kurze Texte aus Lehrbüchern, Zeitungen, Zeitschriften oder um Proben aus literarischen Texten.

In den letzten Jahren wählen Studenten auch immer häufiger das Thema ihrer Diplomarbeiten aus dem Bereich Phonetik und Phonologie. Sie analysieren beispielsweise die in den Schulen benutzten Lehrbücher in Hinblick auf die Vermittlung des phonetischen Lehrstoffs bzw. vergleichen unter diesem Aspekt tschechische und deutsche Lehrbücher. Auf Grund ihrer selbst ermittelten Tatsachen versuchen sie dann, entsprechende phonetische Ergänzungsmaterialen und Übungen zu diesen Lehrbüchern zu erarbeiten. Diese können sie nach dem Studium in ihrem eigenen Deutschunterricht einsetzen.

Das Ziel des Phonetikunterrichts des Deutschen an der Pädagogischen Fakultät in Brno sehe ich darin, dass die künftigen Deutschlehrer für ihre Unterrichtspraxis methodisch gut vorbereitet sind: dass sie sich nicht nur eine gute Aussprache des Deutschen aneignen, sondern die Unterschiede zwischen der tschechischen und deutschen Aussprache beschreiben und erklären können und den Ausspracheunterricht als einen integrierten und ständigen Bestandteil ihrer Arbeit als Deutschlehrer ansehen.

Literaturangaben

DIELING, HELGA UND HIRSCHFELD, URSULA: Phonetik lehren und lernen. Fernstudieneinheit 21, Berlin/München/Wien/Zürich/New York: Langenscheidt, 2000.

HAKKARAINEN, HEIKKI: Phonetik des Deutschen. München: Fink, 1995.

JANÍKOVÁ,VĚRA: Nácvik správné výslovnosti němčiny hrou u žáků s narušenou komunikační schopností. Komenský, Brno: Masarykova univerzita. 2009, vol. 134, no. 2, S. 20-23.

KOVÁŘOVÁ, ALENA: Fonetická cvičení pro nácvik německé výslovnosti. Brno: Audiovizuální centrum Masarykova univerzita, 1994.

KOVÁŘOVÁ, ALENA: Úvod do fonetiky a fonologie němčiny, Brno: Masarykova univerzita, 2003.

RAUSCH, RUDOLF /RAUSCH, ILKA: Deutsche Phonetik für Ausländer, Berlin/München/Leipzig: Langenscheidt, 1992.

Kontakt:
Alena KOVÁŘOVÁ: kovarova@ped.muni.cz

DER PROFESSIONELLE ENTWICKLUNGSGANG VON MENTOREN – BEISPIEL DER MENTORENSCHAFT AM SCHULFACH BILDENDE KUNST

Matjaž Duh und Jerneja Herzog, Universität Maribor, Slowenien

Heutzutage müssen Mentoren in der Lage sein, durch Veränderungen der eigenen pädagogischen Praxis effizient auf die entsprechenden Veränderungen zu reagieren. Sie müssen den Studierenden ein Vorbild sein, sie müssen bei ihnen Interesse für den Lehrerberuf wecken können. Eine moderne Herangehensweise an Planung, Durchführung und Auswertung der pädagogischen Arbeit sollte bei allen Schulfächern vorhanden sein, so auch beim Kunstunterricht beziehungsweise bei Schulfächern mit verwandtem Inhalt.
Im letzten Studienjahr haben wir an der Pädagogischen Fakultät der Universität in Maribor eine Studie durchgeführt, in der Studierende (n = 90) die Arbeit ihres Mentors während ihres Schulpraktikums bewertet haben. Die Studienergebnisse, bei der besonderes Augenmerk auf das Schulfach bildende Kunst gerichtet wurde, haben gezeigt, dass die Kompetenzen der Mentoren, die auf der ganzen Vertikale der Primar- und Sekundarstufe Kunstunterricht erteilen, um einiges unter dem erwarteten Niveau liegen. Für die zukünftigen Lehrergenerationen stellt dies keine erfreuliche Situation dar.

Schlüsselbegriffe: Mentor, pädagogische Praxis, Schulpraktikum, Kunstunterricht

1 Einführung

Die Bedeutsamkeit der Bildung, sowohl des Einzelnen als auch der gesamten Gesellschaft, nimmt zu. Zahlreiche empirische Studien, die sich mit der Ermittlung der Qualität der Ausbildung befassen, belegen diese Annahme. AYPAY (2009) stellt fest, dass Ergebnisse solcher und ähnlicher Studien schon so manche Veränderung der Ausbildung von Lehrkräften zur Folge hatten. Neben dieser Erscheinung gewinnt zudem die Rolle des Mentors an Bedeutung. Der Mentor ist als denkender Praktiker für das Schaffen der Lernfähigkeiten verantwortlich, in denen der Studierende seinen professionellen Auftritt kritisch sucht und kreativ entwickelt. NEUWEG (2008) macht darauf aufmerksam, dass die praktische pädagogische Sachkenntnis und das theoretische Wissen im Bereich der Erziehung und Bildung gegenseitig verbindend und ergänzend wirken. Das Unterrichten ist in seinem Wesen eine praktische Tätigkeit, da die Studierenden mit der Entfaltung des persönlichen professionellen Entwicklungsganges nicht beginnen können, bevor sie nicht in der Klasse stehen (Cvetek, 2005). Lediglich Lehrkräfte, die sich auch selbst weiterentwickeln, können im Lehr- und Lernprozess den Schülern helfen und dadurch zu einer Qualitätsentwicklung im Unterricht beitragen. Die Verantwortung für die persönliche berufliche Weiterentwicklung sollte dem Lehrer überlassen werden. Erst die professionellen Erfahrungen lassen die Erkenntnis zu, dass neben der Biografie des Lehrers, seinem formalen Wissen, seinen Erfahrungen und Werten auch das praktische Wissen eine sehr wichtige Rolle spielt (Gholami, 2009). Für den werdenden Lehrer stellt das Schulpraktikum die einzige praktische Erfahrung, den einzigen Kontakt mit der Praxis und die Möglichkeit dar, schrittweise einen Einblick in die pädagogische Arbeit zu erlangen. In recht vielen Studien wurde die Aufmerksamkeit auf die Bedürfnisse von Lehreranfängern beziehungsweise Studierenden und andererseits auch Mentoren gerichtet. Es gibt jedoch weniger zahlreiche Studien, in denen über eine reflektierende Praxis und die Arbeit des Lehreranfängers beziehungsweise des Studierenden die Rede ist. An dieser Stelle schreiben die Autoren (Harrison, Yaffe, 2008) vor allem über den Stellenwert der sozialen Interaktion im unterschiedlichen Umfeld zwischen den Hochschullehrern, den Studierenden und den Lehrern. Es ist demnach wichtig, wie das Schulpraktikum verstanden, konzipiert und von den Mentoren realisiert wird. Ein Schulpraktikum, bei dem der Mentor die Hauptrolle spielt, wird als tragender Bestandteil der Ausbildung zukünftiger Lehrkräfte verstanden. Während des Schulpraktikums sollten die Studierenden die Fähigkeit zur Planung, Durchführung und Auswertung des unterrichtenden Faches beziehungsweise Fächer entwickeln. LIDSTONE meint, dass Lehrer, die bei der Ausbildung zukünftiger Lehrkräfte mitwirken, eine doppelte Verantwortung tragen: „... Wir müssen die Lebenserfahrungen derjenigen verstehen können, die in der Zukunft den Lehrerberuf ausüben werden, und deren Schüler. Dies sind zwei große Erwartungen an alle, die sich beruflich in einer Welt entwickelten, die zwar nicht perfekt war, jedoch zumindest ein größeres Gefühl der Sicherheit bot, als die Welt, in der wir heute leben" (Lidstone, 2006, S. 11). SWENNEN hingegen ist der Meinung, dass die Tätigkeit des Mentors dann am effizientesten ist, wenn Mentor und Lehreranfänger beziehungsweise Studierender ihre Ideen über die Lehrmöglichkeiten abstimmen und den Unterricht zusammen kreieren (Swennen, u. a. 2008). Ein Mentor muss sich dessen bewusst sein, dass er mit gutem Beispiel vorangehen und dem zukünftigen Lehrer ein positives Vorbild sein sollte. Und dies tun Mentoren, so HARGREAVES (2003), die ihre Arbeit gern tun und auf diese Weise die zukünftigen Lehrkräfte zur bestrebten Ausübung ihres Berufes motivieren. Die bisherigen Analysen der Hospitationen von Mentoren beim Kunstunterricht in den slowenischen Grundschulen (Herzog u. a. 2009a) zeigten, dass die Lage vom fachlichen und pädagogischen Standpunkt aus gesehen nicht gut ist. Das Kerndilemma der Organisation und Durchführung der pädagogischen Arbeit beim Kunstunterricht in der Primarstufe ist vor allem die schlechte Sachkompetenz der Mentoren. Auch anhand der weiteren Analyse (Herzog u. a. 2009b) der Arbeit von Mentoren beim Schulfach Bildende Kunst in der Primar- und Sekundarstufe wurde die oben beschriebene schlechte Lage in diesem Bereich bestätigt.

2 Methodologie

Im Studienjahr 2008/2009 führten wir eine empirische Studie durch, deren Ziel es war, die Qualität der Arbeit von Mentoren während des Schulpraktikums festzustellen. Die Studie beruht auf der deskriptiven und kausal-nicht-experimentellen Methode der pädagogischen Forschung. Die untersuchte Population stellen Mentoren von Studierenden des 3. und 4. Jahrganges der Abteilung für Kunstpädagogik und Mentoren von Studierenden des 4. Jahrganges der Abteilung für Grundschulpädagogik der Pädagogischen Fakultät in Maribor dar. In der Studie wurde die pädagogisch-didaktische und fachliche Arbeit von 90 Mentoren begleitet. Als Instrumentarium für die Datensammlung wurde ein Fragebogen benutzt, der eine Kombination aus der Likert-Skala und offenen Fragen ist. Die Gültigkeit des Instrumentariums wurde mithilfe der Faktorenanalyse überprüft. Unter Berücksichtigung der Tatsache, dass der erste Faktor 37,877 % der Varianz erklärt, was die vorausgesetzte untere Grenze (20 %) übersteigt, haben wir feststellen können, dass das Instrumentarium gültig ist. Zur Bestimmung der Zuverlässigkeit wurde das Verfahren der Primzahlzerlegung benutzt. Alle Faktoren zusammen erklären 86,242 % der Varianz, woraus man schließen kann, dass das Instrumentarium sehr zuverlässig ist. Die Objektivität des Instrumentariums wurde durch einheitliche, eindeutige Anweisungen gewährleistet. Die gewonnenen Daten wurden auf der Ebene der deskriptiven und induktiven Statistik mithilfe der Statistiksoftware von SPSS statistisch bearbeitet.

3 Darstellung der Ergebnisse

Die Ergebnisse des Fragebogens sind tabellarisch dargestellt. Die häufigsten Antworten sind fett geschrieben.

Tabelle 1: Die Ergebnisse der Frequenzdistribution attributiver Variablen (f,f %).

Behauptungen		Dem stimme ich überhaupt nicht zu	Dem stimme ich nicht zu	Ich weiß nicht, ich kann mich nicht entscheiden	Dem stimme ich zu	Dem stimme ich sehr zu	Insgesamt
Bei der Planung und Durchführung der Unterrichtsstunde wurde ich seitens des Mentors/der Mentorin nicht eingeschränkt.	f	0	3	6	30	51	90
	f(%)	0	3,3	10,0	43,3	**56,7**	100
Vor der Realisierung der einzelnen Stunde beim Kunstunterricht hat der Mentor/die Mentorin die Unterrichtsentwürfe gründlich durchgesehen.	f	3	9	6	37	35	90
	f(%)	3,3	10,0	6,7	**41,1**	38,9	100

Während des Schulpraktikums hat mir der Mentor/die Mentorin mit konkreten Tipps und Hinweisen geholfen.	f	3	7	14	40	26	90
	f(%)	3,3	7,8	15,6	**44,4**	28,9	100
Der Mentor/die Mentorin hat eine interessante Hospitationsstunde vorbereitet.	f	2	13	15	41	19	90
	f(%)	2,2	14,4	16,7	**45,6**	21,1	100
Die einführende Motivation dieser Stunde war für die Schüler sehr interessant und hat bei ihnen viel Interesse geweckt.	f	2	12	12	47	17	90
	f(%)	2,2	13,3	13,3	**52,2**	18,9	100
Der Mentor/die Mentorin hat das künstlerische Problem deutlich hervorgehoben.	f	1	14	12	43	20	90
	f(%)	1,1	15,6	13,3	**47,8**	22,2	100
Der Mentor/die Mentorin hat den Schülern mindestens eine hochwertige Reproduktion des Werkes eines Künstlers gezeigt.	f	18	30	6	18	18	90
	f(%)	20,0	**33,3**	6,7	20,0	20,0	100
Der Mentor/die Mentorin hat mindestens ein modernes Unterrichtsmedium benutzt (z. B. Computer, LCD-Projektor, …).	f	31	26	3	11	19	90
	f(%)	**34,4**	28,9	3,3	12,2	21,2	100
Der Mentor/die Mentorin hat die künstlerische Technik und ihre Ausdrucksmöglichkeiten anschaulich demonstriert.	f	17	14	17	23	19	90
	f(%)	18,9	15,6	18,9	**25,6**	21,0	100
Der Mentor/die Mentorin hat ein geeignetes und ästhetisches Tafelbild geschaffen.	f	23	22	11	21	13	90
	f(%)	**25,6**	24,4	12,2	23,3	14,5	100
Der Mentor/die Mentorin hat sehr genaue Anweisungen gegeben.	f	5	2	16	35	32	90
	f(%)	5,6	2,2	17,8	**38,9**	35,5	100
Der Mentor/die Mentorin hatte keine Schwierigkeiten damit, die Motivation für die Arbeit aufrechtzuerhalten.	f	1	9	7	47	26	90
	f(%)	1,1	10,0	7,8	**52,2**	28,9	100
Der Mentor/die Mentorin hat die Auswertung nach im Voraus bestimmten Kriterien durchgeführt.	f	13	15	13	28	21	90
	f(%)	14,4	16,7	14,4	**31,1**	23,4	100

Aus der Tabelle ist ersichtlich, dass die meisten Unzulänglichkeiten in Bezug auf die Arbeit der Mentoren vor allem die Visualisierung der Aufgabenstellung betreffen (Unterrichtsmedien und Tafelbild).

4 Diskussion

Die Mentorenschaft für Studierende während ihres Schulpraktikums ist auf der Primar- und Sekundarstufe des slowenischen Bildungssystems schlecht und unsystematisch, weswegen die vorgestellten Ergebnisse nicht überraschen. Trotzdem können die schlecht vorbereiteten Hospitationsstunden, die wir beim Kunstunterricht begleitet haben, nur schwer gerechtfertigt werden. Die Studienergebnisse deuten auf eher mangelhafte fachliche und pädagogische Kenntnisse und eine oberflächliche Beziehung der Mentoren zur kunstpädagogischen Arbeit hin. Die Antworten der Studierenden, die sich auf das erworbene Wissen während ihres Schulpraktikums, die Arbeit des Mentors bei der Führung und Beratung der Studierenden und die materiellen Voraussetzungen für die Realisierung des Kunstunterrichts beziehen, sind teilweise zufriedenstellend. Weniger zufriedenstellend sind die Antworten, die sich unmittelbar auf den durchgeführten Unterricht des Mentors beziehen. Die Mentoren wählen selbst den Inhalt für die Hospitationsstunden aus, deswegen wählen sie Inhalte und Aufgaben, für die sie glauben, optimal und ein geeignetes Beispiel für die zukünftigen Lehrkräfte zu sein. Für diese Form der pädagogischen Praxis bereiten die Mentoren den Studierenden normalerweise bewährte Inhalte mit bewährter didaktischer Artikulation vor. Eine geringe Motivation der Schüler, ein schlecht vorgestelltes künstlerisches Problem, eine äußerst mangelhafte Visualisierung der Aufgabenstellung und unmittelbarer Kontakt mit hochwertigen (Reproduktionen) künstlerischen Arbeiten, eine schlechte Demonstration der künstlerischen Technik und die Vernachlässigung des Tafelbildes sind auf jeden Fall Elemente, die maßgeblich in die Qualität der Durchführung der didaktischen Einheit eingreifen. In dieser Phase der Mentorenschaft würde man von einem erfahrenen Lehrer auf jeden Fall mehr erwarten. Mit der gegenwärtigen Lage im Bereich der Mentorenschaft für Studierende während des Schulpraktikums im Licht der kunstpädagogischen Disziplin kann man demnach nicht zufrieden sein. Die Mentorenschaft für Studierende während des Schulpraktikums wird in Zukunft noch intensiver zu beobachten sein und es muss dringend ein Weg gefunden werden, wie diese verbessert werden kann. Möglichkeiten zur Verbesserung sehen wir in der Entwicklung eines Organisationsmodels und der prüfenden Begleitung des Schulpraktikums.

Literaturangaben

AYPAY, A. (2009): Teachers' Evaluation of Their Pre-Service Teacher Training. Educational Sciences: Theory & Practice 9 (3), Summer 2009, 1113-1123.
CVETEK, S. (2005): Poučevanje kot profesija, učitelj kot profesionalec. Radovljica: Didakta.

GHOLAMI, K. (2009): Representing the epistemic nature of teachers' practical knowledge. The case of class teachers' general pedagogy. Retrieved January 21, 2010, from: https://oa.doria.fi/bitstream/handle/10024/44850/represen.pdf?sequence=1

HARRISON, J., YAFFE, E. (2008): Teacher Educators and Reeflective Practice. In: Swennen, A., van der Klink, M. ed. (2008). Becoming a Teacher Educator. Theory and Practice for Teacher Educators. Amsterdam. (p. 145-161).

HERZOG, J., DUH, M., BATIČ, J. (2009a): The role of mentoring in the education of prospective classroom teachers. V: The teaching based on the Bologna Process, prispevek na konferenci, College of Nursey School Teachers-Subotica, 2009, str. 269-275.

HERZOG, J., DUH, M., BATIČ, J. (2009b): Teaching practice as motivation for creative art education of prospective art teachers. Journal of elementary Education, 2(4), 67-78

JAVORNIK KREČIČ, M., IVANUŠ GRMEK M. (2008): Cooperative learning and team culture in schools: Conditions for teacher`s professional development. Teaching and Teacher Education 24 (2008), 59-68.

LIDSTONE, J. (2006): Theory and practice in teacher education. V: Peklaj, C., ur. (2006). Teorija in praksa v izobraževanju učiteljev. Ljubljana: Center za pedagoško izobraževanje Filozofske fakultete.

NEUWEG, H.G. (2008): Grundlagen der Lehrer/innen/Kompetenc. Odgojne znanosti, 15-2008. str. 13-21.

SWENNEN, A., L. SHAGIR, M. COOPER (2008): Becoming a teacher Educator: Vices of Beginning Teacher Educators. In: Swennen, A., van der Klink, M. ur. Becoming a Teacher Educator. Theory and Practice for Teacher Educators. (str. 91-102).

Kontakt:
Doz. Dr. Matjaž DUH: matjaz.duh@uni-mb.si
Jerneja HERZOG (Ph. D. student)

Kompetenzen und Kompetenzentwicklung von Hochschullehrer/-inne/-n

Nina Trukhacheva, Nikola Pupyrev, Svetlana Tchernysheva, Liudmila Epryntseva

Altaier Medizinische Universität, Russland

Die überwiegende Mehrheit der Lehrkräfte an den medizinischen Hochschulen der Russischen Föderation hat zwar medizinische Hochschulbildung, gehört aber nicht zu den Experten auf dem Gebiet der didaktischen Methoden und Informationstechnologien. Der vorliegende Beitrag thematisiert die Berufsausbildungsmöglichkeiten der Hochschuldozentinnen und -dozenten in diesem Bereich.

Schlüssenbegriffe: Informationstechnologien, medizinische Hochschulen, Berufsausbildung

1 Einleitung

Die medizinische Aus- und Weiterbildung sollte den hohen gesellschaftlichen Erwartungen entsprechen und auf die internationalen Standards bezogen sein (Wolff, Antes 2007, S. 135). Die Ärzte des XXI. Jahrhunderts sollten nicht nur über eine gewisse ordentliche den internationalen Standards entsprechende berufliche Ausbildung verfügen, sondern zudem auch bestimmte Kommunikationsfähigkeiten im Umgang mit Patienten besitzen und darüber hinaus auf lebenslanges Lernen orientiert sein.
KÜNZI (2009) betont, dass nicht alle Hochschuldozentinnen und -dozenten im Stande sind ihre Studenten und Studentinnen auf die Herausforderungen, mit denen sie in Zukunft konfrontiert werden, vorzubereiten. Die Qualität der medizinischen Universitäten (Hochschuleinrichtungen) als eine wesentliche Grundlage des Bildungssystems eines Landes wird eindeutig von den Hochschullehrern geprägt. Oder anders gesagt: die Verbindung zwischen der Qualifikation der Hochschuldozentinnen und -dozenten und den Leistungen der Studierenden ist unwiderlegbar. Kompetenzen und Kompetenzentwicklung von Lehrerinnen und Lehrern bedeutet erfolgreiche Lehre (Mayr 2006, S. 154).

2 Hauptteil

Die Programme der Kompetenzentwicklung von Hochschuldozentinnen und -dozenten sind in der letzten Zeit zum Arbeitsschwerpunkt an der Altaier medizinischen Universität geworden. Es werden Weiterbildungsmöglichkeiten in verschiedenen Fachrichtungen und auf unterschiedlichen Fachebenen geboten. Unter anderem: ein Universitätsfachkurs „Pädagogik und Fachdidaktik für Hochschuldozentinnen und -dozenten“ sowie „Einführung in das e-Learning“. Unser Arbeitsteam arbeitet an dem zweiten Programm. Wir geben dabei einen kurzen Überblick über die allgemeinen Voraussetzungen, die wesentlichen Grundzüge und Grundgedanken des Kurses, analysieren in erster Linie die Qualifikation der Hochschuldozentinnen und -dozenten im Bereich der Entwicklung der Unterrichtsqualität und besprechen anschließend die vorliegenden Ergebnisse (Erfahrungen). Insbesondere wird das Verhältnis zwischen dem „modernen“ und „traditionsgemäßen“ Unterricht in der medizinischen Bildung diskutiert.

Unsere Forschungsarbeit haben wir mit den Studierenden begonnen. Wie kann man in der medizinischen Hochschulbildung durch e-Learning die Studierenden dem Kompetenzbereich gemäß derart heranbilden, dass sie den Anforderungen an den Arztberuf gewachsen sind und der ausgeübte Beruf ihnen volle Befriedigung bereitet?

Um dieses Ziel zu erreichen sollten solche Lehrer den Unterricht erteilen, die selbst die modernen didaktischen Methoden beherrschen und sich ständig weiterbilden. Für den modernen Unterricht ist ein moderner Hochschullehrer erforderlich (Stelzer-Rothe 2008, S.15).

Die meisten Hochschuldozenten und -dozentinnen an den medizinischen Universitäten verfügen über eine unzureichende methodisch-didaktische Ausbildung und sind der Meinung, dass für den Unterricht an der Universität keine besonderen Gesetzmäßigkeiten und Regeln erforderlich sind. Abgesehen davon, dass das Problem besteht, Hochschuldozentinnen und -dozenten auf solche neuen Unterrichtsmethoden, wie zum Beispiel, e-Learning zu orientieren. Der europäische Aktionsplan e-Learning definiert das e-Learning als Nutzung von neuen Multimedia und Internettechnologien zur Verbesserung der Unterrichtsqualität, indem der Zugang zu den Ressourcen und Dienstleistungen erleichtert wird und ein Gedankenaustausch und Zusammenarbeit im Echtzeitbetrieb ermöglicht wird (Tapio Varis 2005). Kerres schreibt „Der Nutzen neuer Technologien für Bildung hängt nicht von Geräten usw. ab, sondern ein Mehrwert entsteht erst, wenn die Technologie zu einer Problemlösung für Bildungsanliegen transformiert wird“ (Kerres 2002, S.264).

Besonders misstrauisch äußern sich gegenüber e-Learningnutzung im Unterricht die Hochschuldozentinnen und -dozenten der klinischen Disziplinen. Sie bestehen beharrlich auf den „traditionellen“ Unterrichtsmethoden und sind der Meinung, dass man einen Arzt durch e-Learning nicht heranbilden kann. Es unterliegt keinem Zweifel, dass es in jedem Fach Themen gibt, bei deren Behandlung e-Learningnutzung fehl am Platze ist. Wenn es, zum Beispiel, um die Arbeit am Krankenbett geht, so spielt bestimmt rege Anteilnahme des Arztes und ein Gespräch mit dem Kranken die ausschlaggebende Rolle. Jedoch wollen wir es nicht bestreiten, dass es dem Arzt für die Ermittlung von einer umfassenden Information notwendig ist, sich sowohl das Kardiogramm und das Röntgenbild anzusehen, als auch in der Elektronendatenbasis zu der einer oder anderen Nosologie nachzuschlagen. Und dabei kommen die technischen und EDV-Mittel zu Hilfe, die ein Arzt nicht nur kennen, sondern auch in die Praxis umsetzen können sollte. Die Lehrkräfte an der medizinischen Universität sollten nicht nur Kenntnisse vermitteln, sondern auch dem Studierenden das Lernen beibringen. Hierfür müssen Hochschuldozentinnen und -dozenten selbst lebenslang lernen; neue didaktische Recherche- und Informationsgewinnungsmethoden beherrschen und moderne didaktische Techniken, die auf den neusten Erfahrungen der methodischen Didaktik basieren in ihrer Arbeit verwenden können. Ohne elektronische Mittel und Netzwerke wäre das praktisch unmöglich. Es kommt darauf an, dem Arzt und Hochschullehrer die Verwendung von e-Learning in der Lerntätigkeit und im Beruf beizubringen (Trukhacheva 2009, S.174).

3 Verfahren und Instrumentarium

In unserer Untersuchung wurden verschiedene Verfahren verwendet: unter anderem Fragebogenmethode, Interview und Beobachtungsmethode.

4 Forschungsergebnisse

Das Rahmenthema des Lehrgangs „Einführung in das e-Learning“ umfasst inhaltsbezogene Aspekte medizinischer Bildung ebenso wie Fragen von gesellschaftlich notwendigen Informationskompetenzen eines Hochschullehrers im Zeitalter der Informationstechnologien und nicht zuletzt Probleme der besonderen Bedeutung von informationstechnologischen Massenmedien für den Studierenden. Das gemeinsame Ziel ist die Qualitätsverbesserung der Ausbildung an der Altaier staatlichen medizinischen Universität über die Weiterqualifizierung der Hochschuldozentinnen und -dozenten. Ein spezielles Ziel ist der Erwerb von informationsdidaktischen Kompetenzen. Die Ergebnisse unserer Forschung haben wir entsprechend der Zunahme von informationsdidaktischen Kompetenzen unserer Lerner eingeschätzt. Unter informationsdidaktischen Kompetenzen verstehen wir die Möglichkeit die e-Learning-Strategie aktiv zu unterstützen. Bei der Beantwortung der Frage „Halten Sie es für möglich e-Learning beim Erlernen von klinischen und vorklinischen Disziplinen anzuwenden?“ wurden folgende Daten gewonnen (siehe Abb. 1, Abb. 2).

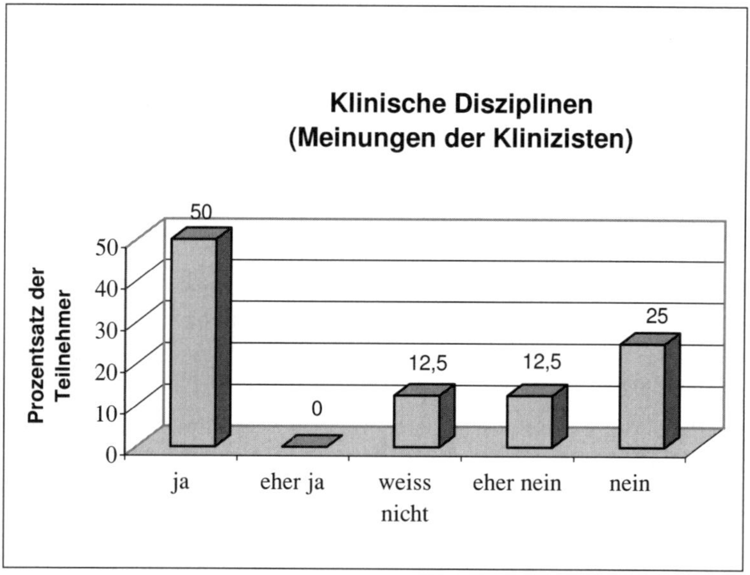

Abb.1: Meinungen der Klinizisten über e-Learning (oben)

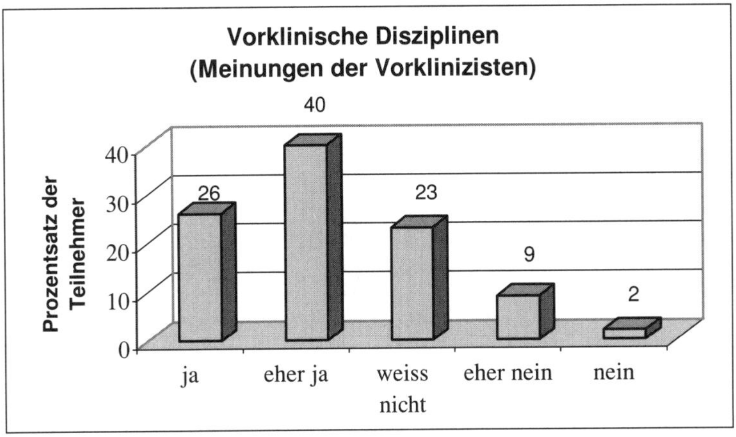

Abb. 2: Meinungen der Vorklinizisten über e-Learning auf die Frage „Wenden Sie die e-Learningtechnologien im Unterricht an?“
Es wurden folgende Daten gewonnen (siehe Abb. 3).

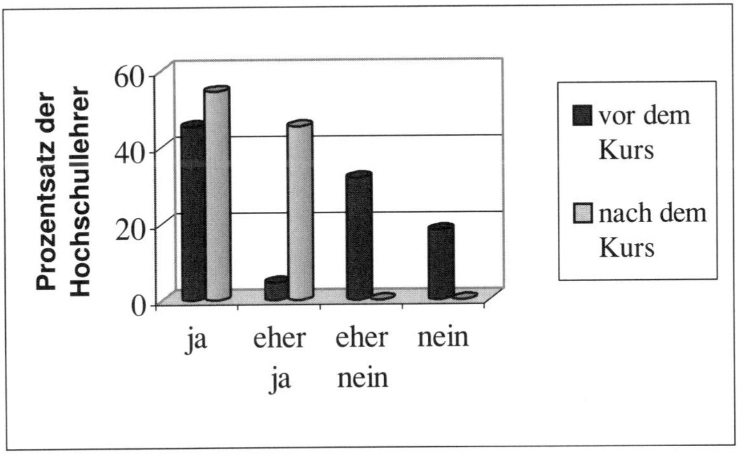

Abb. 3: Anwendung von e-Learningtechnologien im Unterricht
Bei der Beantwortung der Frage „Können Sie mit Kollegen vom Lehrstuhl im Team an der Herstellung von elektronischen Lehrmitteln konstruktiv zusammenarbeiten?“ wurden folgende Daten gewonnen (siehe Abb. 4).

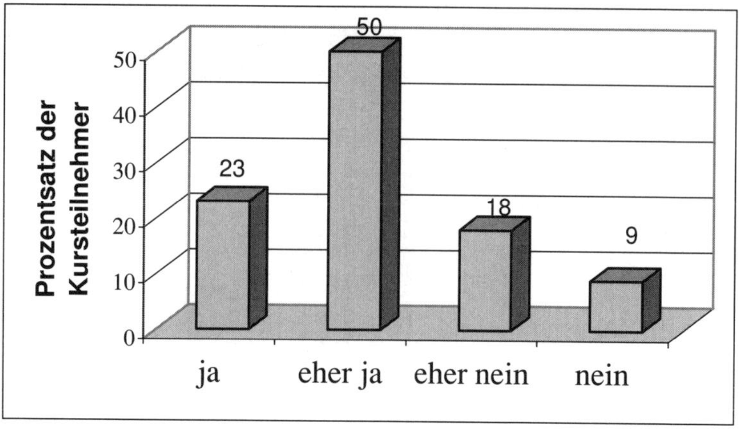

Abb.4: Meinungen der Hochschuldozent/-inn/-en über die Zusammenarbeit

Die Umfrage hat Folgendes ergeben: die klinischen Institute sind weniger dazu bereit e-Learningtechnologien im Unterricht zu verwenden (50 %) als die vorklinischen (66 %). Nach der Teilnahme am Kurs ist der Prozentsatz der Hoch schullehrer, die e-Learningtechnologien im Unterricht verwenden, bedeutend angestiegen, es erhöhte sich auch die Bereitschaft der Hochschullehrer zum Einsatz der neuen e-Learningtechnologien in den Unterricht (73 %).

5 Schluss

Das Forschungsverfahren war anfangs für die Hochschullehrer keine leichte Aufgabe, sie waren es nicht gewohnt beruflich-didaktische und demnach methodisch-didaktische Aufgaben auszuführen. Die Motivation der Teilnehmer, etwas Neues zu erfahren, war sehr hoch, weil sich das auf deren eigenes Berufsfeld bezog, in dem sie täglich tätig sind. Die Arbeitsgruppe der Kursabsolventen zeigte, welche Fortschritte man machen kann, wenn man den Auftrag ernst nimmt: die Gruppenteilnehmer veranstalten zurzeit monatlich nichtamtlich je ein Eintagesseminar für Weiterbildung, machen Fortbildungsarbeit und veröffentlichen anschließend ihre Erfahrungen.

Einige Kursabsolventen können zu Recht stolz auf ihr Qualitätsprodukt sein. Aus eigener Erfahrung zu wissen, dass man zu solch penibler Arbeit fähig ist und dass sie einem Freude bereiten kann, lässt die Kursabsolventen in dieser Richtung weiterarbeiten. Im allgemeinen fördert der Einsatz von e-Learning-

Strategien sowohl die moderne medizinische Bildung als auch und die Unterrichtsqualität.
Die e-Learningnachfrage ist ein Zeichen dafür, dass die Dozenten und Studenten die neuen Herausforderungen auf dem Gebiet der medizinischen Bildungsentwicklung und der Einschätzung der Qualität erkennen und selbst nach Möglichkeiten der Weiterqualifizierung suchen. Für etwa 100 Dozentinnen und Dozenten unserer Universität ist e-Learning eine Möglichkeit ein praxisorientierter Benutzer des Internets und der Fernausbildung zu sein.
Für die Zukunft ist ein Schulungskurs „e-Competence" geplant. Das erforschte Modell für Weiterbildung der Hochschullehrer an den medizinischen Universitäten ist ein komplexer Aufgabenbereich für ein Weiter- und Fortbildungspraktikum und für Forschungen auf dem Gebiet der Weiter- und Fortbildung. Heutzutage besteht kein Zweifel, dass die Ausbildung der Berufspädagogen und der Lehrerfachkräfte im Gesundheitswesen dem Fachgebiet entsprechen auf dem die Heranbildung verwirklicht wird. Wie es aus dieser Vorstellung ausdrücklich hervorgeht, ist der betreffende Weiterbildungskurs von großem Interesse für die didaktische Theorie und Praxis. Weitere Schritte in dieser Richtung werden unserer Meinung nach die Qualität der medizinischen Bildung in Russland auf ein höheres Niveau bringen.

Literaturangaben

KERRES, M., WITT, C.D., STRATMANN, J.: E-Learning. Didaktische Konzepte für erfolgreiches Lernen.- Köln: Luchterhand, 2002.

MAYR, J. (2006): Theorie+Ubung+Praxis=Kompetenz? Empirisch begründete Rückfragen zu den „Standards in der Lehrerbildung". In: Allemann-Ghionda, C., Terhart, E.: Kompetenzen und Kompetenzentwicklung von Lehrerinnen und Lehrern: Ausbildung und Beruf. In: Beiheft der Zeitschrift für Pädagogik, 51/2006, Weinheim: Beltz, S. 149-163.

STELZER-ROTHE, T.: Kompetenzen in der Hochschullehre. Rüstzeug für gutes Lehren und Lernen an Hochschulen. – Rinteln: Merkur, 2008.

TRUKHACHEVA, N.: E-Learning: Aktueller Stand und Chancen in der medizinischen Bildung im Russland. In: Unterrichtsforschung und Unterrichtsentwicklung. – Zürich: Universität Zürich, 2009, S.174-176.

WOLFF, R., ANTES, G.: Evidenzbasierung - Woher kommt die Evidenz und wie wird sie bewertet und genutzt? In: Verhaltenstherapie und Psychosoziale Praxis 39/2007, S.135-141.

http://www.educa.ch/dyn/199391.asp, 20.11.2009, Doris Künzi, Berufsschullehrerin in den Gesundheitsberufen.

http://www.elearningeuropa.info/index.php?page=doc&doc_id=595&doclng=3 10.11.2009 Tapio Varis, Neue Grundkompetenzen und E-Learning-Kompetenzen.

Kontakt:
Nina TRUKHACHEVA, Dr.: tnv10@mail.ru
Nikola PUPYREV, Dr.: pnp57@mail.ru
Svetlana TCHERNYSHEVA, post-graduate: svetlana@agmu.ru
Liudmila EPRYNTSEVA, Dr.

MAGISTER PROFESIONALIS – FACTS OR MYTHS

Małgorzata Jarecka-Żyluk, Akademia Pomorska w Słupsku, Poland

Nowadays the school is a special type of a public institution and at the same time it is a basic organisational unit of the schooling system whose aim is to educate, as well as raise both children and teenagers; it is also a community of teachers and students, a specific form of conveying cultural message which is executed by means of specialised teaching as well as learning actions. The teacher is the one to play a crucial role among various rules governing the school environment. Has teaching, which is one of the oldest occupations in the world, reached the level of professionalisation comparable with other jobs? Undoubtedly there are many objective factors which affect the aforementioned process.

Keywords: teacher, teacher professionalization, teacher's personality, teacher's professional competence

1 Introduction

Since 1825 compulsory education has been implemented in most countries in the world, both as a cultural necessity and legal obligation. School with teachers as its pillars is thus a source of knowledge bestowed upon dark masses. The state, having imposed school duty upon students and their parents, becomes obliged to carry it through, that is, it establishes schools, defines the rules governing them, provides teaching staff.

Modern educational goals determine different styles and competences for the teacher. The effects of learning and the quality of work depend to a large extent on teachers conscious of their role, on their understanding of the world and students. Education based on the student's activity and cognitive independence, learning-oriented and not limited to transmission of data, recognising students as subjects and preparing them to deal with ever-changing reality requires schools open to the world, with the new type of teachers: open-minded professionals, creative, active, autonomous and responsible. In the modern world structure the teacher occupies a special position, that of a border between the realm of great scientific, philosophical and cultural thought, and everyday life, both in its social-institutional and individual, personal dimension.

„Traditional, exclusively or customarily national education of teachers is not enough any more, it is not able to induce impulses necessary for international communication postulated by UNESCO in the field of upbringing and human rights" (Bernardin 1997, p. 89). The teacher of tomorrow is not only a person of knowledge and professionalism, able to think critically, but also a person capable of professional reflection in action and on action, someone with personal predispositions towards solving difficult and complex pedagogical problems, someone aware of *being a teacher*, not merely working as one.

2 Competent master

On the basis of the introductory deliberations it can be stated that professional teacher is, first and foremost, a competent teacher. Among the required competences the most important ones seem to be those which could be referred to as personal competences (Brzezińska 1995, p. 163). They constitute specific basis on which professional competences can be formed and developed. Then, what are those personal competences?

A. BRZEZIŃSKA (1995) distinguishes this kind of competences particularly when discussing the problem of supporting an adult person's development. Apart from them she mentions two kinds of competences in adults: social-organisational and implementation competences (Brzezińska A. 1995, p. 167).

Personal competences pertain to the quality of man's personal, individual functioning, the second type relate to social functioning, and the third type are various skills and abilities, including operational techniques useful in different situations. People with poorly developed personal competences, unable to initiate and maintain contact with other people will not be, according to BRZEZIŃSKA, flexible enough in their actions, or may tend to apply a narrow array of similar operational techniques. Difficult situations will prove very stressful for them, they will find it hard to modify the operational style depending on the changing situation. They will be stiff, authoritative, defending their beliefs and views at all costs, immune to counterarguments. The reason behind such behaviour is that their operational style is not entirely their own, is not based on their individual, personal and social competences, is not their extension (Brzezińska 1995, p. 168).

A. BRZEZIŃSKA treats personal and social-organisational competences as the basis for learning from others and creating one's own strategies and operational techniques, for constructing one's own, personal, individual methods of acting, for forming an individual operational style. People with the sense of competence based on solid foundations (knowledge and skills) are well aware of their abilities, strengths and limitations, they can maintain balance between acting on behalf of others and for themselves, they are more open, flexible, ready to function in new, non-standard conditions, emotionally challenging and stressful.

According to A. BRZEZIŃSKA (1995), competences also correspond well to requirements related to the role of a teacher in modern education. Discussions on new goals for education and the possibility of accomplishing them by teachers are focused around those personal competences. Therefore, in case of teachers personal competences should not only be treated as a basis for development of professional competences, but also as an important element of their professionalism.

It is already visible that teachers' professionalism, their professional formation, covers multiple scopes and dimensions of competences and skills which intertwine, so they are all joined by teachers' personalities, who they are and how they deal with themselves and their development.

Therefore it seems particularly important to consider a special type of the teacher's competences described by M. DUDZIKOWA (1994). They are so-called autocreative competences (Dudzikowa 1994, p. 153-162). They can be treated as a specific condition for the development of the spheres of subjectivity and emancipation, but also as a result of those spheres, since both subjectivity and emancipation competences trigger in an individual natural creativity, which consequently reinforces the process of self-creation, that is an independent forming of oneself.

M. DUDZIKOWA defines autocreative competences as a cognitive structure. It comprises particular skills, and knowledge and experience contribute to it. It is built upon a set of beliefs that those abilities can and should enable to initiate and carry out efficiently tasks in a certain situation in order to introduce in one's personality and behaviour some changes conforming to desired standards. Autocreative competences are especially required, even indispensable for teachers, as the essence of their occupation (work) is preparing others ("immature ones") to self-creation in order to achieve a higher level of personal maturity and rich, complex personality.

D. RUSAKOWSKA (1997) distinguishes communicative, cognitive and interactive competences.

The author understands communicative competences as the ability to speak openly and honestly, to justify undertaken actions with valid arguments, and to communicate with students, other teachers and parents. They determine co-operation and collective decision making.

Cognitive competences correspond to a searching approach, namely introducing innovations, constant learning, analysing, drawing conclusions. The basis for cognitive competences – as in D. RUSAKOWSKA (1997) – is theoretical awareness, which manifests itself in reflexive attitude to undertaken actions. It enables to comprehend the essence of educational processes. In that sense those competences are described also as interpretative. It is the ability to understand profoundly the educational reality and the role of school as a public sphere implementing the idea of democracy.

The third type of competences – interactive – the author defines as the ability to create partnership with students, to treat oneself and others as subjects, as well as to initiate and maintain social contacts (Rusakowska 1997, p. 148-149).

D. RUSAKOWSKA emphasises in particular certain crucial elements in the above mentioned competences of a teacher, which could be treated as indispensable conditions for those competences, namely critical thinking, unschematical and independent thinking, as well as reflexivity, which is a condition for any active pedagogical experience. Thus the category of experience (reflexive) becomes a focal point, a link in the process of initiation and development of the teacher's competences.

3 Summary – facts or myths?

Referring to the above deliberations one may discern two areas of professional competences for a modern professional teacher which are the most desirable nowadays. They are personal competences and implementation competences, of which the most significant ones seem to be communicative, cognitive (interpretative) and interactive competences. They are based on theoretical knowledge ("to know what", "to know why", "to know what for"), and on reflexive practical experience. It is worth mentioning that personal competences constitute specific base for the other ones. They also influence occurrence and development of a critical-reflexive approach in the teacher towards oneself and one's place in education, in the context of its goals and modern conditions. In the light of the newest scientific tendencies, teachers themselves must formulate goals based on their beliefs, they also have to modify their beliefs and goals according to their experience. This sentence succinctly presents the essence of teaching as a profession, and it enlightens one as to the fact that the greatest problem in the process of educating professional teachers is enabling those modifications in a rational manner, through generating in teachers the habit of practical reasoning.

Personality, knowledge and experience are components of a teacher. Major distinguishing features of teacher's work are autonomy, independence, free creativity (not programmed by others) and personal responsibility. Professionalism and competences must be rooted in the person, must be permeated with individuality. A teacher who does not distinguish between teaching a subject and teaching a student about the subject is not a professional.

Possibility of a failure is inscribed in the nature of every occupation. In teaching the probability of a failure is particularly high for this occupation depends on interaction between two independent subjects. Therefore competences, knowledge and interpersonal skills must be the main factor in the work of professional teachers. They must be a fact, not a myth.

References

ANUSIEWICZ, J.: Lingwistyka kulturowa. Zarys problematyki. Wydawnictwo Uniwersytetu Wrocławskiego – Wrocław 1995.

BERNARDIN, P.: Machiavel nauczycielem. Manipulacje w szkolnictwie. Reformy czy plan zniszczenia. Wyd. Antyk Marcin Dybowski – Komorów 1997.

BRZEZIŃSKA A., WILEŃSKI P.: Psychologiczne uwarunkowania wspomagania rozwoju człowieka dorosłego. In Nowiny Psychologiczne Warszawa 1995.

DUDZIKOWA, M.: Kompetencje autokreacyjne – czy i jak są możliwe do nabycia w toku studiów pedagogicznych. In: Kwiatkowska H. (ed.) Ewolucja tożsamości pedagogiki. Warszawa 1994.

HÖRNER, W., SZYMAŃSKI, M. S. (Ed.): Nauczyciel i kształcenie nauczycieli. Zmiany i wyzwania. Wydawnictwo Akademickie Żak – Warszawa 2005.

KRUSZEWSKI, K. (Ed.): Sztuka nauczania. Czynności nauczyciela. PWN – Warszawa 2004.

KWIATKOWSKA, H.: Tożsamość nauczycieli. Między anomią a autonomią. GWP – Gdańsk 2005.

MĘCZKOWSKA, A.: Od świadomości nauczyciela do konstrukcji świata społecznego. Nauczycielskie koncepcje wymagań dydaktycznych a problem rekonstrukcyjnej kompetencji ucznia. Impuls – Kraków 2002.

PEARSON, A. T.: Nauczyciel. Teoria i praktyka w kształceniu nauczycieli. WSiP – Warszawa 1994.

RUSAKOWSKA D.: W stronę edukacyjnego dyskursu nowoczesności, IBE, Warszawa 1995.

WERBIŃSKA, D.: Skuteczny nauczyciel języka obcego. Fraszka Edukacyjna – Warszawa 2004.

ZAWADZKA, E.: Nauczyciele języków obcych w dobie przemian. Impuls – Kraków 2004.

Contact:
Małgorzata JARECKA-ŻYLUK: zyluk_mam@poczta.onet.pl

CONCEPT OF INQUIRY-BASED LEARNING IN TEACHERS' PROFESSIONAL DEVELOPMENT

Iva Stuchlíková, University of South Bohemia, Czech Republic

Inquiry is an intentional process of diagnosing problems, reviewing experiments and distinguishing alternatives, planning investigations, researching conjectures, searching for information, constructing models, debating with peers and forming coherent arguments (Linn, Davis and Bell, 2004). Inquiry-based learning and teaching is therefore seen as potential tool for changing the student's attitude toward school learning and for development of his/her instrinsic motivation. Thus it should be introduced in pre-service teacher training and then cultivated as a core teaching concept in further professional development. The paper will present the data on inquiry-based learning concept as seen by teacher students and in-service teachers.

Key words: inquiry, inquiry-based learning, pre-service teacher, teacher's professional development

1 Background

1.1 Concepts of inquiry and inquiry-based learning

Although the notion of inquiry varies across contexts, common to all variants is an emphasis on active student participation, engaged thought and the investigation of personally valued questions and ideas. The term inquiry-based learning was probably for the first time advocated by J. R. SUCHMAN. He talked about discrepant events, the phenomena that seem to run contrary to what we normally expect. Discrepant events have long been used by science educators to stimulate students' interest and motivation. Observing something that does not fit with what we assume should be happening in school. Such an experience leaves the observer with a "wanting to know" feeling.

But the concept of inquiry has many facets that were described much earlier. Actually, Socratic questioning about personally relevant phenomena is such a generic way of inquiry and its importance for human learning was accented many times by many authors among them J. DEWEY, L.S. VYGOTSKY, J. S. BRUNNER, D. AUSUBEL, M. LIPMAN were probably the most famous ones. Many other terms were used as complementary or in parallel – e.g. problem based learning, inductive thinking, critical thinking, discovery learning, experiential learning, and scientific method of learning.

1.2 Key aspects of inquiry-based learning

The call for inquiry-based learning is esp. evident in science education. It is based on the recognition that science is essentially a question-driven, open-ended process. Students need to have personal experience with scientific inquiry to understand this fundamental aspect of science. Students' inquiry experiences provide the students with understanding of not only science concepts but methods as well (Edelson, Gordin, Pea, 1999).

Talking about IBL we assume: authentic and problem based learning activities where there may not be a correct answer; a certain amount of experimental procedures, "hands-on" activities; self regulated learning sequences where student autonomy is emphasized; discursive argumentation and communication with peers. Inquiry-based learning thus provides the opportunity for developing students' general inquiry abilities, specific investigation skills, and their improved understanding of scientific concepts. Learning from inquiry can enable students to discover scientific principles, but besides discovery the understanding is also developed through recognition of the gaps in their knowledge, through

systematic investigation and its refinement and application of the existing knowledge (Edelson, Gordin, Pea, 1999).
On the other hand, there are some challenges to the successful implementation of inquiry-based learning – students' motivation, skills and background knowledge being some of them. Last but not least, there are the practical constraints of the learning environment – resources, time, schedule etc.

2 Inquiry-based teaching and teachers' professional development

The teacher's understanding of the concepts of inquiry and inquiry-based learning (and/or teaching/education) is anyway very important because it is mirrored in his/her implicit theory of teaching (Marland, 1995) and may foster or undermine the changes of his/her teaching practices. It should be kept in mind that the teacher's willingness to implement inquiry is associated with the orientation to teaching (Magnusson et al., 1999) which influences the development of pedagogical content knowledge.
In teacher education, the assumption is that student teachers' involvement in these teaching/learning practices will lead to re-conceptualization of what the discipline is and how it is learned and taught. However, the transfer of instructional methods seems to be uneasy. „If pre-service teachers have been constituted through discourses that focus on transmission and teacher and textual authority, which now seem so 'natural' to them as to be invisible, how can they foster investigative habits of mind and participation in those they will teach?" (Klein 2004, p. 44).

3 Brief investigation into the student teacher and in-service teacher understanding of IBL

The aim of this study was to describe the notion of inquiry as it is perceived by teacher students and compare it with in-service teachers' perspective.

3.1 Subjects and procedure

Eighteen student teachers (after their initial teaching practice) and sixteen in-service teachers who are studying the two years course of educational counselling were interviewed for their subjective evaluation of inquiry-based learning (IBL). The participants were first discussing the IBL concept to clarify and compare it with other similar notions like PBL, constructivist teaching, etc. Then we asked them to compare pros and cons of the inquiry in the classroom and then summarize it, estimate their subjective real and optimal amount of inquiry-based activities in their lessons (student teachers estimated their own experience as a student and optimal proportion of IBL in their foreseen future teaching). These individual tasks were followed by group discussion to share the ideas.

3.2 Results and discussion

Pros and contras of IBL

Student teachers favoured the core ideas of the IBL; the in-service teachers were more ambivalent.

	Student teachers (n = 18)	In-service teachers (n = 16)
Endorsement (pros prevail over contras)	13	8
Ambivalence	3	7
Disbelief	2	1

Reasons for favouring IBL were: to work on personally important topics, the opportunity to collaborate with classmates, classroom social climate development, having control over one's own learning, ownership of the learning outcomes, deeper understanding of the studied topic, fun, novelty of learning situations in comparison with the routine procedures of transmissive teaching, improvement of teacher-student relationship, more challenge, freedom.

Reasons to avoid IBL were: open-ended nature of the problem, problem with motivation in bigger groups, risk of social loafing, too much time, insecure output practical and organizational constraints – very demanding to prepare the activity for all the students (resources, labs, etc.), less effective, missing structure.

The in-service teachers were much more concerned about the practical constraints and student factors. When summarized, in-service teachers talked about time constraints (81 %), class size (56 %), equipment (81 %), students' motivation (75 %), students' knowledge (56 %), and students' skills (31 %).

Student teachers commented on practical constraints: equipment (61 %), class size (50 %), time constraints (22 %), they saw student factors as less limiting the factors related to student motivation (55 %), knowledge (28 %) and skills (17 %).

The extent of implementation

The inquiry activities were described as comprising the whole range of inquiries: confirmation inquiry (the question and procedure are provided, results are known in advance), structured inquiry (the question and procedure are provided, students generate an explanation supported by the evidence they collect), guided inquiry (the teacher provides the research question, students design the procedure), open inquiry (students ask questions, design procedures, carry out investigations and communicate results).

Proportion of inquiry activities in the classroom	Student teachers (n = 18)	In-service teachers (n = 16)
Reality	17 %	25 %
Optimal	52 %	37 %

The alarming scarcity of "realized inquiry" in student teacher group should be treated very seriously with respect to teacher training curriculum. It could also be associated with the fact, that students hold more the all-or-nothing view of inquiry and are very enthusiastic about the prospective implementation (and thus might be unsatisfied with the proportion which they personally experience in their training).

Relatively modest optimal proportion of inquiry implementation was discussed with in-service teachers, where the curricular limitations, lack of support (e.g. problem design, organization and preparation), the learning outcomes assessments (tests, structured according to the entry exams demands on students knowledge), discipline problems and the need of background knowledge were seen together with the practical constraints (see above) as limiting factors.

4 Conclusion

The main problem with widespread implementation of IBL lies in deeply rooted view that inquiry learning takes too much time and that it is much more efficient for students simply to be given the information they need to know. This point of view is strongly reinforced by the kinds of things students are expected to know to pass the majority of tests they are given. We have to strive for questioning the taken-for-granted assumptions on which this current attitude is based.

The undifferentiated student teachers' understanding of inquiry, which may prevent them from the actual attempts to implement IBL, may be developed only under investigative practices in teacher education. This will not assure „...a specific form of classroom-based instructional change, but at least open up a „new discursive space where old authorities and stereotypical thinking are challenged and where the possibility of creating something new arises" (Klein 2004, p. 42).

References

EASTWELL, P.: Inquiry learning: Elements of confusion and frustration. The American biology teacher, 5/2009, 263-264.

EDELSON, D.C., GORDIN, D. N., PEA, R.D.: Addressing the Challenges of Inquiry-Based Learning through technology and curriculum design. Journal of The Learning Sciences, 3&4/1999, 391-450.

FOSS, D. & KLEINSASSER, R.: Pre-service elementary teachers' views of pedagogical and mathematical content knowledge, Teaching and Teacher Education, 4/1996, 429-442.

JANÍK, T.: Pedagogical content knowledge nebo didaktcká znalost obsahu? Brno: Paido, 2007.

KING, A.: Designing the instructional process to enhance critical thinking across the curriculum. Teaching of Psychology, 1/1995, 13- 17.

KIRSCHNER, P.A., SWELLER, J., CLARK, R.E.: Why minimal guidance during instruction does not work: An analysis of the failure of constructivist, discovery, problem-based, experiential, and inquiry-based teaching. Educational psychologist, 2_2006, 75-86.

KLEIN, M.: The premise and promise of inquiry based mathematics in pre-service teacher education: a poststructuralist analysis. Asia-Pacific Journal of Teacher Education, 1/2004, 35-47.

LINN, M. C., DAVIS, E.A., AND BELL, P.: Internet environments for science education. Mahwah, NJ, USA: Lawrence Erlbaum, 2004.

MAGNUSSON, S., KRAJCIK, J. & & BORKO, H.: Nature, sources and development of pedagogical content knowledge, in: J. Gess-Newsome & N. G. Lederman (Eds) Examining pedagogical content knowledge. Dordrecht, Kluwer Academic Publishers, 1999.

MARLAND, P.W.: Implicit theories of teaching. In: L.W.Anderson (Ed.), International encyklopedia of teaching and teacher education, Oxford: Elsevier Science Ltd., 1995.

SUCHMAN, J. R. (1966): Developing Inquiry, Chicago: Science research Associates, 1966.

http://ec.europa.eu/research/conferences/2004/sciprof/index_en.html , 2004, Europe need more scientists (2004).
http://www.nuffieldfoundation.org/fileLibrary/pdf/Sci_Ed_in_Europe_Report_Final.pdf , 2008, Osborne, J. & Dillon J. Science Education in Europe: Critical reflections.

http://ec.europa.eu/research/science-society/document_library/pdf_06/report-rocard-on-science-education_en.pdf ,2007, Science Education NOW.

The article was supported by the Project 7 RP SiS 234870 „ S-TEAM: Science Teacher Education Advanced Methods".

Contact:
Iva STUCHLÍKOVÁ, PhD.: stuchl@pf.jcu.cz

PSYCHOSOMATIC APPROACH TO SELF-REGULATION OF PEDAGOGICAL KNOWLEDGE ACQUISITION

Vlastimil Švec
Tomáš Baťa University in Zlín, Faculty of Humanities, Czech Republic

Self-regulated pedagogical knowledge acquisition is one of the key factors in an effective professional teacher' training. So far, the cognitive approach to self-regulation has been favoured. The psychosomatic approach is based on the assumption that a student acquires knowledge not only mentally, but also physically. This approach is implemented in psychosomatic disciplines, especially in dialogical behaviour. A student gradually establishes the psychosomatic condition to act authentically and be creative when in pedagogical situations. Self-regulated knowledge acquisition emerges from the nature of psychosomatic disciplines which stimulate students to be aware of what they do and how they do it, and be able to change their behavioural patterns.

Key words: pedagogical knowledge, self-regulation knowledge acquisition, psychosomatic approach, dialogical behaviour.

1 Background

The core of teacher's profession is pedagogical and professional knowledge. Currently, there is a trend to understand pedagogical knowledge in broader sense, with regard to both theoretical and practical dimensions. *Pedagogical knowledge* is seen as acquired proficiency to deal with problems which arise in the teaching profession, e.g. when communicating with pupils. It is obvious that the above mentioned dimensions merge. On the outside, they are explicit and observable. This form of pedagogical knowledge is traditionally referred to as skills.

The theoretical dimension of pedagogical knowledge is hidden to the naked eye and relates to both the teacher's (student teacher's) theoretical knowledge and pedagogical experience. This dimension may be referred to as tacit.

Student teachers and teachers acquire their pedagogical knowledge when dealing with practical pedagogical problems. Today the idea that acquired theoretical pedagogical knowledge is used when dealing with practical problems is seen as antiquated.

Pedagogical knowledge is acquired by a teacher or student teacher especially in situations which need to see their action, even though they may not have acquired any theoretical knowledge yet. One is encouraged to act freely and authentically and rely on one's pedagogical experience. It is a form of experience learning.

Effective pedagogical knowledge acquisition is when a teacher or student teacher is able to control its progress and aims and comment on its results, i.e. to be aware of the results, to evaluate them and change them, self-regulate them.

The existing *approach to self-regulated knowledge acquisition* and in particular to pedagogical knowledge is of cognitive nature (e.g. Schraw, Moshman, 1995). This means that a student teacher or teacher analyses what they consider vital, what they did in a lesson and how effective their behaviour was and only after that they decide what kind of pedagogical knowledge/behavioural approach they need to acquire or adapt.

This paper will deal with a different approach to self-regulated knowledge acquisition, the *psychosomatic approach* which may be complementary to the cognitive one. We will especially comment on how it is used in student teacher training.

2 Excursus to qualitative research of "becoming a teacher" process

Before we attempt to clarify what the psychosomatic approach to self-regulation of pedagogical knowledge acquisition is, let us see some results from the qualitative research among student teachers which we entitled metaphorically "becoming a teacher" process. In this research, we cooperated, among others, with two students for three years when they attended the courses on general and specific didactics and took part in teacher placement. What follows is an excerpt from the author's notes:

I cooperated with Honza and Libor, the student teachers, when they were on their teacher placement (a course in the student's 4th year). I asked them to record each other at the faculty school where the teacher placement was organized. After the placement, we went through the recording of Honza's and Libor's lesson together and commented on it.

V.Š.: How did you feel in the lesson?
Libor: ...I was aware that I had been leaning against that chair almost all the lesson... next time I would try to avoid doing that...
Honza: ... but it's like safe ground there, behind the teacher's desk on the podium, I tried to venture among pupils but came back soon, it felt safer there, in front of all those kids...
V.Š: You only need more time to become more confident, I don't like standing on that podium now...

After that I showed Honza and Libor the recording made by the colleagues two years their junior, who I communicated with in the course of general didactics (which I taught).

V.Š.: Have you seen anything you have got in common with your younger colleagues?
Libor: Well, as for the body language and positioning, it s kind of similar...we both leaned against that desk... and the girls did the same thing...
Honza: It was unnatural to stand there like that... when I think of my trainer, she was natural, spoke calmly and walked around... we were both stiff... I was right back in my second year, the body shows everything, you can't hide it.

After the reflection induced by watching the recording, both students realized that to act means to react with your body to a certain pedagogical situation. The important factor in student's behaviour is not only thinking but also their voice, speech, body movements and gestures.

3 Psychosomatic condition of student teachers and psychosomatic disciplines

The psychosomatic approach is based on the well-tested though often not respected assumption that knowledge acquisition is not only the matter of one's head but of the body as a whole, of psychosomatics.

The psychosomatic approach aspires to show the pedagogical training of future teachers as a "journey of experience and wisdom, the empirical journey accompanied by one's reflection, primary experiences and experience and thus becoming a journey of self-recognition, the journey of creative and innovative practice" (Vyskočil 2000, p. 7).

The psychosomatic approach is founded upon the encouragement of the development of the personality of student teachers which should be oriented towards their "public behaviour" being – (as far as possible) – the presentation, realisation, 'radiation' of a fully-aware, communicative, creative, responsible behaviour and experiencing of situations – a consciously moral personality" (Vyskočil 2000, p. 6).

We have mentioned "readiness" of a student in a certain pedagogical situation which is a precondition for a student to act freely and authentically. This readiness is also referred to as a *psychosomatic condition* by I. VYSKOČIL.

According to VYSKOČIL, condition is "a certain maturity, preparation, readiness to react rapidly and flexibly and, even the need, desire, or internal urge to act publicly, to act and to behave, and to experience directly, without barriers, spontaneously, creatively and productively, independently and responsibly. In feedback loops, in a high-quality manner" (Vyskočil 2000, p. 7).

The psychosomatic condition is more than an acquired pedagogical knowledge (Švec, 2006). It is an array of student teacher's physical, mental and moral dispositions to act (Vyskočilová, 2002). We can understand it as student's readiness to perceive wholly the pedagogical situation; it is looking for harmony, harmonizing the teacher with its curriculum and pupils in the existing context. A student in a certain situation (when stimulated suitably) tries to note their successes and failures and thus they get ready for a certain situation.

The psychosomatic condition of students is developed through psychosomatic disciplines, among which and above all are subjects like Dialogical Behaviour,

Voice and Speech Education, Movement Education and Authorial Readings. The core discipline is Dialogical Behaviour.

4 Dialogical Behaviour

Dialogical Behaviour (DB), is based upon the experience and knowledge that man, usually when alone, speaks to – or plays with – themselves. Their internal partner appears to them and calls to them. And in DB, the whole point is that this dialogue with one's internal partners be reproduced publicly, within a group of their fellow colleagues-students and university-level teachers who have practical experience with this discipline and have experienced it and lived through it themselves.

Students receive virtually no instruction whatsoever as to what they have to do, they are simply told: *Try to hold a dialectical discussion with yourself. With yourself as you would with your internal partner.* I. VYSKOČIL provides several recommendations for students who are beginning with DB (Vyskočil 2005, pp. 20-22, and rounded-out and complemented by the personal experience and experiences of the author of this chapter):

- Do not prepare anything in advance. Inspire yourself by whatever – here-and-now, on-the-spot – comes into your mind, whatever you notice. It is necessary to make this idea public, verbally, or even non-verbally. We will react to this idea immediately or after a while (we will respond).
- Feel, behave and act as if the others present (colleagues, the teacher) simply weren't present (i.e. so-called "public aloneness").
- Concentrate, and perceptively feel what we are doing. Do not think about what to say. Do not concentrate on concentrating – since you will simply fall into a panic.
- As soon as you can, at the very first impulse you feel, give it a form – act it out. But there is no need to feel an immediate duty to enact or say anything on the spot.
- Allow yourselves time to respond to this impulse. Do not hurry or rush, so that you are aware of what it is you are saying or doing; whether and how this other person (internal partner) expresses themselves (i.e. whether they are already speaking or acting).
- Think of nothing. Do not think of anything. Notice what we have done, for instance – what goes on when we alter or change the position of our body, or make some gesture, etc.

- Notice where a certain sequence ends, and where opposition makes itself heard (i.e. our internal partner).
- Maintain tension – that which flows from us, "beyond the footlights", to the others. When we stiffen, for instance our hands, shoulders, are not relaxed; then we rid ourselves of the possibility of expression.
- Seek a productive anti-pole to the previous impulse; contrasts, which complement each other.
- Do not fear changes (which might even surprise us); give it expression. Accept it, act it out.
- Engage yourself fully into the dialectical discussion or behaviour; do not satisfy yourself just with voice, certain movements, grimaces, gestures.
- Enjoy the feelings from this experience and self-testing, taste it to the full.
- Express your experience and feelings from this dialectical discussion or behaviour through self-reflexion in a written form.

DB is an unusual discipline. It places a relatively simple requirement upon students who decide to penetrate its mysteries – that they "act". Of course, "for themselves", since we cannot do anything else. But with whom should they act? The answer is – with their "internal partner" in the given situation of public aloneness. They are given the opportunity to do so in an ordinary faculty auditorium, where one half is reserved for the actions and behaviour of one of them, while the others sit next to each other on seats in the second half, as the audience. However, acting out one's internal partner is not equivalent to or the same as talking to oneself.

The participants are encouraged not to think in advance about what they are going to say (or do); not to prepare themselves in advance – but rather, to begin from scratch, from nothing, from themselves within the situation. The participants are warned not to rush into things and to muffle or dampen their efforts to "be good" (in what they do) – to suppress that "norming" within themselves. That they unnecessarily judge themselves too harshly, curse themselves out, blame themselves; that they do not resist activity, are not unsure of themselves, despair of themselves, are not uneasy about themselves.

Why do student teachers need DB? Student teachers need creativity – they need to know how to make a difference between what to do mechanically, and where a person should not simply remain bound to a habit. They need to understand their own (forms of) expression, what they are inclined towards; where their strengths might lie, their communicativeness. They need to develop their imagination and fantasy; to learn how to react to new situations and to anticipate other situations.

DB requires time; it requires that student teachers rid themselves of their everyday stereotypes in their dealings not only with pupils but also with their colleagues. One university teacher (J.P.), who leads DB training sessions, writes about this in their self-reflective diary as follows: "*Teachers master the art of self-presentation to a high degree, (since) their craft is winning over a class full of pupils. Stepping out before the eyes of others for them automatically means standing up for themselves (doing it well). All those who have tried dialectics know that they have to suffer a moment of helplessness, since this is the first time that a new, unusual, surprising thing is born within themselves; where they see themselves in a light they have never known before.*"

5 Psychosomatic approach to student teachers' self-regulation of pedagogical knowledge acquisition

The psychosomatic approach to self-regulation of pedagogical knowledge acquisition assumes that student teachers (at the beginning or in the course of their studies) attend courses on psychosomatic disciplines, particularly dialogical behaviour, voice and movement management, a course on diction and on authorial reading. These courses are subjectless, i.e. without given contents.

When attending the courses, student teachers gradually realize how to understand oneself, how they come across and what is essential for their communication with others.

This "understanding oneself" is carried out through a number of trials of dialogical behaviour and in other psychosomatic disciplines. The catalyst of this mental process are written self-reflecting analyses of student teachers. A student teacher writes down all the experience and thus gets another view on their actions. It has proven conductive to read one's comments in front of an audience, i.e. in a seminar group. A student teacher becomes an active subject when going through all the psychosomatic disciplines. They become a subject who pays attention to what happens when they act, they notice that and ask themselves what to do so that it would be better next time. It is a new type of qualitative experience which is closely linked to behavioural authenticity and with student's responsibility for one's actions.

This new experience is the fact that student teachers "learn to communicate with their bodies, they try to get involved physically, they activate their imagination, intuition, their mind. All those things they did not take in, feel or realize fully as they understood them as general human, and thus did not factor them into in their actions" (loosely based on Vyskočil).

Psychosomatic disciplines may be followed by pedagogical and psychological courses together with courses on didactics in a certain subject field. Psychosomatic condition of a student teacher (which is being formed and shaped constantly) facilitates self-regulation of pedagogical knowledge acquisition. Questions like "*What did I do? What was the pupils' reaction to it? What did I succeed in? How is it connected with my plans and aims?...*" come to student teachers' mind much more easily after attending courses on psychosomatic disciplines (based on our research).

6 Conclusion

The chapter shadowed out what the psychosomatic approach in self- regulation of pedagogical knowledge acquisition is. We assume there is self-regulation of both outer an inner knowledge. It is desirable to examine further the mechanisms of this self-regulation. We cannot strictly separate cognitive and psychosomatic approaches. It is believed that the cognitive dimension of self-regulation is embedded to the psychosomatic dimension of pedagogical knowledge which is demonstrated in the individual actions of a student teacher.

Bibliography

SCHRAW, G., MOSHMAN, D.: Metacognitive Theories. Educational Psychology Review, 1995, no. 4, pp. 351-371.

ŠVEC, V.: Od znalostí k pedagogické kondici: nový vhled do pedagogické přípravy studentů učitelství? Pedagogika, 2006, č. 1, s. 91-102.

VYSKOČIL, I.: Úvodem. In Vyskočilová, E., Slavíková, E. (Ed.) Psychosomatický základ veřejného vystupování, jeho studium a výzkum. Praha: DAMU, 2000, s. 4-8.

VYSKOČILOVÁ, E.: Psychosomatická kondice jako základ schopnosti vychovávat. In Švec, V. a kol. Cesty k učitelské profesi: utváření a rozvíjení pedagogických dovedností. Brno: Paido, 2002, s. 13-35.

The text is a part of the research grant of Funding Agency of Czech Republic, no. 406/09/1240 (*„Cognitive and Non-cognitive Determinants of the Self - Regulated Learning Development for Auxiliary Services Professions' Students"*).

Contact: Vlastimil ŠVEC: svec@fhs.utb.cz

PEDAGOGICAL PRACTICE AND ITS PLACE WITHIN PROSPECTIVE TEACHERS' PREGRADUATE EDUCATION

Jan Šťáva, Patrik Vacek
Masaryk University, Brno, Czech Republic

The paper deals with the issues of significance and place of pedagogical practice within prospective teachers' pregraduate education. It adverts to the function of every single kind of practice while stressing the importance it possesses as a whole in creating basic competences of any prospective teacher. The content of pedagogical practices should be seen in an array of activities that lead to acquiring familiarity with basic competences for a teacher's profession on every single step of educational architecture. This also has strong ties to precisely described goals for prospective teachers and possible interventions being made during their practices by faculty teachers.

Key-words: professional activity, teacher's profession, pre-graduate preparation, pedagogical practice, educational competences

1 Introduction

In a few past decades there have existed efforts focused at higher level of professionalism in teacher's education. What does that actually mean? Professionals themselves tend to use their expertise originated primarily from their fundamental theoretic and systematic knowledge they have acquired. Such an expertise is not in an everyone's possession and thus it can be quite efficient in the professional's work because of its special relation to knowledge. Briefly said: they are the professionals who inititate knowledge (and education) and while doing so they create new level of experience. But, in which field of inquiry should be a teacher an expert of such-a-kind not to be replaced by other expert and non-teacher? Which systemized sums of knowledge can create the very own core of his or her professionalism? Having said this, we can conclude it is neither a subject of content issue nor education or psychology itself as the theorist from both fields are far more superior (be it mathematician, physicist or biologist) to the teacher. What is, then, very own goal of teacher's efforts? The teacher's profession is a difficult one and a creative process that consists both from two-way teacher-pupil communication and influence through the educational content. That is why we usually perceive the teacher's profession as an expert for this kind of communication, as someone suitable for solving educational issues. The teacher himself must be skilled enough to diagnose educational situations and moreover: he must be capable of dealing with educational decision-making process. Thus, the substantial part of his professionalism lies in the theory of instruction. By saying this, he is the one who integrates specifically education and psychology in the theory of instruction of the fields he has advanced professionally. Simultaneously, he makes specific integration of theory and practice in the process of pupils' education.

2 The signification and content of pedagogical practice's realization

The quality of prospective teachers' educational preparation influences both the quality of our schools and the quality of instruction itself. That is why we have observed recently – and not just in Czech schools but also in a number of other countries – a strong and formiddable discussion concerning the very nature of teacher's education and further advancement of it and it has occurred that it is essential to note the importance of teacher's education curriculum. The key aspect to professionalize teacher's education is the change of teacher's role as a facilitator of every pupil's education in favour of promoting every single pupil's personal growth. With this in mind there even rises the teacher's responsibility for "his" pupil and it also carries along new professional requirements a teacher must meet. For that reason, all schools specializing in prospective teachers' education should address these issues seriously.

Pregraduate teacher's education can be considered as the first significant phase of teachers' education. Its graduates should get familiar with basic teacher competences that could be further developed for granting teacher's competence to them. However, in the Czech Republic there is no official standard term for teacher's competence, not even in the newest documents and requirements by the Czech Ministry of Education. The requirements for teacher's competences are given just by the Accreditation Commission of Czech Ministry of Education and as such they differ greatly in every single accredited teacher's preparation programme. Basically, there exist a few elementary models of teacher's preparation in which the relation of theory and practice can be realized through different modes:

- simultaneously, without a mutually interconnection
- theory prevails, practice is just a complement
- practice is significant, theory only generalizes
- theory and practice makes an unity

As an optimal approach can be seen the last model of preparation and there are efforts leading to its prospective realization: However, for a variety of reasons it is not yet fully implemented. As rather promising there seems to be the Oxford model of preparation (continuous tutorial provided to prospective teacher) or the German model (prospective teacher leaves for a limited time for a real-class experience and just after that he/she finishes his/her study and becomes a teacher). Also, the clinic model is quite hopeful; the practice is being organized at clinic (faculty) schools. Rigorous incorporation of some of the models mentioned above is limited by problems of economic, organizational (too many students) and legislative nature. Though, it is necessary to try to approach these models closer (e. g. clinic semesters, clinic faculty schools, pro-fesssional training, assistance practices, reflexive practices, prospective teachers' practices self-reflexive practices). This is a certain way how to increase the level of future prospective teachers' preparation. However, they are not systematic solutions leading to sustainable qualitative growth of prospective teacher's education efficiency. Those demands can be met only by a practice being realized in the conditions of faculty clinic school that would be an organic part of the university. As it is obvious it is not possible to incept such an exercise institution at the present moment, it is even more necessary to use the current faculty schools and the expertise of well qualified exercise teachers.

The problem of pedagogical practice is not an isolated topic and a mere issue of content, organization, methods and management. It is always necessary to perceive it as a problem of theory and practice in teacher's education. Shaping the professional skills of every prospective teacher is unthinkable without a firm and well adjusted system of practical preparation. Pedagogical practice serves as a connection point between a student's theory preparation and his or her prospective individual school's work. It is a realization of student's preparation towards the teacher's activity; it arms him or her with a complex of competences and routines that are essential for successful solving of educational tasks.

If we are to deal with pedagogical practice as an integrated part of teacher's preparation, we still miss solid theoretical background that would mark it with an approach to conclude and verify the theoretic preparation efficiency. Pedagogical practices in teacher's fields of study have a far more important goal than those fields of study that are not aimed primarily at teacher's preparation. The signification of pedagogical practices as a main part of "practical" education is given by the specific nature of a teacher's profession: contrary to graduates of other faculties, a teacher is expected to be able to deal with all basic professional competences from his or her first days of duty. Thus, the problems of pedagogical practices must be dealt with all seriousness that belongs to the role and function of both school as an institution and a teacher as a profession. In the process of pedagogical practices there is present not only verifying the level of theoretic and practical preparation of a prospective teacher, but there also arise large possibilities for enriching the creative potential of every single teacher. In a system of well-thought and organized pedagogical practice can be also seen the elements of creative schooling and individual work-load of every student. This is, of course, possible only when there is secured an effective way how to get things done with a complex of educational tasks. And as there exists some confusion about different requirements from various faculty departments, there too much often emerges a sort of redundant discussion whether it is necessary to fulfill all the goals assigned or if it is enough to solve some of them. Also, after finishing pedagogical practice, the experience being acquired this way is not always considered as the real school practice.

In the system of a prospective teacher's preparation, pedagogical practice takes a number of different functions. Primarily, it has an educational character and enriches and develops students' theoretical preparation and gives them the possibilites for strengthening and deepening acquired knowledge that serves for further use of theoretical concepts in practice schooling. During pedagogical practices it is evident that there emerges the formation process in the realms of basic professional skills and routines. Every prospective teacher is given a possibility to observe and analyze various aspects of educational process and thus, he or she learns how to manage his or her class and educational situations. The time schedule of any pedagogical pratice should lead a student to certain kinds of research work: be it educational-psychological analysis of the class, complex analysis of the class, complex analysis of the class group and making an experimental sort of work. Nevertheless, the experience put together after checking up students during their pedagogical practice reveals they fulfill a mere minimum of practical work being planned while these activities (a sort of assistance) have a great deal of illustrative character and they do not provoke the cognitive activity. In the structure of educational activities of a student assigned to a pedagogical practice in a school we frequently conclude the aspect of practical educational activity as the weakest point. It is not unusual that a supervisor of a pedagogical practice oversees prospective teachers insufficiently. The student's work during pedagogical practice must be creative one and involve an active aspect. That is why any teacher guarantees the quality of education of every single pupil. The success can be delivered only if every teacher incorporates creatively and responsibly wide array of skills into his or her professional finding the most suitable and effective methods for coping with educational problems. Professional educational work has a peculiarity that lies in the fact that it is not possible to prepare a prospective teacher in a definitive manner. During his/her college year he or she must be guided for active cognitive approach, highly individualized kind of work that overcomes the time schedule of regular class. Then, such a teacher will be able to spread this approach in his or her own schooling.

Creating and shaping professional skills of every prospective teacher is unthinkable without a firm and well thought system of practical preparation. Pedagogical practice must also serve as a connection point between a student's theory preparation and his or her prospective individual and creative school's work. It is a realization of student's preparation towards the direct teacher's activity; it arms him or her with a complex of competences and routines that are essential for successful solving of educational tasks. During the pedagogical practice there is present the process of forming basic professional skills and routines. It is, of course, possible only when the system of pedagogical practices guarantees effective way of solving a whole complex of educational tasks for students – apprentices and prospective teachers. These tasks can be understood as key professional competences (or rather skills) of students that should be familiarized during the run of every mode of pedagogical practice and a subsequent verification. However, this is quite difficult goal to accomplish because most of pedagogical practice of students is conducted out of reach of respective departments' didacticians. Thus, for the success of the system of pedagogical practice it is essential to cooperate among educators, psychologists, didacticians and teacher of guidance. Thus, for the efficiency (and productivity) of pedagogical practices it is important to analyze the system of teacher's key competences and – with this background – to postulate the stages of acquiring those competences during pedagogical practice in the process of realization various kinds pedagogical practices – in accordance with already successfully adopted theoretic concepts of prospective teacher's education. Simultaneously, with out-lining the basic teacher's skills it is necessary to prepare the possibilities of interventions into the process of acquiring professional skills of prospective teacher's practice. If we are supposed to outline the clear scheme of basic tasks and activities being applied during the realization of all modes of pedagogical practice, it is necessary to build upon the analysis of day-to-day teacher's activities which must further be given to accordance with the theory of teacher's key competences (Spilková 1997; Švec 1999, p. 34-36; Švec, respectively Svatoš, Holý 2000, p. 106-107; Filová 1998, p. 9-12). Based on the analysis of approaches to teacher's key competences we can then classify following basic competences considered to become familiar with during the run of prospective teachers' pedagogical practice:

- competences for projects (curriculum, learning unit, didactic transformation of educational content, teaching plan for every single class, precise teaching preparation for a class, specific goals of each class, didactic analysis of educational content, proficiency in choosing appropriate methods that suit pupils' learning styles, an appropriate strategy of progress within a learning unit);
- communication competences (an ability to communicate both with the whole of class and every pupil within it, an ability to react to individual specifics of pupils, to lead various kinds of speech with pupils, be able to create and realize positive climate within the class);
- organizational and managing competences (be able to realize learning units of various kinds, a construction of a didactic test, pupils' activation within the instruction, to react appropriately to individual pupils' needs, to guarantee discipline within the class, managing school documents etc.);
- diagnostic competences (continuous checking of everyday learning, differentiation and integration, pupils' individual needs, gifted and disadvantaged pupils, various methods of classification, diagnoses of pupils' written work etc.);
- reflexive competences (guided observation, class climate measurement, creation of sociogram, an ability to analyze the learning unit and its record, self-reflection etc.).

It is possible to influence the creating of basic educational competences of a prospective teacher by appropriate set-up interventions. Fundamental interventions should be given by precisely described goals for single kinds of pedagogical practices being realized – in the form of stringently described abilities that can be further developed. That said, detailed instructional documents should be prepared for the use by students, teachers and didacticians from the departments. Further possibility of intervention is represented by maintaining a student's educational diary to promote self-reflective abilities of any prospective teacher:

- inception of a self-reflection process, attracting student's interest in the goal of becoming familiar with his or her own educational's acitivity. Indeed, it is very own activity of a student;
- summing up and organizing self-reflection on details concerning reflected educational activity, subsequent analysis and self-evaluation;
- a proposal for a change of a one's educational activity or observed educational activity; this is essential for promoting a one's educational activity (e. g. conclusion of pedagogical practice in one of these ways: final seminar or a talk with teacher of guidance of faculty didactician).

Other possibilities are represented by a concrete intervention by a teacher of guidance to promote professional teacher's competences as follows:

- stimulating interventions (promoting and helping to succeed);
- inhibiting interventions (supressing and removing undesirable and unsuccessful aspects);
- directive interventions (requirements, directions, advises, recommendations, evaluation)
- interventions that call for preparation and realization of teaching;
- interventions to assess the teaching.

3 Conclusions

A significant possibility of futher intervention within the organization of students' pedagogical practices can be seen in very own pedagogical practice's management. At most faculties of education in the Czech Republic there are present official departments of pedagogical practice which are characterized both by the scope and co-ordination of managing activities to guarantee pedagogical practices realization. Such a department should actually have in its possession following competences for prospective teacher's preparation: conceptual, co-ordinative, methodical and organizing. Also, its competences should include a close co-operation with faculty schools. Faculties of education should create methodical materials (methodical manual) that would serve for particular practices' realization and for their students and teachers of guidance.

References

FILOVÁ, H.: Slovo úvodem. In Budoucí učitelé na souvislé praxi aneb rukověť fakultního cvičného učitele. Brno: Paido, 1998, p.9.

SPILKOVÁ, V. :Proměny primární školy a vzdělávání učitelů v historicko-srovnávací perspektivě. Praha: PdF UK, 1997.

ŠVEC, V.: Pedagogická příprava budoucích učitelů: Problémy a inspirace. Brno: Paido, 1997.

ŠVEC, V. Monitorování a rozvoj pedagogických dovedností. Brno: Paido, 2000.

SVATOŠ, T., HOLÝ I.: Vytváření pedagogických dovedností studentů v konvergentním modelu učitelské přípravy. In Monitorování a rozvoj pedagogických dovedností. Brno: Paido, 2000, p.106-124.

Contact:
Jan ŠŤÁVA, PaedDr., CSc.: stava@ped.muni.cz
Patrik VACEK, Mgr.: patrikvacek@ped.muni.cz

THE PREPARATION OF TRAINEE TEACHERS FOR THE RESPONSIBILITIES OF A CLASS TEACHER

Stanislav Střelec, Jana Krátká, Masaryk University Brno, Czech Republic

The aim of the study is to provide an outlook on theoretical and practical aspects of class teacher preparation during their pre-service teacher training courses. The article is a part of the MSM0021622421 research project "The School and Health for 21st Century" developed at Masaryk University Faculty of Education.

Key words: framework programme for education, class teacher, upbringing activities, cooperation with parents, pre-graduate training

1 Introduction

The Czech primary and secondary schools have been going through important changes nowadays. The framework programmes for education and school programmes for education have been declared as a new strategy in Czech education system. Primary schools innovative objectives, key competencies of pupils, educational areas and interdisciplinary themes are the categories outlining the fundamental changes which the Czech school system has been facing nowadays. In this respect, the school is understood as the system of services (assistance) for the pupil developing the necessary preconditions for their optimal, individual and social future employment. The increasing responsibilities of the class teacher are naturally related with all of that. From this point of view, we especially pay attention to the following in this article:

- Common requirements for the educational activities of the class teacher;
- Some practical initiatives for the pre-graduate trainee teachers programmes and their cooperation with the pupils' parents.

2 Common requirements for the educational activities of the class teacher

The Dictionary of Education Terms (Průcha, J., Walterová, E., Mareš, J., 2001, p. 253) characterizes the class teacher as a specialist who instructs, leads and educates the group of pupils in their class, coordinates the educational activities of other educators teaching in the class, cooperates with the pupils' parents, keeps documentation and administration of their class.

Even J. A. COMENIUS in his Didactica Magna stated that the main responsibility for the classroom activities should be laid on one particular teacher. COMENIUS thus anticipated the role of a class teacher even though he had not used that particular term. Notwithstanding, not very encouraging seems the fact that despite such positive experience approved by the centuries, there has not been any coherent official document which would declare the role and the responsibilities of a class teacher in the current Czech school. The Czech Education Ministry (MŠMT) has only mentioned the class teacher role and activities in partial instructions and decrees for teachers in general. Particular activities of a class teacher have so far been determined by appropriate local school authorities and more or less embedded in internal documentation of a particular school. Such documentation supposes that the class teacher:

- Motivates pupils to the development of a set of internal classroom rules in compliance with the school rules and regulations and keeps an eye on observing them (creating open, safe and positive social climate in the classroom); supports the development of positive social interactions among the classmates.

- Intermediates communication among the other members of the teaching staff and guarantees cooperation between the school and the class pupils' parents.
- Acquires and keeps an overview of the personal differences of the class pupils and about their family background.
- Cooperates with a school career counsellor in providing consultancy in deciding about the future education and professional career advancement of the class pupils.
- Cooperates with a school prevention instructor on the detection and screening of warning signals, participates in the implementation of basic prevention projects, screens for the classroom relationships.
- Cooperates with school psychologist and/ or special needs educator on the activities aimed at the prevention of poor academic achievement in the classroom (rectification, guidance, etc.) developing the conditions for the inclusion of the pupils with specific educational needs in the classroom, and, in compliance with the headmaster instructions, in other educational and counselling areas of the work with the class pupils.

3 Some practical initiatives for the pre-graduate trainee teachers programmes

Cooperation with the pupils' parents is considered one of the prime responsibilities of the teacher. The encounter with the pupils' parents brings frequently strain, doubts, anxiety, and some other related side effects. Such situations are uneasy not only for teachers, but for the pupil's parents as well. The class teacher appears in a specific position being a coordinator and integrator with a great number of important educational responsibilities. Most members of teaching staff at primary and secondary schools become class teachers, some of them at the very beginning of their professional career, from which the following question arises: When, where and up to what extent can trainee teachers get the necessary experience for this particular role of a class teacher? Can such practical experience of a class teacher be got during the pre-gradual teacher training course? Without real school environment and invariable groups of pupils, parents, and teachers? Taking all these issues into account, we need to consider current conditions of the teacher training programmes as well (concept, content, and timing). E.g., the course in Theory and Methods of Education is a discipline closely related to the communicative, counselling, and advisory competencies of the teacher at Masaryk University Faculty of Education in Brno. But, due to the disproportion between the course content and the limited number of lessons, the trainee teachers can only be inspired to learning of some issues. The lack of time is experienced especially during our attempts to provide thorough and in-depth skill training as a part of regular trainee teacher courses. Some opportunities can be provided during a continuous teaching practice. During their teaching practice, the trainee teachers were asked to interview a class teacher and report back to the class for a discussion at the faculty. The class teachers were expected to have had the biggest experience in dealing with parents. The trainee teachers were given an outline of an interview and basic information about the application of such exploration in practice. As an illustration, we provide an interview outline for the guidance and interview recording:

Input data:

- Duration of the teacher's work experience:
- Type of school:
- Teaching qualification and specialization:
- Female – Male

The outline of an interview with a class teacher (Introduction – trainee teacher's worries about the communication and cooperation with the pupil's parents, an attempt to avoid wrongs and mistakes).

- How do you estimate the parents' interest in their children's academic achievement (e.g. How many parents [in %] is interested in regular cooperation with the class teacher? What is their motivation?
- In general, what group of parents is interested in a more consistent cooperation with the class teacher? More educated parents? Parents of the pupils with a better academic achievement? Exclusively mothers? Etc.?
- Which forms of cooperation with parents did well? (Individual, group, public, written, office hours, etc.) And in what context?
- What do you appreciate on cooperation with the pupils' parents? What effect does it bring?
- What are the biggest obstacles in the teacher– parent cooperation? How do you overcome them?
- What should the class teacher know about the pupil's family environment?

- What would you recommend to newly qualified teachers for their effective cooperation with the pupils' parents?
- Next question to be formed by the trainee teacher:

The main objective of the interview was to bolster the student's stance towards the professional competence of the teacher, and the interview questions were more informative than "technological" ones due to our worries that the respondents (i.e. class teachers) would not be too keen to share their private in-depth professional experience. However, the follow-up discussion with the interviewing trainee teachers revealed positive feedback dispelling such worries. Based on the positive experience from the interviews, the trainee teachers recommended to enlarge the scope of the outlined issues on some questions related to e.g., the teacher's preparation for parents days, teacher – parent conflict and disagreements and their resolutions, etc.
The trainee teachers were also asked to carry out another interview with the pupil's parents about the class teacher–parent cooperation.
Input data:

- The interview carried out with: a) mother b) father of the pupil
- Type of the school:
- School form (grade):

The outline of an interview with a pupil's parent concerning their cooperation with the class teacher:

- Does your child like going to school or not? Why?
- What level of education and what career do you expect of your child?
- Do you participate in your child's school activities? (On a regular or occasional basis? Do not consider important, ...).
- What kind of cooperation with the class teacher do you prefer? (Individual discussions, school parent's days, written contacts, no cooperation)?
- What do you (as a parent) appreciate in your child's class teacher?
- What should be changed in the teacher – parent and parent – teacher cooperation so that they become better partners?
- What do you think of the school your child goes to? What are you satisfied with? What reservations about the school do you have? What do you strongly disagree with?
- Next question to be formed by the trainee teacher.

During practical seminars, the following ideas proved successful in the development of special communication skills of the class teacher. The trainee teachers were assigned to introduce themselves to the parents in a mock parent's day. They were free to choose the form and the content of their 3-5 minute presentation to their trainee teacher colleagues who represented the parents. The mini-outputs (mini-presentations) were recorded with a camcorder and the best three of them watched during a follow-up discussion in a seminar group. Then the trainee class teacher presenters responded in a self-reflecting way mentioning their initial preparations, analysing the alternatives and discussing possible improvements. During the next seminar, the observers ('mock parents') expressed their impression and views on the trainee class teacher presentations analysing both the role of the mock class teacher and parents (Střelec, 2002).

4 Conclusion

Apart from the above mentioned ideas, several others educational activities bolstering the trainee class teacher experience have proved successful: preparation and implementation of the interviews focused on the pupil's attitude towards the school and particular subjects, pupil's learning styles, interests, hobbies, future career plans, etc. At Brno Masaryk University Faculty of Education, we have positive experience of this special, time-consuming, personal, spatial, and economic form of trainee teachers training. Nevertheless, we have to honestly admit that those are mostly rare optional courses. The core of the pre-gradual preparation of trainee class teachers consists of theoretical foundations, e.g., in case of the teacher–parent cooperation, of the attempt to bolster trainee teachers knowledge of family education (influence of family environment on the personality of the child, typology of parent – child relations, styles of family education, means of parental upbringing influence on their children, deficiency in the child family upbringing, ways of deficiency rectification, etc.). It is questionable whether the special skills trainee teacher programme aimed at the teacher – parent cooperation should or should not be covered besides the pre-graduate phase especially on the postgraduate teacher training level.

References

PRŮCHA, J., WALTEROVÁ, E., MAREŠ, J. (1995): Pedagogický slovník. Praha: Portál. Rámcový vzdělávací program pro základní vzdělávání. Praha : Výzkumný ústav pedagogický, 2005.

STŘELEC, S./KRÁTKÁ, J. (2009): Comparation of opinions of teachers, parents and pupils about social health aspects of form teacher activities. In Řehulka, E. et al. Topical issues in health education. Brno : Masarykova univerzita, pp. 105-118.

STŘELEC, S. (2002): Předpoklady utváření dovedností učitele kooperovat s rodiči žáků. In SVEC, V. et al. Cesty k učitelské profesi: utváření a rozvíjení pedagogických dovedností. Brno: Paido, pp. 184-202.

ŠŤÁVA, J. (2002): Pedagogická praxe v systému vzdělávání na Pedagogické fakultě MU v Brně. In JANÍK, T. (ed.) Úloha fakultního cvičného učitele a fakultní cvičné školy v přípravě budoucího učitele. Brno: MSD, pp. 105–110.

Contact
Doc. PhDr. Stanislav STRELEC, CSc.: strelec@ped.muni.cz
Mgr. Jana KRATKA, Ph.D.: kratka@ped. muni.cz

REFLECTION IN PRE-SERVICE TEACHERS' AUTOBIOGRAPHIES

Alenka Lipovec, Darja Antolin, Sonja Lutovac, Univ. Maribor, Slovenia

In this study we analyze a new approach (for Slovenian circumstances) towards the professional development of elementary teachers. Through writing of mathematical autobiographies, students construct their identities. What creates the identity of the character is the identity of the story and not the other way around. Because one's reflection of mathematical experiences is the main factor of effectiveness of the approach, we present Slovenian pre-service teachers' abilities of critical reflection. We used narrative approach as a qualitative research method on a sample of 214 pre-service teachers. Results show that Slovenian pre-service teachers do not feel the need to think reflectively, especially without instructions. The limitation of the study is in the collection of the data. The size of the sample did not allow the use of narrative interview; therefore written texts were collected and analyzed. Some recommendations for progressive development of reflection in mathematics education of pre-service elementary teachers are given.

Keywords: professional development of elementary teachers, mathematics education, critical reflection, teachers' autobiographies

1 Introduction

A lot of research has been done in the domain of "Teacher change" – meaning a change in teachers' beliefs and conceptions concerning teaching and learning (Leder, Pehkonen, & Törner, 2003; Kaasila & Laurial, 2009a). PAULSEN & WELLS (1998) argue that students majoring in applied sciences are more likely to hold naïve beliefs about the nature of knowledge than those in pure fields. Pre-service teachers seem to believe that knowledge is an organized system of relatively isolated facts that come from an authority, and is acquired quickly or not at all. On the other hand, students of mathematics seem to perceive knowledge as a complex and organized system that develops gradually as a result of reasoning process. Mathematics teachers on elementary level do not share epistemological belief of the domain they teach, which can lead to dissonance between teaching expected by the specific educational domain and teachers' personal beliefs about teaching. This dissonance can be mitigated through critical reflection. Reflection is defined as the intellectual and affective activities, in which individuals engage to explore their experiences in order to gain new understandings and appreciations (Boud, Keogh, and Walker, 1985; p. 19). According to CONNELLY & CLANDININ (2000), for teachers issues of professional knowledge and practice are deeply entwined with individual teachers' past experiences, future goals and with their identities. The importance of the concept of professional identity lies in the assumption that "who we think we are influences what we do", i.e. there is a link between professional identity and professional action (Watson, 2006).

In this study, we investigate reflection through breadth, depth and moral dimension. We examined the breadth of reflection through the number of focuses (Kaasila & Lauriala, 2009a), past and future direction (Conway, 2001) and internal and/or external orientation (Korthagen, 2001). We classified the depth of reflection as descriptive, comparative and critical reflection (Jay in Johnson, 2002). Additionally we took into account pragmatic vs. moral-ethical reflection (Luttenberg & Bergen, 2008). According to RICOEUR (1992), people often develop their sense of identity by seeing themselves as protagonists in different stories. Therefore, if we influence pre-service teachers' mathematical identities by stimulating their reflection process in their narratives (autobiographies), we might enhance their future mathematics practices (see also Lutovac & Kaasila, 2010b). In Slovenia, qualitative research methodology is still finding its way in teacher education. Some examples of research on teachers' professional paths through autobiographies are documented (Javornik Krečič, 2007). POLKINGHORNE (1995) defines narrative research as the 'study of stories'. Narrative methodology using autobiographies was also presented in the field of elementary mathematics education (Lutovac & Kaasila, 2010a), where the cases were taken from Finnish cultural context (Lutovac & Kaasila, 2010a). Qualitative-narrative data can be analyzed paradigmatically through analysis of narratives, going from elements to categories, or synthetically through narrative analysis, configuring data elements into a story.

The aim of this paper is to present some findings that emerged from narrative analyses and analysis of narratives of autobiographies. Narrative analysis was used to present our results as a mathematical prototype autobiography of Slovenian pre-service elementary teachers.

2 Mathematical autobiographies

Two hundred fourteen pre-service elementary teachers wrote their mathematical autobiographies. First, we describe the story that arose as a narrative analysis of all the cases. It starts in the fairytale world of early childhood, where mathematics is perceived as a game. *Sanja: "All the time I played the store, where I was a cashier."* It continues idyllically through the elementary education, where the pre-service teacher perceive herself/himself as a competent mathematician, and the teacher as a good and all-knowing aunt who leads pupils through almost unnoticeable mathematical traps through the game. *Metka: "We had a good teacher, who cared about us."* In the secondary school the feeling of one's own competence partially rocks and the reason for lower success is usually attributed to the teacher's wrong ethical decisions (for instance making differences between pupils) or teachers lack of professional competence. *Marina: "The teacher could not handle us and he had no interest to do so. His lessons were everything but lessons - they were a dinning room, a hairdresser's salon, a meeting room and a time, when I felt awful, weird and trapped into that class, trapped into the time, place and mathematics itself."* The transition to the upper secondary school indicates a major turning point with a consequence of significantly lower grades, repeatedly on the border of acceptable knowledge. Teacher becomes a strict, fear evoking figure, who speaks in incomprehensible language and does not care if pupils understand him. *Sandra: "Teachers were always only lecturing about the content; they had no interest to teach pupils."* Deep panic feelings appear; also resentment towards the teachers from prior school years, who did not provide a strong enough knowledge base. *Veronika: "I felt like a truck full of sand would fall on me, mathematics did not let me breathe and it felt like I would never be able to dig myself out of it."* The period of making more effort follows, often together with attending courses of expensive mathematics instructors. *Kaja: "When I recall what kinds of pain I went through because of mathematics, I am horrified. It was really exhausting; I devoted most of my free time to mathematics."* Then the grades improve, or at least are not negative. The pre-service teacher accepts the state and the meaning of mathematics is minimized with the reference to its lack of connection to everyday life and the nature of ones abilities, both as a defence strategy. Although at university level, positive experiences occur, negative ones are so deeply rooted and it is impossible to cap them.

In analysis of narratives, we holistically graded every aspect of critical reflection. To avoid subjectivity, we included also the grade of first reading, which was completely unstructured on the scale from 1 to 3. It was possible to gather 14 points. In average, pre-service teachers gathered 9 points with small differences between study years, in favour of last year students. The average amount of focuses was 1.78 on the scale form 1 to 3; future aspect 0.41 on the scale from 0 to 1, where fourth year students mentioned more frequently what kind of teacher they want to become (0.47 in comparison to 0.34). The average result in the aspect of internal and external orientation was 1.4 on the scale from 1 to 2. The average result of depth, which was graded based on concentric rule on the scale from 1 to 3, was 2.36, where again older students showed deeper reflection (2.43 in comparison to 2.27). For pragmatic description, we assigned 1 point; if ethical aspect was included, we added another point. The average result was 1.37.

Precisely structured instructions are possible cause for small number of gathered points. In contrast to aspects (breadth of reflection), where we tried to "help" students with instructions, when writing without instructions (for example moral-ethical aspect), the students reached higher levels of reflection. The lack of practical experiences till the third year of studies is another possible cause. It is reasonable to carry out the research again at the end of the study program. We also hypothesise that written data were less narrative than data in a live interview would be.

3 Conclusion

Abilities of critical reflection in mathematical autobiographies of pre-service elementary teachers are relatively low and full of myths and bias towards mathematics and mathematics teachers. The importance of the results is two-fold: 1) they are endorsing the meaning of qualitative research methodology, which gives deeper insight into a research problem 2) they are endorsing the meaning of critical reflection for professional development of pre-service teachers. One of the ways to influence critical reflection is the focus on wider and multiple contexts, for example on the research reading context, on the reflection on the lesson and on describing the experiences when working with pupils. Based on the recommendations of the research literature (Kaasila & Lauriala, 2009a), we already applied these contexts to teacher education. Additionally, we recommend the reflection on *Pedagogical Content Knowledge* through the description of reaction on hypothetical pupils' work (see e.g., Liping Ma, 2008).

References

BAUD, DAVID; KEOGH, ROSEMARY & WALKER, DAVID: Promoting reflection in learning: A model. In: Baud, D., Keogh, R. & Walker, D. (Eds.): Reflection: Turning Experience into Learning, p. 18-40. London: Kogan Page, 1985.

CONNELLY, F. MICHAEL & CLANDININ, D. JEAN: Narrative understanding of teacher knowledge. In: Journal of curriculum and supervision 15./2000, p. 315-331.

CONWAY, PAUL F.: Anticipatory reflection while learning to teach: From a temporally truncated to a temporally distributed model of reflection in teacher education. In: Teaching and teacher education 17./2001, p. 89-106.

JAVORNIK KREČIČ, MARIJA: Proučevanje učiteljevega profesionalnega razvoja z metodo poklicne (avto)biografije. In: Didactica Slovenica, 22 (1/2)./ 2007, p. 3-27.

JAY, JOELLE K. & JOHNSON, KERRI L.: Capturing complexity: A typology of reflective practice for teacher education. In: Teaching and Teacher Education, 18/2001, p. 73-85.

KAASILA, RAIMO & LAURIALA, ANNELI: Student teachers' reflective processes: reflectivity in relation to contextual, emotional and biographical factors. Accepted: CD-ROM of ISATT-2009 conference in Rovaniemi, 2009a.

KAASILA, RAIMO & LAURIALA, ANNELI: Towards a collaborative, interactionist model of teacher change. Submitted: Teaching and Teacher Education, 2009b.

LEDER, GILAH C., PEHKONEN, ERKKI & TÖRNER, GUNTER (Eds.): Beliefs: a hidden variable in mathematics education. Kluwe Academic Publishers, 2003.

MA, LIPING: Knowing and Teaching Elementary Mathematics: Teachers' Understanding of Fundamental Mathematics in China and the United States. - LEA, 1999.

LUTOVAC, SONJA & KAASILA, RAIMO: How to Apply the Process of Employment Using the Narrative Approach in Mathematics Education. Sumitted to Didactica Slovenica (Pedagoška obzorja), 2010a.

LUTOVAC, SONJA & KAASILA, RAIMO: Beginning a pre-service teacher's mathematical identity work through narrative rehabilitation and bibliotherapy. Submittted to Teching in Higher Education, 2010b.

KORTHAGEN, FRED A.: Linking practice and theory: The pedagogy of realistic teacher education. - Mahwah, Nj: Lawrence Erlbaum, 2001.

LUTTENBERG, JOHAN & BERGEN, TEO: Teacher reflection: the development of a typology. In: Teachers and Teaching: theory and practice 14 (5-6)./2008, p. 543-566.

PAULSEN, MICHAEL B., WELLS, CHARLES T.: Domain Differences in the Epistemological Beliefs of College Students. In: Research in Higher Education (39- 4)/1998, p. 365-384.

POLKINGHORNE, DONALD E.: Narrative configuration in qualitative analysis. In: International Journal of qualitative studies in Education, *8*(1)./1995, p. 12-28.

RICOEUR, PAUL:. Oneself as another. - Chicago: University of Chicago Press, 1992.

WATSON, CATE. Narratives of practice and the construction of identity in teaching. Teachers and Teaching: Theory and Practice, 12(5)./2006, 509-526.

Contact:
Phd. Alenka LIPOVEC: alenka.lipovec@uni-mb.si
Darja ANTOLIN: darja.antolin@uni-mb.si
Sonja LUTOVAC: sonja.lutovac@triera.net

Professional Development of Pre-school Educators

Maja Hmelak, University of Maribor, Slovenia

In the first part of the paper, the authors present theoretical foundations for professional development as a segment of lifelong learning of pre-school educators. It is intended to improve work, upgrade knowledge and strengthen professional competences, and is supposed to be based mostly on experiential learning methods that activate the educator's experiences. The empirical research focuses on the fundamental research question, namely, whether professional development of educators is predominantly aimed at traditional or at modern educational concepts. The research is based on Cheng's (1996) definition of traditional and modern education. The authors are interested in the underlying motives for professional development and in the methods of professional development. Based on the empirical data, they find that professional motives are predominant among the motives for professional development, and that the methods are based on experiential learning, among which various forms of active teaching are most common.

Key words: regular professional development, pre-school educators, motives, methods

1 Introduction

Today, knowledge is becoming increasingly important and more and more people are aware that they will have to learn all their lives. As the world is rapidly developing and changing, individuals have to constantly adjust to these changes, which is only possible in case of a solidly educated and innovative work force that regularly upgrades and improves its knowledge. It is due to the constant changes that we cannot expect that the educators will acquire all the necessary knowledge and skills for successful work performance merely through their regular studies, as education of educators is a lifelong process.

2 Lifelong learning of educators

The context of lifelong learning of educators and teachers in Europe also includes professional development (http://www.eurydice.org), which describes several possible ways to develop an educator's or teacher's career. Various models of educators' and teachers' professional development have been developed in Europe. In the late 1960s they were predominately aimed at traditional concepts of transferring knowledge to the individual. In the future, new forms of kindergarten- and school-oriented activities will be required, where those who provide education to educators will engage in long-term cooperation with kindergarten employees and where all participants will strive to improve the quality of the kindergarten. According to PEČEK (2003), training educators is shifting from traditional to more modern educational concepts. In describing the characteristics and the differences between the two concepts of education, PEČEK summarises CHENG (1996, summarised according to Peček, 2003):

- the educational processes of traditional concepts are guided from the outside, the contents are incomplete, whereas the new concepts are kindergarten-oriented (educational activities correspond to kindergarten requirements; the employees participate in the planning of education, they contribute their ideas and test them in practice), their contents are versatile (emphasis is put on development of various employee techniques, values and beliefs);
- traditional concepts of education are directional, concentrated solely on the individual, individual groups and on the kindergarten as a whole and are perpetual and systematic;
- the role of teachers in traditional concepts of education is for the most part played by external experts and lecturers; recipients and participants play a passive role, whereas new concepts of education employ external as well as internal experts as lecturers and the recipients are active;
- employee motivation in traditional concepts is mostly external, e.g. rewards in form of promotion or reduction of work obligations. In case of new concepts, inner and intrinsic motivation is the most important, e.g. tackling employees' desire for professional growth.

Professional development is an integral part of educator training. FEKONJA et al. (2002) consider planning, selection and implementation of various forms of constant learning, diversity of offers, topicality of contents, the number of training hours, accessibility, and use of non-fiction literature to be a part of that. It is intended to improve work, upgrade knowledge and strengthen professional competences. This way, the educators are familiarised with new and alternative forms of work, new contents, new aspects of child development, various ways of motivating a child's development, new technologies, etc. It is supposed to be based on experiential methods of learning, which activate the educator's experiences.

3 The purpose of empirical research

The fundamental research question was, whether professional development of educators is aimed at traditional or at modern concepts of education. In regard to that, we were interested in:

- motives, based on which the educators choose constant in-service training;
- methods of in-service training.

Pertaining to the mentioned aspects, we were interested whether there were any differences in regard to the period of employment, level of education (4 years, 5 years, vocational, higher), status (independent kindergarten, kindergarten as a part of an elementary school) and kindergarten location (city, countryside).

4 Methodology

We used a non-experimental causal method of empirical educational research. The research was carried out on a sample of 111 educators from Slovene kindergartens. The majority of respondents (64.3%) have over 20 years of work experience and have finished a secondary education in pedagogy (56.3%). With regard to the kindergarten's status (kindergarten as a part of a school, independent kindergarten) we find that majority of respondents (51.8%) come from kindergartens which are part of a school, and location-wise most of them work in the city (50.9%).

All questions that were used in the questionnaire were closed questions, expressed through verbal and graded responses.

The data that was collected through the questionnaire was computer processed with the help of the SPSS (Statistical Package for the Social Sciences) statistical programme. The χ^2-test was used to analyse the differences.

5 Results and data interpretation

Motives, based on which the educators decide in favour of in-service training.

We arranged the motives into three major categories: *professional motives* (this category represents the respondents' desire for personal and professional growth and for their usefulness and effective performance. They are expressed through opinions such as: being an educator is a socially beneficial profession, as an educator I can be an example to the children, as an educator I can express my creative side, etc…), *material motives* (this category pertains to external motivation which is based on beneficial socio-economical consequences and opportunities for promotion and further training. This category includes: attractive work conditions, e.g. additional awards, shorter working hours, the chance to further one's education, etc…) and *other*.

Based on the χ^2-tests we found that in all cases the null hypothesis was upheld which means that there were no statistically characteristic differences with regard to the length of employment, level of education, status and kindergarten location. However, the data show that professional motives (81.3%) are the prevailing ones when it comes to the educators' decision process regarding their professional development.

Methods of in-service training

Based on the χ^2-tests we found that in these cases the null hypothesis was upheld. There were no statistically characteristic differences in regard to the length of employment, level of education and status of the kindergarten. However, there were statistically characteristic differences pertaining to the kindergarten location.

Majority of educators (41.1%) believe that the most efficient methods of in-service training are study groups, followed by pedagogy workshops and seminars. Only four respondents chose lectures as the most efficient form. Differences can be found in kindergarten location. While educators working in city kindergartens believe that methods based on experiential learning (study groups 54.3%, pedagogy workshops 53.6%) are more important, employees working in suburban kindergartens prefer lectures (75.0%).

6 Conclusion

Being aware of the complexity of professional development of pre-school educators, we processed the acquired data from the perspective of lifelong learning, which requires constant monitoring and evaluation with the goal of ensuring quality pre-school education.

Using CHENG'S definition of the traditional and the modern perception of education, we studied educators' motives and methods of professional development. Based on the empirical data, we found that among the motives for in-service training, professional motives are the most predominant ones which lead us to conclude that in this segment professional development of educators is oriented towards experiential concepts of education. The prevailing methods are methods based on experiential learning (study groups, pedagogy workshops, seminars), where two-way communication, dialogue and other forms of active learning are prevalent. We speak of a modern oriented concept of educators' professional development.

References

FEKONJA, U., KAVČIČ, T. IN MARJANOVIČ UMEK, M. (2002): Ravni, področja in kazalci kakovosti predšolske vzgoje v vrtcu. V L. Marjanovič Umek, U. Fekonja, T. Kavčič in A. Poljanšek (Ur.), Kakovost v vrtcih (str. 39-51). Ljubljana: Znanstveni inštitut Filozofske fakultete.

Pomembne teme v izobraževanju v Evropi (zvezek 3) Učiteljski poklic v Evropi, profil, trendi, hotenja. Eurydice. Informacijsko omrežje o izobraževanju v Evropi. http://www.eurydice.org (pridobljeno 14. 11. 2006).

PEČEK, P. (2003): Pogledi na osebni in strokovni razvoj. V S. Puš Seme (Ur.), Posvet: zaupaj vase, poskrbi zase (biti vzgojitelj) (str. 23-33). Portorož: Skupnost vrtcev Republike Slovenije.

Contact:
Maja HMELAK: maja.hmelak@uni-mb.si

TEACHER AND INTERCULTURAL COMMUNICATIVE COMPETENCE AS A CHALLENGE

Klára Kostková, University of Pardubice, Czech Republic

Living in a continuously changing multicultural world with frontiers opening, distances getting smaller and relationships becoming closer every day, it is important to realize that this brings new demands into many areas of human existence. In education, a need to respond to them is reflected on various levels, most of them related in some way to the key agent in any educational change: the teacher. This theoretical paper focuses on one specific qualitatively new demand also formulated in curricular documents: the incorporation of intercultural education into the curriculum. Consequently, the teachers themselves should possess a high level of Intercultural Communicative Competence since they are the agents who should bring this concept into life. A meta-analysis of models of the core concept, Intercultural Communicative Competence, will be presented with special attention given to the teacher.

Keywords: teacher's competence, intercultural communicative competence, curriculum

1 Introduction

Living in a multicultural world, it is important to realize that the process of integration requires more than just the ability to live next to each other i.e. what AMARTYA SEN, an economist, calls 'plural monoculturalism'. In other words, groups of people that live side by side but do not touch. More importantly it requires the ability to develop an environment where people of various nations associate, even though it is a colourful mosaic of identities. SKALKOVÁ (2000, pp. 13-22) discusses the complex process of globalization: the expectations, extended human possibilities, broad interpersonal communication and general qualitative improvement of human life on one side, but on the other she pinpoints that it brings along with it some serious problems such as new disputes, pressures and threats. Globalization brings new demands into many areas of human existence, generally speaking the need to be able to live serenely and work effectively together with people from different backgrounds, with different habits and beliefs, with people living according to different values and last, but not least, with people who speak different native languages. Universal agreement that we should reflect the actual need of the globalized multicultural world exists since it simply cannot function without intercultural competence on the behalf of its population. We shall focus on educational context and how we have managed to solve these qualitative new demands. Attention should be paid to conceptualizing intercultural education[9], its incorporation into the curriculum and how well teachers, the key agents in any educational change, are equipped to deal with it.

[9] *'Intercultural' vs 'Multicultural':* These terms are often used synonymously. For instance, *Intercultural education* is a term often used synonymously with *Multicultural education*; however, multicultural is used mainly in the USA, United Kingdom, Canada, Australia, with intercultural used more within the European Union (see e.g. Průcha, 2001). For the purpose of our paper we shall be inclined to use the term *intercultural* since we perceive the meaning of the two above terms differently. *Multicultural*, in our opinion, is a term which represents various cultures, social groups, ethnicities, etc. and their existence in a diversified *multicultural society*; on the contrary, *intercultural* is a term based on the society as a diverse but compatible whole (see e.g. Leeman, 2005).

2 Intercultural education

Intercultural (communicative) competence (ICC) as a key aim of intercultural education is the core that, in various forms, represents an integral part of educational documents at all levels, even though opinions on the desirability of paying attention to it still differ. Its practical application, as well as the theory behind ICC, has been through significant developments and fundamental transformations. However, most authors (Fantini 2001; Průcha 2001; Leeman 2005; Deardorff, ed. 2009 etc.) agree on some critical aspects and challenges for theory, research and practice in this field. These include: a) *Lack of conceptual clarity:* common theoretical agreement on the concept of ICC is hard to find; the theory does not follow available research findings; b) *Lack of research findings:* existing research findings are limited; furthermore, they seem to suggest that the changes in the learners are not in accordance with the exaggerated optimism about the school practice; c) *Theory-practice gap:* the theoretical debate on intercultural education is far removed from daily practice in the classroom; the practical design of ICC development and its theoretical rationale follow different paths; d) *Inadequate assessment:* we are not yet sufficiently capable to be able to critically analyze, nor evaluate, the ICC development of our learners or in society as a whole.

An abundance of various (European) projects with rich financial support are attempting to solve the above mentioned challenges, but have not yet reached any fundamental results and some general policy, including accepted theoretical rationale, content, aims and sharing of research findings, often seem to be absent. With all this in mind, the question is whether teachers are not being forced to sail into unknown waters as they are asked to bring ICC into practice.

3 Intercultural (Communicative) Competence

We attempt to solve the first challenge and provide readers with a general definition of the ICC concept and, consequently, with selected models of ICC and outcomes of their meta-analysis.

3.1 Defining Intercultural (Communicative) Competence

ICC is a multidisciplinary concept that can be approached from various perspectives and is also labelled by different terms; however, this discussion is not the topic of our paper. DEARDORFF (2009) defines Intercultural Competence broadly as appropriate and effective communication and behaviour in intercultural situations (p. xi). In the presented 'definition' it is important to emphasise that DEARDORFF speaks about Intercultural Competence being a must in intercultural situations; however, the question is why 'communication' is not reflected in the 'label' of the competence discussed. This brings us to a broader question concerning the coexistence of two concepts: Intercultural Competence and Intercultural Communicative Competence. In some sources, these two concepts are used, as well as understood, interchangeably (see e.g. Průcha 2010); others claim the possibility and need to distinguish between the two (see e.g. Byram 1997). The distinction states that interculturally competent individuals are able to interact in their native language with people from other countries and cultures; while doing so, they draw upon their knowledge about intercultural communication – their attitudes, skills, previous experience, etc. On the other hand, ICC enables individuals to interact with people from other countries and cultures in a foreign language; their knowledge of other cultures, their values, habits, etc. is linked to their language competence through the ability to use the language appropriately and their awareness of the specific meaning, values and connotations of the language. BYRAM (1997) presents the relationship between Intercultural Competence and Intercultural Communicative Competence as one of degrees of complexity and ability to deal with a wider range of situations of contact in the latter than in the former (p. 71). In simple terms, ICC – the more complex concept – could be perceived as a blend of Intercultural Competence and Communicative Competence in a foreign language.

3.2 Models of Intercultural (Communicative) Competence

Although we leaned towards the investigation of ICC, we shall analyze a variety of relevant models from Czech and foreign literature in order to reach results as comprehensive as possible. The key criteria for selection of the models are that they attempt to capture *appropriate* and *effective communication* and *behaviour* in intercultural situations.

Due to the limited space available, only basic components of the models according to the authors´ structure will be presented. Further meta-analysis will, however, exploit all the components in detail.

3.3 'ICC' models

Concrete models under investigation are of two qualitatively different characters: models resulting from empirical studies (e.g. Delphi methodology employed by Deardorf 2006; Hunter, White, Godbey 2006) and models resulting from an analysis of relevant theoretical sources (e.g. Byram 1997; Ting-Toomey, Kurogi 1999; Common European Framework 2001). Since ICC is a multidisciplinary concept, we not only employ models from an educational context, but also from various other disciplines and backgrounds: socio/linguistics, business affairs, diplomacy/foreign affairs, human resource management, humanitarian help/peace workers, etc.. Nonetheless, this is one of the criticisms concerning meta-analyses, that it may combine too many diversified fundaments; therefore the obtained results might not be as precise as desired. We believe the opposite, as G.V. GLASS (2000) (who coined the term meta-analysis and illustrated its use back in 1976) states: "Of course it mixes apples and oranges; in the study of fruit nothing else is sensible; comparing apples and oranges is the only endeavour worthy of true scientists; comparing apples to apples is trivial" (Glass 2000, http://glass.ed.asu.edu/...). Thus, we decided to investigate the 'apples and oranges' within the scope of the introduced models and definitions that vary significantly in many aspects. Our attempt is to search for common agreement on such components that are conceived as important. In order to do that, we shall uncover the meanings behind the variety of characteristics, descriptors, traits, domains, dimensions, definitions and general terminological plurality of the analyzed models from the perspective of frequency occurrence. We do not have enough space to demonstrate the procedure of our meta-analysis, therefore we shall proceed to the obtained findings, i.e. to the identification of the most frequently occurring components of the ICC construct.

3.4 Findings

The analyzed models mostly share the view of ICC as an integrated whole consisting of domains; their number may vary according to the approach chosen (disciplinary, paradigmatic, etc.). Some of them stress global knowledge, others sensitivity, and others certain skills, positive attitudes or various types of knowledge. Many models examine ICC as an effective cross-cultural adaptation and require experience within foreign culture; others focus on appropriate competent dyadic interactions in intercultural relationships or appropriate and effective interactions on intercultural topics. Our quantitative analysis suggests, however, that ICC is far more complex than any of the individual views. Despite such complexity, the meta-analysis uncovered some common "components" among the seventeen analyzed models. We shall present our findings successively, from the highest frequency occurrence:

- attitudes – 16;
- language – 14; 9 of which are explicitly a foreign language, although this might be influenced by the fact that many of the models are of English language speaking countries origin, as a result of the English linguistic imperialism, meaning English is viewed as the primary language of intercultural communication – *lingua franca*);
- skills – 13;
- awareness of self and others – 13;
- knowledge – 12;
- interaction – 10;
- communication – verbal/nonverbal, C. styles, … – 9;
- context – environment, culture, … – 7;
- understanding and comprehension – 6;
- development/al process/ – 5;
- external and internal outcomes – 5;
- individual/personality – 5;
- effective relationships – 5;
- intercultural experience – 3.

Consequent qualitative interpretation of the analyzed components, as well as the mutual influence of all the variables covered and their position within a newly defined construct, deserve further discussion. Attention should also be paid to the distinction between observable and unobservable components. We lean towards the opinion that competence is tacit, thus cannot be observed directly, although it can be seen through observing how one performs. In other words, 'competence' and 'performance' are closely interrelated, the former being abstract, the latter observable - which also means assessable.

To sum up the analyzed models, five axioms have been derived – domains of: *attitudes, foreign language communicative competence, skills, awareness and knowledge.* ICC is *developmental* – it is viewed as arising from dynamic meaningful *interactive processes* of *(intercultural) communication* of an individual within a given *context.* Such competent (intercultural) interaction based on previous *internal* as well as *external outcomes/abilities* should lead to establishment and maintenance of effective *relationships* - relationships in which one is able to perform effectively and appropriately with members of another language-culture background on their terms.

4 Conclusions – ICC as a challenge for teachers

All crucial components of ICC, as well as other influential variables, have been identified. As a first step towards meeting the demands mentioned in chapter 2, these components have to be operationalized as potential research variables on one hand, and as basics for classroom practice (and assessment) on the other. However, *how* to ensure that teachers and consequently their pupils become interculturally competent communicators still remains unsolved. Teacher educators and their responsibility must not be forgotten either. This vicious circle is by no means easy to break. However, it is the teachers who are expected to incorporate the long-term goal of intercultural education – this newly defined aim of ICC development - into the curriculum of their schools and then enter their classrooms every day and include ICC into the practice of their lessons.

In conclusion, let us summarize the remaining challenges that lie ahead of us. It is mainly the need to include ICC into teacher education. This coin, however, has two sides. Firstly, future teachers' ICC should be developed, so that they would one day become quality mediators of it themselves. Secondly, teachers should be able to conduct didactic transformation of this fundamentally new content of ICC both on the ontodidactic and consequently on the psychodidactic level. Didactic transformation of ICC is by no means an easy task since it cannot be achieved through a cognitive-only approach; attention to the affective domain (Awareness of self and others, Attitudes) and communication is required, which is only then linked to the cognitive one (Knowledge). It is needed to connect the 'formation' of cognition with its 'transmition and mediation' in the means of didactic communication. In order for the learners to reach a certain level of ICC development, or at least to set off on this developmental process, teachers need to meet the demand of a 'communicative approach to didactics' (see e.g. Brockmeyerová-Fenclová, Čapek, Kotásek 2000) by communicating the content of the subject to their learners. In our case, it is further amplified by the need to 'communicate communication'.

References

ARASARATNAM, LILY.: Further Testing of a New Model of Intercultural Communication Competence. 2008.

http://www.allacademic.com//meta/p_mla_apa_research_citation /0/1/1/7/9/ pages11792/p11792-19.php. [accessed 22.2.2010]

BROCKMEYEROVA-FENCLOVA, J., ČAPEK, V., KOTASEK, J.: Oborové didaktiky jako samostatné vědní disciplíny. In: Pedagogika 1/2000, p.23 – 37.

BYRAM, MICHAEL: Teaching and Assessing Intercultural Competence. - Clevedon: Multilingual matters Ltd., 1997.

DEARDORFF, DARLA K. (Ed.): The SAGE Handbook of Intercultural Competence. - USA: Sage Publications, Inc., 2009.

DEARDORFF, DARLA K.: Models of Intercultural Competence. 2006.

http://www.bertelsmannstiftung.de/bst/de/media/xcms_bst_dms_30238_30239_2. pdf [accesses 26.2.2010].

FANTINI, ALVINO, E.: A central concern: Developing Intercultural Competence. 2000.

http://www.sit.edu/publications/docs/competence.pdf [accesses 26.2.2010]

HOWARD HAMILTON, M.F., RICHARDSON , B.J., SHUFORD, B.: Ppromoting multicultural education: A holistic approach. In College Student Affairs Journal, 18/1998, p. 5-17.

HUNTER, B., WHITE, G.P., GODBEY, G.C.: What does it mean to be globally competent? In Journal of Studies in Intercultural Education, 10/2006, p. 267-285.

GLASS, GENE.V.: Meta-Analysis at 25. 2000.
http://glass.ed.asu.edu/gene/papers/meta25.html [accessed 3.3.2010]

GRIFFITH, D.A., HARVEY, M.G.: An intercultural communication model for use in global interorganizational networks. In Journal of International Marketing, 9/2000, p. 87-103.

IMAHORI, T.T., LANIGAN, M.L.: Relational model of intercultural communication competence. In Intercultural Communication Competence, 13/1989, p. 269-286.

KIM, Y.Y.: Communication and cross-cultural adaptation: An integrative theory. – Philadelphia: Multilingual Matters, 1988.

KING, P.M., BAXTER MANGOLA, M.B.: A developmental model of intercultural maturity. In Journal of College Student Development, 46/2005, p. 571-592.

LEEMAN, YVONNE, LEDOUX, GUUSKE: Teachers on intercultural education. In: Teachers and Teaching: theory and practice, 11/2005, p. 575 – 589.

MORGENSTERNOVÁ, M., ŠULOVÁ, L.: Interkulturní psychologie. Rozvoj interkulturní sensitivity. – Praha: Karolinum, 2007.

PÍŠOVÁ, MICHAELA: Klinický rok: Procesy profesního rozvoje studentů učitelství a jejich podpora. - Pardubice: Univerzita Pardubice, 2005.

PRŮCHA, JAN: Multikulturní výchova. Teorie – praxe – výzkum. - Praha: ISV, 2001.

PRŮCHA, JAN: Interkulturní komunikace. - Praha: Grada, 2010.

SKLAKOVÁ, JARMILA: Education in the Context of Current Globalization Trends. In Pedagogika 1/2000, p.13 – 22.

SPITZBERG, BRIAN H., CHANGNON, G.: Conceptualizing Intercultural Competence. In: Deardorff, Darla K. (Ed.): The SAGE Handbook of Intercultural Competence, p. 3-52. - USA: Sage Publications, Inc., 2009.

TING-TOOMEY, S., KUROGI, A.: Facework competence in intercultural conflict: an updated face-negotiation theory. In International Journal of Intercultural Relations, 22/1998, p. 187-225.

TING-TOOMEY, STELA: Communicationg Across Cultures. - New York: Guilford, 1999.

Common European Framework of Reference for Languages: Learning, teaching, assessment. - UK: Cambridge University Press, Council of Europe, 2001.

Contact: Mgr. Klára KOSTKOVÁ: klara.kostkova@upce.cz

ART PRODUCTION AS A TOOL TO REFLECT ON PROFESSIONAL IDENTITY OF FUTURE TEACHERS

Yvona Mazehóová, Jana Kouřilová. South Bohemia University, Czech Republic

Studies have shown that becoming a professional occurs on two levels. First, it takes place on a structural level, such as formal educational and entrance requirements for entry into the profession. Secondly, it occurs on an attitudinal level, such as the individual's sense of "a calling" to the field. Students entering a teacher pre-service training change externally, under the demands of training and in correspondence with their notion of teacher's professional role, and internally, which is in the subjective self-conceptualization associated with the role. This self-conceptualization can be viewed as one's professional identity. To foster changes in self-conceptualization we used some art-therapeutic techniques, which are stimulating conscious as well as unconscious processes.

Keywords: art production, professional identity, future teachers, projective methods

1 Background

Recently, in a greater extent, it is admitted that to create a professional identity it does not suffice to pay attention to gaining a quality explicit basis of knowledge, but it is necessary to develop also the subject's implicit theory. Becoming a professional occurs on two levels. First, it takes place on a structural level, such as formal educational and entrance requirements for entry into the profession. Secondly, it occurs on an attitudinal level, such as the individual's sense of "a calling" to the field. Students entering a teacher pre-service training change externally, under the demands of training and in correspondence with their notion of teacher's professional role, and internally, which is in the subjective self-conceptualization associated with the role. This self-conceptualization can be viewed as one's professional identity. To foster changes in self-conceptualization we used some art-therapeutic techniques, which are stimulating conscious as well as unconscious processes.

The art-therapeutic techniques are assessed as a possibility to foster the self-awareness of future teachers and to study their implicit motivation. The research is aimed at two domains – the collages of professional roles and the expression of anxiety in the art production.

2 Study 1: Profession Roles Collages

The non-verbal projective technique of collage is a method that leads students to explication of frequently unrealized aspects of their implicit theory of teaching. The collage (from French collage – to stick, to paste) is a technique used in painting and graphics, in which the work is composed by sticking the cuts on a pasteboard. The collage elements can be selected either intentionally, or by associations, or absolutely by chance. A stimulus to the collage was a technique called by G. Braque and P. Picasso *papiers collés* (papers stuck together), which originally consisted in sticking newspaper cuts, pieces of wax canvass, wallpapers, and labels on standstill paintings. Later, P. Picasso, G. Braque and J. Gris used the relief character of spatial folded paper and other materials (metal, wood, etc.) to correspond with the spatial perspectives of cubism and its description of reality. The collage technique was also adopted by other artistic styles such as futurism, dadaism, and constructivism. In addition to that, surrealism also widely developed the technique of collage since it corresponds with the surrealistic principle of objective random and associative imaginations.

Our survey uses the collage as a projective technique, i.e. the author projects their own inner contents (motives, wishes, emotions, etc.) into the collage by means of individual elements (cuttings, pictures, labels) without any possibility of their own rational correction. The fact that their artistic interpretation (drawing, painting, etc.) is not led, the author need not be afraid of lacking the artistic skills and being confronted with their own abilities (it does not block them in their work). Our experience shows that the technique of collage is welcomed by students as well as other clients, who otherwise do not like being engaged in artwork.

In our case, the method of collage and its interpretation is based on so-called "Roznov Art Therapy", which uses collages for therapeutic purposes. The task for the student rest in making a collage called "I as a pedagogue in all the forms and roles". They should use various cuttings, pictures, advertisement material (not photos) and stick them on an A3 (or lager) sheet of paper. The student can complete their work by drawing and marking to create their own view on the teaching profession, in which various perspectives on that topic (how they saw it earlier, how it looks now, and what they expect in the future), emotions associated with teaching or possible fears can blend together.

The objective of the collage is to enable the students to deliberate, develop, clarify and re-structuralize their own attitudes, motives and relations to the profession of a pedagogue. However, the motives and emotions are not only conscious (i.e. admitted) but also unconscious, thus often having much more crucial influence on the future profession.

Our experience reveals that working on the topic itself (which takes up several hours, especially if the students are responsible in their work) deepens their contact with the future profession and also leads to the catharsis in a way.

The seminars include another phase, in which a student shares the meaning of individual elements and their arrangements in the collage. Then the leader of the seminar shall facilitate the student also other interpretations, i.e. to find out other interconnections among individual symbols in the collage, which the student is not aware of, has not worked out yet, or does not realize them consciously, but they have been projected into the collage. Certainly, such a style of work is difficult for the leader, who should use not only their knowledge of art therapy, but also their longtime experience with collage interpretations in both clinical and non-clinical environment.

2.1 Tested Persons

Collages of professional roles (N=29 freshmen specialized in pedagogy for kindergartens). The task for the student rests in making a collage called "I as a pedagogue in all the forms and roles". The objective of the collage is to enable the students to deliberate, develop, clarify and re-structuralize their own attitudes, motives and relations to the profession of a pedagogue. However, the motives and emotions are not only conscious (i.e. admitted) but also unconscious, thus often having much crucial influence on the future profession. The seminar discussion on perceiving the profession and professional roles followed and the professional motivations were analyzed.

2.2 Results

Collages General Summary:

- Only a few of students establish relations, more often we encounter narcissism and egocentrism (just because of their egocentrism and immaturity, they can better identify with children);
- Some girls did not put a child on the collage! (they have not worked out themselves, weak self-awareness);
- Naming a role without an experience appears more frequently;
- We repeatedly found problems even in contacts (at least 6 out of 29 collages);
- Frequently students as if did not understand that the collage is not merely about children but also about there roles of a teacher in a kindergarten (apparently it is not a wrong formulation of the task);
- They often realize only a part of pedagogic activities and narrow the content of the profession to guarding the children and teaching them correct habits – they are not aware of the role of their own personality as a tool for educating and cultivating the children in a broader context;
- We have generally (repeatedly) noted "dangerous" creativity, in which authors forget to work out the feelings of themselves, and instead of that they gush plenty of creative ideas;
- Collages are often replete with symbols without any expression of their interrelations;
- Probably only a few of students understand the meaning of their role – their implicit perception of the profession is still beginning to form; unlike implicit theories of teaching, the pedagogy of elementary schools is relatively less differentiated. It can also be related to less personal ex-

periences with kindergartens in comparison with elementary schools. This experience in the role of a pupil forms a basis for the naive implicit theory of teaching (see Stuchlíková, in press).

3 Study 2: Conscious and Non-conscious Anxiety in Artworks

A part of the implicit theories of teaching is emotional experience corresponding with the role of a teacher. Expression of negative emotions, especially anger and anxiety, is created by strong social rules, which determine what is suitable and unsuitable in a social context (Lutz, Abu-Lughod, 1990; Scherer, Wallbot & Summerfield, 1986). These rules are even stricter for so-called helping professions including pedagogy. On the other hand, these professions are more saturated with emotions due to the interactive character of the work. During a working day, teachers must cope with plenty of emotions and some of them, such as anger and anxiety, are under a strong social censorship. Such social rules force teachers to try to suppress or reduce the attacks of anger and anxiety as much as possible. Beside suppression, another method for handling these emotions is repression, i.e. their expulsion accompanied by so-called affective-autonomous separation, when the emotion is passing at the physical level; however the person is not aware of it (Derakshan, Eysenck, 1999). The ideal form of emotional experiencing for helping professions is stability with dominating positive tuning. These social and professional demands together with the repressive style of control can be a reason why some helpers describe their own anxiety as lower than it is in reality.

It can also influence the process of choosing the teaching profession, since the role of a teacher is taken as "interactively safe" because it is relatively well-structuralized and that the asymmetry in the relationship teacher-pupil provides the pedagogue a certain level of dominance. Ego-threatening situations are relatively less probable in the teacher-pupil interactions than in colleague – colleague interactions appearing in other professions.

3.1 Tested Persons

We addressed 174 students of pedagogy (78 % women) to respond the Spielberg State Trait Anxiety Inventory (STAI), Marlowe Crown Social Desirability Scale (MCSD) and projective methods (color version of Wartegg's Drawing Test and color self-portrait).

3.2 Data Evaluation Method

Data pertaining anxiety in the inventory were evaluated according to the population norms; social desirability together with anxiety is applied for de termining the subgroup of repressors and division method by a median is used. Repressors are determined by a low measured level of anxiety and a high level of social desirability. The projective techniques were evaluated at two levels: First, two experts (mutual correlation of classification was .76) assessed the whole product on the basis of their clinic experience, and divided the tested persons into the following subgroups: apparently anxious, latently anxious, non-anxious. The second method of evaluating the projective material consisted in product assessment by appearance of projective indicators of anxiety (e.g. stylization, infantile elements, protective details, monochromatism, unusual comments).

3.3 Results

In comparison with the population norms, the group of future teachers is characterized in the STAI as a bit shifted towards slight anxiety (49 % were placed in the lower third of the population norms, 41 in the central part and only 10 % belonged in the block of highly anxious). In contrast with that, the evaluation of projective production shows that 64.5 % of tested persons were placed into the groups of open or latent anxiety and merely 35.5 % indicated no signs of increased anxiety and their production was rated normal. Further more, attention was also paid to the differences in the group of person with a really low anxiety and those repressors that expressed low level of anxiety, which, however, is much higher in reality. In the projective indexes, the level of anxiety is indicated by appearance of unusual comments, infantile elements and stylization of the self-portrait.

The results show that while the group of future teachers expresses in average a lower level of anxiety, comparing to the population standard, the projective production reveals that this level seems to be considerably higher. Unconscious anxiety can have an effect on choosing the profession (in so-called folk pedagogy, the formal authority of a teacher has seemingly a higher advantage in interpersonal contacts with children), therefore we should pay attention to the work with emotional self-perception of future teachers in developing their professional identity and perception of the profession.

References

DERAKSHAN, N., EYSENCK, M. (1999): Are repressors self-deceivers or other-deceivers? Cognition and Emotion, 13, 1-17.

LUTZ, C.A., ABU-LUGHOD, L. (1990): Language and politics of emotion. New York: Cambridge University Press.

MATHEWS, R.C., ROUSELL, L.G. (1997): Abstractness of implicit knowledge: A cognitive evolutionary perspective. In D.C. Berry (Ed.) How Implicit is Implicite *Learning*? Oxford: Oxford University Press.

SCHERER, K.R., WALLBOT, H.G., SUMMERFIELD, A.B. (Eds.). (1986): Experiencing emotion: A cross-cultural study. Cambridge, England: Cambridge University Press.

STUCHLÍKOVÁ, I. (in print): Implicitní aspekty ve studentském pojetí učitelské profese. Pedagogika.

Contact:
Yvona Mazehóová: mazeh@pf.jcu.cz
Jana Kouřilová: jkouril@pf.jcu.cz

PROFESSIONAL SUCCESS IN BALLET: BALLET TEACHER'S ROLE EVALUATION

Maria Aleksandrovich, Pomeranian University of Słupsk, Poland

Studying the personality traits of successful ballet dancers I was interested in how modern ballet dancers evaluate the role of the teacher in their professional success. Our research was conducted in 2004-2009 at the Belarusian Ballet College (Minsk, Belarus), Comprehensive Ballet School (Gdansk, Poland), Polish Dance Theatre (Poznan, Poland), Dance Group Berezka (Moscow, Russia) and Ejfman Ballet Group (St. Petersburg, Russia). All the participants provided self-reports through questionnaires on professional success (Aleksandrovich, 2004). In my paper I will discuss the results of the evaluation: 1) whether professional success in ballet is a result of collaboration of a teacher and a ballet student or just a personal achievement of the dancer; 2) whether modern ballet dancers are interested in continuing as ballet teachers in the future or not, and why; 3) whether modern ballet dancers are interested in opening and developing their own ballet schools or any other pedagogical practice or not, and why.

Keywords: ballet teachers, ballet dancers, ballet lessons

1 Introduction

Ballet has been considered a highly developed art form that has evolved specific aesthetic and technical ideals. Through trial and error and advice from experienced teachers, these ideals have been developed and handed down for almost four centuries (Clarkson, Freedson, Keller, 1985). To become a professional ballet dancer takes several years of training. Dancing is an extremely competitive sport, and professional ballet dancers need to have the correct body type, well developed and strong joints, incredible flexibility and motivation, but also an experienced teacher who helps to develop self-discipline and strength, grace, balance and an iron will to get through the training, the rehearsals, and the injuries that frequently occur. In the classic studies of talent development (Roe, 1953; Zuckerman, 1977) we can learn about the role of eminent individuals in parenting, educating, and training of the talents. In the recent model of talent development proposed by GAGNÉ (1991) we find such main aspects of this development as: natural abilities, talent, developmental processes, intrapersonal catalysts, environmental catalysts and chance. GAGNÉ names four groups of environmental influences on the development of talents: milieu (culture, family), persons, provisions (programs, activities, services), events.

Teachers of ballet are very different, but they influence the minds of their students. Some of them do it adopting 'old school' approach, i.e. they teach the way they were taught themselves – in a brutal regime, suffering great pain, being screamed at for making the tiniest mistake. Another type is represented by teachers whose professional career has been cut short by injury; they tell students to work hard, but do not inspire them to do so. We may read such evaluation of intensive dance training in the interview with a professional dancer and choreographer (Subotnik, 2002): evidence of disparate training was very significant.

ROBSON, BOOK AND WILMERDING (2002) studied psychological stress faced by dance teachers today. They find out that 78.8% of teachers felt unjustly criticized in their own training, 61.5% had consciously changed their method of teaching to be more supportive of their students. The most stressful aspects of teaching were unmotivated students, 27.9 %, lack of time, 19.8 %, and lack of administrative support, 16.4 %.

In our research we tried to investigate how the role of the ballet/dance teachers is perceived by beginning college ballet students including also the opinion of a group of young professional ballet dancers representing different ballet groups.

2 Investigation

Research questions: the aim of the study was to study how the young ballet dancers evaluate the role of ballet teachers in professional success in ballet. This general aim was further specified in 3 research questions: 1) whether pro fessional success in ballet is a result of collaboration of a teacher and a ballet student, or just a personal achievement of a dancer; 2) whether modern ballet dancers are interested in continuing as ballet teachers in the future or not, and why; 3) whether modern ballet dancers are interested in opening and developing their own ballet schools or any other pedagogical practice or not, and why.

3 Methods

3.1 Participants and Procedure

The research was carried out in the period 2004-2009. The participants included a group of young ballet dancers from different ballet groups: Comprehen sive Ballet School in Gdansk, Poland (58 dancers); Belarusian Ballet College, Minsk, Belarus (59 dancers); Polish Dance Theatre from Poznan, Poland (10 dancers); Ejfman Ballet Group from St. Petersburg, Russia (15 dancers); and Dance Group Berezka from Moscow, Russia (7 dancers). The total research sample was 149 dancers (59 men and 90 women) in the age range from 12 till 45. All the participants had been studying in a ballet school for at least one year. The questionnaires were administered individually or in small groups. Participation in the study was voluntary and anonymous.

3.2 Instruments

For the purposes of this study a, questionnaire was created to assess the level of dance expertise and professional success (Aleksandrovich, 2004). This self-report questionnaire consists of 24 question sections. While constructing the questionnaire for the questions 12-18 transformed data were used from research by URENA (2004). Questions 1-4 connected to demographics, ballet practice history and performance career; questions 5-11 focused on self-esteem in terms of dance expertise and professional success; questions 12-18 investigated the age at which dancers first engaged in dance, and more specifically, when they first engaged in supervised training; question 19 assessed the perception of teacher's importance; question 20 looked at family dance history; question 21 at time evaluation of professional and non-professional activities;

questions 22-24 asked about preferences. Statistical analysis of the data was conducted by using STATISTICA 6.0.

4 Results

We will start the discussion of the results from the analysis of self-evaluation of success in professional career development made by young ballet dancers: 48.3 % of the respondents believed their career development was successful, while 51.7 thought they were unsuccessful in their development as professional ballet dancers.

At the same time if we look at the objective evaluation here, we have 75.2 % estimated as unsuccessful and only 24.8 as successful.

Analyzing the evaluation of the ballet teachers' role in professional success in ballet in the present sample, we found out that 81.2% of participants do agree that the teacher's role is very important, and that success in ballet dance is a result of collaboration of the teacher and ballet students. On the other hand 13.4% of participants evaluate the teachers' role as unimportant, and 5.4% of the participants view their success mostly as their personal achievement.

It is interesting that 34.9 % of the participants would like to have their ballet schools, but only 12.1 % explained why they were interested in continuing as ballet teachers in the future. They offered such explanations as: *I think I can do it well; I think it is very interesting to teach children dancing; I like it very much,* etc. 34.9 % are not interested in owning a ballet school or in any ballet teaching engage ment. And again just 12.1 % included explanations: *I cannot stand it; I think is very difficult to be a ballet teacher; it is a compromise with your conscience; my future is not connected with ballet,* etc. 4.7 % of the respondents had no opinion concerning this topic.

All the responses to this question provided by the participants from different ballet groups were grouped and divided into 9 sub-groups 1) *no,* without ex planation why; 2) *yes,* without explanation why; 3) *yes,* because I like to teach; 4) *no,* because I do not connect my future with ballet; 5) *no,* because it is difficult; 6) *yes,* because it is very interesting; 7) *yes,* because it will allow me to realize my ambitions; 8) *no,* because I am going to fulfill my ambitions in a different way; 9) *I do not know.* Results are presented in table 1.

Answers	No, I do not want						Yes, I want					Sum	Total
Ballet groups/ Sub-groups	EBG	DGB	BBC	OSB	PDT	Sum	EBG	DGB	BBC	OSB	PDT		
1	4	4	20	47	4	79	0	0	0	0	0	0	-
2	0	0	0	0	0	0	4	1	22	2	2	31	110
3	0	0	0	0	0	0	0	0	6	1	1	8	8
4	0	0	0	3	0	3	0	0	0	0	0	0	3
5	2	1	2	0	1	6	0	0	0	1	0	1	7
6	1	0	0	1	0	2	1	0	2	0	0	3	5
7	0	0	0	0	0	0	0	1	1	1	2	5	5
8	1	0	3	1	0	5	1	0	0	0	0	1	6
9	0	0	2	0	0	2	1	0	1	1	0	3	5
Total, N	8	5	27	52	5	97	7	2	32	6	5	52	149
Total, %	53,4	71	46	90	50	-	46,8	29	54	10	50	-	100

Table 1: Would you like to have your own ballet/dance school in the future?

5 Conclusion

Knowing how to do a dance, even at a very high level, is completely different from knowing how to teach it effectively. Being able to dance well does not qualify dancers as teachers. Our results confirm this statement. In our sample the biggest part of the participants (81.2 %) pinpointed an important role of experienced ballet teachers in their professional development, while only 12.1 % of the participants intended to become ballet teachers in the future, and 34.9 % were planning to have their own ballet school in the future.

This research is set within the elite and narrow cultural field of ballet dance, therefore it also provides access to the portrait of a professional ballet dancer and professional ballet dancers' training/education.

References

ALEKSANDROVICH, M. (2004): Uwarunkowania osobowościowe poziomu sukcesu członków grupy baletowej. Badanie realizowane na Uniwersytecie Gdańskim podczas stażu naukowego w ramach Specjalnego Stypendium Rządu RP 2003-2004.

CLARKSON, P.M., FREEDSON, P.S., KELLER, B. (1985): Maximal oxygen uptake, nutritional patterns and body composition of adolescent female ballet dancers Research Quarterly for Exercise and Sport. 56 (2), 180-184.

GAGNÉ, F. (1991): Toward a differentiated model of giftedness and talent. In N. Colangelo and DAVIS G. A. (Eds.), Handbook of gifted education (pp. 65-80). Boston: Allyn and Bacon.

ROBSON, B.E., BOOK, A., WILMERDING, M.V. (2002): Psychological stresses experienced by dance teachers: "How can I be a role model when I never had one?". Medical Problems of Performing Artists. 17 (4), 173-177.

http://www.danceclass.com/dance-teachers.html

SUBOTNIK, R. F. (2002): Talent Developed: Conversations With Masters in the Arts and Sciences. Eliot Feld: Innovator in Choreography and Dance Company Development. *Journal for the Education of the Gifted.* 25 (3), 290-302.

URENA, A. C. (2004): Skill acquisition in ballet dancers: the relationship between deliberate practice and expertise. Dissertation submitted to the Department of Educational Psychology and Learning Systems in partial fulfillment of the requirements for the degree of Doctor of Philosophy The Florida State University, College Of Education. Retrieved July 22th, 2007, from: http://etd.lib.fsu.edu/theses/available/etd-07122004170955/unrestricted/revisedcurena dissertation.pdf

Contact:
Maria ALEKSANDROVICH: mashenka_1976@o2.pl

(PRO)SOCIAL EDUCATION AS (UN)REDUCED ELEMENT OF TEACHER'S IDENTITY

Grzegorz Piekarski, Pomeranian University in Slupsk, Poland

In period of consumption culture simulated by mass media the border between this, what is real and what only seems to be real is blurred. More often we talk about fragmentariness or even the break-up of human identity. This state of things doesn't avoid teachers. Potential teachers' education confronts the challenge of restoring the human identity, restoring of authentic being in reality world not in simulation. Philosophy shows that the road marks prosocial education.

Keywords: teacher's identity, teacher training, consumption's culture, pro-social education

In social sciences the identity paradigm is certainly a problem described by theoreticians as one with long future, but short history. The concept dates back to ancient Greece, yet still it remains mysterious and vague. The mystery and vagueness are by no means caused by invisibility or ignorance. Quite the opposite is the case. Contemporary literature on that matter presents a wide array of approaches to identity as understood by representatives of various disciplines. This is reflected in the widespread identity discourse, abundant in ever new debates and publications, which, however, still remain ambiguous, and as such – elusive. Thus elusiveness would denote „the inability to find one coherent theoretical formula to gather all those various aspects of definition" (Bokszański 1989, S. 124).
Extended conceptualisation of modern identity – presenting, inter alia, reflexive identity, transgressional or transcultural identity – points to the wide interest in the subject, but also to struggling with the problem. Zygmunt BAUMAN claimed that „the question about identity is rooted in the sense of instability of existence, its susceptibility to manipulation, its indefiniteness, uncertainty and lack of finality in any form existence will take" (Baumann 1994, p. 9). It seems that we have learnt how to live with it, since the thesis about the fragmentary character of human identity, or even about its disintegration for which we seek remedy in easy and pleasurable areas of life, has become a truism. There are increasingly more supporters of validating the nonsense of our existence, and, consequently, looking for its equivalents in popular culture. The Dictionary of Modern Polish defines identity as "sameness, authenticity, truthfulness". Nowadays such truthfulness is created by the culture of consumerism with the ideology of pleasure, instant culture accompanied by its eloquent symbol of immediacy: fast food, fast sex, fast car, or the culture of appearances dominated by mass media which are no longer a mirror for the society, but are becoming a specific model for social interaction (Melosik 2007, p. 68-91). Thus the border between what is and what only seems to be real is becoming blurred. Therefore we are facing the problem of discerning between serious matters and trivia, the problem of naming and finding truth, because "when everything wants to be meaningful, nothing is" (Baumann 1994, p. 19). As a result any question about truth becomes pointless. This problem seems to concern also the candidates to teaching profession as well as teachers characterised to a large extent by post-modern superficiality in contacts with students.

It results in dehumanising interpersonal relations, while incoherent and inconsistent behaviour, lack of clearly delineated goals does not bring satisfaction, but leads to disappointment and, consequently, to the loss of identity as relation to the essence of being, the sense of human existence. And we do not have – as Tateusz KOTARBIŃSKI stipulated – the moral right to demand from others any characteristics that we are not capable to acknowledge in ourselves or in our own behaviour. Unfortunately, as we are well aware, without living examples there is no education. Teaching is not only a profession, but also a certain mission of forming harmony between people and their environment. The mission which enables sharing that which extends beyond reality commonly expressed by the words *to own* and *to have*. Therefore, if being a teacher is considered a special vocation, distinguished from other professions, from that point of view pedagogues should understand an extended moral responsibility for their students, first and foremost before themselves. Here we may express understandable anxiety about teachers themselves as the most fallible element. A chance person with a stiff upper lip, unable to gain children's trust or to show trust will never make a good pedagogue. However, such changes, as Maria MENDEL (2001, s. 168) emphasises, are not easy, especially since teachers were not properly prepared during their training to initiate and implement pro-social education or cooperation with students based on it. As a result, the pedagogue is rarely perceived as a person who can recognise educational and pedagogical problems in the social environment, as a person who should reveal certain level of axiological maturity, understood as having one's own internalised, yet open to discussion, axiological orientation. Such changes, then, should be introduced in teachers' formation and modification of their earlier education and experience. An important goal in teacher's didactic and pedagogic work is forming a universally developed personality in students, which would lead to her full and optimal development. However, comments presented by specialists in this field (Olbrycht 2008, p. 15-22; Czerepaniak-Walczak 2008, p. 38) clearly point to the fact that the pedagogue is not sufficiently qualified for upbringing within and towards specific values, for forming attitudes characterised by willingness to help others or by solidarity with others, and for teaching students independent estimation within clearly defined axiological framework. Higher education of teachers/pedagogues is oriented (according to the Bologna Project – mainly the first degree studies) to form instrumental competences. It serves solely the purpose of "producing" graduates who instead of creating an intellectual elite of curious and critical initiators of social change will passively surrender and adapt to status quo. Prospective teachers should not only be equipped in technical competences which will allow them to implement effectively the didactic process, but first and foremost in interpretative competences which render the world more comprehensible. Even the best professional predispositions, the most profound knowledge and the best skills, as Zofia FRĄCZEK (2002, p. 40-41) observes, do not guarantee the teacher's pedagogical success. She adds that such guarantee can be obtained only when knowledge, skills and proficiency are fully completed by axiological values, for a person who does not notice another person's value will never be morally good, even if s/he spent whole life on self-improvement, so s/he will never become a good pedagogue. This role requires, however, a well-defined ethical and pro-social approach, with simultaneous full partnership in interpersonal relations between the teacher and student, pupil and tutor. Unfortunately, the research in that field presents that teachers are of course aware of the utmost importance of their tasks and responsibility for the young generation's upbringing, yet it is still the level of declarations, for on the level of concrete actions it is reduced to using behavioural methods (in class and during recess a pupil is punished, directly or indirectly, every 5-10 minutes) in conveying certain, usually narrow, fragments of knowledge, without understanding or acknowledging students' subjectivity, auto-creation and building of identity. It is saddening that teachers do not see the clear discrepancy between their own declarations and actions. Here is an utterance by a teacher quoted by professor Maria DUDZIKOWA in excellent *Myth of school as a place of "student's universal development"*: "They are [young teachers – G.P.] in a way deprived by a notion that student should be treated as a partner. By no means! A student is my partner. I will not have him pat me on the shoulder, call me Danka and invite me for a beer" (Dudzikowa 2004, p. 66, 233). Apart from wrong interpretation of partnership, this quotation points to specific relations between pupils and teachers which destroy coexistence, and consequently, also the teacher him/herself. Kazimierz DENEK rightly emphasises that „excessive reification of a student deforms his personality. The greater reification, the worse pathology and deprivation of values" (Denek 1998, p. 89). Built on the basis of such attitudes in teachers, accompanied by empty moralism, contacts with children and teenagers, and this example is not isolated, serve only the purpose of making them embarrassed, ashamed, which is very close to rejecting authorities, inability to define one's own goals, lack of trust, sense of alienation at school, inability to make and maintain friendships, increased violence and abusing psychoactive substances.

Hubertus VON SCHÖNEBECK on the basis of his own experience and observation of school events and behaviour of teachers, former colleagues from work, did not hesitate to recognise them as absolutely uninterested in children, their emotions, their world. According to German anipedagogue it leads to dehumanisation of school. He accuses them of falsehood, duplicity and hypocrisy present in only apparent acceptance of a child. In fact, their attitudes take the form of dictatorship, refer to duty and necessity to accept certain foreign, thus incomprehensible for a child, feelings, thoughts, intentions. Similar observations are formulated by Ewa BILIŃSKA-SUCHANEK, for whom very often the teacher, relying on the stereotypes in school's functioning, which emphasise his position and power, deprives students of their subjectivity, which leads to their conviction that they are powerless and to disbelief in any change. "The teacher, who perceives himself as a representative and conveyor of ready truths, does not create any knowledge, and his passive transmission, void of meritorious innovations, confirms students in the belief that school is not a site of creating new qualities for either side.[...] Students [...] with time develop qualities which have nothing to do with creativity, responsibility, intellectual independence, moral sensitivity, personal courage or dignity. With constant tension blocking and insecurity, egoistic attitudes come to light, blocking the student's development on the level of natural identity and role identity" (Bilińska-Suchanek 2003, p. 275-276). As Bogusław ŚLIWERSKI (1996, s. 13) rightly points out, such situations are pseudo-upbringing, in which he seeks the reasons behind destroying human hope and trust by appearances, masks, deceit, destruction and violence. Doubtlessly apt statement is formulated also by Henryka KWIATKOWSKA (1991, s. 26-27), who stipulates the need to prepare pedagogues for responsible actions. Professor KWIATKOWSKA emphasises that modern reality necessitates such changes in education that will mark the move from education of blurred responsibility, power and unquestionable authority towards the education of personal responsibility, based on individuality, cooperation and understanding.

For pro-social activity not only actions for others are important, as it is commonly believed, but also certain intellectual, perceptive and emotional reactions that should be oriented to other people's needs. Only the teacher who can change her way of thinking by developing a relatively permanent readiness to react in a certain way, and the ability to perceive a situation from the point of view of a pupil, can consciously implement not only the teaching process, but also, or maybe first of all, the process of upbringing. Lech WITKOWSKI (1990, p. 12-39) many times at different occasions emphasises that nobility of intentions is not sufficient condition for validating actions. Similarly, for pedagogical processes it is not irrelevant if the message sender (teacher/tutor) has proper skills to present his arguments. Integrity, pro-social attitudes that we postulate must find expression in reflexive sense of duty which cannot be dominated by the force of institutional sanctions, but by specific awareness of personal responsibility which must be incorporated in one's behaviour. It is consistent with the stance of Chantal DELSOL'S who claims that today "when truths are uncertain, when we are surrounded by the atmosphere of nihilism, those who want to transmit [values – G.P.] have only one option: they must be witnesses of what they convey. […] people who prove their faith, not only preach it. Those who want to convey cannot then merely discuss or provide arguments; they must live it" (Delsol 2005, p. 27). Only the pedagogue who believes in the power of change in herself and in others, who improves herself, can inspire another person to her development, to subjective creation of the future for both an individual and the community. Bearing in mind that we are "not what we are, but what we become" (Giddens 2006, p. 105), the following characteristics are worth mentioning: empathy (analysing verbal and non-verbal messages sent by a student, sensing her feelings and extraverbal experiences), responsibility, authenticity, internal need to become an authority, openness, decisiveness, respect, self-acceptance and accepting others, autonomy and reflexivity. These features render pedagogues more aware of reality, whose estimation is based on knowledge and critical evaluation of a problem. Today encyclopaedic knowledge of the teacher does not seem to be the most important factor on any level of education, for modern pedagogue is required first and foremost to possess skills which she could use to fill education with humanism. Therefore it is worth remembering that the time has come to make pro-social, humane values the main goal in training teachers and in their pedagogical work with children and teenagers, who will shape future through their actions. Thus, as Maria CZEREPANIAK-WALCZAK (2008, p. 32) aptly puts it – new cultural patterns formed configuratively and/or prefiguratively determine new types of relations and lead to revision of previous experiences in that context. Therefore, making the essence of pro-social approach a pedagogical aspect has become not only a temporary necessity, but condition *sine qua non* of humanity. Otherwise, given the speed at which changes take place in modern world, neither the teacher-tutor could show her pupils an optimistic, or optimal vision of constructing one's own life strategy, nor will young people change the reality. The possibility of implementing those propositions lies in correct teacher training based on discoveries in social and humane sciences which will help prospective teachers understand the need for social solidarity and civic activity, awaken and deepen sensitivity in students, form correct pro-social attitude and motivation. Particularly valuable here is Lech WITKOWSKI'S thought: "the negative presence in curricula (also academic ones – G.P.) and real educational activities of interest in education and personal formation of sensitivity and moral imagination – in the sphere of behaviour and maturity as to formulating judgements and justifications of one's own preferences as for moral dilemmas and the world's axiological complexity – is reflected in the lack of ability to sympathise with those who suffer, to be humble in evaluating others, to be alert to one's own shortcomings and cultural degradation, as well as to overcome obstacles and to transgress the limitations of our own competence to act and to extend the horizon of perception of evil, harm and pain" (Witkowski 2007, p. 28).

Summing up the meaning of pro-social education in forming the identity of a candidate to teaching profession, bearing in mind that identity is authentic being in the real world, not in the world of simulation we may present its three crucial aspects. Firstly, it provides pedagogical models for new forms of learning social relations; secondly, it promotes developing the ability to act in a purposeful and rational manner, according to socially accepted values and norms (a person living according to values, not their appearances); thirdly, it contributes to emancipation, transforming the processes of socialisation into a practice of gaining skills and competences to free oneself and of reacting outside the framework of institutional conventions.

References

BAUMANN Z: Dwa szkice o moralności ponowoczesnej. Warszawa: Instytut Kultury, 1994.

BILIŃSKA-SUCHANEK E: Opór wobec szkoły. Dorastanie w perspektywie paradygmatu oporu. Kraków: Oficyna Wydawnicza Impuls, 2003.

BOKSZAŃSKI Z: Tożsamość, interakcja, grupa. Tożsamość jednostki w perspektywie teorii socjologicznej. Łódź: Wydawnictwo Uniwersytetu Łódzkiego, 1989.

CZEREPANIAK-WALCZAK M: Aksjologiczne aspekty Procesu Bolońskiego; pytania o jego przesłanki i cele w kontekście akademickiego kształcenia pedagogów. In: Kostkiewicz J. (Ed.): Aksjologia w kształceniu pedagogów, p. .23-40. Kraków: Oficyna Wydawnicza Impuls, 2008.

DELSOL CH: Jak dzisiaj przekazywać wartości. In: Znak no. 2/2005, p. 21-28.

DENEK K: O nowy kształt edukacji. Toruń: Wydawnictwo Edukacyjne Akapit, 1998.

DUDZIKOWA M: Mit o szkole jako miejscu wszechstronnego rozwoju ucznia. Eseje etnopedagogiczne. Kraków: Oficyna Wydawnicza Impuls, 2004.

FRĄCZEK Z: Edukacja aksjologiczna wobec potrzeb współczesności. Rzeszów: Wydawnictwo Uniwersytetu Rzeszowskiego, 2002.

GIDDENS A: Nowoczesność i tożsamość. Warszawa: PWN, 2006.

KROMOLICKA B: Społeczno-zawodowa rola pracownika socjalnego. Szczecin: WNUS, 2002.

KWIATKOWSKA H: Edukacja nauczycielska w optyce pytań o współczesność i przyszłość. In: Materiały z sesji PTP Edukacja nauczycielska wobec zmiany społecznej, Warszawa: Wydawnictwo PTP i Sekcja Kształcenia Nauczycieli ZG ZNP, 1991.

MELEOSIK Z: Kultura popularna jako czynnik socjalizacji. In: Kwieciński Z., Śliwerski B (Ed.): Pedagogika. Podręcznik akademicki, p. 68-91.Warszawa: PWN, 2007.

MENDEL M: Edukacja społeczna. Partnerstwo rodziny, szkoły i gminy w perspektywie amerykańskiej. Toruń: Wydawnictwo Adam Marszałek, 2001.

OLBRYCHT K: Aksjologiczne wymiary kształcenia pedagogów. In: Kostkiewicz J (Ed.): Aksjologia w kształceniu pedagogów, p. 15-22. Kraków: Oficyna Wydawnicza Impuls, 2008.

ŚLIWERSKI B: Klinika szkolnej demokracji. Kraków: Oficyna Wydawnicza Impuls, 1996.

WITKOWSKI L: O nowych polach i wymiarach odpowiedzialności etycznej w pedagogice. In: Sawczuk W (Ed.): Po co etyka pedagogom? Toruń: Wydawnictwo Adam Marszałek, 2007.

WITKOWSKI L: Przekroje analityczne kwestii edukacyjnej (dyskusja społeczno-krytyczna). In: Kwieciński Z. Witkowski L (Ed.): Ku pedagogii pogranicza, p. 12-39. Toruń: UMK: 1990.

Contact:
Grzegorz PIEKARSKI, MA: gpr@wp.pl

INTRODUCING CLIL TO CZECH SCHOOLS

Světlana Hanušová, Masaryk University Brno, Czech Republic

Content and Language Integrated Learning (CLIL) belongs to recent educational trends. Its beginnings in the Czech Republic are challenging due to the high percentage of foreign language teachers without full qualification and rather low foreign language communicative competences of subject teachers. The key to success is thorough teacher education on both the pre-service and in-service level. The author reflects on her experience as a facilitator and co-ordinator of a group of primary and secondary in-service teachers who are currently introducing CLIL into the school educational programmes at their schools. The experience of accompanying practising teachers on their way to innovated teaching procedures serves as a valuable source of research data. The action research carried out in the process of cooperation with in-service teachers is beneficial in the process of introducing modules and courses aimed at CLIL to pre-service teacher education.

Keywords: Content and Language Integrated Learning, CLIL, in-service teachers, communicative competences, school educational programmes

1 Introduction

Content and Language Integrated Learning (CLIL) is a type of bilingual education. Unlike immersion programmes common in America and Canada, CLIL classes are usually taught by teachers who are proficient speakers of the learners' mother tongue (L1). CLIL programmes neither automatically exclude

L1 from instruction nor aim at replacing L1 and depriving the learners of the right to use it.
In the context of the European Union, CLIL is highly promising as it enables the development of language competences necessary for internationalisation and further study as well as the mobility of workers in a unified Europe.

2 The process of teaching and learning within CLIL

Defined as "integrated focus on language and subject matter issues in a coherent framework" (Beardsmore, 2008), CLIL strives to reach dual aims: content-related and linguistic. Mediating content via a non-native language is undoubtedly challenging for both the teacher and the learner. Therefore, the third element that comes into play is represented by the emphasis on the learning process and learning skills (Mehisto et al, 2008). Thus CLIL represents a constructivist approach with a strong learning-centred orientation.
Whereas tertiary CLIL is an inherent component of many university study programmes, without which high quality instruction would scarcely be imaginable, primary or secondary CLIL is sometimes seen as too challenging. The change of the medium of instruction undoubtedly brings about additional demands. However, the increased level of challenge can be seen as an opportunity rather than a threat, as it can trigger the innovation of teaching methods and techniques. MUÑOZ maintains that "the need for permanent comprehension controls leads to more intensive interaction between teachers and learners" (Muñoz, 2002, p. 35).
Research shows that the integration of content and language can have very positive effects on the process of learning content and language provided that it is realised cautiously. The longitudinal research conducted by a team from Prague's Charles University proved that "the use of a foreign language requires a different, deeper way of information processing and leads to enhanced acquisition of both the language and the non-linguistic content matter" (Hofmanová et al. 2008). The results are consistent with Vygotskyan understanding of the ability to express the same thought in different languages as a valuable educational advantage that can also foster understanding of the content.
As for the language component, language teaching and learning in CLIL is inherently communicative. The communicative character of a learning task, which is often difficult to achieve in classical language teaching, is natural and obvious in CLIL. Language does not have to be developed via imaginary materials,

largely unauthentic. The teacher can employ real communication situations and use authentic materials that relate to the learners' learning experience in the content area. MUÑOZ (2002) highlights the added value the CLIL model brings, which consists of the focus on fluency, whereas classical language classes often focus on accuracy.

3 Primary and secondary CLIL in the Czech Republic

Not only CLIL but also other types of integration of different subjects and fields are supported by the main educational documents in the Czech Republic. The Framework Educational Programmes instigate the introduction of new integrated subjects that evolve through the relationships of the subject matter of the various levels, namely topics, areas or educational fields. Unlike bilingual education, schools do not need special accreditation to provide CLIL instruction. Schools are encouraged to introduce CLIL as far as they incorporate it in their School Educational Programmes. CLIL provision is also massively supported by European Social Fund. In 2009 an unprecedented number of OP VK (*Operational Plan of Education for Competitiveness*) projects focusing on CLIL were accepted for financing. Unfortunately, the current Czech context is characterised by an alarming lack of qualified teachers of English and rather low foreign language communicative competences of subject teachers, both of which are serious obstacles to CLIL introduction.

Given the situation, a judicious and careful approach in introducing CLIL is highly desirable in Czech schools. Regular integrated teaching and learning of the language and content can be understood as an advanced form of CLIL which can only be achieved gradually, while carefully reflecting on all possible implications of the innovations. In the initial stages, CLIL instruction in primary and secondary school can be realised as language showers (short periods conducted in the CLIL language while the rest of the teaching and learning in the given class is conducted in the mother tongue) or selected modules in the CLIL language in a given subject or content modules in language classes (Mehisto et al. 2008). CLIL is also apt for project days or project weeks, outdoor schooling, experiential learning projects, or international projects such as e-Twinning.

4 Pre-service and in-service teacher education for CLIL

4.1 Rationale

Although CLIL methodology may appear intuitive, proper teacher training is a necessary condition of successful CLIL application. The development of special educational programmes is recommended by experts, as a mere qualification in a foreign language and another school subject is not sufficient (*Content and Language*, 2006).

Pre-service teacher education might appear as a logical first step, but the fact that in the Czech context even teacher trainers lack experience with CLIL should not be overlooked.

Having considered the complexity of the situation, we decided to launch a project starting from in-service teacher training. The cooperation with in-service teachers enables teacher trainers to research the situation in schools and monitor the piloting of innovations. The experience of in-service teacher trainers cooperating closely with school teachers will subsequently result in the development of modules for pre-service teacher education.

4.2 Current teacher education project

The project planned for 3 years started with an introductory seminar in January 2010. The main aim of the project is to accompany teachers as they introduce CLIL into their practice at Czech primary and secondary schools.

4.2.1 Participants and other stakeholders

The group, consisting of 30 participating teachers from 6 schools and 3 teacher trainers, was established as a professional learning community. We were inspired by STOLL, who speaks about professional learning communities defined as inclusive groups of people cooperating towards a common goal, who are "motivated by a shared learning vision, who support and work with each other, finding ways, inside and outside their immediate community, to enquire into their practice and together learn new and better approaches" (Stoll et al., cited in Mehisto, 2008, p. 94). As teacher trainers, we made it clear from the very beginning that we can facilitate the learning community, coordinate the cooperation and share the professional expertise, but cannot simply transmit all necessary information and *make CLIL happen* regardless of the context at particular schools and the active and creative involvement on the part of the school teachers and school administrators. We acquainted the participants

with research results and guidelines provides by leading CLIL methodologists. However, the experience from different socio-cultural environments cannot be simply transferred to our context. It is vitally important to reflect on every step. The introduction of CLIL has to be continuously analysed and evaluated.
The key prerequisite for successful CLIL provision is the cooperation of language teachers and subject matter teachers, ideally also the cooperation of teaching staff from different schools as CLIL cannot operate on the basis of an initiative of individual enthusiasts. Therefore, a very strong emphasis on team-building and empowerment was a vital element of the project.
Another important factor is the involvement of different groups of stakeholders. Therefore, all school headmasters from the participating schools were invited for the first contact session together with the representatives of local school administration. Other groups of stakeholders, such as parents, pupils, and other teachers at the schools involved and school councils were addressed at the very beginning of the project.

4.2.2 Training methods and techniques

The key principle underlying the in-service training for CLIL we provided has been a so-called *loop input* (Woodward, 1991) that integrates the methods and techniques we want the trainees to use in their practice and the content of the training programme. As trainers, we exposed the participating teachers to CLIL experiences as often as possible so as to provide a model for them to rely on in their own practice. The input sessions offered plentiful possibilities of exposure to the techniques and procedures recommended for successful CLIL practice, such as hands-on activities, experiential learning, drama techniques, creative projects, enhanced reflection of the learning process and cooperative learning. The main topics included lesson planning, the setting of dual aims, team cooperation, scaffolding, innovated methods and techniques, and assessment for learning in CLIL.

4.3 Action research

The format of the cooperation with schoolteachers enabled us to monitor and research the initial stages of CLIL application. Besides contact sessions, the communication with the schoolteachers is also realised online which gives us the possibility of collecting online data. Moodle Virtual Learning Environment (VLE) is used for these purposes (http://moodlinka.ped.muni.cz/course/view.

php?id=1721). Apart from online data, data from questionnaires, reflective diaries and observation notes taken during school visits is also exploited.
The baseline study, conducted at the very beginning of the project, addressed several stakeholder groups, namely pupils, parents, school board members, fellow teachers and school headmasters. The results of the study are currently being processed.

5 Conclusion

The integration of a foreign language and another subject into primary and secondary level CLIL has a potential to enhance foreign language learning, as well as content learning, provided that it is introduced carefully and judiciously. The first results of the study carried out in cooperation with schoolteachers and headmasters who decided to introduce CLIL to their schools confirm that the key aspects that are beneficial in the initial stages of the innovated approaches include team cooperation, the development of learning communities, the stakeholder approach and the emphasis on the reflection of every step towards innovated teaching procedures.
The experience gained in the cooperation with teachers piloting CLIL at Czech schools and research results will be utilised when designing a training CLIL module pre-service teacher trainees in the Department of the English Language and Literature at the Faculty of Education, Masaryk University.

References

BEARDSMORE, HUGO BAETENS: Multilingualism, Cognition and Creativity. In: *International CLIL Research Journal* [online]. Vol.1(1), 2008. Downloaded from http://www.icrj.eu/, retrieved on Feb 22, 2010.

Content and Language Integrated Learning (CLIL) at School in Europe. Brussels: Eurydice. European Unit, 2006.

Framework Education Programme for Basic Education. Downloaded from http://www.vuppraha.cz/soubory/RVP_ZV_EN.pdf, retrieved on Jan 5, 2010.

HOFMANNOVÁ, MARIE, NOVOTNÁ, JARMILA, PÍPALOVÁ, RENATA: Assessment Approaches to Teaching Mathematics in English as a Foreign Language (Czech Experience) In: International CLIL Research Journal [online]. Vol.1(1), 2008. Downloaded from http://www.icrj.eu/, retrieved on Feb 22, 2010.

MEHISTO, PEETER: CLIL Counterweights: Recognising and Decreasing Disjuncture in CLIL. In: *International CLIL Research Journal* [online]. Vol.1(1), 2008. Downloaded from http://www.icrj.eu/, retrieved on Feb 25, 2010.

MEHISTO, PEETER, MARSH, DAVID, FRIGOLS, MARÍA JESÚS: Uncovering CLIL. Oxford: Macmillan Education, 2008.

MUÑOZ, CARMEN: Aprendizaje integrado de contenidos y lengua extranjera. In: Marsh, D. (ed.): CLIL/EMILE – The European Dimension: Actions, trends and foresight potential, pp. 33-36. Jyväskylä: University of Jyväskylä, 2002.

WOODWARD, TESSA: Models and Metaphors in Language Teacher Training: Loop Input and Other Strategies. Cambridge: CUP, 1991.

Contact:
Světlana HANUŠOVÁ: hanusova@ped.muni.cz

USING VIDEORECORDINGS OF LESSONS IN THE EDUCATION OF MATHEMATICS TEACHERS

Naďa Stehlíková
Charles University in Prague, Faculty of Education, Czech Republic

Videos of real lessons are increasingly used in the education of pre- and in-service mathematics teachers, both in the Czech Republic and abroad, mostly to bridge the gap between theory and practice. They have become a part of my mathematics education course at the Faculty, too. The article presents examples of activities from the course in which videos and their analyses were used to develop student teachers' pedagogical content knowledge.

Keywords: Mathematics Education Course, mathematics teachers, pedagogical content knowledge, video-cases

1 Introduction

For some years, I have been teaching Mathematics Education Course (or MEC) for future lower and upper secondary mathematics teachers with the aim of developing their a) awareness of some theoretical concepts from mathematical education, b) ability to didactically transform subject matter, c) ability to observe and evaluate teaching and different teaching strategies, d) ability to diagnose pupils' knowledge and skills and suggest re-education, e) ability (and need) to become a reflective practitioner. (Student teachers will be referred to as 'students'.)

To achieve these goals, I used traditional means such as the study and discussion of texts on ME and of textbooks, various problem solving and problem posing activities, etc. However, I have decided that the best context within which MEC can be organised consists of real cases from mathematics lessons: text-based cases, class observation and video-based cases. Here, I will only concentrate on video-based cases which are used as a springboard for discussion and around which activities are organised. An example is given below (see also Stehlíková 2009).

2 Theoretical Framework

Within ME, videorecordings of mathematics lessons have been used for some time now (Borko et al. 2008; Goffree, Oonk 2001; Krammer et al. 2006; Lampert, Ball 1998; Llinares, Valls 2009; Santagata, Zannoni, Stigler 2007; Sherin, van Es 2005; Star, Strickland 2008; Tichá, Hošpesová 2006; etc.). Given the constraints of this paper, only the main points from the studies will be given. The authors mostly agree that the analysis of video-cases helps students and in-service teachers (among others) to: a) link theory and practice (observable events are discussed and connected to theoretical considerations), b) become aware of the complexities of teaching and learning processes, c) analyse lessons repeatedly from different perspectives, d) reflect on the teaching of others and consequently, on their own, e) develop their ability to notice significant events in teaching, f) get more experience of teaching and be better prepared for the realities of the classroom (overcome the limited amount of teaching experience the students get in their studies).

Many authors also stress that certain prerequisites exist for the videos to be used to their best advantage: a) good cases should be chosen (that is, cases rich in phenomena to be discussed), b) ample opportunities of work with videos are needed as students have to 'learn to see', c) great care should be taken to develop appropriate activities around the videos, d) videos should be chosen with a clear goal in mind (they are a means, not a goal).

In this text, I will show an example of the use of video-cases in order to develop students' *pedagogical content knowledge* (or PCK; Shulman 1986). This notion is well described in literature so I will not deal with it in more detail. I will only stress that, in my opinion, a part of PCK is the ability to notice (Sherin, van Es 2005) and for this ability, the analysis of video-cases is more than appropriate.

3 Illustration from MEC – Pythagoras' Theorem

I have analysed dozens of lessons to determine the ones which might be beneficial, i.e., they have a potential to generate fruitful discussion of pedagogical and subject didactic phenomena and thus to enhance students' PCK. Some techniques which I use in order to guide the students' attention are described in (Stehlíková 2009).

3.1 Context

Pythagoras' Theorem (or PT) is an important topic within mathematics. It has a lot of applications in mathematics and in real life and its teaching has been an object of research. It is quite unique within lower secondary mathematics because "it combines geometric with algebraic reasoning, requires a set of specific prerequisites [...] plus some meta-mathematical understanding (what is a mathematical theorem? Why does it have to be proven? When can it be reversed?)" (Klieme, Pauli, Reusser 2009). It is no wonder that PT and its teaching and understanding by pupils gets a lot of attention in the MEC.

From the point of view of subject didactic, two main types of difficulties with PT appear: *D1*. Pupils remember PT formally as a formula $c^2 = a^2 + b^2$. They often do not realise that in such a case the right angle must be at C and cannot make PT for triangles which are not prototypically labelled (*ABC*) or which are in a non-prototypical position (they are rotated). *D2*. Pupils are not able to distinguish a right triangle in a more complex picture. Often, pupils have mechanical knowledge of PT (Hejný, Kuřina 2009). They can say the equation but then they exhibit *D1* and *D2*. Teaching of PT often relies too much on drilling and on algebraic treatment and manipulatives are rarely used. I want the students to develop the awareness of these important issues for themselves and to this goal, I use a series of activities.

3.2 Activities

3.2.1 Analysis of pupils' solutions

The students are given four pupils' written solutions to a task which involves PT and they are to analyse them. The solutions show that pupils might have difficulties of the above type. The main goal of the activity is to make the students aware of them.

3.2.2 Video-cases

The video-cases are chosen from two Czech mathematics lessons from TIMSS 1999 Video Study (Grade 8 pupils - 14 years old). Neither lesson is an introductory one; they come as the second or third in the sequence of lessons devoted to PT. The extracts will be briefly described. Due to the space constraints, the main 'message' of the cases will be simply stated.

Case 1, Lesson A (4 minutes), Lesson B (3+4 minutes): In Lesson A, the teacher asks a pupil to a) draw a triangle on the blackboard and "not to label it", b) say PT "as a formula because it is easier to remember", and c) manipulate the formula to get other variants (part of the resulting figure is in Fig. 1). In Lesson B, the teacher also starts with drawing a triangle on the blackboard. It is labelled *ABC* and the pupils are asked to write the formula for PT and to "say it in words", too (i.e., they should refer to the areas of squares). Later, the teacher draws 3 right triangles in different positions on the blackboard and the pupils are to label them with different letters and write the appropriate PT equations (part of the blackboard is in Fig. 2).

Implementation: The students watch the three extracts one by one and first discuss them in pairs. Next, the whole class discussion is organised so that each pair is to comment on any aspect of the extracts. As the cases are quite short, the discussion is usually not widely spread. Here, only the subject didactic points of the discussion will be given, while other aspects (such as psychological or general pedagogical) are neglected:

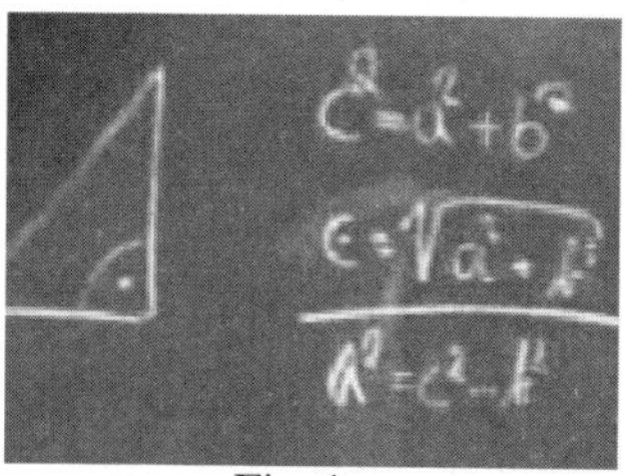

Fig. 1

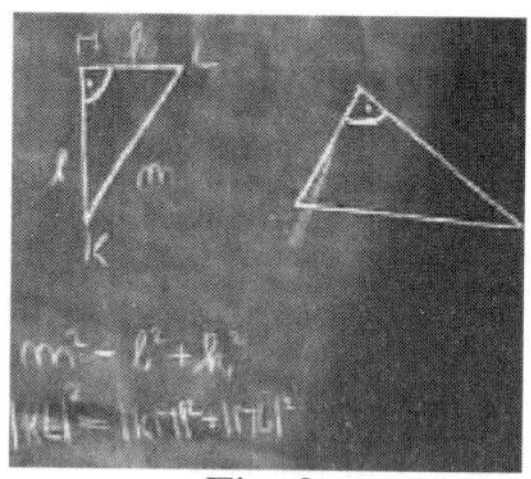

Fig. 2

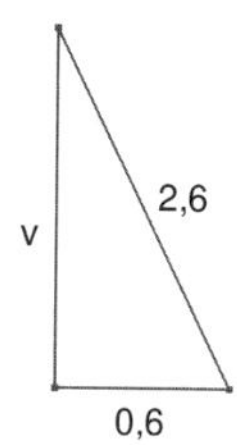

Fig. 3

- Asking pupils to say PT as a formula without any recourse to its conceptual understanding might lead to mechanical understanding (to *D1*). The triangle on the blackboard in Lesson A is not labelled, thus the pupils must use their memorised knowledge of 'prototypical' PT and actually there is no link between the picture and the algebraic expression.
- It is important to vary labels and positions of triangles for which PT is formulated in order to prevent *D1*. More isolated models (Hejný, Kuřina 2009) of triangles and respective PTs are needed for the generic model of PT to originate.
- The teacher in Lesson B seems to be aware of *D1* and tries to prevent it. He prepares situations where mistakes could be made to draw pupils' attention to problematic issues.

Case 2, Lesson A (9 minutes): The teacher introduces a real-life problem about a stepladder and how far it can reach (the situation is to be modelled with an isosceles triangle in which the right triangle must be determined and then one leg calculated with PT). The teacher draws a picture herself and leads pupils by narrow questions towards a solution.

An interesting situation arises when a geometric model of half of the stepladder is on the blackboard (Fig. 3). Two sides of the right triangle are marked with the known measures and the height is labelled v (the beginning letter of the Czech word for height, as is customary). The teacher asks for PT. A pupil dictates and she writes: $v^2 = c^2 - b^2$. The teacher agrees and then adds "I should have written a squared rather than v squared." and rewrites it: $a^2 = c^2 - b^2$.

Implementation: This time, subject didactic points discussed are:

- It is a nice and potentially challenging mathematical problem to be solved by several steps: real life situation – drawing – geometric figure – algebraic expression of PT – solving the equation. The teacher shortens the stage of grasping the problem and concentrates on its algebraic treatment. This results in little understanding of some pupils of what is the basis of the problem – they ask what the question is, where the "second half of the stepladder" is, and are not able to say what the resulting number actually means.
- The situation is not used to prevent *D2*, i.e., to enhance pupils' ability to model a real life situation in mathematics and to analyse the model. In

fact, the teacher uses the problem to drill pupils in creating PT equality, substituting numbers and solving the equation.

- The teacher uses 'question- answer' pattern which soon changes into 'funnelling pattern' (Wood 1998). The pupils are given questions of a low cognitive difficulty and the teacher formulates all the important steps of the solution herself.
- The teacher sticks to the prototypical formulas for PT which leads to a conflict when two prototypical types of labelling meet in one picture: the sides of a right angle (*a*, *b*, *c*) and the height of an isosceles triangle (*v*). She expects pupils to use the prototypical formula for PT even though there are no *a*, *b*, *c* in the picture. Again, there is a danger of *D1*.

Case 3, Lesson B (4+3 minutes): The teacher presents one of the proofs of PT using an old teaching aid (triangles and squares are actually manipulated to show that PT is valid). Next, three pupils are asked to model a right triangle using a rope divided into 3:4:5 parts.
Implementation: For this extract, the discussion focused on the following points: How to show pupils that the proof is necessary and how to involve the pupils in the proof itself and in the discovery that the right angle can be measured in practice using the rope.

3.2.3 Text-case – PT as a generic model

The following description was written by one of my students who tutored a 14-year-old girl: "I asked Jana to draw a picture first and to label it. Each time, she made a frame with $c^2 = a^2 + b^2$ next to the picture. I wanted to know if she only learned PT as a formula or if she was able to use it flexibly. So I gave her a problem where the hypotenuse was *a*. She drew a picture and labelled it correctly (with *a* as a hypotenuse) but she wrote the frame with $c^2 = a^2 + b^2$ next to the picture again. The final solution was correct! When asked why she did so, she answered: 'We always write it like this and only then, we substitute the correct letters and numbers.' I gave her other problems with different labelling and positions of triangles and she solved them correctly."
Implementation: HEJNÝ'S theory of generic models (Hejný, Kuřina 2009) is used in MEC as the theory describing the knowledge construction in mathematics. The students are asked to analyse the above text-case from this standpoint. It appears that Jana has the formula $c^2 = a^2 + b^2$ on the level of generic model,

that is, she can use it flexibly for any right triangles. It is a shortcut of PT, a kind of template into which she can correctly substitute.

3.2.4 Follow-up tasks

The students are asked to do some more reading on the subject matter: different teaching strategies of PT ordered from instructive to constructivist (Hejný, Kuřina 2009); research on the way PT is taught in some countries (Klieme, Pauli, Reusser 2009). Moreover, they read about research on communication patterns in mathematics and on the theory of generic models. Other follow-up tasks may include posing real-life problems for the application of PT, finding an applet to be used in its teaching, suggesting a way technology can be used, etc.

4 Conclusions

The above text illustrates a concrete way in which students' PCK can be developed. In particular, it shows how the theoretical notions introduced in MEC are used for the analysis of situations in the videos. Namely, these are the theory of generic models and communication patterns in the teaching of mathematics (mainly the funnelling pattern). Thus, both video and text-cases helped to link theory and practice in a very meaningful way. Moreover, the videos usually motivate students to suggest alternatives and their possible implications.

The above illustrates how the presented particular cases can be used (and indeed, were used in the autumn term 2009). This can change in the future, depending on factors such as finding new video-cases, new texts, availability of time in MEC, etc. I try to be flexible from this respect because the knowledge base in ME changes a lot which should be taken into account.

References

BORKO, H. ET AL.: Video as a tool for fostering productive discussions in mathematics professional development. In: Teacher and Teacher Education 24 (2)/2008, p. 417-436.

GOFFREE, F., OONK, W.: Digitizing real teaching practice for teacher education programmes: The MILE approach. In: Lin, F.-L., Cooney, T.J. (Ed.): Making Sense of Mathematics Teacher Education, p. 111–145. - The Netherlands: Kluwer Academic Publishers, 2001.

HEJNÝ, M., KUŘINA, F.: Dítě, škola a matematika. Konstruktivistické přístupy k vyučování. Druhé aktualizované vydání. - Praha: Portál, 2009.

KLIEME, E., PAULI, CH., REUSSER, K.: The Pythagoras study: Investigating effects of teaching and learning in Swiss and German mathematics classrooms. In: Janík, T., Seidel, T. (Ed.): The Power of Video Studies in Investigating Teaching and Learning in the Classroom, p. 137-160. - Münster: Waxmann, 2009.

KRAMMER, K. ET AL.: Learning with classroom videos: Conception and first results of an online teacher-training program. In: Zentr. für Didaktik der Mathematik 38(5)/2006, p. 422-432.

LAMPERT, M., BALL, D.: Teaching, multimedia, and mathematics: Investigations of real practice. - New York: Teachers College Press, 1998.

LLINARES, S., VALLS, J.: The building of pre-service primary teachers' knowledge of mathematics teaching: interaction and online video case studies. In: Instructional Science 37(3)/2009, p. 247-271.

SANTAGATA, R., ZANNONI, C., STIGLER, J. W.: The role of lesson analysis in pre-service teacher education: an empirical investigation of teacher learning from a virtual video-based field experience. In: Journal of Mathematics Teacher Education 10(2)/2007, p. 123-140.

SHERIN, M. G., VAN ES, E. A.: Using video to support teachers' ability to notice classroom interactions. In: Journal of Technology and Teacher Education 13(3)/2005, p. 475-491.

SHULMAN, L.S.: Those who understand: Knowledge growth in teaching. In: Educational Researcher 15(2)/1986, p. 4-14.

STAR, J., STRICKLAND, S.: Learning to observe: Using video to improve preservice mathematics teachers' ability to notice. In: Journal of Mathematics Teacher Educ. 11(2)/2008, p. 107-125.

STEHLÍKOVÁ, N.: Using videocases to promote good practice in the teaching of mathematics. In: Kourkoulos, M., Tzanakis, C. (Ed.): Proceedings 5th International Colloquium on the Didactics of Mathematics, p. 325-335. - Crete: University of Crete, 2009.

TICHÁ, M., HOŠPESOVÁ, A.: Qualified pedagogical reflection as a way to improve mathematics education. In: Journal of Mathematics Teacher Education 9(2)/2006, p. 129-156.

WOOD, T.: Alternative patterns of communication in mathematics classes: Funnelling or focusing? In: Steinbring, H. et al. (Ed.): Language and Communication in the Mathematical Classroom, p. 167-178. - Reston: NCTM, 1998.

The article was supported by the research grant "Teaching profession in the environment of changing education requirements" No. MSM 0021620862.

Contact:
doc. RNDr. Naďa STEHLÍKOVÁ, Ph.D., nada.stehlikova@pedf.cuni.cz

THEORETICAL FRAMEWORK FOR DEVELOPMENT OF CPV VIDEOWEB

Eva Minaříková, Masaryk University Brno, Czech Republic

This paper introduces the theoretical background behind the development of CPV Videoweb, a video-based learning environment. Four areas that inform the theoretical background will be described in brief: Reflective practitioner theory, Observation period as silent period in teacher education, Using video cases in teacher education, Cognitive-load theory. Finally, the practical implications for the process of developing CPV Videoweb will be discussed.

Key words: video-based learning environment, teacher education, observation, cognitive-load theory

1 Theoretical Framework for Developing CPV Videoweb

It is unarguable that classroom situations are infinitely complex and that a teacher is forced to make instant decisions in every minute of a lesson (see Wajnryb 1992, p. 1, Rys 1975, p. 97, Day 1990, p. 44 and many others). As WALLACE (1991, p. 89) points out, expecting someone with no training at all to stand up in front of a class and teach could result in them enduring a traumatic experience. Therefore it seems reasonable (as he suggests) to proceed from low-risk activities (such as data collection and analysis) to higher-risk activities (such as microteaching and peer teaching) in teacher training.

CPV videoweb (CPV stands for *Centrum Pedagogického Výzkumu* – Educational Research Centre – see Janík et al. 2009) draws on this idea. Its main purpose is to prepare student teachers for the demands of teaching practice by providing just such a low-risk environment. CPV videoweb is an e-learning environment consisting of short video clips of classroom situations supplemented by other materials, various questions and tasks. It is being developed at the Faculty of Education of the Masaryk University in Brno and is divided into different thematic areas. The main aim is to help student teachers develop their observational skills and so be better prepared for what happens in a real classroom.

The other, no less important, function of CPV videoweb is producing research data. As students work their way through answering the questions and dealing with the tasks, data for further research is generated.

To make such an environment work, the structure needs to be thoroughly thought through and firmly based in theory. The theoretical framework underlying CPV videoweb rests on four pillars:

- Reflective practitioner theory
- Observation period as silent phase in teacher education
- Using video for cases in teacher education
- Cognitive-load theory

This paper seeks to introduce the theoretical background of CPV Videoweb, a video-based online learning environment. First, these four pillars that inform the idea of CPV Videoweb will be introduced, and then the practical implications will be discussed.

1.1 Reflective Practitioner Theory

The theory of reflective practitioner (see Schön 1983, 1987) rests on two basic constructs. The main characteristic of a professional is his *knowing-in-action*, i.e. "every competent practitioner can recognize phenomena ..., for which he cannot give a reasonably accurate or complete description" (Schön 1983, p. 49f.). A professional can also gain insight into his knowing-in-action by *reflection,* i.e. turning "thought back on action" (Schön 1983, p.10). This happens especially when things go very well or very badly and helps them perform better in the future. Teachers do not need to just look back at their own action, but also reflect on observed teaching and identify the similarities and differences with their own practice.

1.2 Observation period as a silent phase in teacher education

Research on teaching practice has shown that if the teaching practice stage comes too early (compare Wallace above) in the course of teacher education, it can be rather harmful. The approach to pupils and to innovative techniques might become wary and student teachers may look at teaching theory and research with suspicion. Furthermore, they might imitate the attitudes and behaviour of their cooperative teachers, which could lead to a limited variety of teaching strategies. Furthermore, cooperative teachers are often regarded as

dominant and overly prescriptive and tell students what to do, providing, of course, that they take their role seriously at all (for overview see Moriner-Dershimer and Leighfield 1995, p. 589f.).
These findings support the idea of including a stage of observation into teacher education, which is by no means new. RYS (1975) pinpoints the fact that observation helps future teachers not only get acquainted with classroom situations, but also develop an "observational feel" and consolidate the terminology they need to talk about teaching and learning. Student teachers also learn to describe, interpret and explain observed situations with the help of previously learned theories. DAY (1990) mentions similar points and highlights the fact that observations help student teachers conceptualise "what goes on in a (second language) classroom" (p. 43).
WAJNRYB (1992) likens the observation period in teacher education to the *silent phase* that is known from theories of second language acquisition (e.g. Krashen 1981). In this phase of acquiring a second language, learners are not asked to produce speech, but merely listen and absorb. The same goes for student teachers. In the observation period, which usually comes in the early phases of teacher education, they are free from the pressure of decision making and operating in a classroom and can look at the lesson from a range of different perspectives.

1.3 Using video cases in teacher education

Having established the importance of observation for teacher education, authors list a number of media through which observation can take place (see Wallace 1991, p. 63; Wajnryb 1992, p. 23). Apart from direct observation, the lists include video clips. These can be viewed and analysed in a seminar session, at home or online. Using video has a number of advantages over direct observation. Videos can be stopped and replayed many times; students' attention can be directed to small details that would otherwise go unnoticed. Putting the videos online can foster students' autonomy by allowing them to work at their own speed (Wuensch et al. 2008).
Mere watching, however, does not necessarily lead to desired outcomes. To promote students' reflection it is important to direct their attention in the requisite way. This can be done by transforming video clips into video cases, i.e. providing background information and tasks to accompany the video clips. This idea draws on ELLIS'S framework for describing teacher training activities (1990). She divides teacher training practices into experiential (actual teaching)

and awareness-raising (develop understanding of underlying principles). Awareness raising activities are a combination of different types of data and different types of tasks. The tasks Ellis lists are: comparing, preparing, evaluating, improving, adapting, listing, selecting, ranking, adding/completing, and rearranging.
Creating video cases follows findings from research, e.g. by VAN DEN BERG (2001): "Multimedia cases may lead to superficial information processing if students are not provided guidance in organising and structuring this type of learning". Thus it is important to stage the difficulty of the video cases so as not to overwhelm the student teachers. Classroom situations, thought captured on video, are still complex.

1.4 Cognitive-load theory

Cognitive-load theory (CLT) is a part of a larger class of limited capacity theories (Goldman 1991) and provides an important perspective on instruction. It is based on the assumption that working memory only has a limited capacity and instruction should be designed with this in mind.
Working memory can only hold about seven (plus or minus two) items or chunks of information at a time (Strickland 2001, p. 416). When processing information, this number can further decrease. On the other hand, the size and complexity of information appears to be unlimited (Sweller et al. 1998). Long-term memory has a limitless capacity. The information is organized in domain-specific knowledge structures known as schemata (Sweller et al. 1998). Schemata categorise information according to how it will be used and are acquired and automated through extensive practice. Their number and complexity makes a clear distinction between experts and novices. Schemata therefore have two functions: organisation of information in long-term memory and capacity expansion of working memory.
Cognitive load is the strain imposed on the cognitive resources of an individual. Of primary importance for instructional design is the cognitive load on working memory. According to CLT, if the cognitive load imposed on a learner in an activity is too high (i.e. the process of solution is too complex), there will be no cognitive resources left for the creating of schemata, which should be the primary focus of instruction.

2 Practical Implications

The first two pillars advocate the need to develop a video-based learning environment and put it into teacher education. The claim for introducing structured observations into teacher education was supported by theory as well as practice. The theory of reflective practitioner gives videoweb its purpose – preparing prospective teachers to be able to reflect on what they (or other teachers) do.
The second two pillars involve generally rather methodological considerations. Video cases allow a move away from simple one video/one question schema and use complex activities with a series of tasks, based not only on video clips, but also on other relevant data (lesson transcripts, textbook extracts, student work, etc.). The nature of video cases lends itself to incorporating into a video-based learning environment where relevant materials can be studied and videos watched multiple times at students' own speed.
Creating the cases and structuring the videoweb is informed by cognitive-load theory. Firstly, we identify the goal of videoweb to be promoting of the creation of schemata. This will help the student teachers on their way from novices to experts. Secondly, we will bear in mind students' cognitive capacity and design the cases in such a way that will reduce extraneous cognitive load and promote the creation of schemata.

3 Conclusion

In this paper we have introduced the basic considerations and pressupositions that were used during the development of CPV videoweb and put them together in a structured theoretical framework. The aim of the paper was to introduce the theoretical background of the practical development of videoweb at the Faculty of Education of Masaryk University in Brno.

References

DAY, R. R.: Teacher observation in second language teacher education. In Richards, J.C. and Nunan D. (Eds). Second Language Teacher Education. Cambridge: Cambridge University Press, 1990, p. 43-62.

ELLIS, R.: Activities and Procedures for Teacher Training. In Rossner, R. and Bolitho, R. (Eds). Currents of Change in English Language Teaching. Oxford: Oxford University Press, 1990, pp. 226-235.

GOLDMAN, S.R.: On the Derivation of Instructional Applications from Cognitive Theories: Commentary on Chandler and Sweller. In: Cognition and Instruction, 1991, vol. 8, is. 4, pp. 333-342.

JANÍK, T. et al.: Exploring different ways of using video in teacher education: Examples from CPV Video Web. In T. Janík a T. Seidel (Eds.). The power of video studies in investigating teaching and learning in the classroom. Münster: Waxmann, 2009, s. 207-224.

KRASHEN, S.: Second Language Acquisition and Second Language Learning. Pergamon, 1981.

MORINE-DERSHIMER, G., LEIGHFIELD, K. Student Teaching and Field Experience. In Anderson, L.W. (Ed). International Encyclopedia of Teaching and Teacher Education, 2nd Edition. Oxford, New York, Tokyo: Elsevier Science, 1995.

RYS, S.: Hospitace v pedagogické praxi. Praha: SPN, 1975. [Observation in Teaching Practice].

SCHÖN, D. A.: The Reflective Practitioner. London: Basic Books, 1983.

SCHÖN, D. A. Educating the Reflective Practitioner. San Francisco: Jossey-Bass Inc., 1987.

STRICKLAND, B. R. (Executive editor): Gale Encyclopedia of Psychology, 2nd Edition. Detroit: Gale Group, 2001.

SWELLER, J., VAN MERRIËNBOER, J. J. J., PAAS, F.: Cognitive Architecture and Instructional Design. In: Educational Psychology Review, 1998, vol. 10, pp. 251-291.

VAN DEN BERG, E.: An Exploration of the Use of Multimedia Cases as a Reflective Tool in Teacher Education. In: Research in Science Education, 2001, vol. 31, p. 245-265.

WAJNRYB, R.: Classroom Observation Tasks (A resource book for language teachers and trainers). Cambridge: Cambridge University Press, 1992.

WALLACE, M.J. Training Foreign Language Teachers (A Reflective Approach). Cambridge: Cambridge University Press, 1991.

WUENSCH, K. L., SHAHNAZ, A., OZAN, E. KISHORE, M., TABRIZI, M. H .N. Pedagogical Characteristics of Online and Face-to-Face Classes. In: International Journal on E-Learning, 2008, vol. 7, is. 3, pp. 523-532.

Contact:
Eva MINAŘÍKOVÁ: eminarikova@seznam.cz

Constructing New Classroom Models in a Teacher Education Course

Nada Vojtkova and Rita Collins
Masaryk University, Dep. of English Language and Literature, Czech Republic

With the goal to provide novice teachers with opportunities to develop skills and knowledge applicable to conditions in the classrooms they soon would be entering, two university teachers integrated their courses using innovative approaches. The trainees in this third year integrated course, which covered teaching methodologies and English (Practical Language), learned about educational theories, tried various methods and reflected critically on new ideas. By using activities such as learning centres, microteaching and dialogue journals, the participants in the course were able to ground their learning in an experienced reality and build conceptual structures that were applicable to their future teaching careers. Based on concepts from constructivist pedagogy, the teachers designed the course to allow trainees to deepen their understanding of learning while exploring elements of teaching within a structured environment.

Key words: innovative approaches in foreign language learning, integrated course, learning centre, microteaching, dialogue journal

1 Introduction

As teacher educators, we want novice teachers to have the skills and knowledge that will enable them to respond to their world and the reality of the 21st century. We also want them to teach in their classrooms in a meaningful way. Aware of the ideas contained within constructivism as a theory of learning (Yilmaz 2008, p. 168), we structured an integrated course of Methodology of Teaching English and Practical Language (English) at a Central European university to provide trainees with an environment where they could study theories, experience methods, reflect on their experiences, apply their ideas and improve their language proficiency.

This paper begins with an overview of constructivism and its application within a teacher education program. This will establish the rationale for why and how we structured the integrated course. Our goal was to have trainees complete the course having developed their thinking, knowledge and views about teacher effectiveness.

2 Constructivism in Education

The concept of constructivism has been discussed by a range of individuals from PIAGET to VYGOTSKY and FRIERE. Summarizing these ideas, YILMAZ (2008, p. 162) concluded "knowledge is not passively received from the world or from authoritative sources but constructed by individuals or groups making sense of their experiential worlds". YILMAZ (2008, p. 163) also pointed out that constructivism is not "a single or unified theory; rather it is characterized by plurality and multiple perspectives". GORDON (2008, p. 324) defined the constructivist approach to education as one where learners "actively create, interpret, and reorganize knowledge in individual ways". BRUNER (1996, p. 19), one of the earlier proponents of constructivism, maintained that "reality construction is the product of meaning making shaped by traditions and by a culture's toolkit of ways of thought".

How is the theory of constructivism manifested in a classroom? CHRENKA (2001, p. 694) described it as a student-centered process where, with the support of a teacher, learners are able to "select and transform information, construct hypotheses, and make decisions". CHRENKA (2001, p. 694) stressed the importance of the teacher's role to provide scaffolding in the learning process as students become "aware, deliberate and responsible participants in the seeming chaos and disorder of the postmodern world". Within the context of teacher education, MARLOWE and PAGE (2005, p. 7ff.) developed four principles concerning the role of constructivism:

Constructivist learning is about

- constructing knowledge, not receiving it;
- understanding and applying, not recall;
- thinking and analyzing, not accumulating and memorizing;
- being active not passive.

Although there has been some controversy over the applicability of constructivism in education, the development of this theory over time and its recognition and implementation in classrooms has demonstrated its value. SEGALL (2002) stressed that it is necessary for teacher education programs to move beyond the traditional, instrumentalist approach, which hampers novice teachers' ability to adapt to changing conditions in schools. Understanding the value of helping trainees to construct their own reality as they go through a teacher education program, we applied the ideas from constructivist pedagogy in our integrated course.

3 Within an Integrated Class Context

The course was a combination of two courses, Practical Language and Methodology of Teaching English that were integrated, meaning a class that met weekly for three-hour blocks was taught by two teachers (Vojtkova was the Methodology teacher and Collins was the Practical Language teacher) with common materials, activities and assessment. The course integration contributed to a greater variety of educational context and the new model provided richer material for analysis. Our trainees were third year students in a Bachelor single-subject teacher education program preparing to be English teachers at the primary level. Some of them had teaching experience, while others had not taught previously. Their overall English level was quite good (C1 according to the Common European Framework of Reference). Our aim was to provide an experiential learning environment in which the trainees would construct their own meanings and concepts concerning teaching. We wanted them to have a strong theoretical background in teaching English as a foreign language and we also wanted the trainees to be willing to take risks, to develop a fluid concept of curriculum and to experience a range of learning modes (Cohen, Lesnick & Himeles 2007).

In the course design we applied the constructivist pedagogy at different levels. As we wanted to meet our trainees' expectations of a university course, we used some traditional ways of providing input (mini-lectures and reading assignments) while also offering innovative ways of learning (learning centers and LMS Moodle forums).

The whole course was topic-based, corresponding to the Methodology syllabus. For each topic one of the teachers prepared a short mini-lecture in which they either emphasized the topic or the language. For example, when dealing with teaching grammar the trainees listened to a podcast about teaching grammar and did listening comprehension tasks based on its content. They were able to gain new vocabulary and discuss the topic afterwards. There were set readings for each topic on Moodle, which the trainees were asked to have read prior to the class session. The trainees' English was enhanced through this reading, writing (electronic forums, dialogue journals and annotated bibliography), listening (podcasts and mini-lectures) and extensive speaking during class activities.

The teachers also modeled good language use, not only using English throughout the class but at times explaining word choice or construction.

We wanted the trainees to experience active learning methods, which is why we used learning centers as a regular classroom activity. During each class session, there were three learning centers that trainees passed through in twenty-minute rotations. Two centers were facilitated by the teachers and one was facilitated by a trainee. The tasks for the centers included microteaching and giving feedback on teaching, discussing educational issues such as teacher roles and values, and teaching grammar.

A trainee would also facilitate a group formation activity at the beginning of each class. The aim of group formation was to divide the class into three groups in preparation for the learning centers and to promote better group dynamics. Our rationale for using these various activities was that if the trainees experienced innovative methods as learners they would be more likely to use them later as teachers. Also the experience of leading a learning center or developing a group formation activity allowed the trainees to be active and to apply what they had gained from the mini-lectures and readings, which is integral to constructivist pedagogy.

We believe that good teachers develop through practice, reflection and critical thinking. Reflection and critical thinking are not innate qualities, but need to be developed in the same way as other teaching skills. We used dialogue journals as a regular part of our course. Trainees wrote into their journals at the end of each session for ten minutes. The teachers replied to these entries outside of class. At the beginning of the course, the reflection was mostly initiated by teachers' questions but later the trainees became skilful and initiated the reflection themselves.

Critical thinking was fostered in numerous ways including methodology discussions, feedback sessions and electronic forums. The learning centers were an excellent method for providing students space to talk in small groups, and to question and reflect on their experiences and the roles of a teacher.

Trainees appreciated the microteaching in learning centers as an introduction into teaching in a safe and supportive environment; however, they needed the experience of teaching in a real school. Each trainee arranged to spend time in a school under a mentor teacher, observing and then teaching. Their practice teaching was observed or videotaped and they were able to discuss their experience and receive written feedback from the methodology teacher. This gave them an opportunity to analyze their experiences, making sense of what occurred and the students' reactions.

4 Conclusion

As teacher educators, we feel it is imperative to provide novice teachers with the skills and knowledge needed to be effective and to teach in a meaningful way. We structured the integrated course based on aspects of constructivism that included active participation, analysis, reflection and knowledge construction. During the course, the trainees had support, materials, models and feedback. We encouraged them to experiment with their own teaching in a variety of ways and gave them opportunities to discuss their ideas, values and experiences. The course contained some traditional methods that were known to the trainees such as lectures as well as innovative methods such as learning centers and dialogue journals, which required the trainees to expand their educational repertoire and to take risks.

We realize that this is just the beginning of developing a teacher education program that fully meets the needs of novice teachers and their potential employers. Twenty years ago GOODLAD (1990, p. 265) pointed out that the "rush to cram it all into the limited time available in teacher education programs appeared to abort the emergence of sustained inquiry and reflection".

We hope our integrated course is a step towards providing the trainees with opportunities for inquiry and reflection.

Bibliography

BRUNER, Jerome: The Culture of Education.- Cambridge, Massachusetts: Harvard University Press, 1996.

COHEN, Jody, LESNICK, Alice, & HIMELES, Darla: "Temporary Anchors, Impermanent Shelter: Can the Field of Education Model a New Approach to Academic Work?" In: Journal of Research Practice. 3(2)/2007, p. 1-21.

CHRENKA, Lynn: "Constructivism and the Role of the Teacher: Misconstructing Constructivism. In: Phi Delta Kappan, 82(9)/2001, p. 694.

GOODLAD, John: Teachers for Our Nation's Schools. - San Francisco: Jossey-Bass, 1990.

GORDON, Mordechai: "Between Constructivism and Connectedness." In: Journal of Teacher Education. 59(4)/2008, p. 322-331.

MARLOWE, Bruce & PAGE, Marilyn: Creating and Sustaining the Constructivist Classroom. – Thousand Oaks, CA: Corwin Press, 2005.

RUSSELL, Tom, MCPHERSON, Suzin, & MARTIN, Andrea: "Coherence and Collaboration in Teacher Education Reform." In: Canadian Journal of Education, 26(1)/2001, p. 37-55.

SEGALL, Avner: Disturbing Practice: Reading Teacher Education as Text. - New York: Peter Lang, 2002.

YILMAZ, Kaya: "Constructivism: Its Theoretical Underpinnings, Variations, and Implications for Classroom Instruction." In: Educational Horizons. 86(3)/2008, p. 161-172.

Contact:
Nada VOJTKOVA: nada.vojtkova@gmail.com
Rita COLLINS: M.Ed. Ed.D.: collinsrita@yahoo.com

Expert's Opinion: Doc. Mgr. Světlana Hanušová, Ph. D.

ARE YOU ASKING THE RIGHT QUESTION? INTERLOCUTOR TRAINING FOR HIGHER SECONDARY SCHOOL TEACHERS TOWARDS STANDARDISED LEAVING EXAM IN THE CZECH REPUBLIC

Marie Doskočilová, Eva Složilová, Milan Kubiatko,
Masaryk University Brno, Czech Republic

In 2011, the new concept of a standardised leaving examination will be implemented in the Czech Republic. For higher-secondary teachers, this introduces a new challenge of standardised language testing, a field that has so far not been adequately tackled by either educators themselves or Czech academia. Apart from comprehending specific language testing theories, there has arisen a need for practical training of teachers to provide them with ample competencies and strategies in order to both carry out an oral exam and, at the same time, apply standardised assessment. This paper focuses on highlighting the demands and challenges that teachers are facing as well as introducing a new project of tester training focused on helping interlocutors-to-be to acquire necessary testing skills.

Key words: tester training, standardised leaving exam, assessment, interlocutor, rater

1 Conducting a Standardised Oral Exam: Theoretical Background And Recent Findings

The theory and practice of assessing second language speaking skill is the youngest subfield of language testing (Fulcher, 2003, p. 1). About 50 years ago LADO (1961, p. 239) stated that testing speaking in a foreign language was insufficiently developed and practised. Research done over the last 20 years has managed to shed some more light on our understanding of what speaking is and what testing it comprises.

To communicate effectively in a foreign language in a test situation, an examinee needs to respond appropriately to what has been said and fulfil their communicative tasks. Their characteristic features and dispositions are also reflected in their performance. However, what they say does not depend entirely on their own abilities, skills and personal characteristics. Many other variables come into play, one of those being the role and performance of the interlocutor.

Interlocutors may differ along a range of parameters that introduce variation into the speaking test, which may affect scores. BROWN (2003, p. 3) mentions the following aspects: the level of rapport that they establish with the candidate; their functional and topical choices; the way in which they ask questions and construct prompt; the extent to which or the ways in which they accommodate their speech to that of the candidate; the ways in which they develop and extend topics. The nature of interlocutor variability has been the focus of considerable recent research interest, for example, in MCNAMARA and LUMLEY (1997, p. 141). LAZARATON (1996) investigated the types of linguistic and interactional support that the native interlocutor provides to the non-native examinee in a one-to-one interview. Results of her study indicate there were 8 types of interlocutor support prevalent in the corpus of 58 CASE (Cambridge Assessment of Spoken English) interviews: priming topics (interlocutors cue examinees on the topic of a question before it is asked); supplying vocabulary or engaging in collaborative completion; giving evaluative responses; echoing and/or correcting response; repeating questions with slowed speech; increased pausing and over-articulation; stating question prompts as statements that merely require confirmation; drawing conclusions for candidates and rephrasing questions. However, their impact on examinees' ratings is unclear. She suggests that rater training should focus on the variable aspect of interlocutor support to make the interactions more similar.

BROWN (2003) addresses the issue of variation among two interlocutors in eliciting qualitatively different samples of communicative competence of the same examinee, its impact on the examinee's performance and, consequently, the raters' perceptions of the two performances. She raises the issue of adequacy of interlocutor training and re-accreditation in interaction-based tests but she does not suggest what form it should or might take. FULCHER (2003, p. 149) explains this by the fact that interlocutor training has not been undertaken as seriously, or for as long, as rater training. At the same time, the score variation associated with raters has been known about for much longer than that associated with interlocutors.
ROSS (1992) analyses 16 oral proficiency interviews and concludes that perceptions of oral proficiency are reflected in the extent of interviewer accommodation which, on the one hand provides a significant factor in assessing oral proficiency, and, on the other, indicates a significant criterion for interlocutor training. The analysis of interview type tasks showed how the interlocutor accommodated to the level of the test taker. It has been suggested that when assessing the oral production, the degree of accommodation should be considered as well, and thus the role of the interlocutor in co-constructing the discourse should be explicitly taken into account.
FULCHER (2003, p. 148) cites BERWICK and ROSS (1996, pp. 50f.) who distinguish the following features of accommodation: display questions, comprehension check, clarification request, or-question, fronting, grammatical, slow-down, over-articulation, other explanation and lexical simplification. As the extent to which the interlocutor provides support might vary, the test-taking conditions are often incomparable for each examinee. The interlocutor training should include practising various degrees and forms of accommodation and support and at the same time eliminate unnecessary support that might lead to scores being affected.
The accommodation issue has introduced the problem of interactional competence and the co-construction of talk. Interactional competence is most often defined … in terms of how speakers structure speech, its sequential organization and turn-taking rules, sometimes including strategies (Fulcher 2003, p. 44). The understanding of speech as co-constructed in all its forms is based on the assumption that individuals do not speak alone, but that performances are constructed with others, or co-constructed (Fulcher 2003, p. 45).

The interlocutor training whose necessity and background have been substantiated by numerous research activities is crucial. Lack of it is perceived by some testing organizations as a shortcoming. This lack can be compensated for by various checklists of tips for good interlocutor behaviour. To mention at least one of them, we need to cite FULCHER (2003, p. 150f.) who considers the advice to interlocutors as demonstrated in the British Council's VOTE Oral Testing Video a particularly good example of interlocutor training. This advice is formulated in "don't do" statements *(Don't correct the test taker when they make mistakes, don't speak too quickly, don't whisper, cover your mouth, or mumble, don't speak too much, don't be condescending, don't be offensive, don't engage in other activities during the test, maintain eye contact with the test taker)*. Nonetheless, this concept can be understood as a general guideline, not as actual interlocutor training.

2 Interlocutor Training Towards a Standardised Leaving Exam in the Czech Republic

As far as the situation in the Czech Republic s concerned, in compliance with *"Maturita"* [Leaving Exam] Regulation 177/2009 (Act 561/2004 Coll. as amended by Act 49/2009 Coll.), the new standardised leaving exam will be conducted by two examiners called *assessor-interlocutor* and *assessor-observer.* Since their responsibility primarily lies in being able to assess in compliance with the *Assessment Criteria,* all examiners are obliged to hold a certificate issued by CERMAT[10] entitling them to conduct the exam. However, most of the both on-line and in-class education towards the new leaving exam focuses primarily on the examiner's ability to assess the candidate rather than to conduct the oral exam as such. Therefore, the "Interlocutor – tester training" project has been developed as an answer to the demand for professional interlocutors and in order to school certified assessors in the art and skill of carrying out an oral exam.

As mentioned above, the *assessor–observer* fully depends and relies on the performance of the *assessor–interlocutor,* since the actual results of the oral exam can only be reliable when it is conducted in a standardised and flawless manner. The project introduced in this paper is only one of the many training sessions

[10] CERMAT: The Centre on Measurement in Education: an institution financed partly by the Czech Ministry of Education, partly by ESF, responsible for the preparation of the new standardised leaving exam tests.

offered to higher secondary teachers and is designed to help them acquire and practise testing skills. This methodical support is originally designed for testers of English as a foreign language, but can nevertheless be adapted for utilisation in the area of testing other foreign languages as well. The project is primarily aimed at the fourth part of the oral exam – the role play, with the potential to convey the acquired skills to the remaining three parts of the exam (immediate response, comparing and contrasting pictures and monologue on a given topic).

To identify the main shortcomings to focus on, 26 video recordings of pilot simulations of the oral exam were analysed qualitatively. The following list presents the key mistakes made by interlocutors, both native English speakers and Czech teachers of EFL[11].

echoing student's answers
yes – no questions
framing/inducing student's answers
drawing conclusions for candidates
wrong formulation of questions
multiple questions asked at once
inability to rephrase questions

lack of accommodation
interlocutor's restlessness
mistakes (grammar, phonetics, lexis)
irresponsiveness
inappropriate familiarity
excessive formality
posture

Due to the time limitations of teachers, there are two available versions: a one-day intensive and two-day in-depth course. As depicted in the schemes below, the principle axis of the interlocutor training is the actual drill of the interlocutor skills on the basis of analysis of selected sections of the video recordings representing the most common mistakes. The performance of trainees will be recorded on video so as to provide a study material, as well as a resource for their further self-evaluation.

Trainees work together at first to grasp the essential theory of conducting oral exams as well as recognise possible challenging areas in an interlocutor's performance. Only then are they divided into two groups in separate rooms (T1 and T2), and each of the trainees attempts to conduct a five-minute role play to be recorded on a video. Tutors serve as interviewees, purposefully accommodating fully to the tested levels B1 and B2[12]. The structure of day one only

[11] EFL: English as a Foreign Language
[12] as defined in the CEFR

differs at the end of the session when the one-day course trainees analyse the video recordings together in a group with both tutors while the two-day course trainees analyse them separately. Group T1 analyses the recordings of group T2 and vice versa. Those who plan to continue the next day are provided with the recordings of themselves to analyse their own performance as homework. After brief revision of the knowledge acquired during the previous day, day two focuses centrally on the interlocutor training and practising the actual interlocutor's skills. At the end of this session, trainees will be videoed again and then provided with both recordings (day one and the end-of-course ones) for further analysis and evaluation of their performance and the progress they have made so far.

This project is designed as a partial contribution to the ongoing debate on the necessity of tester training in general, and particularly to the recent shift of focus towards interlocutor training.

References

BERWICK, R., ROSS, S.: Cross-cultural pragmatics in oral proficiency interview strategies. In Milanovic, M., Saville, N. (Eds.) Performance testing, Cognition and Assessment. Selected papers from the 15th Language Testing Research Colloquium. Cambridge: Cambridge University Press, 1996. s. 34-54.

BROWN, A. Interviewer variation and the co-construction of speaking proficiency. In Language Testing. 2003. roč. 20, s. 1-25. [online], [cit. 16.5. 2007]. URL: http://ltj.sagepub.com/cgi/content/abstract/20/1/1

BYGATE, M.: Speaking. Oxford: Oxford University Press, 1987.

FULCHER, G.: Testing Second Language Speaking. Pearson Education Limited: London, 2003.

HALLECK, G.: Symposium article: Data generation through role-play: Assessing oral proficiency. In Simulation & Gaming. 2007. roč. 38, s. 91-106. [online], [cit. 21.4. 2008]. URL: http://sag.sagepub.com/cgi/reprint/38/1/31

LAZARATON, A.: Interlocutor support in oral proficiency interview: the case of CASE. In Language Testing. 1996. roč. 13, s. 151-172. [online], [cit. 16.5. 2007]. URL: http://ltj.sagepub.com/cgi/content/abstract/13/2/151

LUOMA, S.: Assessing speaking. Cambridge: Cambridge University Press, 2004.

Vyhláška: 177/2009, 561/2004 Sb. po novele zákonem č. 49/2009 Sb. [online], [cit.20.2.2010].
URL: http://www.novamaturita.cz/lkolsky-zakon-a-vyhlaska-1404033137.html.

MCNAMARA, T.F., LUMLEY, T.: The effect of interlocutor and assessment mode variables in overseas assessments of speaking skills in occupational settings. In Language Testing. 1997. roč. 14, s. 140-156. [online], [cit. 22.10. 2007].
URL: http://ltj.sagepub.com/cgi/content/abstract/14/2/140

ROSS, S.: Accommodative questions in oral proficiency interviews. In Language Testing. 1992. roč. 9, s. 173-185. [online], [cit. 26.11. 2007].
URL: http://ltj.sagepub.com/cgi/content/abstract/9/2/173

Contact:
Mgr. Marie DOSKOČILOVÁ: doskocilova.marie@gmail.com
PhDr. Eva SLOŽILOVÁ, M.A.: slozilova.eva@gmail.com
PaeDr. Milan KUBIATKO, Ph.D.: kubiatko@ped.muni.cz

TEACHING ENGLISH TO PRIMARY SCHOOL PUPILS: A NECESSITY, A CHALLENGE OR A BURDEN?

Rumyana Todorova, Zlatko Todorov
Konstantin Preslavsky University of Shumen, Bulgaria

Teaching foreign languages to Primary School pupils has been introduced quite recently. The Bulgarian Ministry of Education has decided that it is a necessity for small children to begin studying foreign languages at an early age. It has its positive as well as negative sides. The paper presents these aspects as well as some perspectives ensuing from this challenge. Apart from this, some ideas are brought to the fore which are closely connected with the practical part of the question, namely some facts about pre-school (kindergarten – 4- to 5-year olds) and primary (5- to 8-year olds) education are presented to support what has been stated.

Key words: English in primary education, early foreign language learning, pre-school, kindergarten

1 Theoretical background

Foreign language acquisition is an important factor leading to a well-balanced and culturally grounded school education. Bulgaria, already a full member of the European Union and an active participant in all educational processes taking place in Europe, strives for unifying the existing educational systems and bringing them in line with European standards. That was one of the reasons for the Ministry of Education to introduce early foreign language teaching from grade 2 in 2002/3. It posed a lot of problems since there are some psychological and pedagogical specificities of children at this age group (7- to 8-year olds) which should have been taken into consideration. Up to year 2002/3 there were some optional classes in which English was mainly taught but there were not any requirements which should have been followed. Another problem was the lack of enough trained foreign language teachers for that specific age group. Early foreign language acquisition puts an emphasis not so much on the acquisition of the language than on the fact that pupils should be aware of the existence of other cultures and should develop competencies for intercultural communication along with the development of their intellectual and linguistic abilities (see Parapulska 2001, pp. 33-36).

2 Aspects of early foreign language learning

According to most researchers in the field of psychology, children up to ten years of age have the intellectual abilities and emotional drive for acquiring foreign languages. As for physiological arguments, some neurologists claim that the capacity of a year to a nine year old child's brain is such that children can remember information much more easily; so, that is the perfect time for them to start studying a foreign language together with the acquisition of their mother tongue. W. PENFIELD, for example, was a proponent of bilingualism from childhood onward (see http://en.wikipedia.org/wiki/Wilder_Penfield). According to R. STOICHKOV, small children can acquire skills for learning from an early age and this can be achieved through the study of a foreign language (Stoichkov 2005, pp. 22-23).

The aim of foreign language learning in the 1970s was for small pupils to learn how to communicate using the language. Since the 1990s the aim has been multiculturally oriented, i.e. communication across cultures through the foreign language. One may wonder how that is possible with the little store of knowledge small children at kindergartens and primary education level have. However, they can be taught very simple but important things, e.g. how to greet their peers, elderly people or their teachers and parents; what polite language to use when asking for some help or favour, etc.

There are cognitive, emotional and pragmatic aspects in learning a foreign language at an early age. Apart from learning English, children are emotionally open for finding out things they do not know about other people in other countries, what their peers from these countries have for breakfast, how they celebrate their holidays, and so on and so forth. Only when a person has learned something about a certain way of life by constantly comparing it with information he/she has about their own standards and norms, only then are they ready for intercultural communication. The pragmatic aspect is related to the reason why pupils should learn the foreign language, namely, that in order for them to be familiar with the other children's culture and to communicate with them they should know the other children's language (see Hubenova 2002, pp. 15-19).

Early foreign language learning corresponds to the Common European Framework (CEF) of Reference for Languages introduced in 1998 (see http://www.coe.int/T/DG4/Portfolio/documents/case_studies_CEF.doc). Its parameters are: multilingual communicative competence; life-long language education; constructing curricula; and achieving partial competence for various education goals. In the CEF some case studies are presented and one of them is related to Finnish education at primary level. It gives a clear picture of what exactly stands at the core of early foreign language learning:

'At the primary level (ages 7-12), Finnish children start learning a foreign language at the age of eight or nine (grade 3). Their ways of learning are strongly influenced by the individual stages of their mental development: young learners are still very holistic and concrete in their ways of thinking and learning; they are not able to approach learning analytically and what is more, in an abstract way. Therefore, in the beginning, the teaching of the first foreign language has to be strongly action-based' (op. cit. pp. 42-43; see also Shopov 2002, p. 116).

One of the prerequisites for children to start learning a foreign language is that at the age between 5 and 10 children are very good imitators, which is brilliant for the acquisition of the foreign language. They can acquire native speakers' pronunciation and intonation to the greatest extent without feeling embarrassment and frustration that they sound somehow odd. Another advantage is that children's cognitive abilities can be developed for both the mother tongue and the foreign language simultaneously.

If we have to sum up the aims of early FLL, we can say that young learners of English should be able to: understand short adapted and abridged texts while listening to them; communicate using simple sentences and phrases; understand the main idea while reading short texts; and use glossaries, tables and graphs that go with their course books.
One of the disadvantages at this stage of people's development is that young learners are easily distracted and cannot be concentrated for a long time. That is the reason why they should be taught the language by using games with a lot of motion and action.

4 Games for young learners of English

We are not going to focus our attention on different theories about games and on various types of games because most academics doing research in this field are well acquainted with both. What matters is that humans of all ages like playing all sorts of games (see Todorova 2008). It is not instincts but drives that are at play. Games are played for pleasure not by necessity. They develop human thinking and imagination. Last but not least, games have an educational role because they are played by following certain rules, something connected with discipline. According to J. HEUSINGA and M. I. GUREVICH games are the driving force of human progress. One of the most important components in games is related to curiosity (see http://www.springerlink.com/content/v716822w28380981/). Language games correspond to the emotional state of pupils and this is something which is in unison with their age group characteristics and interests. Games stimulate children's cognitive activities and provide easier acquisition of language material as young learners do something they like most of all, enjoy it and feel pleasure and fun from it. Games provide entertainment together with learning the language and things about the world and children feel satisfaction from what they are doing because they perform different activities in a relaxed atmosphere and without any stress. Teachers at pre-school and primary-education level teach children not only the language material but the so-called "soft" skills, communicative skills being some of them. Children can be creative enough even though they follow certain rules; they get constant feedback from their teachers, which increases their self-confidence and motivation. Good conduct in games aims at solving various problems, something young learners do subconsciously. In most cases games are about creating a product, either concrete or abstract. What is more, children have to react accordingly and consider subsequent moves at every single moment, which means that they should be concentrated enough if they or their team want to win the game.

Most games imitate real-life situations and in this respect the child learns how to react in similar situations in every-day circumstances.

Games have a competitive nature. This side of games can have positive as well as negative effects on children. There might be children who are always losers and children who always win. In this respect, it is not easy at all for teachers of a foreign language to decide what games to use, when to use them and in what order and participation. It all has to do with the psychology of games and the re-grouping of young learners at the same time.

Something not many teachers do while using games in the FL classroom is evaluate the process of playing games as well as the results of the game. Something that matters a lot for young learners' education.

There are different classifications of games used in the FL classroom but the most common among them is that there are 3 types: role plays, didactic games and language games.

They are all used in internationally recognized exams, one of them being PTE (Pearson Test of English, former London Test of English) for Young Learners. The format of the exam is in accordance with the age group characteristics, i.e. in the form of games. Though the exam is an hour long, having in mind the fact that children's attention is unstable, examiners are advised to stop the exam for a while, take the children out of the room the exam is taking place in, play other games with them in another room and then take them back to the room so that children can go on with the exam. In this case it has turned out that the duration of the exam is not a problem at all.

5 Conclusion

Games in FLT are a necessity, but they are definitely a challenge. They are social activities which teach children to do things not only on their own but in a group/team, which means that they have to show consideration for others. We as humans are inclined to think in frames. With games situations differ each time a game is played and thus children react differently each time. And yet, if there are too many games in the FL classroom children will lose interest in them, get lazy and their motivational role will be brought to an end, so, in this respect games become a burden for the young learners as well as for the teacher.

References

HUBENOVA, M: "Foreign language Teaching at Primary School – Intercultural Communication Education" (in Bulgarian). In: Nachalno obrazovanie, No 4-5/2002, 15-19.

JOHNSON, K./MORROW, K.: Communication in the Classroom. Application and Methods for a Communicative Approach. London: Longman. 1981.

DOBSON, J.: Effective Techniques for English Conversation Groups. Newbury House Publishers. 1974.

MCCALLUM, G. P.: 101 Word Games: For Students of English as a Second or Foreign Language. USA: Oxford University Press, 1980.

MARTIN, C.: Games and fun activities. London: CILT, 1995.

WRIGHT, A./BETTERIDGE, D./BUCKBY, M.: Games for Language Learning. Cambridge: Cambridge University Press, 1994.

PARAPULSKA, Y.: "Foreign Language Teaching at Primary School" (in Bulgarian). In: Nachalno uchilishte, VIII, No 6/2001, 33-36.

SHOPOV, T.: Foreign Language Methodology (in Bulgarian). Sofia: Kliment Ohridski Univ. Press, 2002.

STOICHKOV, R.: "Foreign Language at Primary School – a New Beginning" (in Bulgarian). In: Nachalno obrazovanie, No 4/2005, 22-23.

TODOROVA, R.: "Advertisements – Games for Young and Old, but Mostly for Advanced" (in Bulgarian). In: Episkop Konstantinovi chetenia. Shumen, vol. 13. "Igri I igrachki". Shumen: Episkop Konstantin Preslavski Univ. Press. 2008. 110-116.

http://en.wikipedia.org/wiki/Wilder_Penfield
http://www.coe.int/T/DG4/Portfolio/documents/case_studies_CEF.doc
http://www.springerlink.com/content/v716822w28380981/

Contact:
Assoc. Prof. Rumyana TODOROVA, Ph. D.: r_todorova@yahoo.com
Zlatko TODOROV: zl_todorov@yahoo.com

TEACHER OF PHYSICAL EDUCATION AS AN EDUCATOR OF HEALTHY LIFESTYLE

Danuta Umiastowska, University of Szczecin, Poland

Concern for bettering the condition of Polish people should start with those of youngest age. So, changes in the base program of general education at Polish schools have been implemented. These changes resulted in a greater accent on healthy education. Within the framework of the physical education program, the contents of school lessons and obligatory optional exercises are realized. Four of these exercises have been implemented – in sport, recreation-health, dance and tourism. The main purpose of school physical education is the preparation of the pupil to undertake motor activity for his whole life and to get him used to the arrangement principles of a healthy lifestyle. In the presented work, the author has made an attempt to find an answer to the question: How teachers of physical education and other subjects are prepared to carry out health education?

Keywords: physical education, health education, healthy lifestyle, teachers of physical education

1 Introduction

In the opinion of CIEŚLIŃSKI „a teacher <today and tomorrow> is a humanist, educator and specialist, purposing skill to connect three directions of education and training: humanistic, pedagogic and professional. This kind of teacher knows that the crux of modern physical education embraces shaping of all zones of personality, and thus providing the pupil with instrumental and directional dispositions" (Cieśliński 1990, s. 106). In devising programmes for the preparation of physical education teachers for health education, there is a necessity to take into account that they have to be prepared not only to develop sport, but also to broadly understand how physical activity affects health whilst counteracting against its threats (Huk–Wieliczuk, Marcinkowski 2009).

The purpose of health education is to prepare a human for a role as an active member of democratic society, and allow him to independently or in a group undertake activities to create a healthy lifestyle and environment. This relies on developing competences from: knowledge, skills "to look" inside oneself, commitment and motivation, future vision and experiences achieved as real examples (Jansen 2009). In the opinion of B. WOYNAROWSKA health education is the entire process of people learning how to live to maintain and improve their own health and the health of the others, and in the case of disease or disability to participate actively in its treatment, and then, to cope with and diminish its negative consequences (Woynarowska 2007). However, A. KRAWAŃSKI determines health education as a pedagogic-social process, in which one can use the same methods and techniques as those used in social sciences, e.g. in pedagogy, psychology, sociology and others, to observe behavioural changes of a pro-healthy character in persons and social groups (Krawański 2003).

School health education is a synthesis of education and training, that is a process, in which a pupil will be equipped not only in knowledge, but can also be shaped by this process in directional and personal dispositions, proper attitudes, behaviours and needs.

A teacher of physical education as a promoter of health should then have an effect on his pupils in this way to persuade them to admit health as of superior value, to feel responsible for health and also to consciously aim at its maintenance at the time when the pupil leaves school, thanks to acquired knowledge and habits and the shaping of an affirmative attitude towards health. A program of health education should embrace not only the teacher of physical education, but also other teachers and the entire school community. An investment in health education at school and in a teacher of physical education undertaking health subject matter is fruitful for children's health – one of the essential elements of the school educational process. A school can then be an environment conducive to health only at that time when the teacher of physical education is a central character in the pupils' health education, realizing a health program in a regular and planned way; by this program pupils learn to care about their own health and health of the others.

From 2010, the obligatory general education programme basis opens a new stage for school health education in Poland. In the programme of health education, problems connected with the issue are separated, such as: personal and milieu hygiene, safety and administration of first aid, nutrition and nutritive habits, motoric activity and its using in leisure time, and education to live within a family and within a community. With each problem, two groups of content are separated:

- knowledge – what a pupil should know and understand
- skills and attitudes – what a pupil should be able to do and feel, how to make choices and how to justify them

In this work the author tries to find an answer to the question: *How are the teachers of physical education and other subjects prepared to carry out health education?*

2 Method and material

In this work, a method of diagnostic polling was used based on a research audience questionnaire (environmental). This research was carried out at the work place of the examined people (at school) and was anonymous in character. In this questionnaire, there have been closed, open and semi-open questions. The questionnaire concerns with the knowledge of respondents regarding the basic problems of health education. The research has been carried out at Szczecin City schools, in Poland, among 348 teachers of different subjects.

3 Results

The best mastered knowledge among teachers is knowledge of the proper body posture of pupils (96.7 %). Only 3.3 % of them declare a lack of knowledge in this problem (these are men, teachers of history and foreign language, and teachers with short work experience (from 0–5 years)). Teachers regularly correcting pupils' body posture are teachers of physical education, and among teachers of other subjects each third teacher does it "from time to time". From the respondents, 22.6 % are not aware of the effect in adults of insufficient prophylaxis regarding body posture failures in childhood. Analyzing answers of teachers of particular subjects, teachers of foreign language, religion, and history have a noticeable lack of knowledge in this area. All of them are in the two first age categories in terms of work experience (from 0-10 years). At a lower level, knowledge connected with proper nutritive habits is evaluated. Only 56.1 % of examined persons can enumerate elements of correct diet – to give the correct nutrition – and only 38.9% know how "the nutrition pyramid" is constructed. Definitely, a higher level of knowledge is presented by women (27.4%). There is also a low level of knowledge concerning first pre-medical aid. Persons without problems in "the nutrition pyramid" are in majority teachers of physical education and biology (64.5%). The rest of the respondents signal that they have not come into contact with the possibility of enlarging this kind of knowledge. The majority of teachers can properly describe the meaning of movement for organism function (73.2 % women and 68.3 % men), but admit that it is theoretical knowledge, because they are usually not physically active (86.5 % women and 78.6 % men). Only teachers of physical education (76.2% women and 64.8% men), integrated teaching (36.8 % women), and biology (36.8 % women) declare that they know how to transmit the essence of health education in their lessons (there are no men among teachers of biology and integrated teaching). What is difficult for many teachers is carrying out of exercises discussing the preparation of pupils for caring about their health and enlightenment and the importance of this value for lifestyle (43.9 % women and 54.9 % men). Respondents declare a small range of disposition concerning activating methods. Only 17.5 % women and 13.8 % men use these kinds of methods during educational lessons or exercises with in their subject.

4 Discussion and conclusions

Research realized among teachers from Łódź City, in Poland, indicates that only 25.7 % of them have basic knowledge about dental traumatology and know how to give first aid immediately after an accident (Wochna-Sobańska et al. 2007). With the teachers from Gdańsk City, in Poland, 67.0 % declare they are well prepared to realize pro-health education (Lisicki, Wilk 1999). However, only 13.0% of students from the University School of Physical Education and Sport in Gdańsk City, who will be teachers in future, admit that they are prepared to fulfill the role of health teaching (Wilk 2006). According to the research among teachers from Częstochowa Town, in Poland, (25.0 % teachers of physical education, 19.4 % teachers of integrated teaching, 55.6 % teachers of other subjects) there is a clear will to compensate for a lack of methodical and essential knowledge in the area of health education. 58.8 % from this group would like to participate in courses, 3.0 % would like to undertake post-diploma study, and 22.5 % would like to participate in methodical work shops (Rodziewicz/Gruhn et al. 2006).

Returning to the results from the executed research the following conclusions can be formulated:

- Among Szczecin City teachers, those best prepared to realize health education are the teachers of physical education, biology and integrated teaching.
- The examined persons declare a low level of preparation in first pre-medical aid.

Therefore, to obtain better results in the realization of health education, teachers should be equipped with the following competences:

- knowledge of physical, psychic and psychomotoric education, prophylaxis of the most frequent health problems, health promotion;
- diagnostic skills of the pupil's needs, coordination of activities in health education at school, using methods and techniques of teaching which support the pupils' activity and motivate pupils' care of health;
- establishment of convictions about health as a value for a human being, about readiness to create patterns of health behaviour and activities for multiplication of health (Woynarowska 2008).

References

CIEŚLIŃSKI R.: Nauczyciel wychowania fizycznego jako animator wychowania zdrowotnego [A teacher of physical education as an animator of health education]. Wychowanie Fizyczne i Zdrowotne, 1990, 6, 106-108.

HUK-WIELICZUK E., MARCINKOWSKI J.T.: Uczelnie wyższe wychowania fizycznego wobec aktualnych potrzeb edukacji zdrowotnej [Universities of physical education towards actual problems of health education]. Probl Hig Epidemiol 2009, 90(4), 470-476.

JENSEN B.B.: Edukacja zdrowotna i demokracja [Health education and democracy]. Wychowanie Fizyczne i Zdrowotne 1994, 1: 22-25.

KRAWAŃSKI A.: Interaktywne uczenie się i nauczanie w wychowaniu fizycznym i fizjoterapii [Interactive learning and teaching in physical education an physiotherapy]. AWF, Poznań, 2003.

LISICKI T., WILK B.: Nauczyciele o swoich możliwościach realizacji programu edukacji prozdrowotnej [Teachers about their possibilities in realization of pro-healthful education program]. Akademia Wychowania Fizycznego, Gdańsk, 1999.

ODZIEWICZ-GRUHN J., PYZIK M., PILS W.: Realizacja ścieżki „Edukacja prozdrowotna" w opiniach nauczycieli różnych przedmiotów [Realization of a pathway "Pro-healthful education" in opinions of teachers of different subjects]. Roczniki PZH, 2006, 57, Suplement, 95–99.

WILK B.: Opinie studentów Akademii Wychowania Fizycznego i Sportu o swoim przygotowaniu do realizacji programu edukacji prozdrowotnej w szkole [Opinions of students of the University School of Physical Education and Sport about their preparation to realization of a pro-healthful education program at school]. Roczniki PZH, 2006, 57, Suplement, 43-46.

WOCHNA-SOBANSKA M. LUBOWIEDZKA-GONTAREK B., SZYDLOWSKA–WALENDOWSKA B.: Pierwsza pomoc w urazowych uszkodzeniach zębów u dzieci

– ocena wiedzy nauczycieli, pielęgniarek i rodziców [First aid in injury dental damages in children – an evaluation of knowledge in teachers, nurses and parents]. Zdrowie Publiczne, 2007, 117(2), 179-182.

WOYNAROWSKA B.: Edukacja zdrowotna [Health education]. PWN, Warszawa, 2007.

WOYNAROWSKA B.: Przygotowanie nauczycieli wychowania fizycznego do realizacji edukacji zdrowotnej [A preparation of physical education teachers to realization of healtheducation]. Wychowanie Fizyczne Zdrowotne, 2008, 10, 4-8.

Contact:
Danuta UMIASTOWSKA: umiastowscy@neostrada.pl

PUPILS' OPINIONS ON THEMSELVES AS AN EFFECT OF EDUCATIONAL WORK OF A TEACHER

Danuta Umiastowska, Ewa Szczepanowska, University of Szczecin, Poland

Being a tutor is one of the many important roles of each teacher. A teacher, besides passing on adequate knowledge, has the task of educating a pupil and preparing him/her/her to fulfill different life roles. Children who start the education process in Poland attend a program of integrated teaching for first three years. This program is usually run by one teacher. This period is very important in the child's development, because at that time attitudes towards school duty, activities in a team, and conscious participation in the learning process are shaped. There is much information about psychological development of a pupil in literature, and only a small amount of research discussing self-evaluation of an individual. In this research, using a questionnaire about children's lifestyle aged 9-10 years old, opinions of pupils on themselves were collected. The results obtained allow us to answer the research questions: What are the pupils' opinions of themselves? To what should teachers pay special attention in the educational process?

Keywords: self-evaluation, pupil's opinions, teacher profession, comparative study, questionnaire

1 Introduction

„*Self-evaluation* reflects an all-round relationship of a human to him/her/herself. It is a comparative relationship of different aspects of him/her/herself and his/her behaviour – emotional, intellectual, and social - with some patterns. This inventive approach to self-evaluation is a great determinant motivating a pupil to be active and allowing understanding of him/her/herself, and is an introduction to self-education. Moreover, at a further stage, it carries on to self-steering of the individual's development" (Umiastowska 2004, S. 75). *Self-evaluation* can be understood as the ability for independent comparison of actual status with that required or recognized as valuable (Botwiński 1985). In the theory of self-knowledge of KOZIELECKI, self-evaluation is a method for estimating opinions concerning specific human properties, such as physical features, exterior appearance, health, personal traits, inventive abilities, emotional maturity, motivational structure, relationships with other people, a place in a family and social attractiveness (Kozielecki 1981).

The preparation of pupil to accomplish these kinds of choices is an educational task for each teacher. Different situations in which a child participates at school and out of it require abilities of adaptation, and determination of his/her own role.

The aim of this study is to find an answer to the research question: *What are pupils' opinions of themselves? To what should teachers pay special attention in the educational process?*

2 Material and method

A group of 1026 pupils (544 girls and 482 boys), in nine randomly selected primary schools of Szczecin City (eight public and one non-public school) were studied. During the study, pupils were in their second year of education. The mean age of girls was 9.09, and boys 9.07. The research was realized within the framework of the international research project „Kinder heute – Bewegungsmuffel, Fast Food Junkies, Medienfreaks, Eine Lebensstialanalyse", carried out by Prof. Hans Peter BRANDL-BREDENBECK as the conductor from Deutsche Sporthochschule in Koeln. The work was realized collaterally in seven countries (Belorussia, Belgium, Lithuania, Germany, Poland, Switzerland and Italy). In the study the questionnaire on „Children's and youth lifestyle", worked out by a team of German authors, was used (Brandl-Bredenbeck et al. 2009). A method of diagnostic polling was used, completing questionnaires in the presence of trained pollsters, with whom pupils marked the selected answers. This form of collecting answers was a guarantee that questions were understood, and also gave a reliable answer not suggested by parents or the class tutor. In the presented work, only some of the questions regarding opinions of the examined pupils were used.

3 Results

Tab. 1 and 2 present pupils' opinions about themselves concerning external appearance, condition, self-satisfaction, evaluation of mood and achieved success. Analyzing the results obtained, it is noticeable that boys were more often satisfied about their external appearance than girls (a statistically significant difference at the level of $\alpha=0.05$). Among girls, as many as 17.8% marked the category „I think, my body is not pretty". Girls more often than boys declared reasons to be proud and satisfied of their different achievements (a statistically significant difference at the level $\alpha=0.05$). An almost equal number of girls (71.9 %) and boys (70.2 %) boasted about school successes. A similar number of girls (74.5 %) and boys (75.3 %) also declared the achievement of good sport results. Boys (70.5 %) thought that they learned new exercises very quickly more often in comparison to girls (68.2 %). Girls (71.4 %), on the other hand, thought that they were as intelligent as their peers in greater numbers than boys (69.1 %). Differences in declared opinions about successes and sport achieve ments were not statistically significant. Self-relation to learning evaluated criti cally by „I learn badly" split 12.2 % girls and 14.1 % boys.

Table 1: Opinions of examined girls about themselves [%]

Pupil's opinion about herself	*I do not agree*	*I agree a little*	*I almost agree*	*I entirely agree*
I like my body as it is.	7.2	11.5	22.1	57.3
In comparison with others I look good.	6.7	14.8	21.8	54.5
I will readily change my exterior appearance.	55.9	18.1	8.9	15.0
Generally, I am satisfied with myself.	6.8	9.5	20.6	61.1
I am very satisfied with my body.	9.5	13.4	17.1	57.9
Other children look better than me.	49.4	22.3	13.0	13.2
I look really good.	9.7	11.8	20.2	56.2
I think my body is not pretty.	69.5	10.5	7.8	10.1
I feel bad in my body.	76.2	11.3	4.7	5.7
I look better than the majority of my friends.	43.4	24.4	15.3	14.9
I think that I am intelligent at the same level as my peers.	11.0	15.6	25.2	46.2

Pupil's opinion about herself	*I do not agree*	*I agree a little*	*I almost agree*	*I entirely agree*
I often sit idly because I want to do nothing.	62.9	16.0	9.1	10.0
I am often sad without a reason.	49.8	20.8	14.0	13.4
I laugh very seldom.	65.6	11.1	11.1	10.1
Nothing gives me enjoyment/pleasure.	83.2	4.7	4.9	5.1
I have reasons to be proud of myself.	6.8	8.7	25.1	59.3
I have successes at school.	8.3	17.8	32.4	39.5
I learn badly at school.	73.6	12.1	5.7	6.5
I have difficulties during lessons with answers to questions.	51.5	23.2	14.0	9.2
I have very good sport results.	6.6	16.9	31.0	43.5
I achieve good sport results more often than my peers.	18.9	23.9	27.6	27.6
I learn very often new physical exercises.	12.2	16.7	18.2	50.8
In comparison with others I look good.	64.5	16.2	8.7	8.5

An alarming opinion was that 27.4 % girls and 27.0 % boys of the evaluated pupils declared that they were sad „Often without reason", whereas 21.2 % girls and 29.1 % boys agreed with the statement „I laugh very seldom". A signi ficantly large percentage of respondents also considered that „I often sit idly because they want to do nothing" – 19.1 % girls and 27.4 % boys. Both these categories showed statistically significant differences at the level of α=0.05.

Table 2: Opinions of examined boys about themselves [%]

Pupil's opinion about himself	*I do not agree*	*I agree a little*	*I almost agree*	*I entirely agree*
I like my body as it is.	7.3	6.5	15.8	64.5
In comparison with others I look good.	9.1	13.8	24.8	50.5
I will readily change my exterior appearance.	64.7	10.9	8.5	14.0
Generally, I am satisfied with myself.	7.2	9.1	18.5	63.3
I am very satisfied with my body.	11.3	10.4	15.7	60.7
Other children look better than me.	47.5	23.8	13.7	13.1

Pupil's opinion about himself	*I do not agree*	*I agree a little*	*I almost agree*	*I entirely agree*
I look really good.	9.4	12.3	19.6	56.9
I think my body is not pretty.	73.0	11.3	6.0	7.8
I feel bad in my body.	78.7	6.3	5.3	7.9
I look better than the majority of my friends.	40.1	22.8	19.7	15.5
I think that I am intelligent at the same level as my peers.	14.3	14.7	25.2	43.9
I often sit idly because I want to do nothing.	57.2	13.6	11.6	15.8
I am often sad without a reason.	52.5	18.7	11.4	15.6
I laugh very seldom.	55.1	14.0	12.9	16.2
Nothing gives me enjoyment /pleasure.	80.6	5.8	3.8	8.0
I have reasons to be proud of myself.	6.3	14.5	20.2	59.0
I have successes at school.	9.8	18.2	31.5	38.7
I learn badly at school.	72.0	12.1	6.6	6.5
I have difficulties during lessons with answers to questions.	48.1	22.9	13.4	13.8
I have very good sport results.	7.4	15.5	28.8	46.5
I achieve good sport results more often than my peers.	18.5	18.4	30.9	30.4
I learn very often new physical exercises.	12.4	15.3	20.5	50.0
In comparison with others I look good.	63.7	16.0	8.6	9.9

4 Resumé and conclusions

Participation of teachers in the education process is an inherent element in the Polish educational system. Children spend large part of their lives in educational institutions and because working time is quite often prolonged, parents' contact with children becomes shorter and shorter. Furthermore, pupils should acquire some patterns of behaviour at school. Providing a pupil with co-existence competitions in a peer group, shaping pro-healthy attitudes and getting used to a healthy lifestyle are basic purposes to be realized by all teachers. The school task is to create conditions to realize these purposes. The way to achieve this is school and extracurricular lessons.

Resuming analyzed research results it is noticeable that:

- A gender determinant differentiated opinions of the pupils examined in the evaluation of their own external appearance, achievement of sports skills and satisfaction with their own school and sports achievement.
- A small percentage of examined pupils (13.2%) negatively evaluated their own approach to learning at school.
- Every fourth pupil declared that they were "sad without a reason" and "seldom laugh(ed)".

In applying the results of this study to practical advice for teachers working with children at younger school ages, their attention should be drawn to:

- introducing a wider range of exercises and tasks that bring laughter to the child's face into the educational process,
- giving pupils instructions on how to spend leisure time without sitting idle,
- further shaping proper self-evaluation by preparing pupils to self-steer physical and motoric development.

References

BOTWIŃSKI R.: Kultura fizyczna w szkole [Physical culture at school]. Warszawa, Wydawnictwa Szkolne i Pedagogiczne, 1985.

BRANDL-BREDENBECK H.P., STEFANI M., KESSLER C., BRETTSCHNEIDER W.D., KUSSIN U., BORTOLI L., CARRARO A., LASKIENE S., SEGHERS J., VANREUSEL B., SHPAKOV A., SUDECK G., SZCZEPANOWSKA E., UMIASTOWSKA D.: Children today – Couch potatoes, fast food-junkies, mediafreaks? Lifestyles and health behaviour – first results of an international comparison, International Journal of Physical Education, Koeln, vol. XLVI, Issue 1, 1st Quarter, 2009, p.31-39.

KOZIELECKI J.: Psychologiczna teoria samowiedzy [Psychological theory of self-knowledge]. PWN, Warszawa, 1981.

UMIASTOWSKA D.: Ocena i samoocena ucznia w wychowaniu fizycznym jako przygotowanie do umiejętnego sterowania swoim rozwojem fizycznym [Evaluation and self-evaluation of pupil in physical education as a preparation to skillful steering of oneself physical development]. Zeszyty Naukowe Uniwersytetu Szczecińskiego nr 376, Prace IKF nr 19, 2004, s.75-86.

Contact:
Danuta UMIASTOWSKA: umiastowscy@neostrada.pl
Ewa SZCZEPANOWSKA: eszczepan@poczta.onet.pl

Building a Biology In-Service Teacher Training Model for Development of PCK

Martin Scheuch, Erika Keller, Franz Radits, Günther Pass,
University Vienna, Austria

The aim of this paper is to present the development of an in-service teacher training model in Biology within the last 4 years. We conducted 6 different courses in the field of ecology and their continuous formative evaluations. One goal of the teacher training is the development of the participants' pedagogical content knowledge (PCK). The recent design of the teacher training model is threefold: Module I is focused on biology field work, outdoor education, and didactical implications and it opens opportunities to the teachers to exchange their expertise. Module II is focused on the joint planning of teaching sequences and conducting them. Module III is dedicated to the presentations and the reflections upon teaching activities. Our contribution outlines the model, highlights the process of evaluation and development, and presents some results which have led to the refinement of the model.

Key words: in-service teacher training, module, professional development, pedagogical content knowledge, collaborative learning

1 Introduction, aims of this study

Since 2006 the Austrian Educational Competence Centre of Biology at the University of Vienna has been engaged in the professional development of biology teachers. Our aim at the beginning was to offer an in-service-teacher training with fieldwork in ecology to enlarge the participants' methodological repertoire and to support them to introduce more outdoor biology teaching in their classes. Over the years the courses were evaluated by the teacher trainers and development started stepwise. In 2007, two doctoral theses were started to conceptualize an evidence-based teacher training model for further professional development efforts in Austrian science education. To expand the evaluation, empirical research started by formulating the first concept (Keller et al. 2008) and research design (Scheuch & Heidinger 2009). In this article we want to present the current state of our model and outline the most important steps of the development. Giving a glimpse of evaluation results, we discuss new aspects for further development. The leading question for this contribution is: Which results of the evaluation can help us to elaborate our model?

2 Theoretical background of our model

One central aim of in-service teacher training is the development of pedagogical content knowledge (PCK). We follow the idea that PCK integrates the other knowledge domains and makes them accessible for teaching (Abell 2007). As PCK is mostly developed individually through classroom practice (e.g. Magnusson et al. 1999) it is highly idiosyncratic (e.g. Park & Oliver 2008). Studies on the development of PCK have shown effects of in-service teacher training (Driel et al. 1998; Sullivan-Palincsar et al. 1998; Jong & Valk 2007; Park & Oliver 2008). The duration of the training is a key element: engaging teachers in professional development courses over half a year or even longer with several meetings significantly helps to develop their PCK (all four studies). Integrated classroom practice and the reflection of all the experience seem likewise important. Reflection is crucial in the model of Park & Oliver (2008), moreover they differentiate between "reflection in action" during classroom teaching and "reflection on action" afterwards. Furthermore, an important way of developing PCK in in-service teacher training is the collaborative learning by the teachers in Communities of Practice (e.g. Wenger 2004).

3 The model in its current state

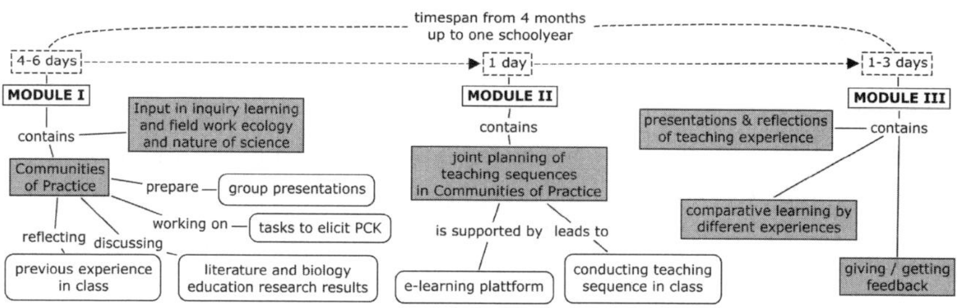

Figure 1: Concept map showing the crucial activities and elements of the tripartite model.

Our model has three modules and contains several determinants of successful in-service teacher training raised in section 2. The teachers' own PCK is addressed directly via guiding questions in discussions and also through group work on specific tasks (e.g. which identification key for plant species suits my teaching and my students best). This way we can focus on different aspects of PCK and link them to course content and to previous experience of the participants. Collaborative work amongst participants is another important key element to support PCK development further from module I: in collaborative planning in module II and in comparative learning in module III.

4 The successive evidence-based development of the courses

From 2006 to 2009, six different in-service teacher training courses were conducted and evaluated with three different topics in different surroundings. Aspects of ecology and, to a different amount, practical field work were common to all six courses. Along with the different content topics, the time schedule varied and instructional aspects differed. Since 2008, we have focused on a certain course to develop the model further. The phases of the development of the model are presented in figure 2. At the beginning the focus of evaluation was very broad. In concentrating on a specific course from 2008 onwards, we started to conduct in-depth research to elicit PCK development (Scheuch, Heidinger 2009).

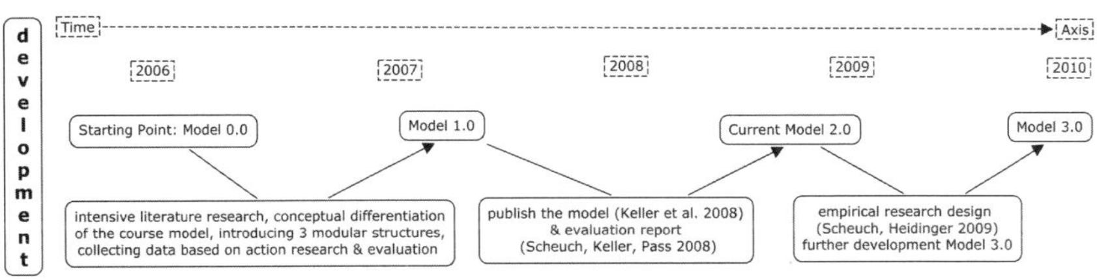

Figure 2: Stepwise elaboration of the model through action – reflection cycles in evaluation.

5 Evaluation methods

Our research is conducted as "second order action research" (Elliott 1991), since we are teacher trainers and researchers at the same time. In biology education this research can be characterized as developmental evaluation research (Krüger 2003). Action research is closer to the continuous reflection of our model; the latter research has broader epistemological interests in PCK development. We combine these approaches. The evaluation questions are closely linked to the course design and further developmental aspects. Exemplary data used in this contribution are: group discussion of the teacher trainers about the goals of a course, written expectations by the participants before the courses and group discussions focusing on collaborative planning. Analysis is done by coding transcripts with inductive and deductive categories derived from evaluation interests and the in-service teacher training model.

6 Key results of the course evaluations

One aspect found in several courses is the gap between the expectations of the participants and the course content. Teachers want to come to university to learn new biology content (Scheuch, Keller, and Pass 2008) and are irritated when methodological aspects, reflection on their own classroom teaching and various other PCK aspects are part of the training. This could be found out in all six courses to a varying degree and evidence is found in previously collected expectations, group discussions and individual interviews as well. Additional evidence for this fact is the high drop-out rate of participants in all courses – on average half of the group. Not all drop-outs can be blamed for this reason, other reasons add to this phenomenon as well. Nonetheless, the remaining participants are very positive about their professional development and their learning outcome concerning their teaching. They stated, however, that they often had to adjust their expectations. Another crucial point is the collaborative work in module II. Teachers are not familiar with collaboration when planning teaching; they report about difficulties in negotiating shared goals and the teaching process to reach them. Very often they remain at the level of brainstorming, which in their view is very fruitful. The teachers don't see any benefit in further collaborative work; their colleagues are not seen as a resource except for the reported brainstorming. What they do like are the presentations and reflections, they report learning from their colleagues in a comparative way. This was also found by DE JONG & VAN DER VALK (2007). A complementary way of collaboration was reported by three teachers with a high commitment to their planned teaching sequence, where all three branded it as too restrictive for their own teaching. They were open enough to plan and work together but felt trapped in the end. Both groups, "the brainstormers" and "the committed ones", were not satisfied with the planning and described their preparing and teaching as individual work; this reflects the real classroom situation, where every teacher has to handle a class alone. This result is similar to the outcome of GRÄSEL et al. (2006), where the highest level of collaboration was an exchange of teaching material and not the desired co-construction of teaching sequences. To sum up, the teachers report the experience to ne very fruitful for their work and they claim that they would never have developed these teaching sequences without the included classroom practice (see Keller, Scheuch, this book) although our intended collaboration is not fully realized.

7 Discussion and outlook

Evaluation results show us so far that module I works very well, and Module III is important for the teachers to exchange their experience and reflect to work on their PCK development. Module II is a weak point at the moment: teachers drop out during the planning & classroom practice phase, those remaining report several difficulties in cooperating with each other. One idea to further enhancement of the model is to start with planning their own teaching already in module I in order to allow the evolvement of a greater commitment among the teachers. Module II could then be more focused on co-constructing teaching sequences. Then we could reach better committed Communities of Practice to enhance PCK development, like SULLIVAN-PALINCSAR et al. (1998) report. What else has to be refined? We should communicate the content and the aims of the courses better so that the participants are not surprised with the amount of biology education in contrast to their expectation of high biological content. In-depth analysis of further data is on the way and we are confident to elaborate our model to enhance the participating teachers' PCK even more effectively in the future.

References

ABELL, SANDRA. K.: Research on Science Teacher Knowledge. In Abell, Sandra K., Lederman_Norman G.(Eds.) Handbook of Research on Science Education. p. 1105-1150 Mahwah, New Jersey, Lawrence Erlbaum Associates, 2007.

DRIEL, JAN. H. VAN., VERLOOP, NICO ET AL.: Developing Science Teachers' Pedagogical Content Knowledge.In: Journal of Research in Science Teaching 35(6)/1998, p.673-695.

GRÄSEL, CORNELIA, FUSSANGEL KATHRIN, ET AL.: Lerngemeinschaften in der Lehrerfortbildung. In: Zeitschrift für Erziehungswissenschaft 9(4)/2006, p. 545-561.

HEWSON, PETER: Teacher Professional Development in Science. In Abell, Sandra & Ledermann Norman: Handbook of Research on Science Education, 1177-1202. Mahwah, New Jersey: Lawrence Erlbaum Associates, 2007.

DE JONG, ONNO, V. D. VALK A. E.: Science Teachers' PCK and Teaching Practice: Learning to Scaffold Students' Open-inquiry Learning. In: Pinto, Roser, Couso, Digna (Eds.) Contributions from Science Education Research. p.107-118. Dordrecht, Springer, 2007.

KELLER, ERIKA, SCHEUCH, MARTIN & RADITS FRANZ: Förderung der Professionalitätsentwicklung von BiologielehrerInnen durch Fortbildung. Weiterentwicklung eines Arbeitsmodells mit den Konzepten der Communities of Practice und des Pedagogical Content Knowledge. In: Erkenntnisweg Biologiedidaktik 7/2008, p. 183-197.

KRÜGER, DIRK: Entwicklungsorientierte Evaluationsforschung – Ein Forschungsrahmen für die Biologiedidaktik. In: Vogt, Helmut, Krüger, Dirk (Eds.): Erkenntnisweg Biologiedidaktik 2/2003. p. 7-24.

LIPOWSKY, FRANK: Lernen im Beruf. Empirische Befunde zur Wirksamkeit von Lehrerfortbildung. In: Müller, Florian H., Eichenberger, Astrid, Lüders, Manfred, Mayr, Johannes (Hg.): Lehrerinnen und Lehrer lernen. Konzepte und Befunde zur Lehrerfortbildung, 51-72. – Münster: Waxmann, 2010.

MAGNUSSON, SHIRLEY, KRAJCIK, JOSEPH ET AL.: Nature, Sources and Development of Pedagogical Content Knowledge for Science Teaching. In Gess-Newsome, Julie, Lederman, Norman G.: Examining Pedagogical Content Knowledge., p. 95-132 - Dordrecht, Boston, London, Kluwer Academic Publishers, 1999.

PARK, SOONHYE & OLIVER J. STEVE: Revisiting the Conceptualisation of Pedagogical Content Knowledge (PCK). PCK as a Conceptual Tool to Understand Teachers as Professionals. In: Research in Science Education 38 (2)/2008, 127-147.

SCHEUCH, MARTIN, HEIDINGER, CHRISTINE: Begleitforschungs- und Evaluationsdesign eines LehrerInnenfortbildungsmodells. In Krüger, Dirk, Upmeier zu Belzen, Annette (Eds.): Erkenntnisweg Biologiedidaktik 8, 2009

SULLIVAN-PALINCSAR, ANNEMARIE, MAGNUSSON, SHIRLEY ET AL.: Designing a Community of Practice: Principles and Practices of GIsML Community. In: Teaching and Teacher Education 14(1)/1998, p. 5-19.

http://www.ewenger.com/theory/communities_of_practice_intro_WRD.doc, 8.3.2010, Wenger, Etienne. Communities of practice: a brief introduction.

Contact:
Martin SCHEUCH: martin.scheuch@univie.ac.at
Erika KELLER: erika.keller@univie.ac.at
Franz RADITS: franz.radits@univie.ac.at
Günther PASS: guenther.pass@univie.ac.at

Five-Year Teacher Training of Primary School Curriculum as a Reflection Transformation

Jiří Havel, Masaryk University Brno, Czech Republic

The paper presents the main trends in the field of innovation of the Primary school teacher education course at the Faculty of Education of Masaryk University. Theoretical basis for their introduction are described and towards the end, feedback on their implementation is summarized, that is based on the analysis of student reflection.

Keywords: primary school teacher education, study programs, curriculum, teachers´ professional knowledge, reflection.

1 Introduction

Primary school teacher education course is a traditional four-year course of study in the Czech Republic. Primary school teacher education courses are offered at all of the nine faculties of education in the Czech Republic, including the Faculty of Education of Masaryk University. Since the beginning of the third millennium – indeed since the beginning of the transformation of the school system after the Velvet Revolution – all these faculties have been faced with the task to innovate curricula both to reflect modern concepts of the undergraduate education of teachers and to fully reflect the transformation of curricula at primary schools. For this purpose, our faculty as the first one managed to prepare for accreditation a new study schedule in order to extend the undergraduate teacher training at primary schools for another year. After thorough preparation, the study program was transformed in the academic year 2002-2003. All departments have been involved in the innovation both of the theoretical and practical part of the primary school teacher education course.
At the beginning, the prolonged course of study was the most obvious change. However, this change was not caused by a technical increase in the number of hours of direct instruction, credits or courses. On the contrary, components have been implemented into the undergraduate training, which were neglected in the original program. Since the introduction of the five-year study program, sufficient time has elapsed to enable us to reflect on the first experiences with its implementation in connection with the original intention to improve the professional preparation of future teachers.

2 Changes in the curriculum of undergraduate teacher education

We realized that the new conception of the teacher professionalism leads away from the idea of a craftsman who needs to consult an experienced expert to deal with professional knowledge to the idea of a teacher who analyzes the causes and effects of practical activities and then gradually accumulates his reflection and knowledge. Logically, the pedagogical-psychological component became the main focus of primary school teacher education at the Faculty of Education, which allowed the unification of teacher education in specific teaching methodology and simultaneously in reflection of the practical disciplines of laboratory (exercise, practice) and field nature (continuous and contiguous practice of different thematic orientation at teacher training schools). The focus on the psycho-didactical competencies as the foundation of teacher professionalism brings neither a weakening of theoretical education nor a strengthening of the practical component of teacher education. On the contrary, the meaning of rationalization and decontextualization of practical activities increases.

It is crucial to find new solutions to the relationship between the theoretical and practical training with the aim to reduce their isolation and achieve mutual unity. The cyclical movement from theory to clinical experience and back is enforced (cf. Svatoš 2000, p. 21). Integrative courses play the key role – subject didactics courses and the teaching practice. Despite such explicitly formulated emphasis, it is still by no means usual for the subject didactics courses to integrate didactic as well as other educational and psychological knowledge that the teacher uses in various educational situations.

It is through elaborate integration that we tried to eliminate the traditional fragmentation and wide range of multidisciplinary courses in the primary school teacher education course. The integration is related to the interdisciplinary form of applied courses, bringing together generally educational-psychology and didactic training, which helps to active and situational conception of teaching. At the same time it was very important to be aware of the gradation. We therefore had to solve another very significant problem. Is it appropriate to design the study program in the consecutive model, in which the teacher students will first pass the first level of tertiary education in any field and then pass the pedagogical studies? The content and didactic components tend to be separated (see Průcha 2002, p. 98). The need for substantial reduction of the fragmentation of the subject in the schedules for each year supported this new model. However, previous good experience from the implementation of the primary school teacher education study program presented arguments against that. That is why the authors have contemplated designing a modular study program for a relatively long time. According to this model, the student would go through specific cycles (typically two semesters) of similar disciplines, thus enabling the students to concentrate better.

In the end, almost all representatives of the participating departments have proposed such a sequence of their disciplines that enabled them to continuously work on each student throughout the study and watch the gradation of the professional skills in the field. The concurrent model was thus chosen, in which future teachers will study in parallel both the general and the specific subjects and, moreover, pedagogical, didactic, psychological disciplines, while undergoing practical training in schools (Průcha 2002, p. 98). In fact, a sort of symbiosis of these models was developed, where the basic platform is presented to all students in the first six semesters of a five-year study program and after that a practical training in which the theoretical knowledge are converted to the real professional expertise is intensified during the next four semesters. However, this practice is often criticized by the students themselves. They feel that they are separated from field experience in the first three years of study. It is an understandable feeling, if the issues in the teachers of the content courses fail to reflect the didactic dimension.

Another basis for modifying the program was the awareness that appropriate integration of theory and practice in the modern conception can be achieved through development of the student's personality, which leads to the development of its professional knowledge of a practical nature. The present conception of teacher education for primary school teachers emphasizes teaching skills, educational decisions and key competences, and requires deep integration of theoretical and practical training, as well as keeping the student in touch with the reality of schools throughout his study (cf. Kosová 2002, p. 10). The idea of scientific construction of teacher education is abandoned, and we rather try to address dilemmas, contradictions and uncertainties of the teaching profession (cf. Štech 2003, p. 17).

According to the formulation of the objectives of undergraduate teacher education, we used the teaching professional competence model of E. WALTEROVÁ (2001, p. 31) who defined the so-called core competences of teacher education:

- subject-specific competences
- didactic and psychological competences and teaching skills
- general teaching skills
- diagnostic and intervention skills
- social, psychosocial and communication competences
- managerial and normative competences
- professional and personality-cultivating competences

The pedagogical module is strongly accented in the current model, which is, from our point of view, the real focus of the undergraduate teacher education. The module contains both pedagogical and psychological disciplines, subject didactics and practical training in the laboratorial form (exercises, practices) and field practice (continuous and coherent practice). The individual components of the professional preparation are divided into ten semesters of study (see the concurrent model) and all departments that are involved in the education of future primary school teachers should gradually be concerned with their content and reflection.

Professional knowledge is formed in four stages:

- *Personal and social education*, verbal and nonverbal communication skills.
- *Diagnostic and interactive phase*, the development of general teaching skills in the specific context of educational process in school (analysis of teacher and student activities during teaching, diagnosis of a pupil).
- *The development of skills of transformation and interpretation of educational content*, development of divergent thinking and action.
- *The development of one's own teaching style*, teaching approach, the skills of examination the effectiveness of its own educational activities, the flexibility to change strategies, approaches and methods of work (finding a distance from one's actual practice).

3 Reflection of the experience

The new module receives very positive feedback from the students. It turns out that the newly included disciplines, such as teaching methodology, pedagogical diagnostics, educational management, project teaching, and optional subjects, such as action learning, alternative schools, etc. are generally perceived as very beneficial for use in practice and they also facilitate its reflection.

The students also feel the need to obtain study skills relating to the competence of education of pupils with special educational needs, for which the program still lacks a wider platform. Furthermore, not even one-hour extension of the wider professional training component did not help to remove other well-known difficulties, such as an inability of students to understand the basic arguments and expert knowledge of research and educational-psychological diagnostic nature, as well as the ability to apply it in the process of school self-evaluation, diagnosis, interventions, etc.

Along with the extension of the study for five years, there was another substantial change in the approach foreign languages. Specifically, foreign language courses are an integrated component of the study program; the previous system of some teachers specializing in teaching foreign language was abandoned. In the new module, each graduate of the primary school teacher education course should be a qualified teacher of one foreign language (English, German, French or Russian). From this point of view, the foreign language was included in the study of teachers at primary school in the group of so-called "major approbation subjects" (as Czech language, Mathematics, Training, etc.). A mandatory final state exam in a foreign language (for primary school teachers) was recently included, which represented a significant quantitative shift that contributed to the fact that the Faculty of Education of Masaryk University is distinguished from other similar faculties.

From our point of view, the basic philosophy of the concept of language training is justified and correct. We base our assumption on the need of qualified teachers of foreign languages, especially English, at primary schools. Nevertheless, in the academic year 2008/2009, the faculty allowed students in their final year, who were supported by the Department of English language, to make a decision as to whether or not to take a final state exam in a foreign language.

However, we expected that the level (foreign-language-wise) of the students at the beginning of their university studies will be positively affected by the quality of secondary education and by clearly defined requirements of the faculty and that the level will have a constantly rising trend. Unfortunately, according to faculty staff, the situation is in general much more complicated on account of a very weak level of foreign language knowledge on the part ofthe students.

Not even a relatively large number of optional courses, which could help students with weaker language skills to balance some deficiency and to continue in the study, have not brought desirable effect yet. Another dilemma lies in the question whether – bearing in mind the current situation in schools – it is still effective to continue providing a choice of four foreign languages. The graduates' ability to find jobs at primary schools speaks clearly against that.

Finally, we want to mention the positive reactions of changes in the practical training, which is dominated by efforts to emphasize the concept of pre-primary school teacher education as a process of continuous gradation of teacher competence, in which the academic and professional component is not separated. It relates to continuous practical training throughout the study. The system focuses on the reflection of all the outputs and thus the time and adequate human resources increase. But the important thing is that the quality of professional knowledge, which students present in their *portfolios*, has significantly improved.

4 Conclusions

The improvements of undergraduate primary school teacher education study program, which started in 2002 by the extension of the field of the study program, starts to pay off. We are convinced that we are on the right track, despite some of the above mentioned difficulties. It clearly highlights the complexity and specificity of multi-subject professional training of teachers in primary education. The low aptitude of many accepted students is not a negligible phenomenon, which underscores the importance of the trend and which affects the overall nature of the undergraduate teacher education programs. Not only the unprecedented transition to accepting students only on the basis of the general expected aptitude (i.e. without any verification of their professional and personal skills and aspirations) is the reason, but also the fact that the number of graduates over the past 20 years has multiplied, and their reported interest in the teaching profession is very low. If this trend does not change, it will be hard to expect significant improvement of the input level of candidates. It is therefore vital to include this element in the teacher education programs.

References

HAVEL, J.: Model praktické přípravy studentů učitelství primární školy v pětiletém studiu. "The five-year study of teacher training for the first grade at the primary school - experience and question marks." In: Pedagogická praxe. Sborník příspěvků z III. celostátní konference. Praha: PdF UK, 2003, pp. 47-51.

HAVEL, J.: Pětileté studium učitelství pro 1. stupeň ZŠ-zkušenosti a otazníky. "The five-year study of teacher training for the first grade at the primary school - experience and question marks." In Za kvalitou vzdělávání učitelů primární a preprimární pedagogiky. Olomouc: PdF UP, 2009, pp. 83-90.

JANÍK, T.: Znalost jako klíčová kategorie učitelského vzdělávání. "Knowledge as a key category of teacher education." Brno: Paido, 2005.

KOSOVÁ, B.: Idea spolupráce univerzity a cvičných škol. "Idea of cooperation between universities and training schools." In Spolupráca univerzity a škol. Banská Bystrica: PdF UMB, 2002, pp. 10-13.

PRŮCHA, J.: Učitel. Současné poznatky o profesi. "Teacher. Current knowledge of the profession." Praha: Portál, 2002.

SPILKOVÁ, V.: *Praxe* současné školy a vzdělávání učitelů v historicko-srovnávací perspektivě. "Practice of contemporary schools and teacher education in comparative historical perspective." Praha: UK, 1997.

SVATOŠ, T.: Individuálně orientovaná pregraduální učitelská příprava. "Individually oriented undergraduate teacher preparation." Habilitation thesis. Hradec Králové: PdF VČU, 2000.

ŠTECH, S.: Praxe jako moment teoretické přípravy učitelů. "Practice as a moment of theoretical training of teachers." In Pedagogická praxe. Sborník příspěvků z III. celostátní konference. Praha : PdF UK, 2003, pp. 17 – 20.

WALTEROVÁ, E.: Učitelé jako profesní skupina, jejich vzdělávání a podpůrný systém. "Teachers as a professional group, their training and support system." Praha : PdF UK, 2001.

Contact:
Jiří HAVEL: havel@ped.muni.cz

The value aspects in undergraduate teacher training

Hana Horká, Masaryk University Brno, Czech Republic

The paper deals with the most important changes in the conception of undergraduate primary teacher training at the Faculty of Education Masaryk University, which were introduced in the association with the complex transformational tendencies in the Czech school system. With regard to the emphasized axiological dimension of education we focus on the so-called minimum values curriculum, value competence of a teacher and the possibilities of its development. The author describes teacher training which is aimed at the competence to specify the value aspects of the school curriculum, to motivate appropriately and functionally combine the affective and cognitive goals.

Key words: values education, undergraduate teacher training, the value-life-orientation competence, the value dimension of education, values curriculum, affective domain.

1 Introduction

The curricular reform of the Czech school system is reflected in the conception of undergraduate teacher training. The changes in the hierarchy of educational goals with the emphasis on the value dimension evoke the need to include the cognition of meaningfulness and significance of human conduct and activities into teacher training as well as functional combination of affective and cognitive goals. The inclusion of the categories of ethics, good and bad or the questions of meaning from the point of view of the development of society and humans means to overcome the prevailing one-sided stress on the cognitive aspects of pupils' learning and thus create sufficient space for other aspects of their personality development. The internalisation of these values and achieving aims in the affective domain is a complicated process which cannot be reduced to simply learning facts and indifferent acceptance of them as given and granted but takes place through "discovering values, identification with them, adopting them into pupils' inner world, overcoming obstacles when following those values" (Kučerová 1996, p. 49).

The focus of our attention is a number of questions: What are the components of the competence, which is crucial for values education? How does it correspond with the "minimum values curriculum"? How are teachers trained (both personally and in terms of methodology) for the development of the value relationship to reality?

2 The value-life-orientation competence

- The basis of all teacher's competences as the "guide" of a pupil in the world of values involves the value-life-orientation competence (Horká, 2005, p. 98). This most general competence implies its components:
- to stimulate *the change of value orientation* in today's world, which is motivated solely by performance and prosperity; for this it is necessary to identify the value orientation, that is to help children solve the problems of everyday life and perceive the *values of humanity*, such as truth, wisdom, beauty, morality, good, love and personal freedom;
- to develop attention, sensibility, interest, positive relationship to a certain thing, aesthetic feeling, moral and other attitudes, opinions, feelings and values (the affective domain);
- to create educational situations in which these values will be a reality and realize that the objective knowledge of things or notions in natural and social world are not a guarantee of right conduct, which is represented by "human meaningfulness of such events, its meaningfulness in the relationship to other people, acceptance of only one meaning and rejection of another" (Dorotíková 1997, p. 19-21);
- to lead systematically to the reflection of meanings, i.e. to the realisation of the consequences of reality for life, the skill to notice them, differentiate among them and decide adequately;
- to satisfy the growing need for the spiritual dimension in human life;
- to assist pupils when establishing a responsible relationship towards themselves and their learning, i.e. to inspire children to develop their skills, teach them how to identify their possibilities, lead them to self-fulfillment, focus on the development of their needs and interests, which may prevent a deficiency of basic human values;
- to help pupils understand the multicultural environment of the world, i.e. to be able to mediate the recognition of differences and inspire attitudes such as respect to the others, tolerance and respect for the differences, friendship, relationship to citizenship, their own nation, culture (cp. competences in helping pupils according to Z. Helus 2001, p. 28);

- to suppress undesirable forms of conduct and behaviour in the context of changing life conditions (e.g. to prevent superficiality, pretence, utilitarianism, intolerance, being inconsiderate, selfish, indifferent, cynical, to encourage preservation of cultural values in the time of contradictory influences, temptations, influence lifestyle, encourage sensitive perception of beauty, warn against doctrines, including advertising, fashion, mass propaganda, etc.);

3 The values curriculum

The "minimum" values curriculum (Lorencová 2000, p. 50), the aims of education in the curricular document Framework Educational Programme for Primary Education (2005) and educational literature (e.g. Blížkovský, Kučerová, Kurelová 2000; Kozlík 1998) have become a starting point for the definition of the content curriculum of values education in the following areas:

- The relationships of pupils to themselves – the art of being original, realize one's own potential and use it at one's maximum; develop one's knowledge, improve oneself (the values of individual personality development); look after one's health, enjoy life and culture (the values of human life);
- The relationship to other people – the art of being with others, respect their opinions, attitudes and rights, being tolerant and helpful (the values of social life); to manage well all the values of human life and world, not only economic, but also spiritual, to work productively and cooperate in the name of social development (the values of the development of democratic civil society);
- Relationship to nature – the art to live naturally in harmony with nature, promote preservation of clean air, drinkable water and habitable Earth as opposed to noise, mess, wasting, etc.; to actively contribute to environmental preservation, human sociability, personally contribute to preservation of peace in the whole world, spread of democracy in the country (the values of environmental protection, sustainable development, "habitable Earth" and the value of peace).

It is obvious that the structure of competence and content curriculum of values education correspond and become a starting point for the conception of professional training.

What is the reality in teacher training? How do we prepare students to:

- solve everyday problems, perceive the values of humanity and encounter them in real life
- find a responsible approach to themselves and their studies
- understand the multicultural environment of the world etc.

4 The development of competences for values education

The teaching strategies of various subjects are discussed in methodology seminars and can be tested during teaching practice. The question is whether students have sufficient theoretical background and practical training for values education. We present experience from professional primary teacher training at the Faculty of Education Masaryk University which develop students' competences:

- Diagnose the current level of children's experience, knowledge schemes, needs and interests. Students observe and analyse the process of children's cognition and learning (preconcepts, individual personality traits), educational strategies leading to understanding of the world.
- Design personality development of pupils and reflect on the results. Attention is paid to how the pupils live, what they think about, what needs and opinions they have, what they are satisfied with, what worries them. Based on these findings, teacher can choose adequate methods for pupil's development.
- Respect the stages of internalisation of specific values and attitudes in pupils, which are by taxonomies defined as a hierarchy process with levels ranging from perception to reaction and appreciation to the integration of values in character.
- Consider that a change in attitudes requires time and no immedite effect can be expected.
- Elaborate and clearly define teaching goals in the affective domain within the curricular elaboration of a topic (goals, content, process) – the aims, their specific form, key competences, subject matter, teaching strategies, approaches, evaluation instruments and activities.

- Specify the target categories and gain personal experience with a broad range of activities for a) emotional learning (to enhance empathy, reflect antipathy and sympathy), inclusion of tasks such as: put oneself in somebody's place, be able to express one's attitude to a phenomenon, be able to appreciate significance, b) social learning (to promote cooperation, solving dilemmas in conflicts, assertive conduct) formulating tasks such as: pair work, group work, solving a conflict together, convince others about one´s truth, c) values education (to influence questions of values and evaluation) setting tasks such as: evaluate, judge, compare values, rank values, solve a moral dilemma, formulate the meaning and significance of an educational situation (cp. Lukášová – Kantorková, 2003, p. 172)
- Specify the content of values education into accessible and attractive activeties for pupils using suitable methods (e.g. the method of solving moral and aesthetic dilemmas using microstories, demonstration of materials – pictures, songs, poems etc., the method of role play in solving moral situations).
- Create favourable conditions for the personality development of pupils, i.e. primarily the climate encouraging, respecting the pupil, the atmosphere of trust, safety, understanding, empathy and honesty, bringing about a certain order and system.
- Boost self-confidence, self-respect, but also the ability to critically evaluate one's own and others´ performance, encourage identity and individuality, independence, authenticity, originality. Students (self)reflect on their skills using portfolio, results of their teaching practice, etc.

5 Conclusion

Our experience proves that the new field of methodology as described and justified by S. ŠVEC (2002, p. 100) as the methodology of social-affective education or methodology (technology) of socioemotional education has its place in professional teacher training.

The implementation of sophisticated values orientation is not feasible by strict enforcement of what should be done but by realistic demonstration of the complex, unstable and ambiguous nature of the reality. It is purposeful to provide subjects for possible (not the only right) decision making (e.g. to learn to view things from different points) for which we always have full responsebility. When students understand this they can also grasp what spiritual values and meaning of life are. Then they can protect their pupils from utilitarism, instrumentalism and pragmatism of the adults' world; they can even teach children the opposite of what "the everyday reality shows as ethical, cognitive, interpersonal and personality standard, the standard of lifestyle and values orienttation" (cp. Kukal 2007).

It implies that we strive for the development of a solid basis of educational competences, which will be shaped according to the reflection of the educational reality and self-reflection. The continuous update of teacher training will proceed alongside the process of establishing the professional standard of teacher's quality in the Czech Republic.

References

BLÍŽKOVSKÝ, B.; KUČEROVÁ, S.; KURELOVÁ, M. A KOL. Středoevropský učitel na prahu učící se společnosti 21. století. Brno : Konvoj, 2000.

DOROTÍKOVÁ, S. Hodnoty a vzdělání. In Občanská výchova v měnící se době. Sborník odborných textů pro učitele. Olomouc : Nakladatelství Olomouc, 1997, p. 31-34. ISBN 80-7182-018-0

HELUS, Z. K tématu „změna školy". Pedagogika, 2001, No. 1, p. 25-41.

KOZLÍK, J. A KOL. Směřování k základní škole zítřka. Praha : Fortuna, 1998.

KUČEROVÁ, S. Člověk, hodnoty, výchova. Prešov : Manacon, 1996. ISBN 80-85668-34-3.

K čemu máme školu. Kukal, P. [on-line] Available on http://www.stolzova.cz/stolzova/view.php?cisloclanku=2007011901 [Quoted 20. 1. 2009].

LORENCOVÁ, J. Společnost – škola - učitel a hodnotová orientace současnosti (o zdroji naší dnešní „krize" hodnot). In Filosofie – výchova-hodnoty. Sborník k významnému životnímu jubileu prof. PhDr. Jaroslavy Peškové, CSc. Studia paedagogica No. 25. Praha : UK, 1999, p. 37- 64.

LUKÁŠOVÁ – KANTORKOVÁ, H. Učitelská profese v primárním vzdělávání a pedagogická příprava učitelů /teorie, výzkum, praxe/ Ostrava : Pedagogická fakulta OU, 2003.

Rámcový vzdělávací program pro základní vzdělávání. Praha : VÚP 2005.

RÝDL, K. A kol. Tvorba profesního standardu kvality učitele. (Vstupní dokument pro veřejnou diskuzi). Praha : MŠMT, 2009.

ŠVEC, Š. Základné pojmy v pedagogike a andragogike. Bratislava : IRIS, 2002.

ŠVEC, Š. Kategoriálne systémy empirickej mikroanalýzy a hodnotenia výučby. Paedagogica 16. Zborník Filozofickej fakulty *UK*. Bratislava : UK, 2002a, p. 72- 100.

VAŠUTOVÁ, J. Kvalifikační předpoklady pro nové role učitelů. In Učitelé jako profesní skupina, jejich vzdělávání a podpůrný systém. 1. díl. Sborník z celostátní konference. Praha : UK, 2001. p. 19-46. ISBN 80-7290-059-5.

The paper was produced under the auspices of the research project of the Ministry of Education, Youth and Sports (MSM0021622421) "School and Health for 21st Century".

Contact:
Doc. PaedDr. Hana HORKÁ, CSc.: horka@ped.muni.cz

CONSTRUCTIVIST PERSPECTIVES ON TEACHERS' LEARNING

Tamara Skolnikova,
Finnmark University College, Norway

The topicality of the problem is determined by the contradiction between requirements concerning qualitative and competitive teachers` education and inelastic requirements concerning the study system. Studies show that even students who score well in exams are often unable to integrate or contrast memorized facts with real-life applications successfully (Skolnikova, T., 2003; Porozovs, J., 2005). The contradiction in its turn requires paying greater attention to the quality of teachers' education process, taking into account the newest approaches in studies. The new insights into the theory of cognition stress the constructivist approach to learning and develop individual learning for every person, because everyone themselves construct their learning, based on their previous experience. Communication and cooperation is carried out during the exchange of experience, enriching mutual socio-cultural environment.

Keywords: constructivism, experience, development, knowledge, interpretation, activation/activity

1 Introduction

Expressions like "constructivism", "construction of knowledge" and similar ones are starting to become a part of the language of teachers' education. Constructivism is a theory of knowledge. We construct knowledge in order to deal with our experience. We can say that "constructivism is the view that reality itself is constructed" by the knower (Kitchener, 1987. 101). This definition has two important consequences:

- "knowledge is never a simple copy of reality, but always results from a construction of reality through the activity of the subject" (Inhelder, 1977, 339).
- "the subject constructs the cognitive schemes, categories, concepts, and structures necessary for knowledge" (Kitchener, 1987, 102).

Students, like all human beings, construct knowledge from their experience, including their school experience. In order for a construction to form, there need to be foundations. The foundations are the students' experience and knowledge gathered in the course of their life. Constructivism is a theory of active learning. Active learning involves the cognitive processes of selecting, organizing, and integrating during learning. The student, acquiring individual experience, forms his learning, the culture of education and interactivity in definite socio-cultural environment (Vygotsky, L. 1984).

In traditional teaching, classes are usually driven by "teacher-talk" and depend heavily on textbooks for the structure of the course. Information is divided into parts and built into a whole concept. Teachers seek to transfer their thoughts and meanings to passive students. There is little room for student-initiated questions, independent thought or interaction between students.

In a constructivist setting, knowledge is not objective. The role of the teacher is to organize information around conceptual clusters of problems, questions and situations in order to engage the student's interest. Teacher assists the student in developing new insights and connecting them with their previous learning. Ideas are presented holistically as broad concepts and then broken down into parts. The activities are student-centred and students are encouraged to ask their own questions, carry out their own experiments, make their own analogies and come to their own conclusions.

2 Theoretical foundations of the constructivist approach

The discussions about the benefits of the theory of constructivism were carried out in 90s of the 20th century when changes the concept of the competent personality. In cognition theories was emphasized the constructivist essence of person`s individual learning, because everyone themselves constructs their learning in connection with the insight that there is no one unified learning mechanism (Reich, 2002).

The ideas of constructivism are based on the basic assumptions of several theories of pedagogy:

- System theory and research about action as system, developed at the end of 50s by Parson (Parson 1976).
- LUHMANN'S investigation about communication as system (Luhmann N. 1984).
- The theory of symbolic interactionalism (Goffman E. 1977) which considers that at the basis of interaction is not the principle "irritant-reaction", but it occurs with the help of gestures and language.
- The theory of subjectivism which considers the space of subjective possibilities (Groeben N. 1986).
- The theory of cognitivism which connects learning with inner psychological patterns, human being's psychic activity, the essential characteristics of which the structuring of new with existing experience and the formation of learning skill (Piaget J. 1990; Bruner J. 1996).

Constructivism, in opposition to behaviourism, pays greatest attention to the student and his/her personal meanings, which are based on student's personal experience, knowledge and interest. Students came with knowledge luggage, which is already organized in a certain way. New information is added to the structured knowledge, thus forming new links with the existing knowledge. Studying with understanding, the personality integrates new knowledge in his conceptual structure.

The strong sides of constructivism:

- Students learn better and enjoy the process more if they are given the possibility to be actively involved in the process, not only be passive listeners.
- The education process is more effective when it focuses on thinking and the formation of understanding, not learning by heart.
- Learning based on constructivism is transferable. Having discovered the principles of their own learning, the student can use them also in other learning situations.
- Constructivism gives the students the opportunity to feel responsible for their learning from the moment since students' learning is based on their own questions, discoveries, as well as assessment process, where the students also have something to say in the matter. Students learn to put questions about things and employ their natural curiosity, inquiring about

the surrounding world.

- Constructivism develops students' social and communicative skills, forming learning environment, where is emphasized cooperation and idea exchange. Students should learn how to converse with others in socially acceptable style.

Constructivism brings us the appreciation of students' efforts of construction. A student confronted with a situation may come up with an account that seems strange for us. One of the possible ways to respond is to try to understand why such a solution or idea seemed sensible to the student. This will tell us a lot about the student and will also help us to step back from our scientific way of looking at the world.

3 Constructivism as a referent for teaching and learning

During last 10-15 years, constructivist approach has gained great popularity in European and American higher education institutions. W. KLAFKI (Klafki W., 1999, 13-35) in the theory of "critical constructivism" emphasizes the activity of the student him/herself, team work and relaxation during studies. With the notion "critical" Klafki understands the development of the skills of self-determination, co-determination and solidarity. The notion "constructive" is connected with the practical disposition of the concept, its tentative and transforming tendency. Learning and teaching, in scientist's opinion, is a process of interaction, during which students acquire larger independence and responsibility for their studies. At the basis of such study process should be creative acquiring of the study material, i.e., it should be really useful, practically oriented, concerning understanding of the material, repetition, versatile exercises. Study process is planed together with students, paying attention to their interests, as well as analysing negative sides of the study process. In group work students have great experience in mutual enrichment, in developing confidence. The aim of Klafki model is to act according to the elaboration plan, but also according to the situation.

KLAFKI in critically didactic sense outlines one of the principles of contemporary didactics, based on a broad notion of "education". Its understanding provides the teacher with the possibility to be competent in definite situation, not narrowing the possibilities of study process with the borders of the theme taught, not reducing teacher's activity to fragmentary acts, but pacing everyday stride with further didactic aim. This thought nowadays confirms the necessity to give teacher academic education, which comprises extensive exercises, the features and expressions of different cultures of mutual information society, raising awareness about global processes and predicting their consequences.

According to VON GLASERSFELD, the main implications of constructivism are:

- If we assume that students have to build up their own knowledge, we have to consider that they are not "blank slates". The knowledge they have is the only basis on which they can build more.
- Whatever a student says in answer to a question makes sense to the student at the moment. To be told that it is wrong is most discouraging and inhibiting for the student. Furthermore, given the way that the student has interpreted the question, the answer may actually be a good one.
- If teachers want to modify a student's concept or conceptual structures, they have to try to build a model of a particular student`s own thinking. Models of students' thinking can, of course, be generalized, but before assuming that a student fits the general pattern, one should have some solid evidence that this is viable assumption in the particular case.
- Asking students how they arrived at their given answer is a good way of discovering something about their thinking; it opens the way to explain why a particular answer may not be useful under different circumstances. By letting the students discover that it can be fun to solve problems, we influence their problem-solving techniques.
- If we want to foster students' motivation into questions that, at first, are not of particular interest (from the students' point of view), you will have to create situations where the students have an opportunity to experience the pleasure inherent in solving the problem. After students have experienced the pleasure of finding a solution by their own thinking once or twice, they will be quite ready to work on problems suggested by the teacher.
- Successful thinking is more important than "correct" answers. As long as evaluation is based on "performance", where the performance means the ability to reproduce answers that were part of instructional process, we are not assessing what would be the important "learning" from a constructivist point of view (i.e., the ability to solve new problems). We have to decide whether we want students to develop their ability to think or

merely to handle standard procedures and give standard answers in a limited set of situations.

- To understand and appreciate students' thinking, the teacher must have a flexible mind because students sometimes start from premises that seem inconceivable to teachers.
- The constructivist teacher can never justify that s/he teaches by claiming that it is "true". In science, s/he can not say more that that it is the best way of conceiving the situation because, at the moment, it is the most effective way of dealing with it (von Glasersfeld 1989).

Summarizing the above mentioned theories and investigations into learning, as performed by several scientists, has worked out the essence and contents of constructive didactic model and pedagogical and psychological pre-conditions, which are depicted in Table 1.

Table 1: The essence and contents of constructive didactic model

The essence of constructivism	*Learning mechanism*	*Learning steps (students` activities)*	*Psychological and pedagogical pre-conditions*
- Studies as self-organized, purposeful and responsible activity. - The construction of individual (self-needed) knowledge, skills, attitudes. - Unity of inner and outer factors in students' motivated activity. - Priority is given to inner factors (meaning, understanding, not behaviour). - Studies are a social process, communication.	Students do not just acquire knowledge, but creatively form (construct) it: - Having discussions during group work, in an accelerated way constructing their knowledge. - Learning is purposeful (with subjectively important information) and showing his attitude to the activity. - During learning the enrichment of one's learning with other participants' experience happens.	- Setting forth subjectively important aim, prediction of the results. Determination of the perspective of learning. - Activation of the previous experience, acquiring new experience. - Mutual planning of the study process. - Critical choice of study material. - Choice of forms and social actions. - Learning as self-assessment of the	*Subjective prerequisites:* - Students' independence. - Collegial relations. Lecturer – an experienced colleague. - Formation of attitude (be able to educate oneself). - Purposefully set priorities. - Students' activity in studies. - Choice of risk, not avoiding the mistakes. - Critical evaluation of the gained experience.

- Studies are emotional experience. - Activation of information and informative space. - Mistakes, trials, successes should be viewed as a sign of learning and information about the level of understanding. - Change of the role of lecturer, s/he becomes an organizer, observer, adviser, as well as learns himself/herself.	- Learning is carried out with understanding (making independent decisions, judging the information choice, etc.). - Learning is conducted with responsibility (about one`s own learning and cooperation). - Assessment and evaluation of the significance of study process and its results by students themselves.	significance of the process and the achieved result.	*Objective preconditions*: - Provision psychologically beneficial and encouraging study environment. - Offer of the perspective and planning versions. - Support of students' activity. Allow students' responses to drive lessons and seek elaboration of students' initial responses. - Providing help in problem solving. - Providing versions of learning contents and methods. - Providing variety of social forms and work organization. - Providing versions of self-assessment of study process and its results. Utilizing peer evaluation.

Understanding constructivism requires a structural shift in students' world view. As they attempt to understand, they are, themselves, constructing. The process of building begins with their initial assimilatory structures which they use to modify, interpret, and transform what they read, hear about and discuss. The methods by which learning can be evaluated should be less goal-oriented; they should assess knowledge construction in relevant real-world contexts requiring authentic learning tasks that represent multiple perspectives and viewpoints.

4 Conclusions

Constructivism is a way of knowing. Constructivism is a way of thinking about knowing, a referent for building models of teaching, learning and curriculum. The central idea of this theory is that meaning must be constructed, that knowledge building is an active process on the part of the learner, not a passive process of information absorption.

Constructivism is also a theory of communication. When you send a message by saying something or providing information, and you have no knowledge of the receiver, then you have no idea as to what message was received, and you can not interpret the response.

Students come to the class with en established world-view, formed by years of prior experience and learning. For students to change their world-view requires work. Students learn from each other as well as the teacher. Students learn better by doing. Allowing and creating opportunities for all to have a voice promotes the construction of new ideas.

A constructivist perspective views learners as actively engaged in making meaning, and teaching with that approach looks for that students can analyse, investigate, collaborate, share, build, generate based on what they already know. To do this effectively, a teacher needs to be a learner and a researcher, to strive for greater awareness of the environments and the participants in a given teaching situation, in order to continually adjust their actions, to engage students in learning, using constructivism as a referent.

References

BRUNER, J.: The Culture of Education. - Cambridge, Harvard University Press, 1996.

GOFFMAN, E.: Rahmen Analyse. - Frankfurt a. M., 1977.

VON GLASERSFELD, E.: Cognition, Construction of Knowledge and Teaching. Synthese, 80 (1), 1989.

GROEBEN, N.: Handeln, Tun, Verhalten als Einheiten einer verstehenderklärenden Psychologie. - Tubingen, 1986.

INHELDER, B.: Genetic Epistemology and Developmental Psychology. - New York: New York Academy of Sciences, 1977.

KITCHENER, R.F.: Piaget's Theory of Knowledge: Genetic Epistemology and Scientific Reason. - New Haven, CT: Yale University Press, 1987.

KLAFKI, W.: Die bildungstheoretische Didaktikk, in Gudjons, H., Didaktische Theorien. - Aufl. Weinheim, 1999.

LUHMANN, N.: Soziale Systeme. - Frankfurt a. Main, 1984.

PARSON, T.: Theorie Sozialer Systeme. - Opladen, 1976.

PIAGET, J.: The Child`s Conception of the World. - New York: Littlefield Adams, 1990.

POROZOVS, J., SKOLNIKOVA, T.: The Attitude of Sports and Biology Teachers Speciality to the Chosen Speciality. - Riga: RTU, 2005.

REICH, K.: Systemisch-konstruktivistische Padagogik.-Luchterhand Verlag (Neuwied), 4. Auflage, Weinheim, 2002.

SKOLNIKOVA, T.: Natural Sciences and Sport: Integration Problems. In: ATEE Spring University. - Riga: LU, 2003.

Contact:
Tamara SKOLNIKOVA: tshk@inbox.lv

Martin Jäggle; Thomas Krobath; Robert Schelander (Hg.) unter Mitwirkung von Edda Strutzenberger und Heribert Bastel

lebens.werte.schule

Religiöse Dimensionen in Schulkultur und Schulentwicklung

Die 33 Beiträge setzen sich differenziert mit Schulkultur und Schulentwicklung auseinander – unter besonderer Berücksichtigung der religiösen Dimensionen im Schulleben. Konkrete Beispiele und Modelle von Schulentwicklung werden vorgestellt und reflektiert, Zugänge zur Wahrnehmung kultureller Unterschiede und religiöser Dimensionen in Schulen und in Schulentwicklung werden aufgezeigt. Das Buch versammelt die Beiträge zu einem internationalen Symposium im Mai 2008 in Wien. Es eröffnet pädagogische, religionspädagogische und organisationsethische Zugänge und richtet sich an WissenschaftlerInnen, LehrerInnen sowie alle Verantwortlichen für Schulentwicklung.

Bd. 5, 2009, 512 S., 29,90 €, br., ISBN 978-3-8258-1392-5

LIT Verlag Berlin – Münster – Wien – Zürich – London

Auslieferung Deutschland / Österreich / Schweiz: siehe Impressumsseite